Tennis in New York

Tennis in New York

*The History of the Most Influential Sport
in the Most Influential City in the World*

By Dale G. Caldwell and Nancy Gill McShea

Published by Intelligent Influence Publishing Group,
an imprint of Intelligent Influence Inc.
www.IntelligentInfluenceInc.com

Printed in the United States by
Printcraft
960 Mamaroneck Avenue, Mamaroneck NY 10543-1631
914.777.7468

ISBN-10: 0983896305
ISBN-13: 978-0-9838963-0-2

Dedication

With deep affection and appreciation to the Caldwell Family; the McShea Family; the Junior Tennis Foundation; the United States Tennis Association (USTA); the USTA Eastern Section; the International Tennis Hall of Fame; and the American Tennis Association.

Tennis in New York

Contents

Chapter	Page
Acknowledgments	*viii*
Foreword	*x*

SECTION I – New York Tennis History

1) *Introduction*	*13*
2) *The Birth of Tennis*	*18*
3) *Tennis Comes to New York*	*23*
4) *New York Becomes the Tennis Capital of the World*	*28*
5) *The Evolution of Tennis in New York*	*31*
6) *Black Tennis in New York*	*36*

SECTION II – Eastern Tennis Accomplishments

7) *Key Moments in Eastern Tennis History*	*44*

SECTION III – Eastern Tennis Hall of Fame Inductees

8) *1988: Ashe, Danzig, Palfrey-Danzig, Fitz Gibbon, Gibson Outerbridge, Stahr, Talbert and Zausner*	*69*
9) *1989: Hoyt, Rooney, Scott and Wood*	*78*
10) *1990: Barker, Holmberg, Lebair, Martin and Williams*	*83*

11) 1991: Budge, Glick, Shields and Sutter   89

12) 1992: Graebner, Hunter, Markin and Shore   96

13) 1993: Dinkins, Llewellyn, Nogrady and Richardson   103

14) 1994: Carillo, Hamilton, Lang and Pate   110

15) 1995: Delatour, Gerulaitis, King and Van Nostrand   117

16) 1996: Hartman, Marmion, G. Mayer and Ward   125

17) 1997: Garry, J. McEnroe, McNeill and Myers   131

18) 1998: Dwyer, Hammond, Pratt and Reese   139

19) 1999: Fitz Gibbon II, Savitt, Viebranz and Weir   147

20) 2000: Fleming, Herrick, Richards and Tully   155

21) 2001: Cranis, Jackson, Seewagen and Stockton   164

22) 2002: Aitchison, Annacone, Horvath and Ryland   173

23) 2003: Amdur, Casale, S. Mayer and Prince   181

24) 2004: Masterson, P. McEnroe, Russo and Smith   190

25) 2005: Benisch, Kovaleski, Nusbaum and Seewagen   199

26) 2006: Gowen, G. Heldman, J. Heldman, Maguire and Vincent   208

27) 2007: Arias, Cullman, Grimes and Rubell   220

28) 2008: K. McEnroe, J. McEnroe, Scheer, Scott and Van Blake   230

29) 2009: Cash, Schmitz, Schwartz and Snyder 239

30) 2010: Buehning, Burling, Flink and Franco 248

31) 2011: Brown, Hainline, Litwin and Picker 258

Acknowledgments

Tennis in New York grew out of our passion for tennis and our belief that life is like a five-set tennis match. We are convinced that tennis is unique because from moment to moment a tennis contest mirrors the universal struggles and joys of daily routine. We come to the sport from different backgrounds and share an obsession for tennis in and around New York City. We collaborated on this book to trace the unusual beginnings and evolution of tennis and to preserve in one volume snapshots of legendary characters that have influenced the game in New York and throughout the world.

Organized tennis in the Tri-State, known formally as the United States Tennis Association (USTA) Eastern Section – Eastern, informally – includes all of New York State and a 35-mile radius around New York City. This area of the northeastern U.S. is home to powerful international organizations in business, politics, construction, entertainment, the arts, finance, law, nonprofit, publishing, fashion, sports and technology.

Some of the power players affiliated with those organizations are mentioned within these pages. Others are featured here in our hall of fame tributes, which were commissioned by Eastern's Junior Tennis Foundation (JTF). We are especially grateful to these legends for their role in creating a fascinating story of tennis in New York.

-- Eugenius Outerbridge, a founder and the first leader of the Port Authority of New York and New Jersey, played a key role in creating the USTA and founded the first national tennis tournament in Staten Island, New York.

-- Jack Nusbaum, once a junior tennis parent and a volunteer attorney for Eastern, is a partner and the chairman of an international law firm. In 1988 Jack was the lead counsel to the Shearson Lehman group…in the $27 billion effort to take over RJR Nabisco.

-- Donald Rubell, a tennis lifer and a prominent New York physician, has created an art collection listed by the Art Review as the fifth most important in the world.

-- Joe Cullman, the Manhattan president and CEO of Philip Morris, helped underwrite the women's Virginia Slims pro tour and sponsored the national televising of the US Open on CBS.

-- Renee Richards, a Queens native and a Yale graduate who became a professional tennis player, is a New York ophthalmologist and one of the world's leading surgeons in Strabismus, the correction of eye muscles.

-- The New York based comedian Alan King threw his golf bags into the lake along with his caddy, bought a tennis racquet and created a professional tennis tournament in Las Vegas.

--Neil Amdur, longtime sports editor for *The New York Times*, was also the publisher and editor in chief of *World Tennis* magazine and a tennis producer for CBS Sports.

-- Eastern presidents – Bob Schmitz, a G.E. executive, introduced the computer to the USTA; and Elaine Viebranz, a force in establishing USTA League Tennis, which today features more than 300,000 tennis players, many of whom play on multiple league teams.

-- Charles Masterson, a New York executive who ranked among the U.S. top 20, joined the Eisenhower White House staff in 1953 as a special assistant/speech writer.

-- George Gowen, a senior partner in a Manhattan law firm, has served 18 USTA presidents and survived countless revolutions in tennis.

-- New York City Mayor David Dinkins, a passionate tennis fan and long-time USTA board member, silenced the planes that disrupted the Open when he ran New York City.

-- Bill Talbert, a lifelong diabetic, arrived in New York by way of Cincinnati and won nine Grand Slam titles – four of them at the U.S. National Championships -- and became a senior vice president of the American Banknote Corporation in Manhattan and the US Open tournament director.

We are indebted to Doris Herrick, who for 30 years was an exceptional executive director of both the Eastern Section and the Junior Tennis Foundation. Barbara Williams and Julius Larkin Hoyt founded and incorporated the non-profit foundation in 1979 to help support junior tennis and special population programs. In 1988, Doris, Alex. B. Aitchison, Harry A. Marmion and Richard A. Scheer pooled their talents and hosted the first annual Eastern Tennis Hall of Fame dinner to honor influential legends and to raise funds for those sectional programs.

We owe special thanks to the late Alastair B. Martin, the major benefactor of the Junior Tennis Foundation who witnessed almost the entire 20th century of American tennis. We are grateful to the photographers Russ Adams, Steve Berman, Ed Goldman, Bob Kenas and Wendy Leroux for sharing superior images of legends who influenced tennis in New York. Thanks also to the International Tennis Hall of Fame which gave us access to its treasured archives and to Warren Kimball for providing unique insights into USTA history. Thanks to colleagues Nick Greenfield, Marc Verebey, Richard Pagliaro, Dave Goodman and Jenny Schnitzer for sharing a passion for tennis in all our publications. We appreciate the talent and patience of Gail Troetti, who designed this book at Printcraft. Finally, we extend a special thanks to Sharon and Ashley Caldwell and to Jerry, Justin, Colette and Jeremy McShea for their constant love and support through the many challenges we faced in writing *Tennis in New York*.

Thanks also to the many staffers of Gene Scott's Tennis Week magazine, Bonnie Barber and our apologies for omitting many New York champions. Space was limited; looking to add many more in future printings and the Tennis in New York magazine.

Foreword

Everyone who is interested in history and the lives of tennis champions, both on and off the court, will enjoy reading this overview of the game's beginnings and its influence in New York . Great tennis champions like Don Budge, Althea Gibson and John McEnroe won multiple titles in Queens at the U.S. National Championships and the US Open – either at Forest Hills or at Flushing Meadows – and they are featured within these pages.

The summer tennis circuit leading up to Forest Hills began at Merion in Philadelphia, then on to Orange in New Jersey, the Meadow Club in Southampton, and finally to Newport. Many other clubs in the Tri-State hosted tournaments on the important Eastern circuit. I learned to play in my early teens at one of them, the Berkeley Tennis Club in Orange , New Jersey , with accomplished Eastern players Jeff Podesta and Larry Krieger. Russell Kingman was the president of both Berkeley and the USLTA at the time and he brought in Jack Kramer, Pancho Segura, Frank Kovacs and Bobby Riggs to play the New Jersey State tournament there. I was a ball boy that year and had never seen the game played on such a high level.

Dale and Nancy document significant information about the sport's game changers – both the champions and powerful volunteer administrators. The leadership of the United States Tennis Association (USTA) was based in New York , so most important decisions were made there. You will see in this history why New York is one of the most influential tennis markets in the world.

-- Dick Savitt

- Dick Savitt -- *1951 Wimbledon, Australian Singles Champion; 1951 U.S. Davis Cup vs. Japan and Mexico: 3-0 in singles; 1976 International Tennis Hall of Fame; 1986 Intercollegiate Tennis Association Men's Collegiate Tennis Hall of Fame; 1999 USTA Eastern Hall of Fame .*

The history of international championship tennis in the New York Tri-State area is the stuff of folklore and Dick Savitt's career is at the center of it, as he connects with several generations. Dick has known and still knows everybody in tennis but his friends say he prefers not to talk about himself, so we outline here some history through his career. In 1951 Dick won singles titles at Wimbledon and the Australian Championships during the Australian-American rivalries. He beat three Aussie champs to win Australia – John Bromwich ('39 and '46), Frank Sedgman ('49 and '50) and Ken McGregor ('52), whom he beat again in the Wimbledon final.

Dick played the U.S. Championships at Forest Hills 11 times, between 1946 and 1959, and was a semifinalist in 1950-51. He played alongside, and sometimes opposed, other big names -- U.S. champs Sedgman, Kramer, Pancho Gonzalez and Arthur Ashe, as well as Bromwich, McGregor, Pancho Segura, Gardnar Mulloy, Lou Hoad, Adrian Quist and Vic Seixas. He also kept meeting the Aussies: he defeated coach Harry Hopman (1948), lost a five-set quarterfinal to eventual champ Ken Rosewall (1956) and prevailed over young Rod Laver in the quarters (1958). Eastern natives or transplants whose profiles appear in this book also competed at Forest Hills during Savitt's years on the circuit, among them Ham Richardson, Fred Kovaleski, Bill Talbert and Alastair Martin, in the 1940s and '50s; and Ron Holmberg, Paul Cranis, Dick Raskind, Bill Tully, Donald Rubell, Sid Schwartz, Eddie Moylan, Bob Barker, Frank Shields, Gene Scott, Don Thompson and Bob Ryland, in the 1950s.

In other important tournaments in the Tri-State, Dick was a three-time champion and retired the cup at the U.S. National Indoors, held from 1900-1963 at Manhattan's Park Avenue Seventh Regiment Armory. Butch Seewagen was Savitt's ball boy. In 1948, Dr. Reginald Weir quietly broke the color barrier there and won his first match. The Nassau Bowl had a 55-year run at Long Island's Nassau Country Club in Glen Cove and featured players who have collectively won 50 Grand Slam singles titles, including Americans Savitt, Kramer, Riggs, Ashe, Seixas, Bill Tilden, Tony Trabert and Australians John Newcombe and Roy Emerson.

SECTION I: New York Tennis History

Chapter 1
Prologue

An Amazing History

For more than 500 years, tennis and its predecessors *"Jue de Paume"* and *"Royal Tennis"* have been linked to powerful people and significant events in history. Documents record the transition of tennis power from France to England to New York City and the sport's enduring influence on the world's culture. Global leaders and celebrities flock to the four Grand Slam tournaments – the Australian Open, the French Open, Wimbledon and the United States Open – all international events that impact their host countries both socially and financially.

The US Open Tennis Championships takes over New York City for a fortnight at summer's end and, like the Super Bowl, the World Series, the NBA All-Star Weekend, the Indianapolis 500 and Golf's Masters tournament, the event is a major highlight on the American sports calendar.

Hosted for 96 years by the United States Tennis Association (USTA) in New York City's borough of Queens, the Open debuted in 1915 at the West Side Tennis Club in Forest Hills. The tournament reigned there for 63 years, originally known as the amateur U.S. National Championships, and later as the US Open after the game turned professional in 1968. In 1978 the Open moved across a couple of Queens' highways to the 1964 World's Fair site in Flushing Meadows and has resided there for the past 33 years. In 1997, Arthur Ashe Stadium replaced Louis Armstrong Stadium as the main venue for the tournament, and in 2006 the whole complex was renamed the USTA Billie Jean King National Tennis Center.

The Open is the largest annually occurring sporting event in the world. Only the Olympics and the World Cup exceed the Open's attendance numbers, but they are not annual events. Studies show that the US Open has a greater economic impact on New York City than all of the Yankees, Mets, Knicks and Rangers games combined.

Credit the Open's success to the influence of legendary Eastern leaders. In May of 1881 representatives of 19 northeastern clubs formed the United States National Lawn Tennis Association (USNLTA) in New York to organize competition in the young amateur sport. That summer the Men's U.S. National Championships debuted on grass at Newport.

Tennis in New York

Newport was grand but New York City was fast becoming the business and cultural center of the United States. In 1907 a reported 11,747 immigrants arrived on Ellis Island in one day and thousands started looking for work. To keep pace with a growing population that depended on public transportation, some of the city's most famous landmarks were erected during years bridging the 19th and 20th centuries, including the Grand Central Terminal (1871), the Brooklyn Bridge (1883), the subway system (1900) and Pennsylvania (Penn) Station (1910), which opened for Long Island Railroad trains via a new tunnel under the East River. To strengthen the voice of the work force that built those landmarks, Samuel Gompers founded the American Federation of Labor (AFL) in New York. In 1886 Gompers began serving as AFL president and labor reform leaders initiated the process of harassing politicians to close the gap between the rich and the poor.

At the same time, New York City was the center of the country's tennis operations. Half of the 260 existing tennis and golf clubs affiliated with the USNLTA were located in the metropolitan area, including the influential West Side Tennis Club, originally a group of 13 players who first rented space in 1892 on Central Park West between 88th and 89th Streets. West Side expanded and by 1912 the membership of 600 voted to relocate to a spacious, 12-acre stretch of lawn at Forest Hills.

A USNLTA Players' Committee formed in 1914 lobbied to bring the men's nationals here. Newport catered to a distracted resort crowd, whereas New York spectators would come from the workplace and appreciate serious tennis. The committee argued that an estimated 25,000 players and many of the 100 top-ranked Americans were New Yorkers, among them future International Hall of Famers Malcolm Whitman, Holcombe Ward, William Larned, Oliver Campbell, Titanic survivor Karl Behr, past USLTA president Henry Slocum, Teddy Roosevelt Pell, Davis Cup captain Harold Hackett, 1908 Australian champ Fred Alexander, Marie Wagner and U.S. national women's champs Ellen Roosevelt, Maud Barger Wallach, Bessie Moore and Juliette Atkinson.

Finally, in 1915 the USNLTA agreed, by a vote of 129-119, and then unanimously, to move the U.S. National Championships to West Side's new home. *The New York Times* editorialized after the first successful event that the game had previously been played more generally in the West than in the East…but New York had begun planting tennis courts in every conceivable place where a vacant lot large enough for a court could be found.

On October 17, 1915 The Times reported: "The grip of tennis on the public was evidenced at the Forest Hills tournament…Instead of a sleepy lawn party, whose decorum was punctuated by gentle hand clapping, you find yourself viewing grueling contests which elicit the wildest applause. In 1915 tennis is a new game…more of a fight and less of a tea party…the tournament attracted as many as 10,000 on closing days…thousands traveled from California…from the far south…from the Atlantic and New England Sections…" California's William Johnston, not yet 20, defeated Nevada native Maurice McLoughlin, 24, by a score of 1-6, 6-0, 7-5, 10-8.

The success of the U.S. Championships at the new site prompted T*he New York Times* to observe in 1915 that "Forest Hills is really the centre of American tennis."[1]

The Influence of Tennis

Some game changers in New York tennis circles continued to influence the organized game throughout the 20th century. **Julie Heldman** benefited from the influential women's movement while the campaign for equal rights was still

---

[1] Robert Minton, Forest Hills, J.B. Lippincott Co., Philadelphia & New York, 1975, pp. 64, 65.

Tennis in New York

in its infancy. Julie graduated from the Dalton School at age 15 and from Stanford in 1962. When she searched for a hiatus from the tennis tour in 1966, she settled for a secretarial job at the "Mad Men" ad agency, Wells, Rich, Greene. After Julie's mother **Gladys Heldman** and **Billie Jean King** established the women's pro tour, Julie ranked No. 2 in the U.S., 5th in the world and in 1981 was named the UCLA Law School Graduate of the Year.

In 1970, Gladys Heldman, the publisher of World Tennis magazine, arranged for the Houston Racquet Club to hold a pro tournament. Nine of the top women players -- the Houston "9" -- signed $1.00 contracts with World Tennis to play in the event – among them Julie, Billie Jean King and Rosie Casals. Gladys enlisted support from Joe Cullman of Philip Morris, who agreed to donate prize money and sponsorship, which was the beginning of the Virginia Slims Circuit.

A week before the 1973 Wimbledon Championships, Billie Jean King, who that year won the fifth of her six Wimbledon singles titles, founded the Women's Tennis Association, uniting women's tennis into one pro tour.

Influential game changers also figured in achieving civil rights on the tennis court. **Althea Gibson** grew up in Harlem in the 1930s and in 1950 she broke the color line in the tennis majors. Althea stood tall that year, becoming the first African American permitted to compete in the U.S. National Championships. She went on to win 11 Grand Slam titles – five in singles and six in doubles.

Arthur Ashe won the first US Open in 1968, the Australian Open in 1970, Wimbledon in 1975 and remains the only black man to ever win a singles titles at those Grand Slam events. Ashe's efforts on behalf of racial equality were intensified after his tennis career when he moved to New York and became an international human rights activist.

Reginald Weir was a New York physician and surgeon who broke the color barrier at the 1948 USLTA National Men's Indoor Championships at the Park Avenue Seventh Regiment Armory on 68th Street. He later won five national senior titles -- three in singles and two in doubles. Barred from USLTA tournaments in his prime, Dr. Weir made tennis history, becoming the first black man to win an official USLTA championship when he captured the 1956 National Senior Indoor title. In 1952, Dr. Weir, by then over 40 years old, and George Stewart, the reigning ATA champion, were the first black men to play at the U.S. National Championships. Well past their best tennis, they both lost in the first round.

Envision the 1931 Wimbledon champ **Sidney Wood** of Southampton, N.Y., and his buddy **Frank Shields**, who grew up in the Bronx, taking turns owning a chic Manhattan laundry service with the great **Don Budge** under the slogan, "Grime Does Not Pay." A much different image of gentlemen decked out in classic white flannel trousers on the tennis court. Rumor has it that Shields, the grandfather of actress Brooke Shields and a man-about-town credited with jumpstarting Errol Flynn's movie career, rose from a sick bed and took it upon himself to lead the St. Patrick's Day parade up Fifth Avenue, and once missed a Grand Slam match because he was partying on a cruise ship that left port.

Dick Savitt, a New Jersey native and a 1950 graduate of Cornell, is observing the 60th anniversary of his 1951 singles victories at both Wimbledon and the Australian Championships. Savitt was the first of only two former Eastern juniors who have won the Australian title -- Vitas Gerulaitis won it in 1977 -- and the second of only four Eastern players who have won in singles at Wimbledon -- Sidney Wood, 1931; Althea Gibson, 1957 and '58; and John McEnroe, 1981, '83 and '84. In fact, Dick just missed winning all four majors in 1951. He lost a five-set semifinal at the French Championships to the eventual champ, Jaroslav Drobny, after leading two sets to love with leads in the next three sets. "My grandmother probably could have won that match," he said. "It was the toughest loss I ever had at that level." In the final four round at the U.S. National Championships in late summer, he lost 6-3 in the fifth set to Vic Seixas while being treated for a knee infection, recalled Savitt contemporaries and fans: Don Budge, Renee Richards, Ham Richardson, Herb Fitz Gibbon and others. In 1973 Savitt helped develop the Israel Tennis Centers. In 1998, he was the

Tennis in New York

International Tennis Association overseas tennis director. Off the court, Dick works as a financial advisor at Morgan Stanley Smith Barney in New York City.

Well known professional players emerged from Eastern's junior ranks in the modern era, among them **John McEnroe** and **Vitas Gerulaitis** of Queens, No. 1 and No. 4 in the world; **Gene and Sandy Mayer** of Woodmere, N.Y., who both ranked among the world's top ten; **Peter Fleming** of Chatham, N.J., ranked No. 8; **Mary Carillo** of Douglaston, N.Y., who today is a prominent broadcaster in sports; and **Kathleen Horvath** of Hopewell Junction, N.Y., ranked No. 10, who at age 23 quit the pro tour to go to college. Kathleen graduated magna cum laude with bachelors and masters degrees from the University of Pennsylvania's Wharton School of Business and worked as a vice president at Goldman, Sachs in private wealth management.

Fred Kovaleski, a gentlemanly type who reached the round of 16 at Wimbledon and the U.S. Championships, started out in Detroit and moved to New York City in the 1970s. Fred was a covert CIA operative in the 1950s and the model for the "I Spy" hit television series -- made famous by Bill Cosby and Robert Culp -- as he traveled undercover through the Middle East in the role of international tennis star and corporate executive. During one assignment, Fred played tennis at the Edgemoor Club in Bethesda with the Russian defector Yuri Rastvorove, who had been moved to a "safe house" in Maryland.

Ham Richardson, a Rhodes Scholar who triumphed over diabetes to rank No. 1 in the United States, migrated from Louisiana to New York City and was the chairman of the board of a New York venture capital and investment banking firm. **Renee Richards** gave a startling account of Ham's response to his sudden collapse during *Tennis Week* Founder Gene Scott's 2006 memorial service. "…Ham was lying semiconscious, soon to be unconscious," Renee said…"I knew he must be in insulin shock as he was an insulin dependent diabetic for 57 years…His wife Midge was trying to negotiate a vial of glucagon into a syringe. I helped, injected the…liquid and he started to focus his eyes. We started him drinking a Pepsi. Paramedics arrived [via a 911 call] and a young medic took Ham's blood sugar - 64! It must have been zero when he conked out. The medic was told that Ham was a former tennis champion, to which Ham piped up, 'I was No.1 in the country!' The medic said, 'Like **Rod Laver**?' Ham immediately responded, 'I beat him!' Everyone knew Ham was back…He was flat out unconscious one moment and the next he was telling this kid he beat Laver!"

Erin Callan of Douglaston, Queens, once a ranked Eastern junior tennis player and a Harvard graduate, rose in 13 years from tax lawyer to investment banker to become the chief financial officer and executive vice president of Lehman Brothers and was known as the most powerful woman on Wall Street.

Tennis in New York Co-Author Nancy McShea wrote **Gene Scott's** profile and later nominated the venerable voice of tennis – an attorney, writer/author, tournament director and co-founder of the National Junior Tennis League -- for induction into the International Tennis Hall of Fame. She mentioned on the application that he had managed tennis players. Gene scoffed, told her to delete that tidbit and said that role was tantamount to running a dry cleaning establishment. It's no wonder. Scott's grandfather, Dr. Eugene C. Sullivan, invented Pyrex, was the chairman of Corning Glass and Gene's first wife Meryl was the granddaughter of the president of Bethlehem Steel.

Seena Hamilton has been a successful New York businesswoman – entrepreneur, broadcaster, editor, journalist, and a public relations and event marketing specialist – yet she gained tennis fame in 1968 when she founded the Easter Bowl in New York, wresting the junior game from relative obscurity and planting it firmly in the national consciousness.

General Robert Shaw Oliver, the first USNLTA president who founded the Albany Tennis Club in upstate New York, was influential in both New York and national politics. He held the positions of Acting Secretary of War and Assistant

Tennis in New York

Secretary of War in the Roosevelt Administration, reporting to future U.S. president and Chief Justice William Howard Taft when Taft was the Secretary of War.

William Larned grew up in Summit, N.J., and served in the Rough Riders, the first U.S. cavalry formed in 1898 to fight the Spanish American War. At the same time, Larned joined Richard Sears and Bill Tilden as the only three men who won the U.S. National Championships seven times. Larned won the title in 1901-02, 1907, 08, 09, 1910 and 1911, and played for the U.S. Davis Cup team in 1902-03, 1905, 1908-09, 1911-12. He later became paralyzed and suffered from severe depression after a bout with spinal meningitis. Tragically, he committed suicide at Manhattan's Knickerbocker Club on December 15, 1926.

Players who rank as Game Changers: (l-r) Dick Savitt, Fred Kovaleski, Ham Richardson, Renee Richards, Gene Scott and Butch Seewagen.

Chapter 2

The Birth of Tennis

Humble Beginnings

Some say the concept of tennis dates to prehistoric times when a caveman might have used a stick to hit a round object back and forth against a tree for fun. But most tennis historians believe that today's modern game is based on a sport called "jeu de paume." The likely origins of this entertaining competition appeared in 11th century France within the confines of cloistered Catholic monasteries. The environment of a contemplative lifestyle is serene, but exercise also nourishes the spirit, so the monks devised a game they called "jeu de paume" or "palm of the hand."

Jeu de paume, which later became known as royal tennis, laid the foundation for the sport of tennis and gave France the distinction of being the first unofficial "Tennis Capital of the World." The country's passion for this sport enabled them to hold this title for almost 500 years.

The rules of jeu de paume were similar to those of modern tennis. Originally played by two people, or four in doubles, the ball, which usually consisted of a wad of wool or sawdust bound together, was hit over a piece of string or rope to an opponent. Players positioned themselves on opposite sides of that makeshift net in a walled courtyard, as depicted in the picture below. One person -- the server -- would start the point by hitting the ball off the wall to a specific area on the other person's -- the receiver's -- side of the court. The receiver would attempt to return the ball in a way that would enable them to win the point.

The two players would continue to hit the ball back and forth until one hit a winner or the other lost the point by hitting the ball out of bounds or into the net. The first person to win four points, and ahead by two points, won the game. If the score was 3 points all they would continue playing until one player led by two points. The player who won 6 games won the set. The player who won two out of three sets won the match.

Tennis in New York

The Game Becomes More Sophisticated

Many historians believe that the original French scoring used in paume was based on the face of a clock. Customized score boards did not exist so players likely used clock faces to score each game. Each player started with a score of "l'oeuf" -- which meant egg and symbolized zero. The first point was "15" or "quinze." The second point was "30" or "trente." The third point was "45" or "quarente-cinq." The third point was eventually reduced to "quarente" or "40" as quarente was quicker off the tongue than quarente-cinq.

The first player to win four points won the "game" or "jeu." If the score was tied at "quarente" then the score was called "deux" -- or "2"-- indicating that the players had to continue until one opponent won by two points. This scoring system has stood the test of time and is still used in both professional and recreational tennis matches.

To prevent sore hands and hit with more pace, the players used webbed gloves. Innovators in the sport eventually convinced players to make the transition from gloves to paddles to racquets -- originally called "battoirs" -- with sheep gut strings in order to drive a new, stronger ball -- stitched together with leather, similar to a baseball -- back and forth consistently with maximum pace and control.

Courtesy of the International Tennis Hall of Fame

The sport spread beyond the monks' courtyard and wealthy citizens started building private courts as early as 1230 A.D. Indoor courts popped up throughout France so that weather could not limit play. The number of courts increased and locals began referring to the game simply as "paume." The game became so popular and time consuming, the Archbishop of Rouen prohibited his priests in 1245 from playing the sport.

By the mid-13th century in France, the sport had become so popular that the Archbishop of Rouen in 1245 prohibited monks from playing paume. King Louis IX also outlawed the sport, insisting that it distracted citizens from daily responsibilities. Players ignored the bans and the game continued to flourish.

A half century later, one French King's passion for the sport cost him his life. King Louis X of France ruled from 1314 to 1316 and died of an illness related to a chill -- probably pneumonia -- from playing an intense game of paume in 1316 at Chateau de Vincennes. Clearly, the addiction to tennis known as the "tennis bug," where people get so caught up in the game they neglect their health and other areas of their lives, existed in the early days of the sport.

In paume, the server would shout the French word "tenetz" before each point --an imperative meaning to hold or take heed -- to alert an opponent that the serve was on its way. Henry V introduced the term to England's influential communities in the 1400s. As the sport gained popularity among the English in the late 1400s, the name changed from "tenetz" to "tennes" to "tennys" and eventually to "tennis." In addition, the French term "deux" was renamed "deuce" in English which is still used today when players are tied with three points or more.

Tennis in New York

The English preferred to call the sport "tennis" instead of "jeu de paume." They eventually renamed it "royal tennis" to acknowledge the sport's popularity among England's royalty. Yet common folk were equally taken with the sport and over the next 400 years the game spread to enclaves throughout Europe until an unusual discovery transformed the game.

Birth of Modern Tennis

Tennis as it is played today evolved from a forgotten invention by the American Charles Goodyear, who discovered the process of vulcanizing rubber in 1839 and patented it in 1844. Tennis balls made of this rubber revolutionized the game by enabling people to play tennis comfortably on surfaces like grass and asphalt.

In the early 1860s in Birmingham, England, Juan Bautista, Augurio Perera and Major Harry Gem, armed with tennis balls made of vulcanized rubber, created a game on a local lawn combining Spanish "pelota" and English "rackets," two sports where individuals or two teams of two people either facing a wall or each other -- separated by a line on the ground or a net -- hit a ball back and forth with a racket.

Perera and Gem used the rubber balls to play a game similar to modern tennis on a croquet lawn in Birmingham's wealthy Edgbaston section. They moved to Learnington Spa in Warwickshire and founded what is considered the world's first lawn tennis club.

In December 1873, Major Walter Clopton Wingfield, a retired British cavalry officer who spent 10 years of active duty in India and China, created a game similar to the one developed by Perera and Major Gem to entertain guests at a garden party at the Estate Nantclwyd in Llanelidan, Wales. He based the game on an outdoor version of jeu de paume, then known as "court tennis" -- and at the suggestion of his friend Arthur Balfour, called it "lawn tennis."

Perera and Gem did not try to market the sport whereas Wingfield understood the value of patenting, packaging and marketing a product. At age 41, Wingfield, regarded as the founder of modern tennis, received provisional letters of patent for "A Portable Court of Playing Tennis" based on his eight-page rule book entitled *Sphairistike or Lawn Tennis*." This important patent signals the birth of modern tennis. He published two books -- *The Major's Game of Lawn Tennis* and *The Book of the Game* -- as well as the very first rules of lawn tennis. The sport was played on croquet lawns and cricket fields and quickly caught on in England and rapidly spread to other major countries.

The Official Birthday of Tennis

Historians still debate the actual date and location of the first lawn tennis match, but there is little doubt that the "birth certificate" of tennis, the provisional letters of patent (Number 685) for a "Portable Court of Playing Tennis", was issued by the British patent office to Major Wingfield on February 23, 1874. That formal recognition of "lawn tennis" is comparable to a newborn child's birth certificate, which is a formal recognition of citizenship. As a tribute to the sport they love, tennis fans everywhere should celebrate the birth of tennis every year on February 23rd.

The Sport Spreads Rapidly

Interest in the sport grew quickly in England in the first year of its patent. Croquet was popular among the world's wealthier communities in the 1800s and the well manicured lawns -- typically 90 feet by 60 feet -- were also perfect for lawn tennis. Publications geared toward regular citizens and members of the military reported rave reviews about the new sport and the global reach of the British Empire added to the enthusiasm. As a result, between 1874 and 1875 tennis courts began popping up all over the world -- in the United States, Canada, China, India and Russia.

Tennis in New York

Packaging the Sport

Once Major Wingfield received the provisional patent for Sphairistike or Lawn Ten-nis he began mass marketing a "Lawn Tennis Kit." His first priority was to create a marketable package that would make it easy for people to set up a tennis court and play the game. He developed a box -- 36 inches long by 12 inches wide and 6 inches deep -- and easy to transport. His kit could be set up on any good sized manicured lawn anywhere in the world. The original packaging, depicted below, was also very attractive.

Courtesy of the International Tennis Hall of Fame

Major Wingfield's Lawn Tennis Box

Major Wingfield's lawn tennis kit cost five guineas and contained instructions, a bag of rubber balls, four oval tennis bats (or racquets), a net with pegs and ribbons to draw the court and the instructions entitled *The Book of the Game* by Major Walter Wingfield. Court dimensions outlined in the directions differ from today's tennis courts. The design listed was significantly shorter than the 78-foot courts used today and was shaped like an hour glass rather than the rectangular shape of modern courts. The court was 21 feet wide at the net and 30 feet wide at the baseline.

Major Wingfield's eight page rule book circulated throughout the Western world, especially among his fellow military members. Some of the instructions were confusing, but the ease with which a person could lay out a court made lawn tennis an instant hit.

Players did not have to buy the full kit to play. Each item was sold separately. In the late 1800s, *The Book of the Game* cost 6 pence, 12 balls could be purchased for five shillings and bats sold for 15 shillings. Consumers could save money because rackets from other racket sports were permitted for play in addition to the official lawn tennis rackets.

The coed benefits of tennis are frequently taken for granted. There are few other sports with a comparable level of popularity that appeal equally to both genders. Coed lawn tennis caught on quickly and at the same time prompted men and women to establish gender based recreational social groups.

Tennis in New York

Major Wingfield published the first rules of lawn tennis in 1874. By 1875 people throughout England were playing lawn tennis so often, interest in croquet dropped noticeably at Wimbledon's All-England Croquet Club.

To stay current, the club's board decided to convert one of the croquet lawns into a lawn tennis court. In 1876, the board of the All-England Club added "Spairistike" courts -- nicknamed "sticky courts" -- to accommodate people interested in playing lawn tennis. This novel recreational activity prompted intense competition among club members, especially men, and increased interest in a formal competition between the best players.

The First Tennis Championships

In 1877, the Wimbledon Club board proposed the idea of establishing a lawn tennis championship and changed its name to the "All-England Croquet and Lawn Tennis Club." A championship would further energize interest in lawn tennis and raise money for a horse drawn roller for the club's croquet lawns. Unofficially, members understood that a major tournament would give the club more influence in the rapidly growing sport of lawn tennis and establish Wimbledon as the premier lawn tennis club in England.

The first Wimbledon Championships, held in 1877, consisted only of men's singles. Twenty-two players of varying abilities entered the tournament that year, quite a modest number by today's standards. People were curious, though, and a crowd of approximately 200 watched the finals between William Marshall and Spencer Gore. They each paid 1 shilling to watch Mr. Gore defeat Mr. Marshall easily, 6-1, 6-2, 6-4. The popularity and prestige of this tournament enabled Wimbledon, England, to lay claim to the title, "Tennis Capital of the World." This was significant because for the first time, in almost 500 years, a country other than France could lay claim to this informal title. It was also unique because a particular municipality, not an entire country, could be considered the center of the racket sports universe.

Chapter 3

Tennis Comes to New York

The Rapid Growth of the Sport

The strategic placement of British military bases around the world hastened the rapid spread of lawn tennis. An experienced British military officer, Major Wingfield understood that the military was, at the time, the world's best distribution network. He used his connections to deliver his lawn tennis kits to as many military bases as possible. His strategy worked. Within a year of its provisional letters of patent, lawn tennis was being played on British military bases in Asia, Europe and even America.

Significant debates still fester about the roots of lawn tennis in America. The first written record, culled from the papers of Martha Summerhayes, the wife of an officer stationed in Camp Apache, Arizona, shows that tennis was played there in 1874. Mrs. Summerhayes wrote in October of 1874 that she observed another officer's wife, Mrs. Ella Wilkins Bailey, playing tennis. Mrs. Bailey and her husband apparently had just arrived from San Francisco, where they were stationed at Camp Reynolds, and presumably Mrs. Bailey had learned to play a form of tennis there.

Some historians claim that Dr. James Dwight of Nahant, Massachusetts, was America's first lawn tennis player. Still others believe that Mary Ewing Outerbridge brought tennis to America after purchasing a lawn tennis kit on a British military base in Bermuda. It is likely that in 1874 British military and merchants introduced lawn tennis in many American enclaves.

Regardless of its exact origins in the United States, the sport grew rapidly throughout the country. Mary Outerbridge returned from Bermuda on the ship S.S. Camina and played one of the first lawn tennis matches at the Staten Island Cricket and Baseball Club. In Massachusetts in 1876, Dr. James Dwight and his cousin Fred Sears organized a local round robin lawn tennis tournament with 15 entries and Dwight beat Sears in the first final. That same year the New Orleans Lawn Tennis Club reigned as America's first lawn-tennis-only-club.

The most successful lawn tennis clubs surfaced in the northeastern United States. New York, Philadelphia and Boston were among the most powerful sites, as the wealthiest and most influential people in business and tennis resided in

Tennis in New York

those areas. These clubs were independent, devised their own rules and used their own equipment for lawn tennis competitions.

Diversity was suddenly an issue when the best players from these clubs participated in the first organized national championships in Staten Island, New York. Players started bickering about rules and equipment which triggered the formation of the United States National Lawn Tennis Association (USNLTA).

America's First Tennis Tournament

The establishment of America's first national tennis championships was in many ways a family affair. One of Mary Outerbridge's six brothers, August Emilio Outerbridge -- an older brother who was an officer on the board of the Staten Island Cricket and Baseball Club -- was so intrigued by the sport his sister brought from Bermuda he convinced the board in 1874 to approve the placement of permanent lawn tennis courts at the club.

However, Mary's younger brother, Eugenius Harvey Outerbridge, had the idea to establish a national lawn tennis championship at the club, which was located on waterfront grounds called Camp Washington, beneath what is now the Staten Island Ferry Terminal.

The growing prestige of The Wimbledon Championships sparked worldwide excitement about lawn tennis. Eugenius, just 20 years old at the time, suggested that the club host an event called "the tournament for the championship of America." The club agreed and the national tournament debuted at the Staten Island Club on September 1, 1880. A silver cup valued at $100 was awarded to the winner. Several of the country's best male players decided to play the tournament, giving it status as the first national tennis championship in America.

Many spectators arrived to view the unique new competition held by the water on beautifully manicured lawns. The accomplished English player O.E. Woodhouse defeated the Canadian J.F. Helmuth in the final to win the men's singles title. Woodhouse had lost earlier in the summer to Herbert Lawford in the finals of the All-Comers tournament at the 1880 Wimbledon Championships. Two local residents won the men's doubles competition. Many of the players, however, considered the tournament a failure because the tournament's rules and equipment differed from those used in their home clubs. The idea of standardizing rules and equipment sparked disagreements between players and administrators.

Top players from New England and Philadelphia questioned three aspects of the tournament – the method of scoring, the height of the net and the type and weight of the balls – which stirred the first major controversy in the history of American tournament tennis. The debate raged on for several months during inter-club play until leaders finally agreed that a governing body should be established to regulate tennis in America.

Founding the USNLTA

On May 5, 1881 a notice appeared in the popular sports publication, *The American Cricketer*, announcing that the inaugural meeting of the United States National Lawn Tennis Association (USNLTA) would take place on May 21, 1881 at the Fifth Avenue Hotel in New York City.

The notice was signed by Clarence M. Clark, president of the All Philadelphia Lawn Tennis Committee; James Dwight of the Beacon Park Athletic Association of Boston; and Eugenius Harvey Outerbridge of the Staten Island Cricket and

Tennis in New York

Baseball Club of New York. The fact that leaders from three of the country's most influential lawn tennis clubs had signed the notice was significant.

Modern tennis is managed by accomplished professionals in their fifties and sixties who play the game recreationally. In contrast, Clark, Dwight and Outerbridge were active, accomplished players in their twenties when they engineered the development of the USNLTA. They were among the best players in the country and possessed the energy and entrepreneurial spirit to create a powerful governing body for the sport.

There was great excitement at the May 21st meeting about the potential for a unified approach to lawn tennis. Thirty six delegates representing 19 clubs -- with proxy votes for another 15 clubs – attended. Each club was allowed one vote. Clubs in attendance included the well respected Albany Tennis Club, Germantown Cricket Club, Longwood Cricket Club, Orange Lawn Tennis Club, University of Pennsylvania and Yale University. They arrived at a consensus to form the USNLTA, develop the rules and regulations of the sport as well as the structure and location of the national lawn tennis championships.

The sport's first national governing body emerged that day, marking the official start of nationally organized tennis, and hundreds of other countries followed suit. Tennis leaders who attended the meeting believed that their respective clubs should have USNLTA voting rights to protect their interests. And they agreed that the first officers must have stellar reputations and impeccable credentials. Albany's General Robert S. Oliver was the popular choice for president, Samuel Campbell was named the vice president and Clarence Clark was appointed secretary-treasurer.

Club delegates decided that the rules and regulations used at The Wimbledon Championships would work well in the United States. A committee was formed to develop lawn tennis rules and regulations based on those used at Wimbledon's All England Club and at the Marylebone Cricket Club.

It was also agreed that the USNLTA would govern the national championships. After some heated debate, a majority of members voted to host the first U.S. National championships at the newly built Newport Casino in Newport, Rhode Island, in August of 1881. The club was considered to be one of the country's nicest lawn tennis sites.

The first United States National Lawn Tennis Championships was a men-only event and entrée was restricted to official members of USNLTA clubs. The old saying -- "First impressions are lasting" -- is very true. The tournament paved the way for 130 years of elite tennis in America. The rules adopted by the USNLTA and used at the tournament were acceptable to both the players and fans. The highlight of the tournament was the exceptional play of a young Harvard graduate, Richard "Dick" Sears, who is acknowledged as the first truly dominant tennis player in American history.

Sears defeated William Glyn of the Staten Island Cricket Club, 6-0, 6-3, 6-2, in that first final, marking the beginning of his amazing streak of 18 consecutive victories and seven straight titles at the U.S. Championships. In men's doubles, Philadelphia's Clarence Clark and Frederick Winslow Taylor upset the heavily favored Sears and James Dwight in the semifinals and then defeated Alexander Van Rensselaer and A.E. Newbold in the final, 6-5, 6-4, 6-5.

The three original USNLTA founders -- we call them America's "Three Musketeers" -- made history. By the second year of the U.S. Championships two of the three had claimed a winner's trophy. Clarence Clark won the first men's doubles title, James Dwight won the second and was later the longest serving USNLTA president.

America's third musketeer, Eugenius Outerbridge, never won a national title. However, he gained legendary status as the president of the Homasote Company, still in existence today in New Jersey and one of the first environmentally

Tennis in New York

friendly American companies. He was also the president of the New York Chamber of Commerce and the first chairman of the Port Authority of New York and New Jersey. Eugenius was so powerful he was immortalized when the Outerbridge Crossing, a bridge connecting Staten Island and New Jersey, was named after him in 1928.

America's three musketeers introduced tennis to the American public as the favorite sport of society's most influential people and turned the U.S. National Championships into one of the country's premier sporting events. First impressions are lasting; tennis has maintained a reputation as the most popular recreational and spectator sport of the wealthiest and most influential people in American society.

Growing Power of the Sections

The U.S. National Championships in Newport were extremely successful. Men's singles and doubles debuted in 1881; women's singles gained entrée in 1887; women's doubles arrived in 1889; and mixed doubles showed up in 1892. Players, spectators and tournament officials considered the tournament a tremendous success. Most USNLTA leaders at the time felt that the tournament site should be the permanent home of the championships.

However, the USNLTA, since its founding, had been controlled by a handful of men residing in the New York, Philadelphia and New England areas. That narrow control combined with the success of the U.S. Championships and rapidly growing interest in the sport beyond the northeast corridor triggered significant conflict within the association in the early 20th century. Local communities gained greater influence in the sport. Lawn tennis associations were established around the country to manage the sport in specific geographic areas. New York tournaments were organized by the New York Lawn Tennis Association and tournaments in Northern New Jersey were coordinated by the East Jersey Lawn Tennis Association.

Profitable local tournaments around the country, combined with the sport's growth in the South, the Midwest and in the West led to widespread disagreement about governance of the association, the definition of amateur players and the location of the national tournament. For the first time people outside the Northeastern U.S. area exerted significant influence on USNLTA affairs.

Association by-law and constitutional changes were traditionally discussed and voted on at the USNLTA Annual Meeting, typically held in February at the Waldorf-Astoria in New York City. Even though the U.S. National Championships were not contested in New York at the time, American tennis power remained in New York with the leadership and staff of the USNLTA.

The growth of tennis, combined with changing world politics and demographics, forced tennis leaders to consider discussing taboo subjects. Topics included changing the division of power within the association; moving the U.S. Championships from Newport; and hosting tournaments where amateurs and professionals could compete against each other, a major area of disagreement until the beginning of the Open era in 1968. Only one of those issues was agreed to at the 1913 annual meeting. For the first time, an organized group of sections was given significant voting privileges in the association.

Each of the then-48 states in the U.S. and the District of Columbia were assigned to a section. According to American Lawn Tennis[2] the sections were as follows: Inter-Mountain (Colorado, Idaho, Utah and Wyoming); Middle Atlantic (Delaware, District of Columbia, Maryland and West Virginia); Middle States (New Jersey, New York and Pennsylva-

---

[2] *American Lawn Tennis (ALT)*, January 15, 1913, Page 398

Tennis in New York

nia); New England (Connecticut, Maine, Massachusetts, New Hampshire, Rhode Island and Vermont); Northwestern (Minnesota, Montana, North Dakota and South Dakota); Pacific States (California, Oregon and Washington); Southern (Alabama, Florida, Georgia, Louisiana, Mississippi, North Carolina, South Carolina and Tennessee); South Western (Arizona, Arkansas, Nevada, New Mexico, Oklahoma and Texas); and Tri-State (Indiana, Kentucky and Ohio) and Western (Illinois, Iowa, Kansas, Michigan, Missouri, Nebraska and Wisconsin).

This realignment of the association's power base -- from complete central control to central leadership with strong regional authority -- has defined the organization since 1913. Major national tournaments, among them the National Clay Court Championships, were established in other regions of the country. This unique period of rapid change in tennis history led to greater sectional power in the U.S. and eventually to greater international influence for both the USNLTA and the U.S. National Championships.

Chapter 4

New York Becomes the Tennis Capital of the World

West Side Tennis Club

The new balance of power between the sections and the national association led to serious discussions at the 1915 USNLTA Annual Meeting about moving the U.S. National Championships from Newport to another location. It was clear that the tournament's great success deserved a larger expanse to accommodate more spectators and generate maximum revenue for the USNLTA. Not surprisingly, many sectional leaders preferred that the tournament be moved away from the popular Northeast corridor of the United States.

However, the revenue issue was important and New York City was at the time the largest and most influential city in the country. Timing is everything, as the saying goes, and most association leaders believed that a club in New York would increase the visibility and profitability of the U.S. Championships.

Luckily, a group of passionate tennis players in New York City had founded the famous West Side Tennis Club in 1892. They first rented space on Central Park West between 88th and 89th Streets and built 5 clay tennis courts. In 1902 the club rented space on 117th Street near Columbia University which allowed for 8 courts. In 1908 the club rented space on 238th Street and Broadway and built 12 grass and 15 clay courts.

In 1911, the West Side Tennis Club hosted a Davis Cup match between the U.S. and Great Britain at the Broadway site. The event attracted thousands of spectators and the club gained the respect and attention of influential USNLTA leaders. But it was clear that that location could not handle large crowds on a regular basis. As a result, West Side club leaders decided to purchase land in a beautiful section in New York City's Borough of Queens called Forest Hills.

Tennis in New York

Forest Hills was founded by Margaret Olivia Slocum Sage in 1906. Mrs. Sage, the widow of railroad magnet and financier Russell Sage and the founder of the Russell Sage Foundation, purchased 142 acres of land in Forest Hills in 1909. Under the guidance of legendary architect Grosvenor Atterbury, the foundation supported the building of a planned community modeled on the garden communities of England. The community was laid out beautifully with exquisite flowers and trees and unique Tudor-style homes.

West Side's leaders fell in love with the beautiful Forest Hills community and for $77,000 purchased property conveniently located near the Long Island Railroad, which had gained access to New York City's Penn Station in 1910. To match the décor of the area, they built a Tudor-style clubhouse for $25,000 in 1914 which established the club as the newest and most beautiful tennis site in New York City.

Julian Myrick, the president of West Side in 1915, was an entrepreneur and a natural salesman who started a successful insurance company, Ives and Myrick. He later became one of the founders of the American College of Life Underwriters. Myrick was so engaging and skilled at selling life insurance and tennis, he convinced the leaders of the USNLTA to move the U.S. Championships in 1915 from the Newport Casino to the West Side Tennis Club in Forest Hills.

The rationale for the move was obvious. New York City would host an easily accessible tournament, on spacious grounds with an iconic clubhouse, and accommodate more spectators, gain greater international visibility and bring in more revenue for the USNLTA. The timing was ideal. In less than a year, amid the early chaos of the First World War, Forest Hills was heralded as the "Tennis Capital" of the U.S. which laid the groundwork for Myrick to become an influential president of the USNLTA.

The Influence of War

The assassination on June 28, 1914 of the heir to the throne of Austria-Hungary, Archduke Franz Ferdinand of Austria, started a domino effect of international conflict that led to the outbreak of World War I in Europe in August of that year. Recreational sports seem unimportant during a time of significant military strife and it was clear that tennis would take a back seat during the conflict in Europe and Asia. As a result, tennis in New York gained greater international visibility.

Initially called The Great War, the First World War forced the cancellation of the Wimbledon Championships in 1915, 1916, 1917 and 1918; the French Championships disappeared in 1915, 1916, 1917, 1918 and 1919; and the Australian Championships closed its doors in 1916, 1917 and 1918. However, since the United States was not directly involved in the War prior to 1917, the U.S. Championships were not cancelled.

The success of the 1915 U.S. Championships at West Side, combined with that year's cancellation of Wimbledon and the French, gave New York a unique status in the tennis world. The increasing success of the U.S. Championships in 1916, 1917 and 1918, years when Wimbledon, the French and the Australian Championships were still in hiatus, coupled with the growing international power of the New York City-based USNLTA, firmly established New York City as the "Tennis Capital of the World," a title it has held for almost 100 years.

Woodrow Wilson was the president of the United States on April 6, 1917 when Congress voted to support his declaration of war on Germany. To support this war effort, the U.S. drafted 2.8 million men to defend the country. The USNLTA, at its February 1917 annual meeting, adopted a resolution supporting President Wilson and the Congress in severing diplomatic relations with Germany. A month later, the association supported proposals for the military draft. Even the USNLTA president, George Adee, was assigned to Fort Dix in New Jersey for military training.

Tennis in New York

This major military conflict intensified the focus of society on the employment resources, cultural and recreational needs of local communities. In fact, President Wilson stated publicly on several occasions his belief that sports and exercise could help the war effort by ensuring that young men would be healthy enough to fight a war for the United States.

Consequently, the USNLTA's sectional associations played a more important role in popularizing grassroots tennis. Local leaders could promote the sport in neighborhoods in a way that the USNLTA national office could not. They were familiar with people's needs and could manage the sport to suit particular locations around the country. This new hyper-local world order increased the influence of sectional associations and paved the way for the establishment of the Eastern Tennis Association (ETA).

Chapter 5

The Evolution of Tennis in New York

Founding of the Eastern Lawn Tennis Association (ELTA)

As tennis spread rapidly worldwide in the early 20th century, the USNLTA sectional associations grew as well. In 1920[3] the USNLTA dropped the word 'National' from its title and became known simply as the USLTA. Moreover, in the century's first decade, sectional associations had demanded more independence, so in the century's second decade, states and regions within the associations demanded more independence as well.

The popularity of the U.S. Championships in Forest Hills significantly increased interest in the sport in and around New York City. As a result, tennis leaders in New York and New Jersey wanted more local control of the sport in their region. Leaders in New York and Northern New Jersey had for years considered separating from the Middle States Section. These two regions, because of their close geographic proximity to the USLTA power base, were the most independent of the Middle States' subdivisions. However, public separation did not become reality until 1921.

That year, the New York Lawn Tennis Association (NYLTA), the organization officially responsible for coordinating tennis in the state of New York, asserted its independence. Its name was eventually changed to the Eastern Lawn Tennis Association (ELTA) and Charles S. Landers, its first president, led the organization from 1921-1922.

Landers was an engineer who became more well known in 1923 when he played a vitally important role in the design and building of the West Side Tennis Club's famous horseshoe stadium, which was financed by Alastair Martin's parents, Bradley and the former Helen Phipps. As was noted earlier, the finals of the U.S. National Championships/US Open were held there from 1924 until 1978 when the tournament moved to the Queens site in Flushing Meadows.

---

[3]American Lawn Tennis; January 15, 1912 and February 15, 1912

Tennis in New York

The influence of the NYLTA was magnified because it was the parent body for the powerful Metropolitan Lawn Tennis Association (MLTA), which was responsible for organizing tennis tournaments and other tennis related activities in Brooklyn, the Bronx, Long Island, Manhattan, Queens, Staten Island and Northern New Jersey. Because of its geographic proximity to USLTA headquarters, the MLTA enjoyed a close working relationship with the national body which enabled the NYLTA to have more input into national tennis policy and operations than any other sectional or local association.

A 1922[4] article in The New York Times announced that Jones W. Mersereau had been nominated for the position of president of both the NYLTA and the MLTA, providing further proof of this association's power. The article indicated that the nominees for the MLTA Executive Committee were as follows: President Jones W. Mersereau, elected the second president of the ELTA, served from 1923-1924 and was later elected the 13th USLTA president, serving from 1925-27; Vice President Walter L. Pate, who would later be elected the third president of the ELTA and serve from 1925-26; Treasurer Louis P. Daily became the fourth president of the ELTA and served from 1927-28; Brooklyn and Manhattan Representative Maskell E. Fox was elected the eighth president of the ELTA and served from 1936-38; New Jersey Representative Holcombe Ward became the sixth president of the ELTA, served from 1932-33 and was later elected the 19th USLTA president, serving from 1937-47. The Queens Representative Charles S. Landers was elected the first ELTA president, from 1921-22, after serving as the president of the West Side Tennis Club from 1918-20. Those nominees were easily elected to their respective positions and were, without question, among the most powerful regional leadership teams in tennis history.

The NYLTA also included the Adirondack Lawn Tennis Association; Great Lakes Lawn Tennis Association; Hudson Valley Lawn Tennis Association; Mohawk Lawn Tennis Association; and the Onondaga Lawn Tennis Association in its membership. These bodies coordinated tennis activities in the areas outside New York City and Northern New Jersey.

As has been noted, the Eastern Lawn Tennis Association (ELTA) was founded to manage and promote tennis in all of New York State and areas approximately 30 to 35 miles from the borders of New York City. Since its founding, the section's geographic boundaries have proven to be the most complicated of any section since they are defined by mileage from New York City rather than by naturally grouped municipalities or counties.

Eastern currently includes the entire State of New York; the geographic areas of Connecticut that are within 35 miles of New York City (excepting that part which is within the city limits of Stamford which is part of the New England section); the entire counties of Passaic, Bergen, Essex, Union and Hudson in New Jersey. In addition, the section covers Monmouth County in New Jersey excepting the boroughs and townships of Allentown, Avon-by-the-Sea, Belmar, Bradley

The West Side Tennis Club celebrated its 100th anniversary in 1992.

---

4 New York Times; December 17, 1922

Tennis in New York

Beach, Brielle, Englishtown, Farmingdale, Freehold, Freehold Townships, Howell, Manalapan, Manasquan, Millstone, Neptune, Neptune City, Roosevelt, Sea Girt, South Belmar, Spring Lake, Spring Lake Heights, Upper Freehold, Wall which are part of the Middle States Section.

Eastern also covers Middlesex County in New Jersey excepting the boroughs and townships of Cranbury, Jamesburg, Monroe, Plainsboro and South Brunswick which are also part of the Middle States Section. The section also includes Somerset County in New Jersey excepting the boroughs and townships of Bedminster, Branchburg, Hillsborough, Rocky Hill and Montgomery which are part of the Middle States Section. Finally, Eastern covers Morris County in New Jersey excepting the boroughs and townships of Chester, Chester Township, Mount Olive, Netcong, Roxbury, Mount Arlington and Washington. The complicated sectional boundaries between Eastern and Middles States (combined with the split of the New York area from the Middle States section) have led to intense sectional battles over the years about membership and revenue sharing.

The ELTA dropped 'Lawn' from its name in 1975 and became the Eastern Tennis Association (ETA). In 1998 the organization's name changed again, this time to the United States Tennis Association (USTA) Eastern Section. Now registered as an independent 501(c)(4) organization with the I.R.S., USTA Eastern has, since its founding in 1921, elected a remarkably accomplished group of board members and presidents.

Eastern's presidents have all been volunteers who have held the title of president with some holding the title of president and chief executive officer (CEO). Initially, the ELTA did not have a full-time paid staff. The organization existed in a one-room office in New York City near Grand Central Station. A part-time employee, Vy Ball, came to the office once a week to open mail and send pertinent information to members. Thanks to the increasing numbers of tournament players and USTA contributions to the sections, Eastern moved to White Plains. In 1977 the volunteer board hired Carol Levy as its first executive secretary.

Outstanding individuals have served Eastern in the role of executive secretary, executive director and/or chief operating officer (COO). The legendary Doris Herrick served from 1978-1997 and again as the interim executive director, from 2005-06. David Goodman served from 1997- 2000; Denise Jordan, 2000-05; and D.A. Abrams, 2006-present. These people have significantly influenced the growth of the organization, which today has an annual budget exceeding $3,000,000.

Volunteers who serve and have served Eastern as president -- or president and CEO -- are charged with the complicated and time consuming responsibility of running the board, volunteers and staff and are ultimately responsible for the organization's success or failure. The influence of this position on tennis, both in the New York region and nationally, historically tags the Eastern president as one of the most powerful volunteers in the tennis world. We list the names below of individuals who have served in that capacity.

1.	Charles S. Landers	1921-1922
2.	Jones W. Mersereau[5]	1923-1924
3.	Walter L. Pate	1925-1926
4.	Louis P. Dailey[6]	1927-1928
5.	P. Schuyler Van Bloem	1929-1931

[5] USLTA President from 1925 to 1927
[6] USLTA President in 1930

Tennis in New York

6.	Holcombe Ward[7]	1932-1933
7.	Russell B. Kingman[8]	1934-1935
8.	Maskell E. Fox	1936-1938
9.	Anton E. Von Bernuth	1939-1941
10.	Richurd M. Hurd, Jr.	1942
11.	Charles E. Hall	1943-1947
12.	W. Dickinson Cunningham	1948-1952
13.	James B. Dickey[9]	1953-1959
14.	Donald O. Hobart	1960-1961
15.	Clifford Sutter	1962-1963
16.	Alastair B.Martin[10]	1964-1965
17.	Henry Benisch	1966-1967
18.	Leslie J. Fitz Gibbon	1968-1969
19.	Ernest J. Oberlander	1970-1972
20.	Eugene L. Scott	1972-1973
21.	George Dartt	1974-1975
22.	Julius Larkin Hoyt	1976-1977
23.	Barbara S. Williams[11]	1978-1979
24.	Harry A. Marmion[12]	1980-1981
25.	Alex. B. Aitchison	1982-1983
26.	Richard A. Scheer	1984-1985
27.	Robert A. Schmitz	1986-1987
28.	Elaine F. Viebranz	1988-1989
29.	Daniel B. Dwyer	1990-1991
30.	Louis C. Dimock	1992-1993
31.	Lois Prince	1994-1995
32.	Marina Nudo	1996-1997
33.	Robert W. Ingersole	1998-1999
34.	Michael N. Gordon	2001-2001
35.	Louis C. Dimock	2002-2003
36.	Stephen B. Cobb	2004-2005

[7] USLTA President from 1937 to 1947
[8] USLTA President from 1951 to 1952
[9] USLTA President in 1964
[10] USLTA President from 1969 to 1970
[11] The first woman President of Eastern and the first woman to serve on the USTA Board of Directors.
[12] USTA President from 1997 to 1998

Tennis in New York

37.	Dale G. Caldwell[13]	2006-2008
38.	Tim Heath	2009-2010
39.	Jeff Williams	2011-2012

Doris Herrick (front, right) joined past Eastern presidents in the early '90s at the United Nations for the annual Hall of Fame dinner -- clockwise from top left: Harry Marmion, Lois Prince, Gene Scott, Barbara Williams, Alastair Martin, Dan Dwyer, Bob Schmitz, Elaine Viebranz and Lou Dimock.

Current USTA Eastern President Jeff Williams (top row, center) chatted with Skip Hartman (l), Laura Canfield (r) and David Dinkins and Lauren Hartman (bottom row) at the 2011 Hall of Fame.

Past Eastern presidents Tim Heath (left) and Dale Caldwell (right) at the Hall of Fame dinner with Dale's parents, the Rev. Gilbert and Grace Caldwell.

The expanding influence of the 17 USTA Sections has forged a healthy balance of power between USTA and Sectional leadership that is comparable to the United States Federal Government and its 50 States and the District of Columbia. Despite differences of opinion on how to legislate their authority, all parties involved in tennis love the sport, all branches of government have a common love of country and both have a common mission to work together to benefit their individual constituencies.

---

[13] The first African American President of Eastern and the first African American to serve as a Section President (2006-2008) and USTA Board Member (2011 to present).

Chapter 6
Black Tennis in New York

Black Tennis Clubs Emerge

The first two decades of the 20th century are remembered as the most remarkable period of growth for the sport of tennis. This expansion of the sport is not as notable for the number of people who started playing tennis as it is for the wide variety of developing organizations whose leaders focused on increasing participation in the sport.

Tennis growth in the country's local communities led to the establishment of USNLTA sectional associations. The popularity of tennis among black players, who were not permitted to play on white-only tennis courts in these sections, led to the founding of the American Tennis Association (ATA).

The amazing growth of tennis clubs for black players mirrored the tennis popularity among other communities around the world in the early 20th century. This was most evident in New York City, viewed as a place of opportunity for blacks who had moved from southern communities that practiced legalized segregation. Tennis became the sport of the 'Black Elite' in New York. The two most famous black tennis clubs there were the Ideal Tennis Club and the Cosmopolitan Club located in the Harlem section of New York City (which many considered the "Capital of Black America").

On Thanksgiving Day in 1916, leaders of the most influential black tennis clubs founded the American Tennis Association (ATA) at the Washington, D.C. YMCA. This organization was established to promote recreational tennis and coordinate competition among players of all races and backgrounds. It is still the country's oldest, continually active African American sports organization. The ATA's New York section has, since its founding, been called the New York Tennis Association (NYTA) and is known historically as one the association's most active sections.

The Ideal Tennis Club was founded in the Harlem section of New York City in 1914 on West 138th Street. It has an important place in history because leaders there organized the first multi-state competitions among black tennis clubs, including traveling teams from Baltimore, Boston, New Haven, Philadelphia, Springfield (Massachusetts) and Washington, D.C. Ideal's founding members wielded great influence as they were among the original founders of the ATA.

Tennis in New York

One of the black community's most successful tennis clubs, founded in 1915, also in Harlem, was the Colonial Tennis Club (whose name was changed to the Cosmopolitan Club). The Cosmopolitan Club would eventually become the most famous black tennis club in America because of its unique connection to two of the greatest champions in tennis history -- Don Budge and Althea Gibson.

In the early 1920s tennis was becoming a very popular pastime among the most successful individuals in both the black and white communities. The powerful white-only clubs were at the peak of their power and greatly influenced USLTA actions. Black tennis clubs in local communities and at Historically Black Colleges and Universities (HBCU) were being formed to increase interest and participation in the sport. Tennis had become the most popular recreational sport for the families of doctors, lawyers, professors and ministers in the black community.

Tennis had become so popular among all influential people in New York City and Northern New Jersey, in fact, that it demonstrated both the regions' influence and affluence.

The Shady Rest Country Club, founded in 1921 in Scotch Plains, New Jersey, showcased tennis courts and a beautiful golf course and had the distinction of being America's very first Black Country club. As in the exclusive white communities, Shady Rest serviced some of the wealthiest people in the New York Region.

By 1928 there were 18 ATA tennis clubs in the New York Tennis Association (NYTA)[14]. These clubs were located in Brooklyn, Flushing, Long Island, Manhattan and New Rochelle. The NYTA member clubs in 1928 included the Arrow Tennis Club (Manhattan); Blue Bird Tennis Club (Manhattan); Brooklyn Tennis and Country Club (Brooklyn); Corona Tennis Club (Long Island); Cosmopolitan Tennis Club (Manhattan); Ebenezer Tennis Club (Brooklyn); E & S Tennis Club (Manhattan); Eccles Memorial Tennis Club (New Rochelle); Flushing Tennis Club (Flushing); Greenville Tennis Club (Manhattan); Huguenot Tennis Club (Manhattan); Ideal Tennis Club (Manhattan); Manhattan Tennis Club (Manhattan); Orion Tennis Club (Manhattan); St. Nicholas Tennis Club (Manhattan); St. Thomas Tennis Club (Manhattan); Utopian Tennis Club (Brooklyn); and the Wicoma Tennis Club (Manhattan);

American Tennis Association champ Jimmy McDaniel (l) and 1938 Grand Slam champ Don Budge (r) played a 1940 exhibition at the Harlem Cosmopolitan Club.
photos courtesy International Tennis Hall of Fame and Museum

There were 15 ATA clubs in the New Jersey Tennis Association (NJTA) by 1928[15]. The clubs were located in Asbury Park, Bordentown, Camden, Elizabeth, Hackensack, Jersey City, Newark, Orange, Plainfield, Trenton and Westfield. In the 1920s tennis was as popular in New Jersey's black community as it was in New York's black community.

The NJTA member clubs included: Asbury Park Tennis Club (Neptune); Bordentown Tennis Club (Bordentown); Camden YMCA (Camden); Capital City Tennis Club (Trenton); Carlisle Tennis Club (Newark); Douglass Tennis Club

---

[14] *Black Tennis: An Archival Collection: 1890-1962* by Arthur A. Carrington, P.13
[15] *Black Tennis: An Archival Collection: 1890-1962* by Arthur A. Carrington, P.13

Tennis in New York

(Westfield); Hackensack Tennis Club (Hackensack); Imperial Tennis Club (Newark); Plainfield Tennis Club (Plainfield); Shore Players Tennis Club (Asbury Park); The Bachelor's Tennis Club (Orange); The Musolits Tennis Club (Jersey City); The North End Tennis Club (Elizabeth); The Orioles Tennis Club (Montclair); and the Triune Tennis Club (Newark).

Beginning of the End of Tennis Segregation

The segregation of tennis was tested many times over the years. Reginald Weir and Gerald Norman of New York mounted one of the most notable challenges to tennis segregation when they paid an entry fee to participate in the 1929 USLTA Junior Indoor Championships at the 7th Regiment Armory in New York City. Their entry was initially accepted because the tournament director did not know that they were African Americans.

Unfortunately, when they checked into the tournament they were denied spots in the draw because of their race. The National Association for the Advancement of Colored People (NAACP) filed a formal grievance against the USLTA claiming discrimination against the players. The USLTA responded by stating that it did not allow 'colored' players in their championships.

Historic Budge-McDaniel Encounter

Despite the blatant discrimination against Weir and Norman, progress was being made. One of the most important tennis matches in history took place in 1940 at the Cosmopolitan Club. Don Budge proved that he was the best white player in the segregated white tennis world by becoming the first male player to win all four of the Grand Slam Championships -- Australian, French, Wimbledon and the U.S. – in a single year in 1938. To date only Budge, Rod Laver (1962), Maureen Connolly (1953) and Steffi Graf (1988, won the Golden Slam – all four majors and the Olympics gold medal) have accomplished this incredible feat.

Budge turned professional in 1939 and dominated his pro matches in the same way he dominated the circuit when he was an amateur. He had proven that he was one of the greatest players of all time because for several years he consistently beat all of the top white players in the world. However, as a true competitor, he wanted to test himself against all of the best players in the world, regardless of race, and especially the top black players who, because of racial discrimination, were not allowed to compete at the Grand Slam Championships.

In 1940 Budge took a social risk when he played a talented black player named Jimmy McDaniel on the clay courts of the Cosmopolitan Club in Harlem. Jimmy was a left hander with smooth strokes who proved that he was the best player in the black tennis world when he won the 1939 ATA men's singles championships at Hampton University in Hampton, Virginia. He went on to dominate the black tennis world in much the same way that Budge dominated the white tennis world. McDaniel won the ATA Championships in 1940 and 1941, confirming his place as one of the best black male players in history.

The social implications of this match in New York City were enormous. Not only was this a contest between a black and white player -- six years before Jackie Robinson was allowed to play in baseball's major leagues -- it was a symbolic match between the elite of the white and black communities. At that time many people in white society believed that blacks were not capable of competing with the smarter and more athletic whites in sports like baseball, football or basketball. These racist individuals were also convinced that blacks would never be able to compete with whites in the elite and highly intellectual sport of tennis.

Tennis in New York

However, Budge knew that a person's color had nothing to do with his or her tennis ability. In the minds of those people who did not understand the passions of an elite athlete, Budge had nothing to win and everything to lose in this match. Historians have not given Budge the credit he deserves for doing the right thing and voluntarily breaking the color barrier in tennis. If Budge had lost that match, the results of white-only tennis championships around the world would have been called into question.

The Cosmopolitan club was filled to capacity for this historic match. Before the first serve the largely African-American audience was filled with anticipation and hope. A good showing by McDaniel would help to legitimize African American tennis and the ATA. A win would be a historic victory for African Americans, the likes of which the world of sport had not yet seen because of the implications for upper class white society. The sports color barrier had been broken before this match. However, the class based color barrier had not been penetrated.

The match was much more competitive than the final score indicates. Don Budge won the match 6-1, 6-2. However, afterward Budge stated that he believed McDaniel was playing at a level comparable to the world's top ten players. He also implied that if McDaniel had the opportunity to practice against the best players he could eventually compete for the world's No. 1 ranking. This match helped to pave the way for the integration of the sport by another talented player from the Cosmopolitan Club in Harlem.

The Color Barrier is Officially Broken

Althea Gibson was born in Silver, South Carolina, and moved to New York when she was just 3 years old. She was a talented athlete who won the New York City Police Athletic League (PAL) paddle tennis championship as a teenager. The PAL Director Buddy Walker introduced her to tennis which she picked up quickly. Gibson's obvious talent in tennis enabled her to earn an honorary membership in the Cosmopolitan Club where she got lessons from the legendary one-armed tennis instructor Fred Johnson.

Gibson became so good that she won the ATA 18 and under national championships in 1944. In 1946 she lost a very close ATA women's singles championship match in Wilberforce, Ohio, to Roumania Peters by the score 6-4, 7-9, 6-3. Gibson was not used to losing and was heartbroken. However, she was committed to doing whatever was necessary to become a champion. Gibson moved south to improve her game under the tutelage of Dr. R. Walter Johnson in Lynchburg, Virginia, during the summers and Dr. Hubert Eaton in Wilmington, North Carolina, during the school year. These tennis and life coaches helped to improve the games of some of the best players in the black tennis community. In 1946, they began the very involved process of developing Gibson's mind and body in a way that would enable her to become one of the best female athletes in the world.

This arrangement was exactly what Althea needed. She won the 1947 ATA women's singles title and went on to win 9 other women's singles championships, from 1948-56 and 8 ATA mixed doubles national titles, from 1948-55 with Dr. Johnson. In much the same way that Don Budge wanted to test his skills against all of the best players regardless of race, Althea Gibson wanted to play against the world's best white players.

After more than a half-century of fighting the national governing body of tennis for equal rights on the tennis court, black players were finally allowed to play in some USLTA tournaments in the late 1940s. Gibson made history at the USLTA National Indoor Championships in 1950 by becoming the first black player to be seeded in any USLTA national championship. She lost in the finals and became the first black player to reach a final of a USLTA national championship. However, Gibson longed to become the best player in the world and recommitted herself to working as hard as she possibly could to win a Grand Slam Championship at least once in her life.

Tennis in New York

In spite of the integration of some tennis tournaments, Gibson was not allowed to play at the U.S. National Championships. The reasons given by the USLTA were that her record was not strong enough for entry into the tournament. Even though she had done well in indoor tournaments the USLTA wanted her to prove her skills at the outdoor tune-up events for the championships which were held at "White-Only" tennis clubs that would not allow her to play.

Her success at the indoor tournament proved to many influential people that she had the ability to compete with the women playing the U.S. National Championships. Betram Baker of the ATA and others in the tennis community lobbied the USLTA to allow her to play in the tournament. The pressure on the USLTA to do the right thing intensified when former world champion Alice Marble had a letter published in the most influential tennis publication of the time, *American Lawn Tennis,* that publicly criticized the USLTA for not letting Althea play the national championships.[16]

In her career, Alice Marble ranked No. 1 in the world, won the 1936, 1938, 1939 and 1940 U.S. National Championships and a total of 18 Grand Slam titles (five in singles, six in doubles and seven in mixed doubles). No one could question her ability to assess a player's ability to compete in the U.S. National Championships. Parts of her letter read *"Miss Gibson is over a very cunningly wrought barrel, and I can only hope to loosen a few of its staves with one lone opinion. If tennis is a game for ladies and gentlemen, it's also time we acted a little more like gentle-people and less like sanctimonious hypocrites.... If Althea Gibson represents a challenge to the present crop of women players, it's only fair that they should meet that challenge on the courts."* She went on to say that if Gibson were not given the opportunity to compete, *"then there is an ineradicable mark against a game to which I have devoted most of my life, and I would be bitterly ashamed."*[17]

The intensity of her support convinced the USLTA to allow Gibson to compete in the Eastern Grass Court Championships and the National Clay Court Championships. She performed well in these tournaments and became the first African American to gain entrée into the U.S. National Championships at Forest Hills, in 1950. On her 23rd birthday, August 25, she beat Barbara Knapp in the first round of the U.S. National Championships 6-2, 6-2. Gibson lost a close three set match in the tournament's second round to three-time Wimbledon Champion Louise Brough.

Gibson proved with certainty, however, that she could compete effectively with the top white players in the world. She was the first black player to grace the winner's circle in a Grand Slam event, winning singles and doubles titles at the 1956 French Championships, and the first to gain entrée into the Wimbledon draw at the All-England Club. She won five titles at Wimbledon: two in singles, in 1957 and 1958, and three in doubles, in 1956, 1957 and 1958; three titles at the U.S. National Championships: two in singles, in 1957 and 1958, and one in mixed doubles, in 1957; and one Australian doubles trophy, in 1957.

Astonishingly, she earned 11 Grand Slam victories within three years, was the No. 1 ranked player in the world, in 1957 and 1958, and the first African American to be voted the Associated Press Female Athlete of the Year, in 1957 and 1958. Finally, she was inducted into the International Tennis Hall of Fame in 1971.

Althea Gibson's first Wimbledon victory was so historic she was honored with the same type of ticker-tape parade in New York that the legendary New York Yankees receive when they win the World Series. She retired from tennis fairly early in her career and became the first African American woman professional golfer. She will always be a New York City and global tennis legend because she broke virtually every racial tennis barrier in the world.

---

[16] *American Lawn Tennis*; July 1950
[17] *American Lawn Tennis*; July 1950

SECTION II: Eastern Tennis Accomplishments

Chapter 7

Key Moments in Eastern Tennis History

In the overview that follows here, we honor Eastern tennis personalities as well as the section's All-American champions, who grew up training in the New York area and advanced to the "Final 8" in Grand Slam singles and doubles competition. We also shed light on a few of the movers and shakers who influenced the expansion of the game.

1915-1945

The post World War I era in America, and especially in the New York area, was the time of the Roaring Twenties and F. Scott Fitzgerald's "Great Gatsby" with its images of Long Island as "a fresh, green breast of the new world," where the rich played tennis in elegant flannel trousers and crisp, cotton dresses. Many players owned estates and belonged to private clubs here. A manicured lawn was the only surface deemed appropriate for play, and miles of grass courts were installed, often before golf links. The idea of women playing sports had been frowned upon, but croquet and lawn tennis were socially acceptable coed activities and caught on quickly among the enclaves and clubs of the wealthy and growing middle classes, especially in Boston, Newport, Philadelphia and New York.

Alastair Martin, a member of the International and USTA/Eastern Halls of Fame, and a past Eastern and USTA president, recalled almost the entire century of championship tennis in Queens. "I saw Tilden beat (William) Johnston in 1925 when I was 10, and I remember (Henri) Cochet used the excuse that he lost to (Ellsworth) Vines (in '32) because his seven-day boat trip from France was delayed," said Martin, whose parents, Bradley and the former Helen Phipps, financed construction of the famous horseshoe stadium at Forest Hills.

Martin watched U.S. champions George Lott, Helen Wills, Mary K. Browne, Maud Wallach and U.S. finalist Frank Shields practice for the nationals on his parents' private courts in Westbury. "Mrs. Wallach wore a black dress and a black hat and served underhand when she hit with my mother, who was a good player," he said. Martin later practiced there with Bobby Riggs, Panchos Segura and Gonzalez when he played Forest Hills himself before and after World War II. He took some lessons with Don Budge, tried to get his backhand-- "The best player I ever saw," he said-- but it didn't do any good.

Tennis in New York

THE CAST...

Frank Hunter (New Rochelle, N.Y.). Played in first men's U.S. Championships in 1915 at Forest Hills. Teamed with Vinnie Richards in 1924 in Paris to win the last U.S. Olympic gold medal for tennis until the game was reinstated as a medal sport in 1988. Twice a national singles finalist (lost in five sets to Cochet and Tilden, in '28 and '29); won doubles title with Tilden in '27. Wimbledon, singles finalist, 1923; men's doubles champ, 1924, '27; mixed champ, 1927, '29. Davis Cup, 1927-29.

Vinnie Richards (Yonkers, N.Y.), U.S. Championships, four-time singles semifinalist, 1922-26. Won two Olympic gold medals in Paris in 1924, in singles and doubles (with Hunter). Won five U.S. doubles titles (three times with Tilden), Wimbledon in 1924 and the French in '26. Turned pro on the Pyle tour in 1926. Davis Cup, 1922, '24-26.

Charles Landers (Manhattan), first president of the Eastern Lawn Tennis Association, 1921-22, which originated as a local governing section of the Middle States Section of the USNLTA. Landers was an engineer and past president of the West Side Tennis Club who helped form plans for Forest Hills stadium.

Frank Shields (Bronx, N.Y.). U.S. Championships, singles finalist, 1930; semifinalist, 1933; four-time quarterfinalist. Wimbledon singles finalist, 1931. Davis Cup, 1931-32, '34. Part-time movie actor with MGM. One of the first top players to run free tennis clinics for kids, mostly in the Bronx and Manhattan's lower East Side. "Frank was a real lover of the game," Martin said. "He worked very well with kids who continued to play tennis because of his influence."

Sidney Wood, Jr. (Manhattan and Southampton, L.I.). Wimbledon, singles champion, 1931; U.S. Championships, finalist, 1935; semifinalist, 1938. Davis Cup, 1931, '34. The son of a mining engineer who once was a partner of Wyatt Earp, Wood overcame serious childhood illness to qualify for Wimbledon's Gentlemen's Singles at age 15.

Gregory Mangin (Newark, N.J.). U.S. Championships, singles quarterfinalist, 1930, 33, 36.

Walter Pate (Glen Cove, L.I.). Played in first U.S. Championships in 1915 at Forest Hills. ELTA president, 1925-26. Captained three victorious Davis Cup teams, in 1937, '38 and again in 1946.

Holcombe Ward (Manhattan). ELTA president, 1932-33. USLTA president, 1937-47. Member of first U.S. Davis Cup team, 1900. U.S. Championships, singles champ, 1904; six-time doubles champ, 1899-1906 (a record), twice a singles finalist. Developed American twist serve. "He was a big shot, very influential, a superb player," Martin said.

1945-1960

Post-World War II America was a relatively peaceful prelude to the onslaught of upheavals in the 1960s. Men returned from the war, life centered on family and television was the exciting, new entertainment. Television coverage of tennis began in the 1950s and by the 1960s, Bud Collins was introducing a new core of tennis fans to the mythical net judge, Fingers Fortescue, on the PBS network. The era was also notable as the period in which sports, specifically baseball and tennis, finally included African-Americans.

THE CAST...

Reginald Weir (Manhattan). A New York physician and surgeon who broke the color barrier at the 1948 USLTA National Men's Indoors at the Park Avenue Seventh Regiment Armory on 68th Street. Later won five national senior titles (three in singles, two in doubles). Once a tennis captain at the City College of New York, Weir won the ATA national

Tennis in New York

men's singles title from 1931-33 before leaving tennis to attend medical school. Following graduation, he promptly regained the men's title in 1937 and captured his fifth singles title in 1942. USLTA president Martin appointed Dr. Weir to the organization's Administrative Committee in 1969.

Sidney Schwartz (Great Neck, L.I.). U.S. Championships, singles quarterfinalist, 1950.

Dick Savitt (Bayonne, N.J.). Australian, Wimbledon singles champion, French semifinalist, 1951. U.S. Championships, singles semifinalist, 1950-51. Davis Cup, 1951. Has been involved with Israel Tennis Centers for 37 years to develop world-class players and improve quality of children's lives.

Althea Gibson (Harlem). First African-American to play in U.S. Championships in 1950 at Forest Hills. First African-American to win French singles title, 1956. First African-American to win Wimbledon and U.S. Championships singles titles, 1957-58. Australian doubles champion, 1957; Wimbledon, 1956-58; U.S. Mixed, 1957. Wightman Cup, 1957-58. First African-American to be voted Associated Press Female Athlete of the Year, 1957-58.

Gladys Heldman (Manhattan). Founded World Tennis magazine in 1953. Owner, publisher, editor-in-chief of the magazine for 20 years. Influential in forming the women's Virginia Slims professional circuit in 1970.

Betty Rosenquest Pratt (Bronxville, N.Y.). U.S. Championships, singles semifinalist, 1956; Wimbledon, semifinalist, 1954, quarterfinalist, 1957. Wightman Cup Captain, 1967, 69.

Ron Holmberg (Brooklyn). U.S. Championships, singles semifinalist, 1959. French singles quarterfinalist; Canadian singles and doubles champ. Beat Rod Laver to win junior Wimbledon, 1956. Davis Cup, 1956.

1960-1978

These were the crossover years between amateur and professional tennis. Alastair Martin, a product of the genteel amateur game, was an early supporter of Open tennis when he was Eastern's president in 1964-65. He said it might help project the stars and rid the game of "its stuffed shirt image." He supported the British revolt which led to the International Tennis Federation's sanctioning of Open tennis when he was USLTA first vice president in 1967-68; and in 1969-70, when he was USLTA president, he worked to consolidate the transition into the Open era. At the 1970 US Open, Martin approved use of Jimmy Van Alen's sudden-death nine-point tiebreak. "Billy Talbert, the tournament chairman, suggested it," he said, "but I shouldered the burden of giving official approval. I'm not known to be foolhardy... My heart was in my throat waiting for one of the star players to criticize it in the heat of battle."

In 1975 the Forest Hills tournament switched from grass to clay after the men's players' association threatened a walk-out. Shortly afterward, the USLTA and the ELTA dropped "Lawn" from their names. In 1978 the Open resurfaced on hard courts at the USTA National Tennis Center because it had outgrown Forest Hills.

Eastern leaders stepped up the campaign to introduce tennis to children in every community, regardless of economic status. Martin founded the Eastern Tennis Patrons in the 1960s and was president of the National Tennis Foundation in 1970. Both organizations sponsored free junior clinics in public parks and lobbied school boards to include tennis in their physical education classes. "Tennis is a challenging and intricate game that you can play all your life," reasoned Martin when asked why he had consistently supported the growth of the sport.

Tennis in New York

THE CAST...

Hy Zausner (Manhattan). Built the Port Washington Tennis Academy in 1966 as a non-profit, charitable institution to help children channel their energies in a positive way. Home of the International Junior Tennis Championships (formerly sponsored by Rolex) since 1977, and the national Winter and Easter Classics. Training ground for some of Eastern's greatest players under coaches Harry Hopman and Tony Palafox.

Seena Hamilton (Manhattan). Founded the national junior tournament, the Easter Bowl, at the Midtown Tennis Club in Manhattan, 1968.

Eugene Scott (St. James, L.I.). U.S. Championships, singles semifinalist, 1967. French quarterfinalist, 1964. Wimbledon, winner of Gentlemen's Silver Plate, 1963. Davis Cup, 1963-65. Co-founded National Junior Tennis League, 1969. An attorney, Scott filed the papers for the not-for-profit charitable corporation, a free, team-oriented program for kids in city parks. Founder, Publisher, Editor-in-Chief of *Tennis Week* magazine, the tennis publication of record, 1974. Professional tournament director: Masters in New York, Kremlin Cup, Orange, Westchester and others.

Skip Hartman (Manhattan). President, New York Junior Tennis League, 1971-present. Developed the New York chapter of the NJTL when the national program moved to Washington. Pioneered the NYJTL Schoolyard Program in 1984, a model for the USA Schools Tennis Program. To date, the schools program in the Eastern Section has introduced tennis to 1,400,000 children. Also pioneered Play Tennis New York, the model for the introductory USA Tennis 1-2-3 Program.

Julie Heldman (Manhattan). U.S. National Championships, singles quarterfinalist, 1973. Wightman Cup, 1969-71, '74.

Mary Carillo (Douglaston, N.Y.). French mixed doubles champ, 1977. Television sports commentator for CBS, ESPN, HBO and USA Networks. Voted the "Most Powerful Woman in Tennis" and "Top Female Personality of the Decade" in the 1990s by Tennis magazine and Tennis Week.

Dick Stockton (Garden City, L.I.). US Open, singles quarterfinalist, 1977; mixed doubles champion, 1975. Won 20 USLTA national junior titles in the 1960s, the most ever recorded by an Eastern junior.

Barbara Williams (Larchmont, N.Y.). Eastern president, 1978-79. Broke the "old-boy network" as the first woman president of a USTA section. Later, as USTA treasurer, she became the first woman to serve on the organization's Board of Directors.

1979-2000

In 1979, the tennis boom was in full swing and John McEnroe of Douglaston met Vitas Gerulaitis of Kings Point in the US Open final that crowned a king of Queens. McEnroe emerged with a 7-5, 6-3, 6-3 victory to claim his first Grand Slam singles title and first of eight U.S. Open titles. "We played in the same places growing up," McEnroe has said. "Vitas was the big shot player in the East. We all looked up to him and suddenly I'm 20 and he's 24 and we're playing in the US Open final. There was an emotional connection there...I don't think it will ever happen again – two guys from Queens playing for the US Open title."

Tennis in New York

THE CAST...

Vitas Gerulaitis (Howard Beach, N.Y.). US Open, singles finalist, 1979. Australian singles champ, 1977; Italian Open champion, 1977, 79. Wimbledon doubles champ, 1975. Supported free tennis clinics sponsored by the New York City Parks and Recreation Department under Tony Mitchel and Mike Silverman. Davis Cup, 1977-80.

John McEnroe (Douglaston, N.Y.). Won 17 Grand Slam titles, seven in singles: four at the US Open, in 1979, 80, 81, 84; three at Wimbledon, in 1981, 83, 84, and ten in doubles: four at the US Opens, in 1979, 81, 83, 89; five at Wimbledon, 1979, 81, 83, 84, '92, and one French, 1977. Compiled 154 combined singles and doubles titles --77 in singles and 77 in doubles. Posted the most victories in Davis Cup competition, 59; most years played, 12; most team matches played, 30. Played on five Cup-winning teams, 1978, 79, 81, 82, 92. Ranked first in the world 14 times during his career. Davis Cup Captain, 2000.

Peter Fleming (Chatham, N.J.). Won 66 doubles titles. US Open doubles champion, 1979, 81, 83. Wimbledon doubles champion, 1979, 81, 83, 84. Davis Cup, 1979-84. Recorded a 14-1 Davis Cup doubles record with McEnroe. Teamed with McEnroe to win seven straight Masters titles in Madison Square Garden, 1978-84.

Gene Mayer (Woodmere, L.I.). US Open, singles quarterfinalist, 1982, '84. French doubles champ, 1978-79. Davis Cup, 1982-83.

Sandy Mayer (Woodmere). Wimbledon, French doubles champ, 1975, 1979.

Jimmy Arias (Buffalo, N.Y.). US Open, singles semifinalist, 1983. French mixed doubles champ, 1981. Davis Cup, 1984, 86-87.

Kathleen Horvath (Hopewell Junction, N.Y.). French singles quarterfinalist, 1983-84.

Melissa Brown (Scarsdale, N.Y.). French singles quarterfinalist, 1984. Wimbledon Ladies' Plate, 1984.

Molly Van Nostrand (Brightwaters, L.I.). Wimbledon singles quarterfinalist, 1985.

Terry Phelps (Larchmont, N.Y.). French singles quarterfinalist, 1985.

Patrick McEnroe (Douglaston, N.Y.). US Open, singles quarterfinalist, 1995. Australian singles semifinalist, 1993. Davis Cup, 1995. A member of the USTA Board of Directors and a tennis commentator for ESPN.

Justin Gimelstob (Essex Fells, N.J.). Australian, French Mixed doubles champion, 1998.

2000-Present

September 11, 2001 -- In Memoriam

Dick Lynch was a defensive back for the New York Giants from 1959-1966, twice leading the NFL in interceptions, and was later the voice of the Giants on radio. Dick passed away in 2008 at his home in Douglaston, N.Y. Family and friends who believe in the after life were certain that Dick was happy to meet his son Richard again, who was lost when the plane crashed into his building at the World Trade Center on Sept. 11, 2001.

Tennis in New York

Richard Lynch had been a top-ranked national junior tennis player and a standout at the University of South Carolina . After college, Richard went to work as a bond trader for Euro Brokers on the 84th floor of Tower 2 at the World Trade Center . After the 9/11 attack, Dick established a permanent tribute to Richard and asked USTA Eastern to name the Boys' and Girls' 12 sportsmanship award after Richard Dennis Lynch 11.

"My father's courage and grace somehow made a difference...", Dick Lynch's daughter Nancy Lord said. "At Richard's memorial mass, he said, 'It took that building to take my son down.' And then he said: 'Forgive those guys, for they know not what they do.' Even in utter anguish he showed us that you go on, you live your life." Amen.

The best news of the decade for both Eastern and American tennis was in December of 2007 when the U.S. defeated Russia to win the Davis Cup. It was America's first Davis Cup victory since they edged Russia 3-2 in 1995. The 2007 championship team featured two New York natives – Davis Captain Patrick McEnroe of Douglaston, and the No. 2 singles player, James Blake, who was born in Yonkers. On the opening day of the contest, Andy Roddick beat Dmitry Tursunov, 6-4, 6-4, 6-2, and Blake outlasted Mikhail Youzhny in one of his typical nailbiter, 6-3, 7-6 (4), 6-7 (3), 7-6 (3). The Bryan brothers clinched the victory in doubles.

The business of tennis grew rapidly in the beginning of the 21st century. The leadership of the USTA invested considerable resources and time in transforming the US Open from a major international tournament and the 4th leg of the Grand slam to one of the world's most important entertainment events. During this decade the Open continued to be "The Place" to see-and-be-seen at summer's end, to hobnob and do business, whether the visitor be a corporate CEO, a celebrity, a super model, musician, politician, an athlete from other sport or simply a passionate tennis fan. This wildly successful entertainment event, which takes advantage of all that New York City has to offer, has become the standard by which other events around the world are judged.

Interest in tennis grew rapidly around the world in the beginning of the 21st century. The good news is that the sport's global resurgence gave the US Open even higher visibility around the world. The bad news is that globalization in the upper echelons of the sport has intruded on the excitement of the once-dominant American-Australian rivalry. During much of the 20th century players from New York, Southern California, Florida and Australia were the best in the world. Now small countries like Serbia and Switzerland are producing higher ranked players than the U.S. Consequently, fewer New York region players have earned success in the professional ranks. Since 2000, only Scott Lipsky of Long Island -- who won the 2011 French Open Mixed Doubles title with Australian Casey Dellacqua – has won a Grand Slam event.

In an attempt to increase interest in tennis in the United States and in developing the number of top American players, the USTA has stepped up its focus on growing the game in younger and more diverse communities. For the first time the organization has invested millions of dollars on programs designed to increase the number of 10 and under tennis players. Countries like France that are approximately one-fifth the size of the U.S. can boast five times the number of players under 10. As a result, more players from other countries are ranked among the world's top 100 than the United States. The 10 and under initiative has successfully increased interest in the sport among young people and should lead to a resurgence of American professional tennis players.

Beyond the obvious goal of developing more accomplished young players, the USTA is beginning to work more closely with groups like the American Tennis Association (ATA) to increase interest in tennis in African American, Latino and Asian communities. The International Tennis Hall of Fame (ITHOF) has also focused on growing interest in the game by developing very successful exhibits like the *Breaking the Barriers* exhibit on black tennis history, for which *Tennis*

Tennis in New York

in New York Co-Author Dale Caldwell was the Curator with Arthur Carrington, and the *Vive el Tenis* exhibit on the expansion of tennis in Latin America. This focus on diversifying tennis participation indicates a very bright future for tennis in America and the multi-cultural region of New York.

THE CAST...

Since 1978, when the Open moved to the USTA Billie Jean King National Tennis Center, no less than 90 players who came up through the USTA Eastern junior ranks have competed in the qualifier and main draw of men's and women's singles. A sampling includes, with early hometowns: MEN--Arias, Fleming, Gerulaitis, Gimelstob, the McEnroe and Mayer brothers, Stockton, Paul Annacone (East Hampton, N.Y.), Bobby Banck (Williamsville, N.Y.), Barry Bindelglass (Clifton, N.J.), Martin Blackman (Manhattan), Fritz Buehning (Short Hills, N.J.), Marco Cacopardo (Forest Hills, N.Y.), Rod Crowley (Orange, N.J.), Bill and Tom Csipkay (Wyckoff, N.J.), Larry Davidson (New Rochelle, N.Y.), Ray Disco (Forest Hills, N.Y.), Miguel Dungo (Staten Island, N.Y.), Howard Endelman (Roslyn, N.Y.), Ted Farnsworth (Englewood, N.J.), Mike Fishbach (Great Neck, N.Y.), Tom Fontana (Matawan, N.J.), Marcel Freeman (Port Washington, N.Y.), Mark Freedman (Purchase, N.Y.), Eric Fromm (Glen Head, N.Y.), Chris Garner (Bay Shore, N.Y.), Mike Grant (Roslyn, N.Y.), Jim Gurfein (Great Neck, N.Y.), John Hayes (Cos Cob, Conn.), John James (Mt. Kisco, N.Y.), Bryan Koniecko (Jericho, N.Y.), Andy Kohlberg (Larchmont, N.Y.), Cary Leeds (Manhattan), Scott Lipsky (Merrick, N.Y.), Matthew Litsky (Roslyn, N.Y.), Richard Matuszewski (Hopewell Junction, N.Y.), Ricky Meyer (Great Neck, N.Y.), Jon Molin (Yonkers, N.Y.), Billy Nealon (Rochester, N.Y.), Willie Notar (Douglaston, N.Y.), Hugo Nunez (Rockaway, N.J.), Guillermo Oropez (Montclair, N.J.), Evan Ratner (Smithtown, N.Y.), Peter Rennert (Great Neck, N.Y.), Butch Seewagen (Old Westbury, N.Y.), Sven Salumaa (Huntington, N.Y.), John Schmitt (Brookville, N.Y.), Larry Scott (Merrick, N.Y.), Bill Stanley (Rye, N.Y.), John Sullivan (Rockville Centre, N.Y.), Eric Taino (Jersey City, N.J.), Greg Van Emburgh (Stony Brook, N.Y.), John Van Nostrand (Brightwaters, N.Y.), Phil Williamson (Mt. Vernon, N.Y.) and Mike Zimmerman (Great Neck, N.Y.); WOMEN: Brown, Carillo Horvath, Phelps, M. Van Nostrand, Kristie Ahn (Upper Saddle River, N.J.), Leslie Allen (Manhattan), Bea Bielik (Valley Stream, N.Y.), Sandra Birch (Huntington Bay, N.Y.), Gail Brodsky (Brooklyn, N.Y.), Pam Casale (Fairfield, N.J.), Kyle Copeland (Montclair, N.J.), Cathy Farrell (Dunkirk, N.Y.), Jennifer Fuchs (Dix Hills, N.Y.), Ruta Gerulaitis (Howard Beach, N.Y.), Grace Kim (Ridgewood, N.J.), Christina McHale (Englewood Cliffs, N.J.), Sheila McInerney (Rome, N.Y.), Kathy May Mueller (Glen Ridge, N.J.), Patti O'Reilly (Ridgewood, N.J.), Nancy Ornstein (Matawan, N.J.), Kerri Reiter (Woodbury, N.Y.), Renee Richards (Manhattan), Tina Samara (Laurel Hollow, N.Y.), Caroline Stoll (Livingston, N.J.), Eileen Tell (Aberdeen, N.J.), Keiko Tokuda (Clifton, N.J.) and Carol Watson (St. Albans, N.Y.).

Eastern Game Changers Influence Tennis in New York

Maud Barger Wallach (New York City) won the 1908 U.S. singles title in Philadelphia. Sidney Wood gave her his 1931 Wimbledon trophy (after Frank Shields defaulted) and told her to give it to the winner the next time he played Shields on grass. Wood beat Shields at the 1934 Wimbledon Queen's Club warm up and Maud gave Wood his trophy. International Tennis Hall of Fame

Holcombe Ward (New York City), a member of the first U.S. Davis Cup team, won the 1904 U.S. singles championship at Newport. International Tennis Hall of Fame

Frank Hunter was a singles quarterfinalist at the 1915 U.S. National Championships, the year the tournament debuted at Forest Hills. Titanic survivor Karl Behr advanced to the round of 16 in the 1915 championships while Walter Pate made it to the 3rd round.

Sidney Wood, Jr., the 1931 Wimbledon singles champ and singles finalist at the 1935 U.S. National Championships, played for the U.S. Davis Cup team, 1931-34. International Tennis Hall of Fame and Museum

Eastern Game Changers Influence Tennis in New York

Frank Shields, a 1931 finalist at Wimbledon and the U.S. National Championships, eyed USLTA President Louis Dailey (right) presenting the trophy to singles champ John Doeg, who prevailed 10-8, 1-6, 6-4, 16-14.

Frank Shields (left) and pal Errol Flynn (r) pictured at a tennis exhibition with (center) England's Wimbledon champ Fred Perry (1934, 35, 36) and Elmer Griffin.
Willie Shields

Frank Shields (center) signed a 7-year movie contract with MGM and was an assistant director on "The Goldwyn Follies" movie set.
Willie Shields

The 1932 U.S. Davis Cup team -- (l-r) Frank Shields, Wilmer Allison, Bernon Prentice (captain), John Van Ryn, Lawrence A. Baker and Ellsworth Vines -- defeated Canada, Mexico, Australia, Brazil and Germany but lost to France in the Challenge Round.

Eastern Game Changers Influence Tennis in New York

Dr. Reginald Weir broke the color barrier at the 1948 U.S. (Lawn) Tennis Association National Men's Indoor Championships at the Seventh Regiment Armory.

1957 Sports Illustrated cover girl Althea Gibson, the first African American to play at the U.S. National Championships at Forest Hills, in 1950, and the first to win a singles title there, in 1957.

Dick Savitt (right), pictured with members of the 1951 U.S. Davis cup team (l-r) Ted Schroeder, Tony Trabert and Vic Seixas, won 3 singles duels vs. Japan and Mexico.

Fred Kovaleski (l), pictured in the January 15, 2006 issue of The Washington Post Magazine, was a CIA operative in the 1950s and the model for the "I Spy" hit television series -- made famous by Bill Cosby (r) and Robert Culp -- as Fred traveled undercover through the Middle East in the role of international tennis star. Washington Post.

Eastern Game Changers Influence Tennis in New York

Arthur Ashe won the first US Open in 1968 and won Wimbledon (above) in 1975. International Tennis Hall of Fame and Museum

Tennis goes mainstream: (l-r) Paul Cranis, Eastern Junior Development chair; Seena Hamilton, founder, national junior Easter Bowl at Manhattan's Midtown Tennis Club; Eastern president Gene Scott; and umpire Lee Jackson prepare for 1973 tournament.

John McEnroe (l), who defeated Larry Gottfried (ctr.) to win the 1973 Easter Bowl boys' 14 title under the 59th Street Bridge, accepted his award from Freddie Botur (r).

WTA pioneers Billie Jean King and Gladys Heldman (l & r) thanked Joe Cullman (ctr.), CEO of Philip Morris, who helped underwrite the women's Virginia Slims professional tour, chaired the US Open from 1969-70 and provided sponsorship to make possible the national televising of the Open on CBS.
International Tennis Hall of Fame and Museum

Eastern Game Changers Influence Tennis in New York

Enter the tennis boom. Gene Mayer (l) and his brother Sandy (r) won the 1979 French doubles title and achieved career-high world rankings of No. 4 and No. 8 respectively.
Steve Berman. Russ Adams

Vitas Gerulaitis won the 1975 Wimbledon doubles crown with Sandy Mayer and was ranked No. 3 in the world in 1978.
Russ Adams

Vitas Gerulaitis and his family -- (l-r) Vitas; sister Ruta, who also toured on the pro circuit; and their parents, known affectionately as Mama and Papa G.
Mel DiGiacomo

John McEnroe won his first major singles title at the 1979 US Open in Flushing Meadows and won 8 Open titles overall-- 4 in singles - 1979, '80, 81, '84 and 4 in doubles - 1979, '81, '83, '89.
International Tennis Hall of Fame and Museum

Eastern Game Changers Influence Tennis in New York

Douglaston childhood pals Mary Carillo and John McEnroe won the 1977 French mixed doubles title and almost 30 years later, in 2006, they presided -- with Chris Evert, Venus Williams and others -- over the ceremony renaming the US Open site as the USTA Billie Jean King National Tennis Center. Carillo-John. Russ Adams.
Chris Evert, John McEnroe, Venus Williams and Mary Carillo. Ed Goldman

Kathleen Horvath, pictured practicing for the Eastbourne Wimbledon warm up, ranked No. 10 in the world in 1984.

Eastern Game Changers Influence Tennis in New York

Leslie Allen, who ranked No. 17th in the world, founded Win 4 LIfe to help city kids achieve success.
Steve Berman

(L-r) Melissa Brown visited with Lynda Carter and Martina Navratilova between matches on the pro circuit in the early 1980s.

Neil Amdur (l) collaborated on autobiographies in 1980 with Chris Evert (r)and in 1982 with Arthur Ashe.
Maria Eugenia Garcia

Mary Carillo (r), the venerable voice of TV sports, used to mix it up with Gene Scott, the venerable voice of the printed word of tennis.
Steve Berman

Eastern Game Changers Influence Tennis in New York

The New York Junior Tennis League honored Billy Davis (r) and Louis Marx Jr. (3rd from left) in 1996 at the 11th annual NYJTL Civics Awards Luncheon at the Grand Hyatt Hotel. Cheering them were (l-r) Skip Hartman, Tim Mayotte, David Dinkins, Peter Malkin, Nick Bollettieri, and Bob Davis.

In 1995, Justin Gimelstob celebrated his first ever victory in the main draw of the US Open, a 6-4, 6-4, 4-6, 4-6, 6-3 decision over David Prinosil of Germany.
Ed Goldman

Bob Ingersole, USTA Eastern president in 1998-99, is the director of tennis at the West Side Tennis Club and president of Eastern's Junior Tennis Foundation, which funds scholarship programs for young players and special populations. .
Steve Berman

Mike Silverman (l), sports director for the City Parks Foundation, which provides free lessons and clinics citywide for 7,000 kids in 40 N.Y.C. public parks, with Billie Jean King, one of the program's most ardent supporters.

Eastern Game Changers Influence Tennis in New York

Past Eastern president Les Fitz Gibbon, 1968-69, founded the USLTA Information Booth at West Side and then he and Barbara Williams moved the operation over to Flushing Meadows.
Nancy Gill McShea

Past Eastern presidents Mike Gordon (l) and Marina Nudo (r) have assisted Charlotte Gordon at the US Open in the USTA Membership Booth.
Nancy Gill McShea

Kay and John McEnroe, general chairmen, 1989 Eastern Tennis Hall of Fame.

U.S. Davis Cup Captain Patrick McEnroe cheered on James Blake (l) on their way to winning the 2007 championship.
USTA

Eastern Game Changers Influence Tennis in New York

(L-r) USTA Eastern Executive Director D.A. Abrams and his wife Shelia joined Eastern President Dale Caldwell and his wife Sharon at the 2007 Eastern Hall of Fame dinner.
Ed Goldman

Brian Hainline (r), chief medical officer for the USTA, and David Schobel (l), director of USTA Leagues, presented the 2007 US Open Wheelchair competition awards to David Wagner of the United States and Peter Norfolk of Great Britain.
USTA

Larry Scott, (r), former chief of the Sony Ericsson WTA Tour, was joined at his 2008 induction into the Eastern Tennis Hall of Fame by colleagues Mark Miles (l), former CEO of the men's ATP Tour; and Anne Worcester, tournament director of the Pilot Pen tournament and former CEO of the WTA Tour.
Ed Goldman

Bob Ryland, a 2002 Eastern Tennis Hall of Fame honoree, was cheered by his friend and Eastern staffer Larry Dillon.
Steve Berman

Eastern Game Changers Influence Tennis in New York

The McShea family enjoys annual trips to the US Open with friends: (l-r) Sue Fanning, Jerry McShea, Tracy McNeill, Justin and Colette McShea.
Nancy Gill McShea

Dale Caldwell was joined by his wife Sharon and daughter Ashley the day he was elected president of the USTA Eastern Section in 2006.
Andy Jacobs

Elaine Viebranz (r), honored in 2004 by the International Hall of Fame with the Samuel Hardy award for her long service to the game, congratulated 1996 US Open champ Pete Sampras for surviving his rough quarterfinal match with Spain's Alex Corretja.
Steve Berman

Eastern Game Changers Influence Tennis in New York

(L-r) Nancy McShea, New York City Mayor David Dinkins, Arvelia Myers, David Goodman and Nick Greenfield enjoyed the festivities at the Eastern Tennis Hall of Fame.
Steve Berman

1991 U.S. Davis Cup semifinals, Kansas City, MO, U.S. 3, Germany 2. U.S. group (l-r) David Pate, Jared Palmer, Andre Agassi, Luke Jensen, Captain Tom Gorman, USTA President Robert Cookson, Bob Russo, immediate past USTA president David Markin, Jim Courier, George Fareed and Scott Davis.
Russ Adams

Andre Agassi danced with Alan King on Arthur Ashe Kids' Day.
Steve Berman

David Dinkins (center) with 2008 USTA Tennis & Education Foundation Board members, from left, Rosalind P. Walter, President Patrick McEnroe and Executive Director Karen Martin Eliezer.
Ed Goldman

Eastern Game Changers Influence Tennis in New York

Bea Bielik (l) upset two seeds in her tour debut to reach the 3rd round of the 2002 US Open and Scott Lipsky (r) won the 2011 French mixed doubles title.
Ed Goldman

John McEnroe enjoys entertaining with his guitar.

A future influential player, perhaps -- Nancy McShea's granddaughter Tatum, pictured at a clinic with Anna Kournikova.

The Celebrities

Alec Baldwin (center) joined Eastern staffers at the 2003 US Open in the President's Box: (l-r) -- Mali Circle, Aaron Segal, Jenny Schnitzer, Lara Schneider, Julie Bliss and Shelley Brazely.
Nancy Gill McShea

Jane Gill, Christie Brinkley and friends enjoyed the view at the 2010 US Open.
Bob Straus

President Bill Clinton and Connecticut's Senator Dodd understand intense competition.
Ed Goldman

Charlize Theron was surprised to see her image on the big screen.
Ed Goldman

Virginia Wade (l) and Stanley Tucci liked the action. Ed Goldman

Tony Bennett is a fixture at the Open.
Ed Goldman

Jack Nicholson maintained his usual demeanor.
Ed Goldman

Harlem Junior Tennis Program rates a presidential salute

On January 14, just six days before he left office, former President George Bush honored the Harlem Junior Tennis Program as the nation's 999th "Daily Point of Light" at a special ceremony in the East Room of the White House.

Karin Buchholz, executive director of the Harlem program, and Kris Burrell, 16, a junior member whose determination and desire exemplify the program's ideals—both academically and on the tennis court—traveled together to Washington, D.C., to accept the award from the president.

"It was so thrilling, we felt overwhelmed," said Buchholz, herself a graduate of the Harlem program who later played tennis on scholarship at the University of Arizona and competed on the women's pro circuit for three years before returning to her roots in 1990.

"Kris and I started out on a huge line with 49 other (Points of Light) honorees and their families, but the national security people motioned us to move to the front. They said, 'You are going onstage with the president.' During the ceremony, President Bush turned toward us and acknowledged us personally."

Beginning in 1989, and continuing through his last day in office January 20, when he named the 1020th Daily Point of Light, the president had recognized outstanding individuals, businesses and organizations of every conceivable type who engaged in voluntary community service to combat our most pressing social problems. Moreover, the president had initiated the idea to urge all people to make serving others central to their lives and work.

Karin Buchholz (c) accepted "Daily Point of Light" honor for the Harlem Junior Tennis Program.

In paying tribute to the volunteers of the Harlem program, New York state's lone representative to be recognized personally by the president as a Daily Point of Light, Bush said the organization exemplifies his belief that, "From now on in America, any definition of a successful life must include serving others."

The Harlem Junior Tennis Program was founded 20 years ago by volunteer Claude Cargill, 76, a retired police officer and tennis coach, and operates out of the 369th Regiment Armory as a special training center for children ages 7 to 17.

Through the years, the program has received much acclaim for helping more than 1,000 young people avoid the temptations of the inner-city by taking them off the streets and putting them on the tennis court. The Eastern Tennis Association honored the program as its 1990 "Member Organization of the Year," and featured its juniors on the section's 1991 yearbook cover.

Sponsored by Mutual of New York, and supported by well-known community leaders and spokesmen—New York City Mayor David Dinkins, Arthur Ashe, Bill Davis, Earl Monroe and Tony Guida, to name a few—the program's success depends in large measure on the service of local volunteers who play an integral role in the day-to-day operations. For example, more than 75 of the juniors' parents prepare food that is sold during fund-raising tournaments, and they participate in parent-child Junior Olympic events.

The program primarily attracts youngsters from Harlem, but all the city's kids are welcome. To be eligible, juniors must maintain at least a "C" average in school. Tutors are provided for those whose grades fall below the requirement and for those who want to raise their grades above a "C."

Perhaps due to the emphasis on academics, graduates of the program have earned tennis scholarships to universities like Duke, Howard, Syracuse, Tulane, Temple, Rutgers and Fordham.

SportsActive / Tennis

Port Tourney Will Get Format Change in '95

By Nancy Gill McShea

When the Port Washington International Junior Tennis Championships get under way Christmas Day, it will be the last time this multi-age international Har-Tru tournament will be played under one roof.

Due to an adjustment in the International Tennis Federation's schedule, the event will resurface September 18. The tournament format will also change from a multi-age indoor Har-Tru event to an 18s-only outdoor hardcourt tournament, in order to strengthen the sequence of top-flight international junior play in the United States. The tournament will coincide with similar international junior events scheduled during that time period in Canada at the Sega Junior International Championship, at the U.S. Open and at the USFNG Insurance Sugar Bowl International Tennis Classic in New Orleans.

The tournament's history reads like a "Who's Who" of tennis. A 14-year-old Tracy Austin was one of the first winners in 1977, the first of a long line of future stars to walk through the club's doors. Austin became the youngest girl (16 years, nine months) ever to win the U.S. Open singles title.

"The Port tournament had an international flavor which was important for me at the time," said Austin, now 31, who beat four top foreign players to win the Girls 18s title. Six months later she won Junior Wimbledon. "I had played in international team competition before Port, but I had never played as an individual. It was a great tournament to play in my own country."

Austin said the change in format at Port Washington was unfortunate. "It's been a great part of junior tennis history in our country," she said. "And great for kids of all ages."

Future Open champions Stefan Edberg and Mats Wilander won at Port Washington, too. So did Goran Ivanisevic and Luke Jensen. Boris Becker, Ivan Lendl, Yannick Noah and Mary Joe Fernandez all played it, but didn't win. Nor did a 9-year-old Jennifer Capriati, who in 1985 clutched her Cabbage Patch doll on the way to the girls' 12s semifinals.

Port Washington's impressive list of former players also includes local players who have fared well. The locals have netted more than two dozen titles at the Port international, which has showcased more than 12,000 players from 50 countries in the boys' and girls' 12, 14, 16 and 18-and-under age groups.

"Pressure is not a real factor here," tournament organizer Dick Zausner said. "Ranked juniors at all levels are used to competition. They welcome an international tournament to get an idea how the No. 1 junior from Sweden plays. They might never have another chance to do that."

Some have. Chris Garner of Bay Shore, for one, won the 12s in 1980, ranked first nationally in several junior categories and later advanced to the men's round of 16 at the 1993 Ford Australian Open. Garner also reached the 18s doubles finals at Port Washington in 1983 with Keith Kambourian of Manhasset. That same year, Kambourian beat Argentina's Javier Frana (now ranked 110th in the world) in singles before losing in the quarters to Austria's Thomas Muster.

"I played at Port five times a week," said Kambourian, a Duke graduate, who is now the head pro / manager at the Bethpage Tennis Center. "The tournament

Newsday File Photo
A 14-year-old Tracy Austin used a two-fisted backhand to win in 1977 Port Washington Junior Championships.

was a great chance to play the best foreign players on my home court only 15 minutes from my house. You really have to see what's out there."

Molly Van Nostrand of Brightwaters, who also trained at Port Washington, captured the 14s trophy in 1978. "I definitely had the homecourt advantage," she said. "Winning there was a stepping-stone in my career; it gave me confidence that I could compete on an international level." Seven years later, Van Nostrand advanced to the quarterfinals at Wimbledon.

Local champions who will return this year include Ron Nano of Great Neck and Olivia Dubovikov of Staten Island (both 12s winners, in 1990 and '92) and Vania Yui of Bayside (last year's 16s winner and twice the N.Y. State singles champion), who will all play the 18s. Other young hopefuls to watch are: Bruce Li of West Hempstead (an 18s quarterfinalist in '93); Agnes Wiski of Flushing (a USTA national 14s champion who will play the 16s); Brooke Herman of New York City (18s); David Hauser of Rockville Centre, Scott Lipsky of Merrick and Hiroyuki Nakamura of Whitestone (16s); and Jonathan Chu of New York City (the 12s).

Spectators are welcome to attend the event which runs Christmas Day through Jan. 1. Admission is free. For more information, call (516) 883-6425.

Nancy Gill McShea works for the USTA and is a freelancer who writes about tennis.

Mike Lupica Bids Farewell to Arthur Ashe, The Daily News, February 7, 1993.
Mike was at a dinner when he heard the news that Arthur Ashe had died. He wrote the following obituary in longhand and dictated it to the newspaper over the phone.

42 ☆   DAILY **SPORTS** NEWS   Sunday, February 7, 1993

Arthur Ashe, Champion

MIKE LUPICA

PORTRAIT OF A WINNER: Arthur Ashe hoists Wimbledon trophy in 1975 after upsetting Jimmy Connors to become the first black to win the tournament.
AP

The blessing that was Ashe

HE STOOD ON this golf course in New Jersey on a fine summer day, one of those days when the whole world will live forever and Arthur Ashe, all these years with AIDS by then, said he never asked, "Why me?"

"If you start asking that," Arthur Ashe said, "when do you stop? If I asked why I had a bad heart, or why I got AIDS, do I also have to ask why I won Wimbledon? Or why I had this kind of life? When something bad happens, people have this way of forgetting their blessings. I don't. I've had a wonderful life."

He had a wonderful life, an American life of this century that will always be remembered. He died at 3:13 yesterday afternoon at New York Hospital-Cornell Medical Center in the city of New York, the place where he had to come a long time ago because the world had not changed enough in other places for him to get the great chance in tennis his talent deserved.

And so Arthur Ashe went on to find all those blessings of an extraordinary tennis life. He won the United States championship, and he won that Wimbledon in 1975 from Jimmy Connors. And it was a career of grace and skill and dignity and as much heart as anyone I have ever known. He was my friend. It is a club as big as all the corners of this world, all the places that Arthur Ashe enriched.

But to call Ashe a tennis player, to limit him that way, is to say Jackie Roosevelt Robinson was nothing more than a baseball player. Ashe was like Robinson in this way: He did not just change a sport, he changed the way we looked at things, thought about things. All the important things.

Tennis was just the beginning, a way for Ashe, great American, to become an ambassador to all the important things. Arthur Ashe should have been a United States senator. He should have been so many things. Older, mostly. He should have gotten to see more than six years from a beautiful daughter, Camera. He should have grown old with a strong, beautiful woman, a dream partner named Jeanne Ashe.

"In your private thoughts, you always want to do things that will be remembered," Arthur Ashe said to me once. "Not in an egotistical way. Not in a bragging way. Just so people will know that you left your mark."

Arthur Ashe did that every day of his public life. He came out of Virginia with this sweet backhand, and thick glasses that always looked too big for his sweet face, and really a dazzling talent for striking a tennis ball. And he became a Jackie Robinson for men's professional tennis. It was just right, of course.

Arthur Ashe always said that when he was a boy, all his black friends ran with him to second base on the first day of baseball tryouts, and all of them wanted to wear No. 42 because Jackie Robinson wore No. 42.

"He was all we wanted to be," Ashe said.

In his way, Arthur Ashe did as much, and was cut down almost as young. Ashe wrote books and went to South Africa when others were afraid, and when he went it really wasn't about tennis. He would say much later that he went to show the black children of South Africa that there were other ways, in other places across the world. "There was this one boy who followed me around the first couple of days I was there, just staring at me, not saying anything," Ashe said a little over a month ago, when Sports Illustrated made him Sportsman of the Year. "I finally asked him why he was following me. And the boy said I was the first free black man he'd ever seen with his own eyes." Ashe smiled that December day at the Pierre Hotel and said, "It was then that I considered my trip a success."

In the end, he became one of those amazing figures, standing on the right side of all the big issues. Even with AIDS, Arthur Ashe traveled and lectured and inspired all who saw him, or heard him. Everywhere he went, they gave him awards, because it was late in the game now for Arthur Ashe, and everyone wanted to tell him what they thought about him.

"I'm busier than I've ever been in my life," he said at the Pierre. Jeanne Ashe looked at him and shook her head and said, "I have lost the capacity to be amazed by my husband."

After fighting his whole life for racial equality and fighting against apartheid, and everything else, after his book about black athletes in this country, and being Davis Cup captain and being a television commentator, now he had AIDS to fight, and not too much time in which to do it.

Arthur Ashe, you must understand, was blessed with everything except enough luck.

He was too young for heart attacks, but he had one at the end of the '70s, and more heart trouble in 1983.

He needed transfusions after his heart surgery in '83 and it is believed that that is when he contracted AIDS from contaminated blood.

It was not discovered until five years later, and the world did not find out until last April, when the newspaper USA Today discovered Ashe's condition, and called him about it.

He decided to call his own press conference. Arthur Ashe was never one to let the other guy dictate anything.

So he stood there in April in the crowded room high above the Avenue of the Americas and said that it was true, that he was suffering from AIDS. It was moving and eloquent and a little bit defiant. Somehow you left feeling better. Arthur Ashe did that always.

There was a moment that day, and I have written about it more than once, when words failed him, and the emotion of the day started to make Arthur Ashe break down. AIDS could do that, even to Ashe, we discovered. So the tennis player, in that moment, needed a partner worthy of him. There was one right behind him. His wife stepped forward with a clear voice and took the paper with his speech on it from him with steady hands and continued for her husband.

Soon there was the Arthur Ashe Foundation, 100 Park Avenue, to fight AIDS. There was a splendid sunny day before the United States Open, when 10,000 people came into Louis Armstrong Stadium to watch some tennis and send some money to Arthur Ashe's foundation. Finally, there was the Sportsman of the Year award and on that day the award felt like a Nobel prize for sports. Which means it felt exactly right.

I ASKED HIM during our round of golf last summer if he was angry, and that is when he talked about his blessings and finally Arthur Ashe said, "Growing up black was harder than having AIDS."

He had said it before. He meant it. This was one of those storied American lives and it ended yesterday afternoon. A storied voice is stilled and we all are poorer. We are the ones blessed, now in memory.

ETA NEWS

by Nancy Gill McShea

Vitas Gerulaitis Remembered

As the tennis community continues to mourn Vitas Gerulaitis, who died suddenly on September 18th in Southampton, NY, at the age of 40, his many friends and acquaintances are consoling one another and his public with cheerful remembrances of his warm generosity, sharp sense of humor and flashy athleticism.

Most Eastern fans had never met Vitas personally, but they will always remember his dazzling presence at the center of the tennis boom in New York during the 1970s and early 1980s. He was from the neighborhood! And he sparked an exciting generation of ETA junior players—many of whom trained alongside him at the Port Washington Tennis Academy—becoming the first among them to rise to the top of the world's pro ranks by winning both the Australian Open and the Italian Championships in 1977. Together, Vitas' Port crowd and other local favorites brought fresh vitality to the game in the East, inspiring kids of all ages to pursue tennis in droves.

"Vitas was the first one of us that did anything," said Mary Carillo, who trained at Port with Gerulaitis, John McEnroe and Peter Fleming, to name a few. "I remember when he first played Wimbledon (Vitas and Eastern's Sandy Mayer won in doubles there in 1975). I couldn't believe I knew somebody who was playing Wimbledon."

When Gerulaitis and McEnroe battled for the 1979 U.S. Open men's crown, with McEnroe emerging the winner to claim his first of four Open singles trophies, Eastern players turned America's Grand Slam event into a virtual hometown celebration. That same year, McEnroe and Fleming won their first of three Open doubles championships, while other members of the Port entourage—Carillo, Vitas' sister Ruta, Eric Fromm, Ricky Meyer and Peter Rennert—competed in women's and men's singles along with Eastern's Leslie Allen, Kathleen Horvath, Andy Kohlberg, Gene Mayer, Renee Richards, Jon Molin and Caroline Stoll.

Throughout his playing career, Gerulaitis devoted much of his off-court energies to recruiting thousands of young players into the fold, especially at free junior clinics sponsored by the NYC Parks Department before the Open. Big cars would drive up to Central Park and Vitas would burst onto the scene like a movie star, cracking jokes with friends, John McEnroe, Bjorn Borg and Guillermo Vilas by

Mike Silverman

Vitas Gerulaitis, the world's No. 3 tennis player in 1979, was often the center of attention at free junior clinics sponsored by the NYC Parks Department.

his side. His young audience would stand awestruck. Then he would engage the group in a flurry of joyous activity. Tennis balls would soar through the air until every child had a chance to hit with the pros. Between 1979 and 1989, Vitas donated 30,000 tennis racquets to the Parks' effort through a foundation in his name.

In his last few years, Vitas dazzled us at the Open with lively insight and a bit of mischievous candor in the TV booth. And finally, this past August he stopped in to greet his loyal fans at an ETA benefit during Jimmy Connors' Citibank Champions tournament in Westchester. He had looked forward to playing before his home crowd again. He felt there would be warmth and humor revisited there. There was.

Vitas Gerulaitis was more than one of our great tennis champions. He was familiar to us; he was like an old friend. We will miss him.

TENNIS WEEK **49**

OCTOBER 20, 1994

Pallbearers at the tennis star's funeral included McEnroe (third from left), Borg (rear) and Connors (right)

John McEnroe (l), Bjorn Borg (rear) and Jimmy Connors (r) were pallbearers at Vitas's funeral.

by Nancy Gill McShea

EUGENE L. SCOTT (1937-2006)

The late Billy Talbert used to say he had to read Gene Scott's "Vantage Point" column in *Tennis Week* with a dictionary by his side. But Talbert also added that he always got the point of the columns.

Many tennis fans got the point about Scott, who came up through Eastern's junior ranks in the Long Island community of St. James and made it to No. 11 in the world. A lifelong friend of Eastern tennis, he was the section's president in 1972-73 and the vice president of the Junior Tennis Foundation. In 1989, he was inducted into the Eastern Tennis Hall of Fame.

Sadly, Gene's voice was silenced on March 20, when he died of amyloidosis, a condition that can cause organs such as the heart and kidneys to malfunction. He was 68.

"It will never be the same without him," said his friend Lois Prince, who, like Gene, is a former Eastern president and Hall of Fame inductee. He was at once witty, intellectual, demanding, impatient and, most of all, loyal to friends. He believed people had to stretch themselves to reach their full potential or they would make a pact with the status quo.

Doris Herrick seconds that. "I will always miss Gene," said Herrick, Eastern's longtime executive director. "He challenged me to do my best and was the first person I would call for [advice] about Eastern tennis."

Gene graduated from Yale, where, according to *The New York Times*, he earned nine varsity letters (in tennis, soccer, hockey and lacrosse), more than all other athletes in Yale sports history, with the exception of football legends Walter Camp and Amos Alonzo Stagg. After Yale, he graduated from the University of Virginia Law School and then proceeded to earn an international reputation as a player, writer, editor, publisher and entrepreneur who influenced the visibility of tennis and created a positive public perception of the sport for more than 40 years — especially through the written word.

He possessed great integrity in meeting personal goals within multiple tennis roles and believed everyone, including himself, should be held accountable. He founded and was the publisher of *Tennis Week* (1974 to present), America's second-oldest nationally distributed tennis magazine still in publication. His "Vantage Point" column, which numbers close to 1,000 in the more than 30 years of the magazine's existence, is regarded as "the conscience of tennis" and is one of the most widely read in the sport.

Gene used his column to present and analyze important issues and/or conflicts that are a source of constant distraction in a volunteer-based sport, which serves tennis players from the grassroots novice to the professional level. He met issues head on and argued persuasively to influence those in authority to reach a logical, objective conclusion. In doing so, he risked alienating authorities within the game's power structure.

On the court, Gene was the ultimate gentleman and sportsman, always applauding a good shot and congratulating an opponent, win or lose. Besides achieving a career-high No. 11 world ranking in 1965, he was a playing member of the U.S. Davis Cup team, 1963-1965, and ranked five times in America's Top 10. He was a singles quarterfinalist at the French Championships, a semifinalist at the U.S. Championships, and reached the finals or won every American grass court tournament except Forest Hills. (In 1967, he lost in a five-set semifinal there to eventual-champion John Newcombe). He was also the U.S. Open court tennis champion from 1973 to 1977.

He continued to play tennis competitively until the end of his life. He won more than 40 world and USTA national senior men's (35s to 65s) singles and doubles championships, many of them following double hip replacement surgery almost 20 years ago. He said he continued to compete to see if tennis truly is a game for a lifetime, but everyone who watched him play could see that he simply loved the game.

In 1963, he won the William Johnston Award, this country's highest honor for sportsmanship and contributions to the game. He was a co-founder of the National Junior Tennis League in 1969. In the role of attorney, he filed the papers for America's most prominent grassroots tennis program, a free team-oriented program for kids in city parks.

As a producer of televised professional tennis events worldwide, Gene was actively involved over the past 25 years in the promotion and management of important tennis championships. From 1986 to 1990, he directed the Nabisco Masters at Madison Square Garden, the most significant indoor championship in the world. In 1990, he developed and for 10 years produced Russia's most celebrated annual sporting event: Moscow's Kremlin Cup. In 1994, he directed the inaugural President's Cup in Uzbekistan and also explored developing and/or expanding the professional tennis scene in Uruguay, the Caribbean, Cuba, Kazakhstan and China.

He had multiple bylines in *The New York Times*, *Sports Illustrated*, *Newsday*, *Harper's Bazaar* and *Esquire* and authored 20 books on tennis. He was an occasional tennis TV commentator, one of his most notable matches being the Billie Jean King vs. Bobby Riggs "Battle of the Sexes." He produced four award-winning documentary films for CBS Television and served on many boards.

All of Gene Scott's friends at Eastern will miss him. He accomplished so much in such a short time. May he rest in peace.

SECTION III: Eastern Tennis Hall of Fame Inductees

Biographies of Eastern Tennis Hall of Fame Honorees

The following chapters contain a unique insight into the lives of some of the most influential people in the New York region. We provide 102 snapshots -- by induction year -- of legendary tennis players, contributors and volunteers who have been inducted into the Eastern Tennis Hall of Fame. Eighty seven biographies were researched and written by *Tennis in New York* Co-Author Nancy Gill McShea; nine were written in 1988 by a public relations firm; and seven were written by Cara Griffin in 1996-97.

Each of these individuals has made an important contribution to tennis in New York and the surrounding areas. The sum of their diverse backgrounds, skills and experiences proves that tennis is a sport for a lifetime for all people. It provides further evidence that people who play an influential role in tennis in New York are often influential figures in business, politics and entertainment.

Chapter 8

1988: Ashe, Danzig, Palfrey-Danzig, Fitz Gibbon, Gibson, Outerbridge, Stahr, Talbert and Zausner

Arthur R. Ashe, Jr.

Few athletes of our generation have combined superlative talent and performance with the warmth, dedication, leadership and sportsmanship of Arthur Ashe.

Ashe was the first winner of an "open" tennis championship in the United States, in 1968, as competition rules were changed to permit both pros and amateurs to compete for the national title. He couldn't accept the prize money, however, because he was a U.S. Army lieutenant receiving his hotel and $20 a day expenses. But the Richmond, Virginia, recreation leader, who specialized in working with youngsters, gradually made up for lost time by winning the Australian Open title in 1970, the World Championship Tennis (WCT) singles crown in 1975, and 27 of the 32 singles matches he played in Davis Cup competition.

In 1975, Ashe accomplished one of the greatest feats in tennis when he won the coveted Gentlemen's singles title at Wimbledon. A nagging injury slowed him down in 1977 and 1978, and in 1979 Ashe suffered a heart attack. He returned to the courts in 1980 as the U.S. Davis Cup captain. Under his leadership, the U.S. won the Davis Cup the next two years.

Ashe attended UCLA, where he was a three-time All-American and the 1965 NCAA singles and doubles champion. In addition to his US Open, Wimbledon and Australian Open titles, Ashe has won the U.S. Clay Court Championships. He was ranked number one in the world in 1968 and 1975 and in 1985 was inducted into the International Tennis Hall of Fame.

Ashe has served for over twenty years as a dedicated and hard working volunteer within the Eastern Section and at the national level with the USTA. A longtime resident of New York, Arthur Ashe has been a U.S. emissary, traveling extensively as one of the game's most highly regarded authorities and most widely respected individuals.

-- Junior Tennis Foundation

Allison Danzig

Allison Danzig's many contributions as a tennis journalist more than established him as one of the greatest authorities on the sport. He was respected by many and always wrote with sagacity and precision. Remembered by friends as the "Gentleman from The Times," there were very few players, officials or colleagues in the media who did not seek his guidance.

The Texas born Al Danzig, who later resided in Ramsey, New Jersey, was the first journalist ever to be elected to what is now the International Tennis Hall of Fame. His college years at Cornell University demonstrated a well thought out blend of athletics and academics. In addition to his involvement with the varsity football team, he earned an A.B. degree in journalism in 1921.

Throughout his illustrious career, he was acclaimed for his distinguished sports reporting. His first job after graduation was with the now defunct *Brooklyn Eagle* as a sportswriter. It was there that he covered his first big tennis tournament in Bay Ridge, Brooklyn. In 1923, he began his 45-year career with *The New York Times* as a sportswriter covering tennis, football and crew racing. He covered five Olympic Games - Los Angeles, London, Helsinki, Melbourne and Rome - as well as every national tennis championship. During his affiliation with *The Times*, Danzig managed to find the time to write and edit several books. These include "*The Racquet Game?*" and "*Elements of Lawn Tennis*" and "*The Winning Gallery, Court Tennis Matches and Memories*."

A long time member of the U.S. Tennis Writers Association, which he served as its president, he was honored by many prominent organizations. Columbia University developed the Allison Danzig Cup, which is awarded to the winner of the annual Columbia-Cornell tennis matches. Also, the Longwood Cricket Club has established the Allison Danzig Award for distinguished tennis writing.

Among many other posts, Danzig served on the Board of Directors and Executive Committee of the National Tennis Foundation and the Hall of Fame.

It is a pleasure to acknowledge a man whose zestful and unrelenting lifetime contributions to tennis and to those around him made him a leader in the sport.

-- Junior Tennis Foundation

Sarah Palfrey Danzig

If a course was given on "How to Conduct Yourself as a Champion," Sarah Palfrey Danzig would be the ideal teacher and role model. While she certainly competed furiously, it always was with tremendous grace, charm and sportsmanship.

Palfrey Danzig, who was elected "Massachusetts' Greatest Woman Athlete" in 1953, was best known for her sweeping backhand and keen competitive spirit. A winner of 24 foreign national events, including the 1938 and 1939 Wimbledon doubles titles, she twice won the U.S. Grass Court singles title and was a nine-time U.S. Grass Court doubles champion. She also captured U.S. Clay Court and Indoor singles titles and from 1930-39 was a member of America's Wightman Cup team, which recorded eight victories during those years.

She was elected to the International Tennis Hall of Fame in 1963.

A resident of New York City, Palfrey Danzig has dedicated much of her post-competitive tennis life to contributing to the growth and popularity of the game, as well as bettering her community and society. Among her involvements have been serving as a member of the Eastern Tennis Patrons, from 1962-67; serving as chairman of special events for the Child Study Association of America, from 1963-67; and participating as a member of the Trustee Community Service Society of New York, from 1966-76. Her active associations today involve membership on the Executive Committee of the International Tennis Hall of Fame, Inc., as well as the Lawn Tennis Writers Association of America. She is the author of two popular tennis books in addition to contributing numerous articles to prestigious magazines.

-- Junior Tennis Foundation

Leslie J. Fitz Gibbon

If there is one word that would sum up Leslie Fitz Gibbon, it might be "involved." Fitz Gibbon has dedicated his time and energies to the development of the Eastern Tennis Association and the United States Tennis Association for more than 40 years, as a volunteer administrator and player.

From 1968-1969, Fitz Gibbon served as president of the ETA. He also has been chairman of the ETA Membership and Delegate Committees and from 1966-1967 was the section's secretary. Fitz Gibbon has been the director of the USTA Booth at the U.S. National Championships, and then the US Open, since 1966, and he was the treasurer of the USTA from 1977-1978. He has been a member of the USTA's Nominating, Membership, Information, Budget and Finance Committees and is presently involved with the USTA Davis Cup and Olympic Committees. Since 1978 he has been the chairman of the Stevens Cup Committee and the ITF International men's 45 team competition. He serves as chairman of the USTA Senior Grass Court Championships and is the captain of the Britannia Cup, an ITF International men's 65 team competition.

The Garden City, New York, resident was ranked in ETA men's doubles and is presently a top senior tournament player. Although he has always enjoyed tennis as a participant, he counts as one of his greatest thrills having his son, Herbert S. Fitz Gibbon, compete at Wimbledon. Les and Herb have teamed up throughout the years in several tournaments, including both the Eastern and National Grass Court Father and Son events. In 1962, they won the national title.

Les Fitz Gibbon graduated in 1935 from the Massachusetts Institute of Technology (MIT) and has since been the president of the Pilot Packing Co. Inc., a manufacturing representative in the railway supply business.

-- Junior Tennis Foundation

Les and Herb Fitz Gibbon won the 1962 National Father-Son Grass Court title.

Althea Gibson

Emerging from a childhood in Harlem to reign as the tennis champion on the magnificent green lawns at Wimbledon, Althea Gibson has been a dynamic and successful pioneer in the sport. She was the first African American to compete in the U.S. National Championships, in 1950; the first to grace the winner's circle in a Grand Slam event, with singles and doubles victories at the 1956 French Championships; and the first to gain entrée into the Wimbledon draw at the All-England Club. In 1957 and 1958 she won two singles and three women's doubles titles at Wimbledon, two singles and one mixed trophy at the U.S. Championships and one doubles crown at the 1957 Australian, bringing her grand total to 11 within three years.

A 1953 graduate of Florida A&M, Gibson also won the 1950 USLTA Eastern Indoor Championships and that same year was the runner-up to Nancy Chaffee Kiner at the USLTA National Indoors. In 1956, 1957 and 1958 she won the Wimbledon doubles title with a different partner each year.

Teamed at Wimbledon with Darlene Hard in 1957, Gibson won the doubles title and at the conclusion was introduced to and congratulated by Queen Elizabeth II. When she returned to New York, she was greeted with a tickertape parade and an official reception.

Turning pro after her second victory at the U.S. Championships, and expecting more from her talents, she became a professional golfer in her forties. Gibson, who resides in East Orange, New Jersey, retired a few years ago and is now a top teaching tennis professional.

Her autobiography, entitled *"I Always Wanted to Be Somebody,"* which was published in 1958, is a true depiction of her struggle. She made her mark in tennis history and served as an inspiration to many as she broke barriers on her road to victory. Althea Gibson was inducted into the International Tennis Hall of Fame in 1971.

-- Junior Tennis Foundation

International Tennis Hall of Fame

Mary Ewing Outerbridge

drawing (artist unknown)

It is only fitting that Mary Ewing Outerbridge, "the Mother of American Tennis," be honored at this evening's inaugural Eastern Tennis Association Hall of Fame gala. She is credited with introducing lawn tennis to the East more than a century ago, when she was a young, 22-year-old socialite from Staten Island. Thus, all tennis players, writers, administrators, umpires and fans owe her their gratitude.

Outerbridge brought a set of tennis equipment with her on a return voyage from Bermuda to Staten Island in the winter of 1874. She had been visiting family in Bermuda and participated in the new game of lawn tennis there with some officers of the British garrison. She liked the game and purchased some balls, racquets and a net from the regimental store. When she arrived in Staten Island, dressed fashionably in a petticoat and long skirt, she was halted at customs by an agent who did not know what duty to charge for the tennis equipment.

Mary's brother, A. Emelius Outerbridge, who was famous in shipping circles, was able to help get the tennis set through customs. Emelius was also an active cricketer and director of the Staten Island Cricket and Baseball Club at Camp Washington (later St. George) and helped his sister obtain permission to set up the first lawn tennis court there. Soon after, courts were built in Newport, Rhode Island; Plainfield, New Jersey; and in Tuxedo, New York.

Mary and her sister Laura were the first pair in the East to play lawn tennis on a court, which was laid out using white tape. The game soon became popular among the Outerbridge family and their circle of friends, and later, with other elite groups. Mary's most famous brother, Eugenius H. Outerbridge, the first chairman of the New York Port Authority, who lent his name to the Outerbridge Crossing between Staten Island and New Jersey, was a driving force in the formation of the United States National Lawn Tennis Association, now known as the United States Tennis Association. It was Eugenius who decided to hold the first national lawn tennis tournament in 1880.

Mary Ewing Outerbridge, who made her mark in the East and across the U.S., was enshrined in the International Tennis Hall of Fame in 1981, which was also the 100th anniversary of the USTA.

-- Junior Tennis Foundation

Jack Stahr

Family photo courtesy of Jeanne Stahr

If he was not writing the rules, Jack Stahr could be found at any major tournament calling the shots. He was a top chair umpire for more than 20 years and was the chairman of the first USTA Rules Interpretation Committee. His book, *"Friend At Court,"* is considered by many experts to be the definitive authority on rules interpretation.

After graduating from Butler University in 1927 with a B.A. in English, Stahr's career moved along rapidly. In 1929, he became sports editor of the *South Bend Tribune*, a position he held for four years. He served as a sportswriter with the Associated Press in Chicago and New York from 1933-1936, and then began his 38-year public relations career as the editorial director of Carl Byoir and Associates, Inc.

A native of Indiana, Stahr resided in Larchmont, New York, for 40 years. He took an interest in officiating in 1958 after attending several tournaments at Forest Hills. He became a member of the USTA Umpires Committee and served as the chairman from 1973-1974. Stahr officiated the No. 1 court at Wimbledon in 1973 and 1977 and served as the chair umpire for the US Open and the Davis Cup Challenge Rounds for three years. In 1976, Stahr became the first administrator of the USTA Umpires Council.

Stahr, who was inducted into the International Tennis Hall of Fame in 1984, has refereed such tournaments as the National Collegiate Athletic Association finals, Family Circle Cup and the Murjani Women's Tennis Association Championships.

From 1963-1981, he authored the "Decisions" page in *World Tennis* magazine and in 1966 was honored with the McGovern Award for his highly respected *"Friend At Court,"* which many umpires claim to be the bible of tennis regulations.

-- Junior Tennis Foundation

William F. Talbert

Steve Berman

Although Bill Talbert achieved his greatest on court success in the 1940s, the world of tennis has felt his impact over the past four decades. A true sportsman, Talbert has enjoyed a successful tennis career both on and off the court.

In 1942, 1945, 1946 and 1948 he was the United States national doubles champion with Gardnar Mulloy. A consistent player, Talbert was ranked in the top 10 by the United States (Lawn) Tennis Association for a remarkable 12 consecutive years. He was a member of the U.S. Davis Cup Team from 1948-1954.

As his playing career drew to a close, Talbert devoted his knowledge of the game, candor, sensitivity and perseverance to being a tennis coach, administrator and philanthropist. From 1953-57, he captained the U.S. Davis Cup Team, successfully leading his squad to the Challenge Round in each of the five years he served.

Inducted into the International Tennis Hall of Fame in 1967, the Cincinnati-born Talbert turned his attention to tournament administration, becoming the tournament director of the US Open, then at Forest Hills, in 1970.

On his first day at his new administrative post, one he would hold for 15 years, Talbert made a major change in the tournament format; he instituted the sudden-death tiebreak which had been devised by Jimmy Van Alen.

"Tennis needed a finish line," stated Talbert. "Sudden-death provided the same kind of excitement found in football and basketball in the final few minutes."

In addition to overseeing many on court aspects of the Open, it was Talbert who first introduced charity involvement to the game, having the US Open benefit the American Diabetes Association. An accomplished author, the New York City resident has penned such tennis books as "*Playing For Life,*" "*Tennis Observed*" and "*The Game of Singles in Tennis,*" as well as being a contributing editor to *Sports Illustrated* magazine.

Talbert, a holder of 39 national titles, is currently a senior vice president with the American Banknote Corporation and the vice chairman of the International Tennis Hall of Fame and Foundation. He has done much to elevate the game of tennis in the United States and internationally to the level of popularity that it enjoys today.

-- Junior Tennis Foundation

Hy Zausner

A gentleman of distinction and goodwill, Hy Zausner has unselfishly left his mark on Eastern tennis and the many youths whose lives he and the Port Washington Tennis Academy (PWTA) have touched.

In the early 1960s, Zausner began working with problem children in the metropolitan area, most of them drug abusers with little or no future. Viewing the growing problem of drug addiction first hand, he realized that a permanent cure to a young person's dependence on drugs was usually impossible. Children were often able to "clean up" for a short period of time, but without challenges or goals toward which they could direct their energies, they often reverted back to drugs. The problem youths, Zausner realized, needed an activity through which they could learn discipline, self-control, honesty and sportsmanship. It was then that be met Nick Bollettieri, who suggested Zausner try channeling the youngsters' energies toward a more positive outlet - tennis.

Under Bollettieri's personal instruction, Zausner picked up a racquet for the first time and saw the potential of tennis as a tool to reach troubled kids. In 1966, Zausner founded the PWTA with the underlying idea, "If we can get kids hooked on tennis, they will not get hooked on drugs."

He started the academy with a few outdoor courts and a further theory about the influence of peer pressure -- by motivating children to perform with other juniors at their highest level, then drugs, alcohol and other harmful substances would not be a part of their lives. Zausner's concept proved successful and he has expanded the original facility into a fully equipped modern sports academy, including 13 indoor courts, six outdoor courts, whirlpools, exercise classes, a library, study hall, and most importantly, career counseling.

Although Zausner's aim was not necessarily to develop outstanding tennis champions, but rather to provide a healthy learning environment, his academy has graduated such great tennis stars as John McEnroe, Vitas Gerulaitis and Peter Fleming. "We did not make champions out of them," Zausner states modestly, "but…our program and method of teaching gave them the opportunity to develop their championship potential."

The PWTA is a non-profit, charitable institution. Tuition is charged only to those parents who can afford to pay, while those who are unable can apply for scholarships for their children. Tuition does not cover all of the academic expenses. The PWTA operates each year at a deficit which is made up by contributions from the friends of the academy and the Zausner family, who work without salary. Zausner will do what he can for those who cannot afford to join, including making them feel equal to others. He claims to grow more fond every day of what he has created. As he states: "Kids keep me going."

-- Junior Tennis Foundation

Chapter 9

1989: Hoyt, Rooney, Scott and Wood

Julius Larkin Hoyt

Julius Larkin Hoyt could be characterized as a modest, low-keyed country lawyer. He has been a practicing attorney in Newburgh, N.Y., since 1950, after he earned three degrees from Cornell University and served on Guam during World War II. But in the world of tennis he has national clout in the unlikely area of finance. His innovative contributions to the sport on the administrative level, including four terms as treasurer of the U.S. Tennis Association, date back to the beginning of the Open era in 1968.

Initially, Hoyt became involved in the game as the typical tennis parent. His son Bert showed promise at a young age and the local pro suggested that the Hoyts contact the Eastern Tennis Association so Bert could play the juniors. They mailed in the $5.00 membership entry fee and were on their way. Interestingly, the Hoyts spent much time in the company of another 1989 ETA Hall of Famer, John J. Rooney, who in those days ran the boys' 12 tournaments.

Bert was an ETA-ranked junior through the 18s and in 1974 he joined the pro circuit. He competed as a pro for eight years, including a stint with the Bundesliga club team tennis structure in Germany. He ranked among the world's top 200 on the ATP Tour and remained in Germany after his playing days to work for the company, Puma, in product development.

While Bert's tennis star was rising, the elder Hoyt became increasingly aware of the financial realities of the game, coincidentally, through yet another 1989 ETA Hall of Famer, Gene Scott. "Scott accomplished a great deal when he was the ETA president (1972-73)," Hoyt said. "They were challenging times in tennis...There were no national support funds for the East. Scott inherited a deficit, reversed it with standard marketing techniques and went out leaving a surplus."

Scott and his playing cronies, Paul Cranis and Herb Fitz Gibbon, also inspired Hoyt with their dedication to the juniors. "The three of them got up at 5 a.m. every morning to work with kids wherever they could get court time," Hoyt continued. "They were knowledgeable and committed so it was not hard to join in with them."

Twenty-one years later, Hoyt has received numerous distinguished service awards for his contributions to the game. The International Tennis Hall of Fame honored him this past March with the Samuel Hardy Award at the USTA Annual Meeting in Hawaii. The Hardy Award is presented annually for long and outstanding service to tennis. Hunter Delatour, chairman of the Hall of Fame Awards Committee, cited Hoyt's "significant contributions and selfless devotion to all levels of tennis. . . Tennis is a better sport today because of Julie Hoyt's efforts."

Hoyt served on several ETA committees involved with junior affairs and in 1976 was elected president of the section. Accomplishments recorded while he held that office included the restructuring of the ETA into five regions with regional vice presidents, rewriting the constitution and rules, improving the financing and budgeting process and establishing a system of periodic reporting. He received the Distinguished Service Award for leadership as president in 1978 and accepted the Outstanding Leadership Award in 1980.

Significantly, in 1979 he was a founding member of Eastern's Junior Tennis Foundation (JTF), which has prospered for years as the section's major fundraiser. He served as the foundation's president until 1988 and received three more Distinguished Service Awards for his work with the JTF -- in 1981, 1982 and 1983.

During the years he served as the USTA treasurer, Hoyt earned distinction as a member of several national committees, including the US Open, budget and finance, sanctions and schedule, and membership. He chaired the USTA Education and Research Committee and also served for three years on the USTA Management Committee as the regional vice president of the North Atlantic Region.

Robert Garry, acting executive director of the USTA and the organization's director of finance and administration, applauds Hoyt's dedication to the game. "He embraced the USTA as a personal opportunity for public service," Garry said. "He is as gracious and energetic as he is creative and effective, and his homespun humor and personal warmth are always welcome. His ability to set goals and priorities within the volunteer structure has had a great impact on the USTA."

-- By Nancy Gill McShea

John J. (Pat) Rooney

Steve Bernau

"There is a twinkle in his Irish eyes, a smile...and a warm glow on his grandfatherly face," wrote Maury Allen in *The New York Post* in October, 1987. Add to that his trademark Brooks Brothers tweed cap and sports jacket and his habit of arriving with flowers whenever he's a dinner guest, and a picture emerges of John J. (Pat) Rooney. He is a gentleman and a scholar, and not incidentally, a tennis legend in his own time!

The son of a judge who wrote for the financial pages of *The New York Times*, and a Harvard elocution teacher, Rooney was born and educated in New York City. At age 15 he graduated from Townsend Harris High School (today's equivalent of the Bronx H.S. of Science); and he earned an A.B. degree from Fordham University in 1924 with a major in philosophy/psychology and a minor in mathematics. He never took a tennis lesson, yet he was undefeated in doubles for four years on Fordham's Varsity Tennis team. In his post-graduate years he continued to play the game, competing in amateur tournaments while pursuing career interests -- as an oil field surveyor in Oklahoma, a bond salesman on Wall Street, owner of an aircraft parts business, and service in the U.S. Navy as a Lieutenant Commander during World War II -- until he returned to Fordham in 1947 for a masters degree in nuclear physics to prepare for a life in the aeronautics field.

While he was a graduate student, Rooney taught math at Fordham Prep. As fate would have it, however, tennis began to dominate his time there -- he has since coached the Prep's Varsity Boys' team for 40 years, and simultaneously coached their arch rivals, New York City's Xavier H.S. team, for 15 years. The two squads practiced together amicably on the 207th Street courts (due to Rooney's gift for reconciling natural adversaries; he stressed what a privilege it was for them to play there on clay while confiding to a friend that the surface was actually dirt), but when they squared off against each other in a dual match representing their respective schools, the "coach" wisely vanished from sight. "I understand everything perfectly," he quips, using a favorite Rooney expression. "Do you follow me?"

In 1974 the new coeds at Fordham College persuaded Pete Carlesimo (then the Athletic Director) to establish a women's varsity tennis program, and Rooney signed on as the head coach of the Lady Rams. They have since compiled a record with the highest winning percentage of any Fordham athletic team in recent history. Today, Rooney, who is about 85 years old and hedges with appropriate Irish ambiguity about his age, is probably the oldest active college coach in the business -- and the most vocal. Ever the realist, he insists tennis is for fun. "Academics are first!" he says firmly. "We don't have a pro team here...We win (of course!) but we have a good time." Indeed they do. One former team member recalled trying out for the women's squad: "He took a pen knife from his pocket, cut a rose and presented it to me. He said, 'The roses on the outside of the fence belong to the Jesuits, the ones on the inside belong to Rooney.'" And he's not above tantalizing his girls with his Tiffany's charge card; they regularly beg to borrow it for a couple of hours.

Inevitably, coaching led Rooney to a life in tennis. He is the Bronx delegate to the Eastern Tennis Association Board of Directors and the section's Scholastic Ranking chairman since 1950 and is most familiar to generations of young Eastern tennis players as a veteran tournament director. He has hosted literally hundreds of ETA junior invitational high school events for boys and girls, where he has observed Eastern's most promising players come up through the ranks, including future greats John McEnroe and Vitas Gerulaitis. Rooney is also shrewd; that's how he hand-picks his Fordham women's team.

On the national scene, Rooney came into contact with tennis legends such as Bill Tilden and Bill Talbert, first as an umpire and later as the USTA chairman of ball boys and ball girls -- at the U.S. National Championships, the US Open, and at Madison Square Garden's Nabisco Masters and the Virginia Slims Championships -- for more than 25 years. Martina Navratilova has stated repeatedly that "Mr. Rooney's ball people are the best in the world!"

In 1986 Rooney won the ETA "Coach of the Year" award for his successful seasons and his long service to the game. He loves his work and claims he goes non-stop seven days a week. "I'm working as fast as I can here," he says with obvious delight. "I'm going a mile a minute. It's just overwhelming, but what the heck!"

-- By Nancy Gill McShea

Eugene L. Scott

When one considers Gene Scott the tennis writer, the tendency is to compare him to the political writer, William F. Buckley, Jr. As Buckley is the guru of the conservative party through *The National Review* and his nationally syndicated column, "On the Right," so, too, is Scott the conscience of the tennis world via his column, "Vantage Point," in *Tennis Week*. Like Buckley, Scott challenges people to think about issues -- specifically what's right and wrong in the tennis business. The use of lofty language and the slight trace of acerbic wit lend truth to the comparison as well – a possible throwback to their days at Yale when both were members of the eclectic secret society, "Skull and Bones."

A New York City native, Scott grew up in Long Island's St. James community, where he started playing tennis at the age of 12. He received no formal instruction but credits Elizabeth Ryan (Italian, French and Wimbledon champ) with being his inspirational teacher. As a Yale undergraduate, Scott set a record that still stands, earning four varsity letters for four consecutive years in tennis, soccer, hockey and track. After Yale, he graduated from the University of Virginia Law School.

Scott showed an independent streak early, traveling alone by bus on the summer tennis circuit when he was 18. He looked like the classic "preppie" before it was fashionable, the same image he projects today. (However, rumor has it that he pitched hay in his younger days, although his hands seem to have recovered from the callouses; and he currently wears a pair of 25-year-old Gucci loafers with holes in the soles.) Even then he was his own man, as he talked often to friends about someday becoming a writer and running a country newspaper.

Writing would have to wait, though, while Scott was establishing himself on the international tennis stage during the 1960s as Eastern's world class player. In 1963 he competed on the U.S. Davis Cup team and earned the No. 4 U.S. national men's ranking. He advanced to the singles quarterfinals at the 1965 French Open and that year achieved the No. 11 world ranking. In 1967 he was a semifinalist at the U.S. Championships, where he surrendered in five sets to the eventual champion, John Newcombe of Australia. Scott ranked among America's top ten five times, was the U.S. Open Court Tennis titlist for five years and the U.S. Amateur champ for ten. A competitive tennis player to this day, he has been the USTA Senior Grass Court champion for the past two years.

Tennis magazine has called Scott "The Renaissance Man," and so he is. He is a columnist, author, tournament director, attorney, film producer, TV commentator, public speaker and athlete. His book, *Bjorn Borg My Life and My Game*, was No. 5 on the *London Times'* best seller list, and he wrote and produced three award winning documentary films on the US Open. He has also promoted more than 150 professional men's and women's events since the start of the Open era in 1968 and was the color commentator for the "Battle of the Sexes" match between Bobby Riggs and Billie Jean King at the Houston Astrodome.

Scott was a co-founder of the National Junior Tennis League, with Arthur Ashe, Charlie Pasarell and Sheridan Snyder. He is also the current director of Madison Square Garden's Nabisco Masters professional men's tournament, a member of the U.S. Tennis Association executive board, a vice president of the International Tennis Hall of Fame, president of the U.S. International Lawn Tennis Club and a past president of the Eastern Tennis Association. He has tennis bylines in *The New York Times, Sports Illustrated* and *Esquire*, along with a lighthearted article about champagne in *Harper's Bazaar*. He has lectured for the Practicing Law Institute and is a member of the Board of Arbitration of the New York Stock Exchange.

Scott inherited his independent nature, intellectual curiosity and loyalty to friends from his family. His grandfather, Dr. Eugene C. Sullivan, invented Pyrex and was the chairman of the Corning Glass Works. His mother, Dorothy, is a writer and his father, S. Lytton -- a treasurer of the ETA in the 1960s -- was the most decent human being Scott has ever known.

All of which seems to confirm and explain what friends say: "Gene Scott is a very gifted and demanding individual. He wants to experience everything, to learn and grow at every level....He believes people either stretch themselves to reach their full potential or they will make a pact with the status quo."

-- By Nancy Gill McShea

Sidney B. Wood, Jr.

International Tennis [Hall] of Fame

The son of a mining engineer who once was a partner of the legendary Wyatt Earp in a Nevada mining claim, Sidney Wood overcame childhood illnesses to become a world class tennis player on Wimbledon's Centre Court, in 1927, at the tender age of 15. A few years later, in 1931 at the age of 19, he won the Gentlemen's singles championship at the All England Lawn Tennis Club.

Born in Black Rock, Connecticut, in 1911, Wood spent his early years in California when his father, Sidney, Sr., moved the family to the YouBet mining camp there. Three years later the family moved to Berkeley. According to Wood, he was a semi-invalid during that time, between the ages of four and eight, but he liked to hit the tennis ball so his father built him a court out of crushed stone from the mine's rock pile. He says laughingly, "The ball never bounced straight, which accounted for my very short backswing."

Wood played casually until he moved to Berkeley. When he was 11 or 12 years old, his uncle, Watson Washburn, left for Australia to compete on the U.S. Davis Cup team, and he gave Wood one of his racquets. Sidney met Helen Wills Moody and Helen Jacobs, who combined had won Italian, French and Wimbledon championships, and he practiced with them at a Berkeley country club until he was 14. Then he returned to the East coast to live with his grandmother on 79th Street in New York City and began to play on Eastern's 15-and-under boys' circuit and the junior 18s. His success qualified him for an important men's tournament at the time, the Arizona State Championships, and he won that title while he was still 14.

By 1927, Wood had won several men's tournaments, and he qualified for the French Championships. Surprisingly, he advanced to the third round there which earned him a spot in the main draw of Gentlemen's singles at Wimbledon. He would play the defending champ, René Lacoste, in the first round on the All England Club's famous Centre Court. Said Wood, "He was very gentle with me."

In 1931, the year Wood won Wimbledon, he beat Fred Perry in the semis to set up a meeting in the final with his roommate and doubles partner, Frank Shields. But Shields had sprained his knee in his semifinal victory over Jean Borotra and was unable to play the final. Wood won by default. However, the two friends had a private understanding that Sidney would not consider himself the Wimbledon champ until he actually defeated Frank. He did so the following year in England's Queen's Club final, the warmup for Wimbledon.

Wood continued his education while he was playing tennis, graduating from Connecticut's Cheshire Academy in 1929 and attending the University of Arizona in Tucson. He was nationally ranked among America's top ten from 1930-1935, and again in 1938. He was a finalist at the U.S. National Championships at Forest Hills, N.Y., in 1935 and a doubles finalist at the U.S. National Indoors, with Eugene McCauliff, also in 1935. He was a member of the U.S. Davis Cup team from 1931-1934 and won the 1956 U.S. National Father-Son Championships with his son, Sidney III, who competed on Yale's Varsity Tennis team with Gene Scott and Donald Dell.

A resident of Southampton, N.Y., for 60 years, Wood, at age 77 today, calls himself "a mad inventor of tennis courts." He remains active in the tennis business as the chairman of Grandstand International Corp., a firm which manufactures the tennis court surface, "Courtship." He has been a member of the International Club (IC) of the United States, an international member of the IC of France and an honorary member of the IC of Great Britain.

Sidney Wood was inducted into the International Tennis Hall of Fame in 1964.

-- By Nancy Gill McShea

Chapter 10

1990: Barker, Holmberg, Lebair, Martin and Williams

Robert M. Barker

Like any ambitious junior analyst who works for a firm on the New York Stock Exchange and commutes on the Long Island Rail Road, Bob Barker should have been studying *The Wall Street Journal* the morning of Sept. 2, 1955. Instead, he turned to the sports section of *The New York Times* to check out the featured opening day matches at the U.S. National Championships (now U.S. Open) in Forest Hills, N.Y. He was shocked to see that HE was scheduled to play at 1 p.m. that very day.

"I was so startled and excited," Barker recalls, "I read it several times!" He immediately put in an SOS call to his father Richard who collected Bob's tennis gear and met him at Forest Hills for his historic debut on grass. He lost that match in five sets, but at age 25 he was just beginning his long, successful career in competitive tennis.

The story is revealing. Bob did not expect to get in to the U.S. Championships that year; he had not received written notification and had been rejected the year before. Plus, he had never played the junior circuit so his tournament experience at the game's highest levels was limited, except for outstanding results on tennis teams at Manhasset High School on Long Island and at Colgate University. But he was never rejected again. He competed in the men's draw at the U.S. Championships until he was 35, won titles at the USTA National men's 35 and 45 Clay Court tournaments, and set Eastern records for 35 years.

"Bob has been one of the most respected Eastern players over the past three decades," says tennis promoter Lloyd Emanuel. "In addition to his national titles, he dominated every ETA adult age division, and remarkably, held his own against top players well into his forties. His achievements are a tribute to his intense spirit and excellent physical conditioning."

Barker, who is often described in the press as "a stockbroker capable of tennis heroics," has accumulated more than 60 ETA and USTA rankings, including being ranked in ETA men's singles for a record 20 consecutive years while earning the No.1 ranking in every age category. At age 29 in 1959, he was ranked No. 6 in ETA men's singles right behind Ron Holmberg and Dick Savitt, who that year ranked 4th and 5th, respectively, in the U.S. top ten.

Earlier, in 1956, Barker was runner-up in the Suffolk County Championships in St. James, Long Island. That draw featured three ETA Hall of Famers spanning three generations. Barker, then 26, beat Alastair Martin, 41, in the semis. Later that day Bob lost to Yale freshman Gene Scott, 18, in the final. It was Scott's first title in men's singles and he remembers it well. "Bob is a cross between a pit bull and a poodle," says Scott. "Off court he's a gentle fine guy, but he's a great competitor."

Barker has achieved his greatest success on clay, his favorite surface. In 1961 he met Arthur Ashe in the finals of the Eastern Clay Court Championships at the Oritani Field Club in Hackensack, N.J. Barker was 31 and Ashe was 17. Mel Woody of the *Newark Evening News* reported, "There must have been 40 or 50 key points in the grueling five-set match...Barker twisted his ankle early in the third set which may have cost him eight or nine points...It took four match points before Ashe pulled out the 6-3, 2-6, 6-3, 4-6, 6-4 marathon victory." Losing has its compensations, however. Smiling wryly, Barker says, "I played the tournament (at Oritani) for 18 years. I was getting older and never won it so they felt sorry for me and gave me the sportsmanship award."

Barker is also an author. His 1975 novel *Love Forty* about a stock broker obsessed by tennis drew rave reviews from some of the sport's experts -- Bobby Riggs, *Times* reporter Allison Danzig, Dick Stockton, Ashe and Scott. Said Riggs, "Only a top player could have written *Love Forty*. This is what competitive tennis is really like." Scott added, "Barker thoroughly explores the psychological aspects of a semi-professional's daily routine, and his own on court experience provides a real-life tone that has rarely been duplicated."

Along with his busy tennis schedule, a Wall Street career and the labor involved in writing a novel, Barker found the time to direct a junior tennis program in Great Neck, N.Y., in the 1970s. He has also worked as an ETA tournament director and as the volunteer chairman of several ETA committees.

-- By Nancy Gill McShea

Ron Holmberg

Russ Adams

From the late 1950s through the '60s, reporters and editors at *World Tennis* magazine frequently paid tribute to Ron Holmberg's tennis ability. "Holmberg can do more with a tennis ball than any other player of his era," they wrote. "There is no shot that is beyond his aptitude...His touch, power and strokemaking are beautiful to watch..."

The *U.S. Tennis Association Official Encyclopedia of Tennis* cites Holmberg as one of "the leading tennis players of his day." He ranked 10 times among the top ten in U.S. men's singles during his prime and was a semifinalist at the U.S. National Championships and a quarterfinalist at the French Championships. He also won the singles and doubles crowns at the Canadian Open in Toronto, among other titles.

Holmberg's record was impressive, but more importantly, he was a spectator's delight. Steve Flink, the editor of *World Tennis*, says, "Ron was his own kind of player, a consummate stylist, which made him stand out. He reminded me of

(Ken) Rosewall in that he was so effortless. He could hit winners from everywhere." Flink remembers watching him play Rosewall in the Wimbledon warm-up at the Queen's Club in the late '60s. Holmberg was down a set and 2-love, but after a rain delay he found his timing and completely took over the match. "He was brilliant!" says Flink.

Ron learned the game in his native Brooklyn at Fort Greene Park and progressed through the New York City parks system. He played No. 1 singles for Bishop Loughlin High School in Brooklyn and won the City's Public Parks Championship. His potential carried him beyond his roots into the national arena when he was 14 and met the famous teaching pro John Nogrady, who was a tremendous help, especially with match-play strategy. In 1953, at age 15, Ron won the boys' 15-and-under doubles title at the junior national championships, was triumphant in both singles and doubles at the Indoors, and won his first match at the U.S. National Championships in Forest Hills.

At 16 he was an early protégé of the USTA's Junior Davis Cup program, and in 1956 he capped off his successful junior career by beating his old friend Rod Laver for the junior singles title at Wimbledon. He was also a playing member of the U.S. Davis Cup team, in 1956 and '57, and was twice the NCAA doubles champ during his college days at Tulane, in 1957 and 1959.

During the past 20 years Holmberg has established an international reputation as a junior and adult coach. He ran a junior camp at the Kent School in Connecticut and coached at the U.S. Military Academy at West Point. In the summer of 1989 he taught at an adult camp with his pal, Australian Roy Emerson, at the Palace Hotel in Gstaad, Switzerland.

"Teaching is terrific," says Holmberg. "It's fun to work with a group when everybody enjoys being there...I do not choose to teach people strictly on ability, but on their desire to learn. For this reason all my lessons are enjoyable."

His teaching reflects his approach to life. "Ron is a direct person and uncompromising in his principles," says one former student. "But he's also carefree and his personality comes across on the tennis court. He talks about the game in very precise terms yet he believes players should spend time just fooling around on the court. He feels that when players have fun experimenting with crazy shots, they learn to love the game and become creative." The Holmberg philosophy: "Hit the ball as hard as you can and as close to the lines as you can, but don't miss!"

Ron Holmberg also worked as an ESPN broadcaster over a three-year period, including calling the play-by-play during the United States' 4-1 winning effort over Czechoslovakia in the 1981 Davis Cup match. And he's a jet setter, always on the go, socializing with many successful people in the entertainment and sports industries who have become his good friends. His daughter Holly -- "She's the light of my life," he says. -- has gone off to college at Emory University in Georgia so he has more flexibility to travel. For a change of pace, he plays in regular pickup basketball games all around the country every opportunity he gets. "Basketball is my first love," he says, "probably because I was better at tennis...My good friend John Andariese (the voice of the N.Y. Knicks with Marv Albert) knows basketball the way I know tennis, but we both love the other sport...Life is that way."

-- By Nancy Gill McShea

Harold A. Lebair

Harold Lebair devoted more than 40 years of service to promoting the game of tennis. He was widely respected for many administrative contributions to the sport, but he was perhaps most well known as a tennis umpire and linesman.

In 1949 Lebair was the first American (and non-British) chair umpire to call the men's singles final at Wimbledon. Ted Schroeder of the United States edged Czechoslovakia's Jaroslav Drobny for the title in five sets. Lebair recalled feeling a little nervous that year climbing to his perch on Wimbledon's famous Centre Court. At one point during the tournament he inadvertently announced the wrong score and later recalled: "To my horror and shame, 14,000 voices cried in unison, 'Oh, no, Mr. Umpire!' It could have been worse, I suppose. Imagine what a baseball or basketball crowd would have done to me!"

As a linesman he made headlines when the U.S. beat Australia at the 1938 Davis Cup match in Philadelphia. His famous foot fault calls on Australian Adrian Quist prompted banner headlines: "Lebair Wins Davis Cup for America!" He had called seven foot faults on Quist, a number unheard of in those days. "I can still hear the boos," he would say 20 years later. "But the umpire backed me up. What's more, Harry Hopman, the Australian captain, got up and defended me before the crowd."

Among Lebair's fondest recollections was a sporting gesture he doubted would ever be repeated. Gottfried von Cramm, the German tennis player, was locked in a duel with America's Don Budge. Von Cramm served an ace, then turned to Lebair, who was a linesman for the match, and said, "I foot faulted then, didn't I?"

Lebair was treasurer of the U.S. Lawn Tennis Association from 1958-1967, and as chairman of the USTA umpires from 1941-1952 he was the first to use female officials in the Forest Hills stadium during the U.S. National Championships. He chaired and/or was a member of 11 USLTA committees, including chairing the president's committee that revised and modernized amateur tennis rules in 1953. He was also a tennis member of the U.S. Olympics Committee, from 1958-1965.

He also received two prestigious tennis awards. In 1948 the Tennis Writers' Association honored him with its annual award as the man who had done the most for tennis that year; and in 1951 he received the John T. McGovern trophy, given annually to the umpire who does the most for tennis officiating.

Harold Lebair was born in Philadelphia, attended the University of Pennsylvania and worked as a reporter for the *Philadelphia Public Ledger* before moving to New York in 1908. He was later a member of the national advertising staff of *The New York Times*, from 1936 until he retired in 1965. Personally, he was described as a tall, lean erect man who dressed smartly and often wore a homburg. He was distinguished for his brisk walk, rapid speech and brimming energy; yet he always found time to be friendly.

Born in Philadelphia, Lebair attended the University of Pennsylvania and worked as a reporter for the *Philadelphia Public Ledger* before moving to New York in 1908.

He settled on the South Shore of Long Island in Lawrence with his wife Lucile and three daughters, and launched a long career in tennis, advertising and local community service. He died in July of 1967.

-- By Nancy Gill McShea

Alastair B. Martin

International Tennis Hall of Fame

In early 1969, a piece by Neil Amdur in *The New York Times* featured a banner headline: "Martin, New Tennis Chief, Seeks Twin Goal of Unity, Expansion." Alastair Bradley Martin of Glen Head, Long Island, and New York City, who had rated newspaper headlines for 30 years both as a tennis player and administrator, was about to assume the presidency of the U.S. Lawn Tennis Association.

Martin thought like a player and believed that former players should have a say in the way the game is run. The USLTA presidency in 1969-1970, however, was a tough assignment. Tennis was in turmoil with the advent in 1968 of "open competition" between professionals and amateurs. It was a time of dramatic growth, unlimited commercial opportunities, power struggles and uncertainty. Martin had supported a British revolt which led to the International Tennis Federation's sanctioning of Open tennis, and now it was his turn to consolidate the transition into the Open era.

Tennis writers in the New York dailies were quick to point out that although he was a product of the Park Avenue-Princeton-Eastern establishment, a man who had enjoyed a wealthy upbringing and aristocratic heritage, Martin was a realist.

When he was the president of the Eastern Lawn Tennis Association in 1964-1965, he said, "One of the drawbacks we face in trying to improve the situation in tennis is its stuffed-shirt image. We haven't projected our stars; Open tennis might help."

Alastair was also an early supporter of introducing tennis to children in the public sector. The Eastern Tennis Patrons, of which he was a co-leader, donated several thousand dollars to the New York City Board of Education in the 1960s. "We sponsor annual clinics in the parks of New York, Long Island and New Jersey," he said, "and we were instrumental in having tennis put into the regular curriculum of physical education training in the schools...this is a major breakthrough." In 1972 when he was the president of the National Tennis Foundation, he increased the organization's support of junior tennis programs in major cities; and privately, he organized a joint effort with the Boy Scouts of America.

Martin played tennis in prep school, at Deane in California; and at Princeton, where he was graduated in 1938. He competed on the Eastern clay and grass court circuits before and after World War 11 (during the war he served as a Captain in the U.S. Army). In the 1950s he ranked among America's best tennis players in singles and held an ETA ranking in singles and doubles for 11 straight years among some of the most accomplished players of the day – Dick Savitt, Bill Talbert, Sidney Wood, Jr., and this year's fellow hall of fame inductees Ron Holmberg and Bob Barker.

He also achieved national and international stature in court tennis during the 1940s, '50s and '60s. He was the U.S. National Court singles champ eight times, its doubles titlist 10 times, and the British champion in singles. But the reporter Allison Danzig noted in *The Times* that even though "Martin happens to be the best amateur court tennis player in the country and probably the world...it is for his contributions to lawn tennis that he has been singled out by the pros." The U.S. Professional Lawn Tennis Association honored him with its annual award for distinguished service to tennis in May of 1956.

When Martin retired from the USLTA presidency, Danzig wrote, "I regret that you are stepping down...There never was a time when tennis was more in need of the leadership of men like yourself – men of character whose only interest is to serve the game...Too often profits and prize money are the only yardsticks of success and progress. Hardly anyone seems to give a thought to the future (champions) or takes steps to make it possible for more of the youth of the land to be introduced to a game that will give them pleasure and good health for life...I know you are concerned about this...I have so great a respect for you as a man of integrity and honor who says only what he means and believes."

Appropriately, Alastair Martin was inducted into the International Tennis Hall of Fame in 1973.

-- By Nancy Gill McShea

Barbara S. Williams

In her role as the first woman to serve on the Board of Directors of the U.S. Tennis Association, Barbara Williams commands the highest visibility of any woman in tennis administration in the United States, and perhaps the world. Presently the treasurer of the USTA, she is also the first woman to serve as an officer on that board, and the first to be elected the president of a USTA section, the Eastern Tennis Association, in 1978-1979.

In addition, Williams was honored in 1985 with the "USTA Service Bowl," the sport's most prestigious award for women. The award, which is presented "to the player who yearly makes the most notable contribution to the sportsmanship, fellowship and service of tennis," lists tennis greats Billie Jean King, Chris Evert, Alice Marble, Maureen Connolly Brinker and Sarah Palfrey-Danzig among its most well known recipients.

However, Barbara's first priority is her family -- her husband Jack; six children: David, Sally, Sue, Bobby, Amy and Andrew (tennis players all); 12 grandchildren; her 87-year old mother, Anna Lisa Seaquist; her brother Kenneth; and her longtime companion Sylvia Jones. Fortunately, the whole group shares Barbara's commitment to the game. It is not unusual for them to spend a weekend working behind the scenes processing a 15,000-piece tennis mailing; and in 1988 the Williamses were honored as the ETA Family of the Year.

Honors and position do not distract her, though. Barbara has been dedicated to Eastern tennis for more than 30 years, and she continues to be interested in helping people at the lower organizational levels of the sport, and those who are just getting involved as players.

She grew up in Evanston, Illinois. Her Girl Scout leader taught her to play tennis in the public parks there when she was 11, and she won the City's tennis title three times in her youth. After she graduated from the University of Illinois, she moved east to Larchmont, N.Y., in the late 1950s and quickly became known as a tennis leader. She founded the Metropolitan Inter-Club Tennis League at the Orienta Beach Club in Mamaroneck, N.Y., and was its president for 18 years. The league, which fields both adult and junior teams, has succeeded because of Barbara's personal involvement. She gathered key tennis players from various clubs, inspired them to volunteer their time, which led to an extensive recreational tennis network in Westchester County.

During her years as an ETA administrator, she founded and is still a member of the Junior Tennis Foundation. She organized and chaired the Foundation's first major fundraiser for junior tennis, an outing to the movie premier of "Players" followed by a party at New York's hot spot at the time, Studio 54. The event raised $50,000. She initiated programs for the young novice player and the disadvantaged: the Caravan program of free tennis clinics, the "Ups" circuit for unranked players, as well as district tournaments and rankings. She has also captained ETA team events, started intra-sectional team matches for men and women, worked as a tournament director and served on and/or chaired some 14 ETA committees.

Barbara has etched her legacy in the game simultaneously in both the national and international arenas. Since 1980 she has been a member of more than a dozen USTA committees, most notably the Olympic Games and the Federation and Wightman Cups. She chaired the Maureen Connolly Brinker Cup, a team competition between the U.S. and Australia, which the U.S. hosted from 1980-1987; and her trademark, the USTA's Individual Membership Committee, from 1981-1985.

Friends agree unanimously that Williams is a true ambassador for tennis. ETA Executive Director Doris Herrick, who has worked with Barbara for years, has said: "She has been a gracious hostess at the US Open [in the USTA Information Booth] since the tournament moved to Flushing Meadows in 1978. People from all over the world and across the U.S. stop to say hello to her every year. What's amazing is that she remembers all of their names!"

Not if you're Barbara Williams!

-- By Nancy Gill McShea

Chapter 11

1991: Budge, Glick, Shields and Sutter

J. Donald Budge

Before tennis, Don Budge loved baseball while he was growing up in California. He liked to think of himself as a slugger and figured sluggers play the outfield, so center field was his territory. Later, when he was king of the tennis world, he had the thrill of his life when his idol, the legendary Babe Ruth, presented him with the "World's Greatest Athlete" award, the Gold Laurel Wreath, at the 1939 World's Fair in New York.

One year earlier, of course, Budge had become a legendary slugger himself when he achieved the first Grand Slam of tennis at age 23, winning singles titles at the four majors – Wimbledon, the Australian, the French and the U.S. National Championships – a record that stood for 23 years. And he won two other national championships in 1938, the Czechoslovakian and Irish titles, to bring the total to six, unequalled by anyone!

One tennis expert said recently, "The awesome presence of Don Budge can be summed up in the fact that 20 years after his prime, it was still more important to have his name on a racquet than a manufacturer's."

The following is a sampling of the man's brilliant amateur tennis career, from 1934-1938:

1934 - U.S. National Championships: singles round of 16; USTA Clay Courts: doubles winner; ranked No. 9, U.S. men's singles.
1935 - U.S. Championships: doubles finalist; U.S. Davis Cup team, 7-2 record; ranked No. 2, U.S. men's singles.
1936 - U.S. Championships: singles finalist, doubles winner; Wimbledon: mixed doubles finalist; U.S. Davis Cup team, 4-1 record; ranked No. 1, U.S. men's singles.

1937 - Wimbledon: singles and mixed doubles winner; U.S. Championships: singles, mixed doubles winner, men's doubles finalist; U.S. Davis Cup team, 12-0 record; ranked No. 1, U.S. men's singles; winner, Associated Press "Athlete of the Year" (only male tennis player ever so honored); *Time* magazine cover story; Starred in New York's Broadway "Ticker Tape" parade; winner, "Sullivan Award," given annually to greatest amateur athlete (only tennis player ever to win award).

1938 - first winner of Tennis Grand Slam – Australian: singles winner; French: singles winner; Wimbledon: singles, men's and mixed doubles winner; U.S. National Championships: singles, men's and mixed doubles winner; ranked No. 1, U.S. men's singles; U.S. Davis Cup team, 2-1 record.

Budge was such a crowd favorite with his easy-going manner and good humor on the court, the press reported his every move. After he beat Bunny Austin in the quarters on Wimbledon's Centre Court in 1935, he turned to bow to the Royal Box and casually wiped his brow. The press immediately interpreted the gesture as a friendly wave to Queen Mary and headlined the story around the world. Two years later, when he was presented to the Queen after winning his first Wimbledon title, the Queen said, "Mr. Budge, I did not see you when you waved to me. Had I, I would have waved back."

History shows that England's Queen had countless opportunities to wave to Budge, as he is the only player ever to win all three events at Wimbledon – twice. And he accomplished the same feat at the U.S. National Championships, albeit not in succession. Between 1936 and 1938, he won 14 Grand Slam titles (Gene Mako teamed with him forever in men's doubles, while Alice Marble and Sarah Palfrey Danzig shared the mixed winners' circle with him). In Davis Cup play, he was 25-4 overall, winning 18 singles matches (fifth on the all-time list despite a brief amateur career). In 1937, he won a historic fifth and deciding match against Germany in the Davis Cup tie, rallying from 1-4 down in the fifth set to defeat Gottfried von Cramm, 6-8, 5-7, 6-4, 6-2, 8-6. Bill Tilden said it was the greatest match in tennis history.

The Budge era is noted for his sportsmanship and defense of professional tennis. Based on the amateur system, Budge felt promising players could not hope to compete successfully if they had to support themselves outside of tennis. With the incentive of financial reward, he reasoned, fewer stars would leave the game before they reached their full potential.

Budge turned professional in 1939 and was the world's pro tennis champ from 1939-1946, thereby sacrificing his chance to win another Grand Slam, earn a U.S. ranking, or play Davis Cup. In fact, he was on his way to winning the first Professional Grand Slam in 1939, having won the U.S., French and British titles, and was en route to Australia in September for the final leg when World War 11 broke out and the trip was cancelled. That year, he challenged Ellsworth Vines, who had been the reigning world pro champ for five years until Budge surpassed him and Fred Perry. The top tennis pros played a series of matches

Don Budge and Nancy McShea at 1991 Eastern Hall of Fame.

against one another to determine the annual champ. In 1939, Budge prevailed over Vines 37-22 in 59 matches, and he routed Perry 28-8 in 36 matches. They worked hard for their money! World War 11 interrupted his pro tennis career, but Air Force Lieutenant Budge staged morale-boosting exhibition matches for the troops in the Pacific. In 1943, he and Jack Kramer played an exhibition in New York's Seventh Regiment Armory for a U.S. War Bond drive and raised close to four million dollars for the war effort.

Budge played an aggressive game, most notable for his backhand drive. He transformed the stroke from a defensive groundie to an offensive weapon. Willie Shields says his pop, Frank X., admired Budge's "roll-over corner-to-corner backhand." The elder Shields would say, "Watch this! You'll never see a more beautiful backhand than this!"

After his playing days, Budge moved to New York in 1954 and opened the Town Tennis Club on East 56th Street. Shields and Sidney Wood, Jr., who were inducted with Budge into the International Tennis Hall of Fame in 1964, ran a chic New York laundry service. Budge later bought out Shields and re-named it "Budge-Wood" under the slogan,

"Grime Does Not Pay." Then they sold out to Arnold Palmer, who subsequently sold the business to NBC. Today, Budge and his wife Loriel travel extensively in the interests of tennis. He is a spokesman for Prince Racquets and conducts junior clinics and teacher forums around the country.

Who was the greatest tennis player? Budge says that "Vines was the best player on a given day, but Kramer was the most consistent 365 days a year." Don Budge wasn't bad either!

-- By Nancy Gill McShea

Dr. Irving V. Glick

George Kalinsky

Back in the 1970s, Dr. Irving Glick wrote a regular column for *Tennis Week*, "The Doctor's In," until, he says with a chuckle, "I ran out of anatomy."

Gene Scott, the publisher and editor-in-chief of *Tennis Week*, recently summed up that particular columnist's unique impact in tennis: "In a business world where power, money and a threatening-tone-of-voice carries sway, Irving Glick is an anomaly. He is our game's best example of how the world should change its priorities. This doctor is 'always in', and he is always quiet and modest with a tone of voice almost inaudible. But listen up. You do want to hear what he has to say."

Indeed, Dr. Glick, a New York City native and a certified Diplomate of the American Board of Orthopedic Surgery since 1952, returns to New York tonight fresh from the French Open in Paris where he participated in a meeting of the International Tennis Federation (ITF) Medical Commission. He pioneered new concepts in sports medicine long before they were accepted procedure, recommending fitness training, conditioning and strengthening and agility programs for the "Who's Who" in professional tennis – Stan Smith, Ilie Nastase, Martina Navratilova, Bjorn Borg, John McEnroe, Vitas Gerulaitis and Tracy Austin, to name just a few.

In terms of nutrition, Dr. Glick's 1980 brochure, "Eating for Fitness," stressed the importance of complex carbohydrate as the chief source of energy, a revolutionary concept at that time.

"When it comes to the orthopedic problems of tennis players -- tendons, muscles, bones, pulls, tears and fractures -- there is probably no man with more world-class experience than Dr. Glick, the orthopedist who serves as official physician of the US Open," asserts John Sharnick in his 1986 book, *Remembrance of Games Past*.

In addition to the US Open, Dr. Glick has served as, or is now serving as, the tournament physician for the Virginia Slims, the Nabisco Masters, the W.C.T. Tournament of Champions, the Maureen Connolly Brinker Cup and the Port Washington Tennis Academy Rolex International Junior Championships. He is the orthopedic surgeon and team physician for the St. John's University Basketball team, the medical advisor to the ATP Tour and the honorary chairman of the U.S. Tennis Association Sports Science Committee. He was also the International Tennis Federation medical representative to the 1988 Olympics in Seoul, Korea. Along with other professional responsibilities, he maintains a thriving private medical practice on Long Island and plays tennis four days a week!

The Doctor combines his medical expertise with a "great big shoulder to lean on," which is why he is one of the most visible and popular characters in Eastern tennis. He has a reputation for genuinely listening to people, for letting patients and friends articulate their physical (and emotional) symptoms at length rather than hurrying them along with a quick diagnosis. Not surprisingly, he likes to refer to everybody as "family."

Tommie Glick (ctr.) congratulated Don Budge (l) and her husband Irving (r) for their special contributions to tennis in New York.

Of his own family he says with obvious delight, "I have two children -- John and Betsy -- two grand-children, but only one wife, Tommie, who hails from Texas...And she's a lovely lady."

Dr. Glick clearly enjoys life and people. His friends and tennis cronies at the Port Tennis Academy say the twinkle in his eye and easy smile complement a wry sense of humor which is contagious. "He always brings humor into the conversation and picks up people's spirits," they say. "Doc started an epidemic here at Port with his puns -- we call them 'Glickisms' -- to the point that we all imitate him now..."

He is trim and fit, a walking advertisement for his health formulas. He plays tennis regularly at Port despite a staggering work schedule, which prompts the academy's head pro, Bob Binns, to marvel at his stamina. "Doc's a very good player," Binns says. "But what's amazing is he'll come to play after he's been up working all night, and he'll climb the stairs so slowly you worry about him. As soon as he gets out there, though, the man starts sprinting around the court like he's Carl Lewis!"

Dr. Irving Glick regards tennis as one of the consolations of age and believes that the quality of senior tennis keeps improving with better conditioning and proper diet. "Tennis is physical, emotional therapy for me, it's recreation," he says with his usual chuckle, eyes twinkling all the while. "I've been playing for more than fifty years...They talk about a runner's high. I get a tennis high...That's enough to keep us seniors playing."

-- By Nancy Gill McShea

Francis X. Shields

Armed with devastating good looks, irresistible charm, superior athletic ability and an extraordinary constitution, Frank X. Shields made a run through life on earth which few people had seen before and few have seen since. Such was the consensus of the press who reviewed Willie Shields' 1986 biography of his late father, "Pop," entitled *Bigger than Life*.

Born in the Bronx in 1909, Shields was heralded as the self-taught tennis champion with the big serve and all-court game who began by collecting USLTA national junior titles in the 1920s and finished his career in the Forest Hills twilight in 1947. He was a finalist at the U.S. National Championships in 1930 and at Wimbledon in 1931. He was a playing member of the U.S. Davis Cup team with an overall record of 19-6, including victories over Perry, Crawford and Hopman, and was the captain of the Davis Cup team in 1951. Ranked No. 1 in the U.S. in 1933, he was in the U.S. top five six times and top ten eight times from 1928-1945. He ranked in the world's top ten five times. In the 1950s, he won the National Court Tennis Championships with Ogden Phipps.

Finally, in 1964, Frank Shields was inducted into the International Tennis Hall of Fame

But he was more than a great athlete who chose to play tennis. He was a true sportsman whose gregarious spirit mirrored the innocence of the 1930s and '40s when the world was younger and tennis was an amateur sport. Says Willie, "Pop loved to bring people together so they could enjoy each other. He had a genius for connecting directly to a person's soul; he could find the lost child in a tycoon and the dignity in a sanitation worker. He was brought up to believe that what counted was how hard and attractively a man did what he did, that making money was a vulgar way of keeping score."

Having fun was a big part of living well in those days, perhaps because of the reality of The Great Depression and the immediacy of World War 11. In between tennis matches, Shields partied with the rich and famous (often changing into his tuxedo right after a match), was as proficient at the bridge table as he was on the court, joined the U.S. Army and took a shot at Hollywood. He also introduced his friend Errol Flynn to Jack Warner. Next scene: Flynn launches career with lead in "Captain Blood." Tennis players had to earn a living, so Frank and his tennis pal Sidney Wood ran a laundry business which catered to the New York society set, and he was involved in a successful 30-year insurance venture with his early childhood friend and tennis partner, Julie Seligson. (The pair won the USTA Boys' 18 Indoor doubles title in 1927 and were both ranked in the U.S. top ten in 1928.) Frank's friends will tell you that his trousers' pocket was his bank and that he was generous to a fault. Through it all, he experienced a series of triumphs and catastrophes, eventually falling victim to the latter.

"Frank was special, he never made judgments about people," says his third wife, Katharine Mortimer Blaine. "He loved everybody, he was totally non-selective. I never knew him to refuse an appeal for help, and no one was too seedy or disreputable to qualify for one of his rehabilitation projects. Everyone he met felt that Frank was his best friend. He spent 25 percent of his day selling insurance and the other 75 percent solving other people's problems." Shields also supported many charitable causes. He started the first Pro-Am Celebrity Golf Tournament to benefit the Boys' Club of New York. With the proceeds, the Club constructed a second building, which was known as "The House that Shields Built."

Francis X. Shields died in 1975 at age 66, and the flag at the Meadow Club in Southampton flew at half mast the day he was buried. Wood, who was inducted into the International Tennis Hall of Fame with Shields in 1964, wrote: "Frank's heart was as warm and stubborn as any that beat...His abilities exceeded his exploits, however notable... In his first year as an insurance broker for Equitable, he led the entire national sales force with more than a million in volume. But he was forever more giver than taker...Wherever he played, Frank was the gallery favorite...No athlete of his era evoked more admiration, envy, wonderment...on and off the court...He is surely the only man, before, or since, who landed in Paris for the French Championships and, following an extended celebration, found himself back aboard an ocean liner en route home to the U.S.A. with only a dinner jacket for luggage...A sentimental Irishman, he once took it upon himself to lead the St. Patrick's Day Parade up Fifth Avenue, without invitation, when he was ill and confined to bed...The overworked word, charisma, came much later than my unforgettable, beloved friend Frank. But if ever such a term was formed to fit a man, that man was Shields."

-- By Nancy Gill McShea

Clifford S. Sutter

Steve Bernan

When Cliff Sutter's father and a few friends built two grass courts near the Sutter home in New Orleans during the early 1900s, they set the stage for the emergence of a future U.S. tennis champion. Personally, young Sutter would fit the image of the gracious old South, while combining art and artifice on the tennis court with a beautiful blend of coordinated movement and racquet work.

"I started playing on those courts when I was five," says the 80-year-old Sutter, who went on to win seven tournaments in a row in 1932, the year he ranked No. 3 in the U.S. and fifth in the world. "My whole family played, including my mother and sister who wore long skirts and big bonnet hats."

"Cliff was so elegant in long flannel trousers, you thought it almost indecent if he donned white shorts," says a friend. "Opponents, however, who thought elegance and competitiveness couldn't go together made this mistake at their peril. The crease in his pants was sharp as a razor, but so was his fighting edge."

Two memorable Sutter performances illustrate that point. In 1930 at age 19, he beat 37- year-old Bill Tilden in an Eastern grass court tournament at Rye, N.Y. Sutter was leading, 6-0, 4-1, in the two-out-of-three-sets match when the gallery began chiding Tilden for his temperamental behavior. Tilden defaulted, citing an old knee injury as the reason. A week later at Newport, the two were again paired as opponents, and Sutter faked a limp when he saw Tilden. Tilden yelled, "I never said it was my knee, Cliff...!" to which Sutter responded, "I'll finish this match anyhow, even with my bad knee!" Tilden beat Sutter 8-6 in the fifth.

In 1932, a determined Sutter faced Ellsworth Vines -- still considered one of the world's best players ever -- at the U.S. National Championships. A prominent tennis analyst wrote: "In one of the great semifinal matches of all time, Vines ran into Sutter, a young player of consummate style and consistency. Sutter won the first two sets, 6-4, 10-8, and came within a stroke of match point three times in the third set and once in the fourth...Vines gradually came around, winning the third 12-10, the fourth 10-8, and the last one, when Sutter was tired, 6-1...The packed Forest Hills Stadium went wild when it ended. Sutter's magnificent challenge was the highlight of the tournament."

Sixty-one years later, Sutter is still resolute when he discusses the Tilden and Vines encounters. Of Tilden's default, he says, "I had him!" As for Vines, he insists, "I shoulda had him!"

Sutter traveled on the USTA junior tennis circuit when he was 12, ranking as high as No. 8 nationally. He was later a singles semifinalist and four times a quarterfinalist at the U.S. National Championships, during which time he ranked in the U.S. top ten five times -- in 1930, '31, '32, '33 and '34; and he was undefeated in U.S. Davis Cup team play in 1931 and '33. Cliff and his brother Ernest are the only brothers ever to win the NCAA singles title, and each won it twice as a student at Tulane -- Cliff in 1930 and '32, Ernest in 1936 and '37 -- and together they won the 1961 national senior doubles crown.

Cliff joined New York's business commuters in 1933 at age 23, eventually becoming a vice president and account supervisor with the advertising agency, BBDO. He was later the marketing manager of Bancroft Sporting Goods until he retired in 1975. During those years, Sutter was involved in USLTA tennis administration, as chairman of the Amateur Rules Committee and advisor to Russell Kingman (Eastern president, 1934-35; USLTA president, 1951-52). "The game was getting a bad image with press reports of under-the-table payments, and my friends on the Greenwich Railroad platform needled me about 'that game of mine' and how much better amateur golf was run," says Sutter, who served as Eastern's president himself in 1962-'63. "We worked to give tennis a better image and we did...Then the whole game changed with registered players and Open tennis."

Interestingly, the lives of Cliff Sutter and this evening's fellow inductee, the late Frank Shields, intertwined during their playing days and later. Cliff first met Frank at a junior tournament in Chicago. Shields, then 16, hitched a ride to New York with Sutter, who was 15. In 1931, the pair, together with Sidney Wood, defeated Argentina 5-0 in a U.S. Davis Cup match. Sutter and Shields were later married to sisters -- Rebecca (Billy) and Suzanne Tenney, respectively, after Frank introduced Suzanne to Cliff.

Cliff and Suzanne Sutter recently celebrated their 55th wedding anniversary on Cape Cod, where they retired in 1977. They have four daughters, one son, nine grandchildren and two great grandchildren.

-- By Nancy Gill McShea

Chapter 12

1992: Graebner, Hunter, Markin and Shore

Carole Caldwell Graebner

Carole Graeber quietly blazed the trail of the "modern woman" before it was fashionable. While Betty Friedan and Gloria Steinem were urging women across the country to take control of their own lives in the 1960s and '70s, Carole had already taken that quantum leap into the evolving future. A future characterized by unprecedented complexity and opportunities in women's lives.

In the summer of 1959 at the tender age of 15, Carole emerged from her sheltered child-hood in Santa Monica, California, and traveled East to compete in the international tennis arena for the first time. The adventure would impact her life -- it would lead to world-class tennis stardom in the 1960s; the luxury of financial independence in her teens; the joy of raising her two children, Cameron and Clark; and the eventual transition to a successful business career in 1976.

Beginnings often shape one's destiny. Carole says that her mother Berniece and grand-father, John Joseph Keefe, alias "Gramps, provided good moral fiber and helped her to grow into a strong independent woman. And they supported her first step in that direction – playing tennis.

To ease the loneliness of being an only child in a neighborhood with few children, Carole invented her own brand of tennis by hitting against the garage door of her Spanish-style home. "I had one of those old wooden paddles with a rubber ball attached to it," she explains. "I stole a tennis ball from a dog down the street and used the paddle to create design games (similar to tick-tack-toe) on the door. I would target particular spots, like hitting cross court or down the line. I got so good at it, Gramps said it was about time I had strings. He bought me a wooden racquet for $2 and I branched out to the tennis courts across the street. I was 10."

Gramps signed her up for free clinics on Saturdays and she played in her first junior tournament at 11. "I lost 6-0, 6-0," Carole says, recalling the humiliation with some amusement now. "I was so mortified I burst into tears. But Gramps insisted there was no reason to cry, that I had nothing to be ashamed of, that the girl was clearly a better player. He said if playing tournaments and risking losing were going to make me cry, then we shouldn't do it. He said, 'What do we need to do?' I said I guess I've got to practice, and then maybe I'll win."

She became a regular on the Southern California junior circuit and was a member of the local Junior Wightman Cup team with, among others, Billie Jean Moffitt (King), Eastern's Jana Hunsaker, and Karen Hantze (Susman). In the summer of 1959, Carole and five other members of the squad debuted on the Eastern summer circuit. The highlight of Carole's trip East was her acceptance into the women's draw at the U.S. National Championships. She lost her first-round match to No. 4 seed Sally Moore 9-7 in the third set, but she was ecstatic.

"That summer changed my life," she says. "I was like a star gazer. Margaret DuPont had invited us all to her home in Wilmington, Delaware, to practice on the estate's indoor and outdoor courts. I realized what her trophy room represented -- not just wins and losses -- but interaction with hundreds of people, visiting incredible places around the world, learning to appreciate great art treasures and understand the deeper meanings of history and life. It was so appealing I wanted a piece of it. And I realized it would require a total commitment."

Carole returned to California and reality. "I went back to school and played tennis all the time," she says. By 1962 at age 18, she was self-assured and traveled alone to Europe to play Wimbledon. She was sponsored by the Santa Monica Recreation Department, but had saved enough money working nights at J.C. Penney (for $1.25 an hour) to buy her own luggage for the trip, plus a brand-new car.

Her celebrity status was rising rapidly now, and she was asked to be the tennis hostess at the Beverly Hills Hotel. She played regularly with Hollywood stars like Katharine Hepburn, Sam Goldwyn, and Sydney Janis of New York's famous Janis Art Gallery, who introduced her to abstract impressionism through his private collection of Jackson Pollack. Her impressive tennis resume carried such clout, her clientele tipped her $50 to $200 an hour.

Carole was ranked No. 4 in the world in singles in 1964, the year she reached the final of the U.S. National Championships, and a year later she captured the U.S. National and Australian doubles titles with Nancy Richey, earning the world's No. 1 doubles ranking. The trivia buff will note that Carole and Richey set the record for the longest match in women's doubles at the 1964 Eastern Grass Courts, recording 81 games in a 31-33, 6-1, 6-4 winning effort. Carole also won gold and bronze medals at the 1963 Pan American Games in Sao Paulo, Brazil.

Carole joined Billie Jean and Darlene Hard to win the first Federation Cup match ever played, at the Queens Club in London in 1963. In addition, she posted a 12-1 record in 10 Federation Cup appearances, played for the Wightman Cup team from 1963 to '71, and is the only woman who has doubled as player/captain for the Federation, Wightman and Bonne Bell Cup teams.

Today, Carole brings her vivacious personality to the daily repartee of business. One of her clients and friends, Jim Baugh, the general manager and vice president of Wilson Racquet Sports, says, "We've always looked at Carole as part of our family. And we laugh about the only family feud we've ever had -- getting her off the T-2000 racquet (she only plays with Wilson). Nobody loves the sport, and what it really stands for, more than Carole."

Carole is the vice president and the national advertising director of *Tennis Week*, chairman of the United States Federation Cup, vice chairman of the U.S. Wightman Cup and a member of the U.S. Olympic committee. She has also been affiliated with many sports media outlets and corporations over the years, including *Sports Illustrated* and *World Tennis* magazines, ABC's Wide World of Sports Radio, Madison Square Garden Cable Network, for whom she has worked as a tennis color commentator for television, and as a spokesperson and lecturer.

Tennis Week's publisher and editor-in-chief Eugene L. Scott, who toured on the summer tennis circuit at the same time Carole did, and who was also her lawyer, witnessed the transitions in her life. "It is interesting to note that this year's inductees have an all-too-rare combination of tennis and business skills," Scott points out. "Carole Graebner has moved with grace and facility from the playing field to the field of business. In Carole's case, neither is a Field of Dreams but instead a veritable meadow of reality."

Does Carole Caldwell Graebner believe she's missed out on anything? "Yes, I wanted to be a song leader in high school at football games," she sighs, "part of the group of girls who marched together with the band, twirling batons and carrying flags. My tennis denied me that opportunity. I was heartbroken! And in my next life I assure you I will do it."

-- By Nancy Gill McShea

Francis T. Hunter

Francis T. (Frank) Hunter was right out of the "roaring twenties" in New York, a handsome charming man about town, a wonderful fellow to be around. He was also one of the earliest tennis players to combine a prosperous business career with international celebrity in the sport. In 1924 Frank emerged as a tennis hero in Paris, when he and fellow New Yorker Vinny Richards teamed up to earn the last U.S. Olympic gold medal for tennis until the game was reinstated as a medal sport in 1988.

Born in 1894 in New Rochelle, N.Y., Frank exhibited a zest for adventure typical of that age. After he graduated from Cornell in 1916 (where he captained the men's tennis team), he immediately left the States to serve as a Lieutenant Commander aboard the U.S.S. New York with the British fleet in the North Sea during World War I. When he returned to civilian life he became a business entrepreneur. During the next decade he operated three coal mines in West Virginia, controlled a fleet of cargo steamships, and founded the New Rochelle *Standard Star* newspaper. By 1929 he owned and published an entire chain of Westchester County newspapers. All the while, he was a contender among the world's top four tennis players.

On the tennis court, Frank was a burly, aggressive player with great determination. He relied on a forehand that was rated among the more powerful in the game. Although his backhand was mainly a defensive stroke, and he danced around it to hit the forehand, his fighting spirit carried him through to many victories. Frank announced his arrival on the world tennis scene at the USTA Indoor Championships. He was the Indoor singles champ in 1922 and was the runner-up to Vinnie Richards in 1923 and 1924.

The record shows that Frank was ranked among the top 10 U.S. singles players five times, from 1922-1929 (ranking second behind Bill Tilden from 1927-1929). At the U.S. National Championships, he won the doubles title with Tilden in 1927. He was twice a singles runner-up, losing in five sets to Henri Cochet in 1928 and again in five sets to

Tilden in 1929. At Wimbledon, he was a singles finalist in 1923, captured two men's doubles titles (with Richards in '24 and Tilden in '27), and two mixed doubles crowns (with Elizabeth Ryan in '27 and Helen Wills in '29). He was also a playing member of the U.S. Davis Cup team in 1927-1928.

In 1930, Frank repeated as the Indoor singles champ, his last amateur title before turning pro. He later ran the first professional tennis exhibition in Madison Square Garden, featuring Ellsworth Vines and Fred Perry. Frank was inducted into the International Tennis Hall of Fame in 1961.

Cliff Sutter, who was inducted into the ETA Hall of Fame in 1991, and who crossed paths with Frank on the tennis circuit, says, "Frank Hunter had bulldog determination on the tennis court…What a forehand! And he was a man of great charisma who lived life to the hilt. The last time I saw him, he was lounging comfortably on the porch of the Meadow Club in Southampton entertaining the crowd. That was so typical of Frank. He had been a successful, wealthy man before the crash of 1929 (I knew he was wealthy because he always traveled with a trainer, Bill O'Brien) and he would rise again after the crash with '21' Brands."

Indeed, through his connection with the Westchester Embassy Club in Armonk, N.Y., Frank became friends with Jack Kriendler and Charlie Berns of New York's famous '21' Club. After the repeal of prohibition in December of 1933, Berns left '21' and he and Frank founded '21' Brands, Inc. An importer and distributor of wines and Ballantine Scotch, the company became famous worldwide. Frank served as president of '21' Brands until 1963 and afterward was a member of the executive committee.

An accomplished sportsman, Frank roamed the world on hunting and fishing expeditions: from shooting bears in Alaska, to safaris in Africa and India. The walls of his New York penthouse were completely covered with the trophies he brought back from his adventures -- lions, tigers, birds and fish…and silver tennis cups. In 1962, the B'nai B'rith Sports Lodge in Manhattan honored him as its "Citizen of the Year."

Frank's daughter, Barbara Tailor, remembers her father as a warm, friendly pal, someone with a great sense of humor. "Everybody loved him," she says. "He cared about others and was so generous. He helped many a needy family and friend anonymously."

Frank Hunter died in Palm Beach, Florida, on December 4, 1981. He was 87 years old.

-- By Nancy Gill McShea

David R. Markin

David Markin commands instant recognition as a man of prominence in the complex worlds of international tennis and Fortune 500 corporate business. Outside the competitive arena, he is married to the former Susan Schnell; and he is the father of three children -- John, 22; Christopher, 20; and Maggie, 17.

One longtime associate says, "Because David is committed in so many different directions, he might appear to be a man of contradictions on the surface. He is indeed complex. He is very witty, extremely generous, and has a real sense of community and family. For example, his schedule is impossible, yet he finds time to communicate almost daily with his three grown children who are off in different directions now. He is intolerant of mediocrity yet he displays an unbelievable patience for those trying to over- come it. And of course his love of tennis amazes us all."

One of the most effective and accomplished volunteers in the sport of tennis during the past 35 years, David is the immediate past president of the United States Tennis Association (USTA) and a past chairman of the US Open. His current responsibilities include chairing the U.S. Davis Cup committee and serving on the International Tennis Federation's Davis Cup committee. He is also the overseer of the new US Open project, an ambitious plan that he says will upgrade the event into the "world's finest Grand Slam tournament."

This past March, David was honored with the 1991 USTA Samuel Hardy Award at the Association's annual meeting in Amelia Island, Florida, for long and outstanding service to the game. Prior to his term as USTA president, he had served as the first vice president, second vice president and as secretary. He was chairman of the Junior Tennis Council and the Boys' Junior Davis Cup committee, as well as the Boys' 14 and Men's 35 ranking committees. On the sectional level, he was president of the Western Tennis Association, among other titles, and he served as the assistant referee and referee of the USTA Boys' 18 and 16 National Championships in Kalamazoo, Michigan, for the past 25 years.

One USTA executive and colleague sums up his contributions succinctly: "David has been unique in the tennis world, aware of the political needs, aware of business demands, and having the willingness to fully commit to accomplishing his responsibilities. He doesn't lead by pointing and telling people some place to go. He goes to that place himself."

In business, David is the president and chief executive officer of International Controls Corp. (ICC), a Fortune 500 corporation; and he is the president and chairman of the board of Checker Motors Company, based in Kalamazoo. Since his affiliation with Checker dates to 1953, David was ready to assume the leadership role for the largest taxicab manufacturer in the country in 1970 when he was 39 years old. He took the reins as Checker's president, led the company through its expansion from 200 to 1200 employees and from manufacturing a single product to becoming a major supplier to the automobile industry.

In 1982, Checker halted production of the world-famous Checker Taxicab and has since focused on expanding the auto supplier business. In 1989, David and three other investors gained control of ICC, which now owns Checker Motors and all of its subsidiaries. In addition to running the facility in Kalamazoo, his business activities include operating taxicab fleets, running an insurance company in Chicago and traveling to subsidiaries located in Savannah, Georgia, and in South Charleston, West Virginia.

According to those in his inner circle, David thrives on the multiple challenge of serving tennis and managing his private business interests simultaneously. To do it effectively, he surrounds himself with competent, loyal and organized people.

Although David is a native of New York City, his tennis roots can be traced to his youth in Great Neck, Long Island, where he was a member of the high school tennis team (he still refers to himself as the kid from Great Neck who first fell in love with tennis at Forest Hills). He later played tennis at the Cheshire Academy in Connecticut and at Bradley University in Peoria, Illinois, before making his permanent home in Kalamazoo. He has held national rankings in various age categories throughout the past 35 years, in both singles and doubles. Yet some of his peers claim he's an even better tennis teacher than he is a player. He helped coach a Kalamazoo high school team to two Michigan State Championships; he chaired the YMCA Tennis Excellence program for juniors there; and he has given hundreds of free tennis lessons to aspiring young players. Many of his former students continue to correspond with him throughout college and into the adult ranks, thanking him for his help in coaxing them to reach their potential.

Everybody who knows David Markin agrees that his dedication to developing U.S. tennis players is matched only by the great satisfaction he derives in working with America's largest volunteer organization, the United States Tennis Association.

-- By Nancy Gill McShea

Sam Shore

Sam Shore -- no generation barriers

He started his career on Wall Street, but it was a chance tennis match with a friend in 1929 in Brooklyn that started Sam Shore on his athletic career.

"That day was my fondest recollection of tennis," Sam has said. "To think that I could take that racquet and hit the ball wherever I wanted stunned me. I never stopped trying after that."

Sam grew up in New York City between Madison and Fifth Avenues on 105th Street when tennis didn't qualify as a neighborhood game. He played all the street sports, rooted for baseball's New York Giants, and quit football when he was beaned on the head. But on that special day in 1929 tennis would become his sport for a lifetime.

That year also marked the beginning of the depression, a reality which closed the door on Sam's future on Wall Street and opened the door to his future career in tennis. By 1931, he was working nights as a linotype operator for the *Daily News* and spending his days teaching tennis at Vinnie Richards' indoor courts at Manhattan's 71st Regiment Armory. He continued juggling the two careers until 1956 when he retired from the *News* and devoted himself exclusively to teaching and playing tennis.

Sam celebrated his 86th birthday this past March 22nd and on April 17 he toasted his wife Jessica on their 50th wedding anniversary. They were surrounded by their children, Annabelle and Edward, grandchildren and friends. All Shore loyalists will share yet another milestone with him this evening, his induction into the ETA Hall of Fame.

On court, he is the gentleman who stands tall and trim, a vision in Wilson tennis whites, his thick silver hair framing an easy smile and twinkling blue eyes. His brisk stride clearly sends a message -- Sam Shore is a man of determination who meets life's challenges with dignity, grace and style.

Since joining the Eastern tournament circuit 63 years ago in 1929, he has been a presence not only in the section, but also nationally and internationally. According to Seena Hamilton, the 1990-91 ETA Hall of Fame chairman, in 1973 Sam captivated the European tennis set with his talent, charm and sportsmanship and collected a series of international over-65 trophies when Hamilton invited him to play for the American team at the Los Montero's Senior and Veterans International Tennis Tournament in Marbella, Spain.

Sam has been nationally ranked since 1972. Of the 10 USTA national titles he has won, his most recent victories include the 1987 over-80 clay court singles and doubles crowns and the 1988 over-80 grass court doubles championship, which he shared with his ETA partner Ed Tarangioli. Sam was a rookie in the 85s in 1991 and was a doubles finalist at the clay courts. In addition, he is a former vice president of the U.S. Professional Tennis Association (USPTA) and a past president of the Eastern Professional Tennis Association. He won the USPTA Player of the Year Award in 1982, 1983 and 1988.

Everyone who knows him understands that Sam's real achievement goes beyond his many tennis titles and awards. His long love affair with tennis and spirited interaction with people have inspired the same love of the game in countless young children, advancing juniors and adults of all ages and skill levels. He has crusaded for tennis all over the Eastern Section, first teaching the sport at the Manhattan Regiment Armory, in Central Park and at Hempstead Lake on Long Island. From 1948 to 1978, he ran his own popular club, Shore's Tennis, in Port Washington, N.Y. Since the late '70s, he has taught at the Port Washington Tennis Academy.

"Sam has been a national treasure," said Lois Prince, a friend and the vice president of the Eastern Section and chairman of the section's Junior Tennis Council. "I have known him for many years and no matter what his accomplishments -- and they are many -- he is always there for the little guy, especially kids. He is one of a kind.

"Shore's tennis was 'the place to be' on Long Island for many years," Prince continued. "That's where all the action was because Sam's spirit and energy are contagious. When he would say, 'Come on girls, I'm coming out on the court with you,' it was the highlight of their day."

Sam is nothing short of a wonder to the thousands of junior players who stream in and out of the Port Academy every year. As one former junior recalled, "Every match I ever played at Port, Sam was there. I used to sneak in a few extra minutes during the warm-up. But he was always aware of my allotted time. I'd hear him walking toward my court and he'd say, 'Start taking serves.' Then he'd walk to the next court and tell the players they had only three minutes left. It was unbelievable. It was like he had 13 separate clocks in his head -- one for each court."

On court, he is something else. Kids love to test him by whipping forehands at him unmercifully, but power doesn't faze him. He scoops up the ball effortlessly, returns it with his own mustard and flashes that famous smile as his young opponents stand in awe. Perhaps just as famous as the smile is the "Shore Shuffle," the small quick steps he takes to scoot back to the baseline after winning a point.

In a recent piece about him in Long Island's *Newsday*, sports columnist Steve Jacobson asked a rhetorical question: "...You don't know Sam Shore? Almost everybody who's held a tennis racquet around here knows Sam..."

-- By Nancy Gill McShea

Chapter 13

1993: Dinkins, Llewellyn, Nogrady and Richardson

David N. Dinkins

Famous tennis fan David Dinkins and famous Open champ Monica Seles.

The Honorable David N. Dinkins, perhaps the City's most visible tennis fan and recreational player and the 106th Mayor of the City of New York, was inaugurated on January 1, 1989 with the pledge to make the streets safer, offer children more hope and opportunity and secure the City's fiscal stability, among other high hopes.

Despite assuming this office during very difficult times, the Mayor has given the people of New York compassionate and effective leadership. And considering his high profile, it is not surprising that he advances some of his favorite causes as a volunteer for the sport he loves.

Conveniently, the Mayor has also been advised -- under doctor's orders -- to play the sport he loves five times a week! Singles, of course. Since taking over as mayor, he has reportedly raised his game one whole level by adding a topspin backhand to his repertoire and becoming much more aggressive and powerful on the forehand side. His regular tennis opponents understandably view his new prowess with a certain envy, but they admit that the ability to improve one's game so dramatically, in one's sixties, is consistent with being an effective mayor in New York City.

Besides, as his friend David Markin points out, "Not every great man has a topspin backhand."

Among the Mayor's proudest accomplishments are those that improve the quality of life for the City's most vulnerable people, especially children. During his tenure, he has instituted a comprehensive criminal justice program: Safe Streets, Safe City. The youth component of the plan helps prevent crime by giving young people new opportunities for learning and recreation. Nowhere is that ideal more evident than in the Mayor's enthusiastic support of junior tennis programs in the metropolitan area. He is praised often for publicizing his belief that tennis offers children a healthy, positive alternative to the dangers of the street.

In 1990, Eastern's Junior Tennis Foundation added a scholarship in the Mayor's name to the awards agenda at this annual Hall of Fame celebration, which is also the sole fund raiser for the ETA's junior programs. Part of the funds benefit needy children in the inner city who might otherwise never have a chance to learn the game. The Mayor has thoroughly enjoyed presenting two scholarships each year to two deserving youngsters from among the City's tennis programs: the Department of Parks and Recreation, Pyramid Tennis and the Harlem and New York Junior Tennis Leagues (NYJTL).

The Mayor not only supports these programs as a matter of principle, he regularly joins the children on tennis courts throughout the City decked out in the insignia jackets of his favorites -- at Eastern/USTA schools programs, pro-celebrity clinics, awards ceremonies such as the NYJTL-sponsored Mayor's Cup All-Scholastic Championships, and at fund raisers.

In 1991, when he was honored as the ETA's "Tennis Man of the Year," the Mayor reiterated his faith in the inherent goodness of children. "There are highly publicized situations regarding problem kids," he said that evening. "People think all kids are like that today. Well, they're not. Most youngsters are good and kind and wonderful and fair."

He has also fostered a positive image for New York nationally and worldwide through special events, which bring additional revenue to the City. The City hosted the successful 1992 Democratic National Convention and plans are underway to bring the 1998 Goodwill Games to New York. Moreover, the Mayor has enthusiastically supported the USTA's plan to improve and modernize the US Open site at Flushing Meadows-Corona Park to ensure that the Open remains the world's pre-eminent Grand Slam tennis tournament.

The Mayor knows all too well that New York City needs a world-class economy to thrive and he has taken aggressive steps to invest in business and build the City's economic base. Part of that effort has included trying to expand economic opportunities for small businesses. In fact this past January, the Mayor attended the official opening of the Roosevelt Island Racquet Club, a new privately-owned tennis facility, in recognition of small business development in the City.

Mayor Dinkins was born in Trenton, N.J., on July 10, 1927, and began his career in public service in 1966 as a N.Y. State Assemblyman. He was president of the Board of Elections from 1972-1973, served as the City Clerk from 1975-1985 and as the Manhattan Borough President from 1985-1989. He is a graduate of Howard University and Brooklyn Law School, and a veteran of the United States Marine Corps. He and his wife Joyce have two children: David, Jr., and Donna Hoggard; a grandson, Jamal; and a granddaughter, Kalila.

During warm celebrations such as these, the Mayor's charming personality and warm sense of humor shine through -- even at his expense. At last year's Hall of Fame dinner he told a story about driving through Harlem with Joyce. They saw a street sweeper who was also one of Joyce's former boyfriends. The Mayor said, "Aren't you glad you didn't marry him?" To which Joyce replied,"…I'm not so sure because if I had married him he'd be the Mayor."

-- By Nancy Gill McShea

Sydney Llewellyn

Sydney Llewellyn arrived in New York in 1930 from Jamaica, the West Indies, a young man in his twenties who later emerged as one of the most accomplished and influential tennis coaches in the East.

In the mid-1940s, he joined the Cosmopolitan Tennis Club in Harlem where the famous Fred Johnson tutored him in the game. Sydney would go on to inspire people of all ages to play tennis, including those at the highest level of the sport. He guided his most notable pupil, Althea Gibson, to five Grand Slam singles titles: the French in 1956, and both Wimbledon and the U.S. National Championships in 1957 and '58. And in 1959, Sydney launched Althea's professional career by arranging for her to play tennis prior to the Harlem Globetrotters' basketball games.

"Sydney is among the world's greatest tennis coaches," says Althea, who in 1988 was among the first nine people to be inducted into the ETA Hall of Fame. "His knowledge of tennis is outstanding. Through his coaching, I developed my game and gained confidence. It was a great moment for us both when I won my own country's championship for the first time."

How did this man, who was first introduced to tennis as a ball boy at the exclusive St. Andrew's Tennis Club in Jamaica, integrate all his life experiences -- as a research assistant, inventor, author, soccer player, swimmer, painter, dancer, taxi driver, seaman and master pool shooter -- and become one of the great American tennis coaches?

Friends say he had an experience at age 16 which gave him confidence and changed his life. Drs. Morris Steggerda and C.B. Davenport came to Jamaica to conduct an anthropological study for the Carnegie Institute on *Race Crossing in Jamaica*, and they selected Sydney to work as their research assistant. When the work was published --stating in part that black people possess an exceptionally well-developed sense of rhythm -- Sydney received an unusual commendation, which read: "Sydney Rhoden Llewellyn, a sixteen year-old boy, acted as an assistant recorder. His work was efficient and thorough." The field research gave him an opportunity to travel outside of Jamaica, and the whole experience provided him with a range of skills -- technical and social --that would serve him well throughout his life.

In 1967, he invented an exercise training device called "Equiform" to allow tennis players to simulate the various strokes of their game. A cable device which connects to the foot and wrists, Equiform trains the muscles and assists the motion of the various strokes. It is still in existence today.

Sydney's students have labeled him variously as a philosopher at heart, a keen observer and a master of the inner psychological game. They point out that early on he espoused the theory that tennis for kids is a healthy alternative to the dangers of the street. "Tennis is more than a game, it is a habit," he has said. "And if we can give kids this habit, they won't have to seek others."

One of his admirers is former student Bill Davis, the assistant commissioner for equal opportunity for New York City's Department of Parks, and a five-time champion of the American Tennis Association (ATA, which was founded in 1916 as a predominantly African-American national tennis association).

"Sydney believes in the power of the 'word,' and that by the word one lives in dignity," says Bill. "His hobbies are drawing and painting, but he is better known for painting pictures with his words, which flow like an art form in which one can visualize his concepts…When he explains the tennis grips, he associates it with the holding of a bird. 'Don't squeeze it to death,' he says, 'but don't let it get away.'"

Don Ringgold, another ATA champ and former student who went on teach tennis at the University of Pennsylvania, has said, "You know, he used to cite Kahlil Gibran's *The Prophet*. He knew it verbatim. Coach is an amazing man."

In 1977, Sydney coordinated and managed this country's first prize money tournament for African Americans in Myrtle Beach, S.C., with Horace Reid emerging the winner. In addition, over the past 40 years he has taught more than a dozen ATA champions and has influenced more black tennis players to become teaching professionals than perhaps anyone else in history. A sampling includes: Bill Davis' brother, Bob, who teaches in the ABC Cities program; Zack Davis; Arthur Carrington; Terrance Jackson; Lisa Hopewell; and Dot Kornegay. He has also taught fellow Hall of Fame inductee David Dinkins, the celebrated photographer Gordon Parks and other celebrities.

Through the years he has been an active member of the U.S. Professional Tennis Association, treasurer of the Eastern Professional Lawn Tennis Association and a contributing writer for *Professional Tennis* magazine.

Sydney Llewellyn often preaches a motto that applies to all of life's endeavors; "Start where you are, with what you have, make something and never be satisfied."

-- By Nancy Gill McShea

John Nogrady

For more than a half century now, famous Eastern coach John Nogrady has been challenging and cajoling tennis players to give it their best shot. He approaches his craft with unusual analytical skills and with an engaging joie de vivre. Not to mention an irreverent teaching style! Depending on which side of the net you're on, John's teaching methods may be viewed as either insightful or inciteful.

People from all walks of life have felt the sting of the familiar Nogrady challenge. "You're playing great, marvelous, fantastic," he will say. And then he'll give you the needle to bring you down to earth: "You're almost mediocre."

A few of his notable Eastern disciples responded to that challenge by capturing top prizes in tennis. For example, in 1951 John helped prepare Dick Savitt for his victory at Wimbledon. And in 1954, Alan Roberts beat the heavy favorites to win the USLTA Boys' 15-and-under Nationals in Kalamazoo, Michigan, by adhering to John's strategy patterns. Amazingly, Alan had never even been considered a dark horse.

John originally abandoned baseball for tennis at Crystal Gardens in Astoria, Queens. "I was 15 or 16 and had this big western grip from baseball," he says. "I hit myself in the nose on a high forehand drive and figured there must be an easier way to play this game. I tried every stroke and learned through trial and error. I practiced on one of the first ball machines and learned to take the ball on the rise. Then I challenged everybody and anybody, giving people two courts while confining myself to one."

By age 17, he won the singles and doubles titles at Eastern's junior sectional championships and went on to play No. 1 singles for St. John's University. He turned pro at 19 and earned the No. 2 professional ranking in the United States for three consecutive years -- in 1943, 1944 and 1945. While on the pro tour, he won 16 of 42 encounters against the great Don Budge, whom he faced in the semis of his first pro tournament. He also toured with Budge promoting Wilson Sporting Goods all over the U.S. and Canada.

John's teaching methods were so successful, he was invited to be the resident pro at various Long Island estates -- at the Phippses and the Martins in Old Westbury and at the Fairchilds in Lloyds Neck --- and for several years he lived at William DuPont's estate in Delaware. Through those associations he worked with, and entertained, many of the great tennis names and celebrities of the 1930s, '40s and '50s, among them Louise Brough, Alice Marble, Bill Talbert, Margaret Osborne, Gussie Moran, Vic Seixas, Errol Flynn, Grace Kelly and other bright lights.

In the 1950s, the U.S. (Lawn) Tennis Association tapped John to work with Eastern's top juniors throughout the summer – including ETA Hall of Famer Ron Holmberg and Herb Fitz Gibbon -- to make sure that at least four boys from the section qualified for the nationals at Kalamazoo. One year he actually secured qualifying berths for 20 youngsters, which was unheard of in those days. His boys trusted him to the extent that they would call him from tournaments around the country for counsel. "I can't hit my forehand over the net," was the usual cry for help. "What should I do?"

John recalls that he worked with the kids on indoor courts at the Phipps' estate and also accompanied his boys to Eastern summer tournaments and chaperoned them at Kalamazoo. "Mr. and Mrs. Phipps were very kind," he said. "They would send down an elaborate buffet lunch that looked like a banquet on a movie set...In passing, I told Ogden Phipps that I thought Alan Roberts could win Kalamazoo if I scouted his opponents and directed his patterns in each match. I reasoned that most good players have all the shots but don't know how to use them. Mr. Phipps said 'No way! I'll give you $100 if he does it.' I gave Alan specific instructions every night and sure enough he won the tournament. Alan's an orthopedic surgeon in California now, but I won the hundred."

John teaches patterns and introduces students to the game's "common denominators." First, there is always a weakness. There's no way the mind will accept two weapons on a given day, and since the mind always measures the forehand versus the backhand, one stroke suffers by comparison. So you must compensate. Second, when you hit a tennis ball, the key to accuracy depends on how well you go through the length of the four-foot timing box -- which starts as your stroke goes forward and extends to where you direct and follow through on the shot -- at a minimum of 20 miles per hour. "The steady player has a four-foot timing box most often," he says. "However, when you hit harder, you have to be closer to the ball because the timing box becomes shorter. You have to be quicker and prepare earlier."

No discussion of John Norgay is complete without witnessing his wry sense of humor and gift for telling a good story. "I used to teach a psychiatrist whose wife commented that I get paid more per hour than her husband," he will muse. "I said to her, 'He's just a psychiatrist. I'm a tennis pro and a psychiatrist.' That kept her quiet."

He immediately follows with another anecdote. "A psychiatrist named Harry couldn't beat his friend, Joe, who was also a psychiatrist. Harry said he'd like to take some lessons so he could beat Joe. After a few weeks, Harry did beat Joe. Then Joe came with Harry to one of his lessons and asked if he could watch. When Harry went in to change for the lesson, Joe took $200 out of his pocket and said, 'Here, throw the lesson.' He was absolutely serious; he wanted me to put Harry back to where he was."

Herb Fitz Gibbon, who regularly trained with John during his Eastern junior days, reminisces about his coach with a smile. "I remember him as a nomadic type with a great sense of humor and a huge appetite for life. He was always playing cards, going to the horse races or making a deal to buy a new Cadillac. He only got angry at me once -- when he caught me playing basketball."

-- By Nancy Gill McShea

Hamilton F. Richardson

Hamilton Farrar Richardson was born in 1933 in Baton Rouge, Louisiana, and grew up to become the personification of the "American Dream." He is a gentleman of diverse interests who has earned distinction in the elite circles of academia, tennis, business and politics.

Ham's accomplishments are so numerous and the influences in his life so varied, any attempt to pinpoint a defining experience would be folly. Certainly his origins gave him a good head start. When he and his three brothers distinguished themselves in college as members of Phi Beta Kappa, they were simply upholding a proud family tradition. Ham's maternal grandfather, Hamilton Johnson, had been a Phi Beta Kappa at Vanderbilt University. And both of his parents, Cary Richardson (a writer-sculptress) and Roger Richardson (dean of engineering at Louisiana State University and a research engineer for Standard Oil of New Jersey) achieved that honor at LSU.

Yet Ham's response to a childhood illness might well have been the defining moment of his life. "At 15, I discovered I had diabetes," offers Ham, who in 1956 was honored with the Joslin Award for outstanding service to diabetes, and who has served as director of both the American Association and the Juvenile Foundation for Diabetes. "It matured me. Like most kids, I was not very disciplined and a challenge is always good. Diabetes gave me more determination to prove I was as good as anyone else...I didn't regard it as much worse than a cold because Bill Talbert had it. And if he could be a great tennis champion, there was no reason I couldn't be."

Indeed in 1954, barely four years after he was diagnosed, Ham experienced a memorable year when he was a junior at Tulane. In quick succession he repeated as the NCAA and Southeastern Conference tennis champion, won the USLTA national Father/Son doubles title with his dad -- for the second time -- was a member of the victorious American U.S. Davis Cup team -- and a part-time playing captain as well -- and was honored with the William Johnston Award for outstanding sportsmanship and service to tennis. Off the court, the U.S. Junior Chamber of Commerce named him one of the "Ten Most Outstanding Young Men in America," an honor he shared with Chuck Yeager, Senator Ernest Hollings and Robert F. Kennedy, among others. Ham was the youngest man ever to receive the award.

In 1955, when he graduated number one in his class from Tulane with a B.A. degree in Economics, Ham was one of 32 people selected to study as a Rhodes Scholar at Oxford University's Trinity College in England. Among his group were Reynolds Price, a famous author and professor at Duke; and Senators Paul Sarbanes of Maryland and Richard Lugar of Indiana. "An extraordinary group of people," says Ham, who acknowledges that tennis was an important factor in his selection.

In 1956, while he was still studying toward B.S. and M.A. degrees at Oxford's Honours School of Philosophy, Politics and Economics, from which he graduated in 1957, he also claimed the No. 1 tennis ranking in the United States. He reclaimed the No. 1 U.S. ranking in 1958, the year he won the doubles title with Alex Olmedo at the U.S. National Championships in Forest Hills. Ham ranked among this country's top 10 for 11 years, posted a 20-2 record in his seven-year stint as a playing member of the U.S. Davis Cup team -- 17 of those wins in singles, placing him seventh on America's all-time list with Barry MacKay -- and won more than 50 tournaments in his career, including 17 U.S. national titles. In addition, he was elected as the original inductee into both the Tulane and Southern Tennis Halls of Fame, and he is a member of the Louisiana Sports Hall of Fame.

Kevin Richardson, who was twice a finalist with his father at the USTA Father/Son National Championships, in 1975 and 1977, corroborates his father's belief that overcoming diabetes and achieving success in tennis gave him a strong sense of himself. "...Tennis gave him a confidence that led to success in other fields," says Kevin, who writes for the *Newark Star Ledger*. "He's very focused, loves challenges and viewed tennis that way. His friend Bill Talbert demonstrated that he could be a diabetic and still be a tennis champion."

Kevin adds that his father loves to teach – particularly doubles strategy -- and is incredibly knowledgeable. Business is his career, yet his interest in politics is ongoing. For example, Ham first worked for Senator Russell Long, from 1957-1960, as a legislative assistant and executive secretary, later served as the New York City finance chairman for Richard Gephardt's 1988 presidential campaign, and has been a supporter and a financial backer of Mayor Dinkins. He is also a financial consultant for the National Commission on Urban Growth Problems and the director of the CORO Foundation, which trains young people who are interested in a public service career.

Ham has engaged in various phases of the securities industry since 1960, when he joined Smith, Barney & Co. He was affiliated with several other investment firms until the 1970s when he moved to New York and became an independent investor and a principal in investor groups. In 1979, he formed Richardson & Associates, a privately held venture capital and investment banking firm, of which he is chairman of the board.

"No one ever doubted that Ham was going to achieve in life," reasons Gene Scott, a longtime acquaintance who competed against him in the early 1960s.

"It was just a question of which direction he would choose. The obvious pursuits for any kid are sports and academics. Characteristically, Ham took on both when most rivals would have opted for one or the other. Presto, a Rhodes Scholar and America's No. 1 tennis player!"

When asked to cite his proudest achievements, Ham Richardson mentions the thrill of being in contention for top honors in national Father/Son competition over a span of two generations -- first winning with his father and later reaching the finals with his son Kevin. "And I am very proud of my family," he says, "my three children: Kevin, Kenneth and Kathryn; and my wife, Midge."

-- By Nancy Gill McShea

Chapter 14

1994: Carillo, Hamilton, Lang and Pate

Mary Carillo

Russ Adams

You know what's great about Mary Carillo! She reaches through the television set, grabs you, and makes sure you're paying attention.

Through the sheer force of her personality, quick mind and knowledge of tennis, Mary leaped fearlessly from the women's pro ranks to the broadcasting booth 14 years ago, breaking through the gender barriers to become one of the most visible tennis analysts in the world today.

"Bill Talbert was scraping the bottom of the barrel when he interviewed me at the Garden during a late-night match (on MSG) during the 1980 Avon Championships," said Mary, who refers to her early broadcasting years as her "Vaudeville Days."

She was so good, Talbert gave her the mike. A USA Cable network producer who caught the broadcast hired her six months later. In 1983, when she was passing notes to Al Trautwig and Barry MacKay during a US Open men's match on USA, Trautwig refused to use them, believing the words should come from Mary herself. After the show, Trautwig explained to the executive producer that Mary should be calling men's matches too. The next day she was there.

Today, you, the fan, analyze matches with Mary -- and sometimes get into verbal debates with her -- much the same way you call Knicks' basketball with Marv Albert and John Anderiese or Mets' baseball with Tim McCarver and Ralph Kiner. The fact that she's a woman is incidental. Mary's instinct for spontaneous humor, vivid in-your-face language and perceptive observations are the hook. You relate to her immediately even if you don't always agree with her.

"I'd like to wish 'me sainted Irish mother' (Terry Carillo) a Happy St. Patrick's Day," Mary exclaimed on the air during the March Lipton Championships. Then without pause, she might say, "Watch this guy, he looks like the type who enjoys hoisting a beer with the boys."

Mary's appeal is so universal that when her credentials for calling a men's tennis match were questioned at last year's US Open, a guy from Corona, Queens, chased after her for an autograph. "Hey Mare, you're the best," he shouted. "I don't care if you are a chick!"

"I don't pay attention to my reviews, whether they're positive or negative," said Mary, who is certain she will be the last non-Wimbledon winner to have this kind of broadcasting career. "I just try to stay focused on the job at hand."

Mary has been honored with more than a dozen broadcasting awards during her affiliation with CBS Sports and the ESPN and USA Cable networks, including accolades from such industry powerhouses as the Women's Tennis Association and *Tennis* and *World Tennis* magazines, for whom she's written volumes of lively prose. Moreover, she was recently voted the "Top Female Tennis Personality of the Decade" by *Tennis Buyer's Guide* (a publication of *Tennis* magazine which polled its readers and the national press corps of tennis writers). And last December, *Tennis Week*'s editorial staff elected Mary as "The Most Powerful Woman in Tennis." In both instances, she overwhelmed the competition, including such tennis legends as Martina Navratilova, Billie Jean King and Chris Evert.

Blessed from birth with a strong presence and an unwillingness to compromise her integrity, Mary first captured the hearts of the New York media during the 1970s tennis boom when she was a top-ranked ETA junior player out of Douglaston, N.Y. She took the seaweed off an old Alex Olmedo wood racquet she used for crabbing at the local dock and followed her dream all the way to the pros, inspiring hundreds of girls to play tennis in the East along the way. She won the 1977 French Open mixed doubles title with her childhood friend, John McEnroe, and was ranked as high as No. 32 in the world in singles.

A well-known sports writer has said of her appeal, "When Mary came into the interview room after matches, the reporters always flipped open their pads because she was so quotable."

Mary once recalled her first impression of the US Open at Forest Hills in a colorful piece for *World Tennis* magazine. She wrote that when she was still in her early teens she was naturally captivated by the ball kids who looked terrific, all decked out in white. And she decided that would be a cool thing to do. But by the end of the day, after she had seen Chris Evert play for the first time, she knew that that's what she wanted to do.

She took John McEnroe's advice and started taking tennis lessons, trailing after him to the Port Washington Tennis Academy, and played her first ETA tournament in the 14s division. "It was up in Westchester," Mary said. "I had short curly hair and showed up in a pair of shorts with one racquet. Lee Jackson promptly put me in the boys' draw. And I had to try to convince her that I should've been in the girls' draw.

"Junior tennis was fun. We had a pretty good group. Ruta Gerulaitis and I were always trying to duke it out. Vitas [Gerulaitis] was the first one of us that did anything. I remember when he first played Wimbledon. I couldn't believe I knew somebody who was playing Wimbledon."

Terry Carillo was relieved when her daughter retired from the pro tour and began a career in the broadcasting booth after her third knee operation (Mary later had a fourth operation). "She has to walk on those legs for the rest of her life and be able to bounce her kids. Besides, she'll look great on TV in red silk shirts. Red is her color," said Terry, who was always too nervous to watch Mary play. "I would sit in the locker room counting the tiles on the ceiling and my husband, Tony, would tell me, 'You're missing all these beautiful moments.'"

Mary, who at 37 is the youngest person to be inducted into the ETA Hall of Fame, is enjoying many beautiful moments today. And she has the luxury of bouncing her children, Anthony, 6 1/2, and Rachel, 2 1/2, on her knee.

"This kid Rachel is a real Italian," Mary bellowed recently. "All she eats is macaroni!"

-- By Nancy Gill McShea

Seena Hamilton

Steve Bernun

Seena Hamilton's mother, Helen, once advised her impressionable young daughter to remember that "no experience is ever lost." Seena took her mother's advice literally.

In a lifetime notable for its furious pace and lists upon lists of accomplishments that leave one somewhat breathless, Seena has forged five separate business careers - as an entrepreneur, broadcaster, editor, journalist and public relations and event marketing specialist.

Her late husband, Dr. S.K. Fineberg, sometimes cautioned her against taking too many detours, yet he believed that her versatile background in journalism and business -- especially Gulliver's Trails, a children's sightseeing service she devised for hotels -- prepared her to run the independent national junior tennis tournament, the Easter Bowl, which made junior tennis famous.

Dubbed the "Mother Superior of Junior Tennis" by her friend, Bud Collins (she's not crazy about that label), Seena founded the Easter Bowl 26 years ago in New York, wresting the junior game from relative obscurity and planting it firmly in our national consciousness. While her feisty temperament demands recognition as a virtuoso in the grown-up business world, she speaks more softly about the generations of young tennis players who have participated in the Easter Bowl.

"I love kids," said Seena, who often resembles the child within us all. "It's been a great 26-year detour. I have met thousands of tennis families and I hope maybe some of my efforts have made junior tennis a happier place for them."

Indeed the Easter Bowl, which has long showcased our nation's future pros -- including Eastern's Mary Carillo, Ruta and Vitas Gerulaitis and the McEnroe and Mayer brothers, among others -- also serves as a springboard for the good things Seena has accomplished on the business side of tennis. She used a journalist's eye to publicize junior trends and programs, and used her marketing skills to enlist corporate support to help ease the financial burden of training a top player. In the 1980s, her New York-based sports marketing firm, Seena Hamilton & Associates, commissioned the first national survey on junior tennis for the Omega Watch Corporation, which helped launch the ETA Omega/Tourneau National 16s team. She also personally directed the first seminar for tennis parents.

Her influence in the marketplace has been so strong, Seena has received dozens of citations – notably from the White House, foreign governments and Cable TV – as well as awards from *USA Today* and *World Tennis* and *New York Woman* magazines, naming her a power in tennis. In addition, the ETA elected her its "Woman of the Year" for helping to organize the Junior Tennis Council, among other innovations.

Eugene L. Scott, the publisher and editor-in-chief of *Tennis Week* who has supported the Easter Bowl, particularly in the early 1970s during his tenure as ETA president, smiled when he heard of Seena's induction. "Seena is surely not her real name," Scott said. "Seena suggests a tall, frail, willowy woman. Moreover, the letters in the name 'Seena' are the first five letters of the expression 'seen and not heard,' also inappropriate for this founder of one of the noblest junior tournaments on the calendar. Seena Hamilton is seen and heard plenty in our game. And you'd better listen."

Seena's early history indicates she has thrived on challenge since the night her late father, Leonard Hamilton, came home with several formidable gentlemen, woke his precocious five-year-old daughter and invited them to "ask her anything." During her teens, she boarded at the Sanford School in Hockessin, Delaware, which further shaped her strong personality.

"Sanford believed in individuality," said Seena, who pointed out that she was not phlegmatic to begin with. "The school's head mistress, Ellen Sawin, instructed us never to follow the herd. I once headed straight for the proofreading test at a Middle States scholastic editorial competition because I knew I would win it. Ellen redirected me to creative writing, admonishing me not to take the easy route. I came in second."

Seena moved on to the College of William and Mary in Virginia, and the summer before her senior year she took a job as a copy girl at the *Daily News* in New York. After graduation, she was named a scriptwriter for the *Daily News'* radio and TV station, responsible for four shows a day. She was 21 years old.

At age 22, she detoured briefly from journalism to work as the publicity director of MGM records - the year she met her husband - but she jumped back into the publishing game as the associate editor of *Apartment Life* with hopes of cracking into the big time. Then she saw an ad in *The New York Times* for *Today's Woman* and ended up as the magazine's home planning editor.

"There I was, me, who was afraid to move a chair without my decorator telling me what to do," laughed Seena, who at 26 finally found her niche as the editor of the *Hotel Gazette*, the industry's leading publication.

"Those nine years with the *Gazette* were some of the happiest of my life," Seena recalled. "I had total control of publishing an issue every other week. I didn't know how to dummy up a magazine but I learned in a hurry. When my son, Bryan, was about to be born, I called the owner of the magazine and said, 'I can't come to work today, I think I'm about to have my baby.' He said, 'You can't do that... you're on deadline.' He sent a production man to my home, we put the issue to bed at 10 p.m., and Bryan was born at 8 the next morning."

The *Gazette* led Seena to the hotel lecture circuit, and in 1962 she recommended that the Hilton chain offer children's programs to increase summer occupancy. She pioneered Gulliver's Trails in New York; and to publicize the children's service, she picked up her first young passengers at the Waldorf in a Rolls Royce. The idea caught on rapidly throughout the world as a convenient service for members attending conventions with their children. In 1965, during an AMA convention in New York, Seena actually escorted 800 children to the World's Fair in one day.

But by 1968, when Seena's son, Bryan, had zoomed to the top of the ETA boys' 12 tennis rankings and trained in an invitational New York program for the top three juniors in each age group, she tried to raise money to expand the program and instead was talked into starting the Easter Bowl. She has run the tournament like an extension of Gulliver's Trails, proving the wisdom of her mother's axiom, "No experience is ever lost."

Charles Friedman, a former writer for *The New York Times*, has said of Seena, "Her drive for the good of the game is like the forehand she loves to smack on the court. Her determination and dedication represents the best that one can give to tennis, which surely needs more like her."

And people who know say she has a very good forehand!

-- By Nancy Gill McShea

Millicent Hirsh Lang

Steve Berman

Millicent Hirsh Lang's tennis memories are preserved in a scrapbook whose pages overflow with newspaper stories written by her friends, Allison Danzig of *The New York Times*, and Fred Hawthorne of the old *New York Herald Tribune*.

Millicent's joyous tennis career began in 1928 when, at age 11, she won her first women's tournament at St. James Park in the Bronx.

"When I won that tournament, there was no trophy," recalled Millicent, who that same year gave up a promising future as a concert pianist to pursue tennis. "But someone got to New York Mayor Jimmy Walker, who quickly corrected the oversight, and my victory was noted on the front page of *The Times*."

In the 66-year interim leading to her Hall of Fame induction, Millicent's life intertwined with many tennis greats -- including ETA Hall of Famers Barbara Williams, Alastair Martin, Gene Scott, and the late Frank Shields and John 'Pat' Rooney – as she first gained stature in the 1930s as a national and Eastern champion, and later as a dedicated volunteer tournament director and senior player.

It all started when Millicent's Dad, Morris Hirsh, became interested in tennis. "Being the eldest of three daughters, if Dad said, 'Let's go,' I did. I was eight years old. We lived on the Grand Concourse in the Bronx across from the Kelton Tennis Courts and there we started," she said. "On weekends we traipsed to St. James Park and many kindly gentlemen would hit with me."

Millicent quickly distinguished herself as a junior player, capturing three titles in the early 1930s at the Anne Cumming Memorial tournament (a Jersey State girls' event). She also won both the singles and doubles trophies at the 1933 USLTA National Indoors and ranked first in the Eastern section for several years.

By 1936 when she was 19, Millicent, who had been attending New York University, was already a veteran on the women's circuit. In November of that year, when the USLTA National Indoors debuted at the 7th Regiment Armory in New York, she was a singles runner-up to Sylvia Hemrotin of France and advanced to the mixed doubles semifinals with Shields, who had been one of her more famous hitting partners during her early youth.

"Frank and I were very good friends, we grew up together since we lived only one block apart," Millicent said. "I copied his big forehand and Helen Jacobs' slice.

"That particular indoors was quite a gala. Ted Heusing narrated my final match with Sylvia over the radio. My father was there and he always made me nervous. I was leading 5-3 in the first set and lost it 7-5. After I won the second set I went up to the gallery (during my 10-minute rest period) to sit with my father, and then promptly lost the match."

After the Indoors, Millicent, Frank Froehling, Sr. and Helen Pedersen -- a Wimbledon semifinalist who ranked among the U.S. top 10 for nine years -- toured the winter circuit together from February to June. They started in Bermuda; trekked to Chicago, where Millicent won the Western Indoors singles, doubles and mixed titles; on to Houston; the Carolinas; Atlanta; Chattanooga; and finally ended the road trip in New Haven and Hartford.

"It was a wonderful experience, we all got on well," she said. "The three of us toured in Frank's (Froehling) 1928 Model A Ford. He was known as the 'blond bomber,' so naturally he received a lot of attention and fan mail."

In the early 1940s, Millicent ranked 14th in U.S. women's singles and lost to Louise Brough in the singles quarterfinals of the U.S. National Championships at Forest Hills. She also married Nathaniel (Nat) Lang, and after the war, she and

Nat stayed close to home in Great Neck, N.Y., raising three daughters. Later, Edith Martin asked her to run Eastern's women circuit. Millicent enlisted Barbara Williams to help her organize the New Jersey/New York States and the Eastern Clay Courts. Alastair Martin secured the Piping Rock Club on Long Island for her invitational grass court tournament, which often attracted future Grand Slam champions such as Billie Jean King and Virginia Wade.

Millicent also captained and played on Eastern's Sears Cup teams for several years. And in the late 1960s and early '70s, she started the senior circuit, ranking first in that division with four different partners.

"When I was running Eastern women's tournaments, I would call Gene Scott and request that he get some of my players into the US Open draw at Forest Hills and he did," she said. "Gene was counsel to the US Open in the early 1970s and accepted entries for the tournament. I didn't know him at all, yet he was most considerate."

Millicent has enjoyed the whole adventure, especially such larks as playing exhibitions with the great Vinnie Richards at various clubs in the East, and reigning for several years with Lady Woodall as Bermuda's doubles champs. Each spring, Pops Merrihew invited Millicent to participate in two Bermuda invitationals. On one occasion in the mid-1950s, Sir John Woodall, the governor general of the Bermudas, actually held up the departure of a commercial Pan-Am flight so that she and Lady Woodall could finish a final match. Millicent boarded the plane soaking wet but was happy to make the flight back to New York with Nat and the children.

"This Hall of Fame honor is an acclamation of my small accomplishments, but the real issue is how many friends did I make? Quite frankly, the old tennis friends are still my friends," Millicent said.

About four weeks ago, the Langs' Long Island home was burglarized and every bit of silver was taken, including all of Millicent's tennis trophies. Soon afterward, she had lunch with her longtime Eastern tennis rivals and friends, Helen Pedersen (McLoughlin) and Norma Taubele. "Norma had retired the New Jersey State trophy, having won it three times," Millicent said. "In a gesture of friendship, she asked me if I would like to have it since I had won it twice. So I took it and now I have a trophy again."

-- By Nancy Gill McShea

Walter L. Pate

The late Walter Pate secured his place in tennis history off the courts as the captain of three victorious U.S. Davis Cup teams, in 1937, 1938 and 1946. Yet in 1915, Pate, a native of Glen Cove, Long Island, qualified on his home turf for one of the most significant events in tennis history -- the first U.S. National Tennis Championships ever played at the West Side Tennis Club in Forest Hills, N.Y.

Although Pate lost early in that landmark tournament, which, according to *The New York Times*, "established Forest Hills as the center of tennis in this country," the experience undoubtedly helped shape his future as an important leader at the center of the game he loved.

A graduate of Cornell and a partner in the New York law firm of Cooke, Brown and Pate, Walter was president of the Cornell Club in New York, where he maintained a residence. He also had a home at the Nassau Country Club in Glen Cove. After a freak accident forced Walter to abandon any dreams of court stardom – he broke a hip while playing a match on wet grass, which left him with one leg shorter than the other -- he took on the role of tennis administrator, serving as president of the Eastern Lawn Tennis Association in 1925 and 1926.

He captained this country's Davis Cup teams when tennis, especially Davis Cup tennis, commanded a greater share of attention among American sports fans and the press.

Historically, the tennis supremacy of the world rests with the country that wins the Davis Cup trophy, and the 1920s, late '30s and '40s were among America's best Davis Cup decades. The United States retained the Cup from 1921 to 1926 -- the longest stretch of possession in the competition -- until France and Great Britain dominated for the next 11 years.

In 1937, the U.S. came roaring back under Captain Pate, defeating Great Britain 4 -1 at Wimbledon in London. The U.S. team, which was sparked by a young Don Budge, who won three matches -- two singles and one doubles with his longtime partner Gene Mako -- returned home to a hero's welcome and a Broadway Ticker Tape parade. (Frank Parker, Wayne Sabin and Bryan 'Bitsy' Grant were also members of that squad.)

The U.S. repeated as champions under Pate in 1938, defeating Harry Hopman's Australian squad 3-2 at the Germantown Cricket Club in Philadelphia. But Australia retaliated in 1939, edging the U.S. 3-2 at the Merion Cricket Club in Haverford, Pennsylvania.

Davis Cup matches were suspended from 1940-1945 during World War II, but Captain Pate returned in 1946 with the team of Bill Talbert -- who later served as Davis Cup captain from 1953-1957 -- Gardnar Mulloy, Ted Schroeder, Frank Parker and Jack Kramer, who routed Australia 5-0 at the Kooyong Tennis Club in Melbourne, Australia.

Mulloy later wrote, "The seventh and final member of our (1946) team was non-playing captain, Walter L. Pate, a short middle-aged Wall Street lawyer, with a tremendous enthusiasm for the game. In his younger days, he had broken a hip and now walked with a limp. He had captained pre-war teams, among them the one which lost to Australia in 1939. It was a fitting gesture to give him the opportunity to bring back the Cup, and one for which his experience qualified him. Loyalty to his team, and an aversion to hurting anyone's feeling, though he could put his foot down with unshakable firmness when necessary, were qualities for which the boys adored him. And before the tour was over he was to become one of my best friends in tennis."

Talbert and Budge, both ETA Hall of Famers, agree that Captain Pate was a very modest, fine gentleman who understood very well the nuances of tennis.

"Cap was like a second father to me, he was instrumental in getting me and Gene Mako on the 1935 (Davis Cup) squad for experience when our records weren't good enough at the time," said Budge, who also credits Pate with suggesting that he change from a Western to an Eastern grip and helping him to do it. "Cap knew tennis. Bill Tilden once said to him, 'I hit my forehand even with my belt buckle,' and Cap said, 'No you don't, you hit your forehand out in front of your hip.' He bet Tilden $5 and took photos to prove it.

"Gene and I often stayed with Cap out in Glen Cove when we were in town," said Budge, adding proudly that his mentor, who was a great authority on bridge, edited "The Four Aces" for Ozzie Jacoby. "Once when Gene and I popped into his office for a visit, he was sound asleep in his chair. Rather than embarrass him, we asked his secretary to wake him and announce us. When we went back in, he said he was as busy as the dickens."

In 1915, *The New York Times* stated prophetically that "Forest Hills is the center of tennis in this country...and New York may produce more potential tennis champions in the future." There were 25,000 tennis players in the New York area then but only 128 men qualified for the debut of the U.S. National Championships at West Side. Tennis champion Walter L. Pate was one of them.

-- By Nancy Gill McShea

Chapter 15

1995: Delatour, Gerulaitis, King and Van Nostrand

Hunter L. Delatour, Jr.

Steve Berman

Call him "Mr. Tennis." Read his list of accomplishments, from his first involvement as a USLTA umpire in 1935 to the present day, and you'll see why.

An active player all his life, Hunter Delatour first played tennis in the late 1920s on Long Island, where he nurtured his game on the Great Neck High School tennis team and in local Eastern tournaments. He went on to play for the Princeton tennis team under famous coach Mercer Beasley. During those formative years, Hunter also managed the Twilight Park Tennis Club in Haines Falls, N.Y., where his parents spent their summer months.

"Twilight was one of the old line, well-respected USLTA member clubs," he said. "It was noted for an annual tournament which I ran during my tenure. Bill Tilden had played it, and while I was there Gardnar Mulloy was a regular participant. It was during this period that I would hold the proxy and represent the club at the USLTA Annual Meeting, which was held each year at the Vanderbilt Hotel in New York."

In the 57 years that have elapsed since he left Princeton in 1938, Hunter has managed to combine two rewarding careers -- as a high profile volunteer in tennis administration and as an innovative leader in his own optical business. He manufactures and markets products designed to preserve and improve eyesight, and serves on the Northern California Society to Prevent Blindness. During the war years he took a brief detour into another worthy endeavor. From 1941-1946, he served in the U.S. Navy, entering as an Ensign and retiring in the rank of Lieutenant Commander. He was honored by the British government as a member of the Order of the British Empire -- "It's an honor I cherish," he said. -- and was also awarded a commendation ribbon by the U.S. Secretary of the Navy. While serving in Washington, he met his wife, Eugenie, who was working in the British Embassy. They married in 1944 and later returned to civilian life, spending the next 18 years on Long Island's North Shore.

In 1962, Hunter's good friend and Princeton classmate Alastair Martin recruited him to serve on the Eastern Lawn Tennis Association Board of Directors as a delegate from Long Island. From that point on, he maintained a steady involvement on the administrative side of the sport and was elected to the USTA presidency in 1983-1984.

"Hunter has always had an instinct for knowing what is best for tennis," Alastair Martin said recently. "And perhaps his greatest contribution to the game has been his subtle ability to get officials to accept his views. He has always had great respect for good sportsmanship and has championed a liberal view toward Open competition -- more tennis for more people."

In 1966, Hunter and Eugenie, who have three grown daughters -- Anne, Debbie and Susie -- moved to Portola Valley, California. He was elected to the board of the Northern California Tennis Association and in 1972-1973 served as Northern Cal's president. In 1975 he was elected secretary of the USTA, followed by two-year terms as second vice president, first vice president and president. His two years as immediate past president culminated 12 years of service on the USTA Board of Directors. He has also served as president of the International Tennis Hall of Fame, vice president of the International Tennis Federation and in many capacities on various USTA committees.

"Being involved in tennis has resulted in our having traveled to all corners of the earth to be with people interested in the game...We can go anywhere in the world and find a fellow tennis player who is already a friend, or who will be, once the tennis relationship is cemented," Hunter said. "I have enjoyed doing all I could to encourage grass-roots tennis at all levels. During my term as USTA president, the schools program was inaugurated. The National Junior Tennis League (NJTL) and the USTA merged, and the USTA formed a closer relationship with the International Tennis Hall of Fame and collegiate tennis."

The recent unrest between labor and management in professional baseball, hockey and in tennis reminds us that the art of merging ideas among any sport's diverse organizations to promote growth and harmony can be a complex challenge. And tennis leaders from New York to California regard Hunter Delatour, Jr., as one of the great diplomats in that effort for tennis.

"Hunter has diffused much of the acrimony that is present at the tennis bargaining tables," according to one source who reflects the consensus. "His image is one of a gentleman and a conciliator."

Tennis Highlights:
USTA Board of Directors (1975-1986): Secretary, Second Vice President, First Vice President, President and Immediate Past President.

USTA Committees (1972-present): Men's Ranking; Management and Executive Committees; Scholarship Awards; Olympic Pan-Am; Constitution & Rules; Credentials, US Open; Tennis Rules; Ranking Committees' general chairman; Davis Cup; Olympics; USTA/International Tennis Hall of Fame chairman; Budget & Finance; Federation Cup; and Governance & Planning.

Member, Committee of Management, Vice President, Honorary Life Counselor, Life Trustee: International Tennis Federation; Director, National Tennis Foundation/Hall of Fame; President, International Tennis Hall of Fame; President, Northern California Tennis Association; elected to Northern California Tennis Hall of Fame; member, International Lawn Tennis Club of USA; honorary member, International Lawn Tennis Clubs -- Great Britain (All England Lawn Tennis & Croquet Club), France, Sweden, South Africa, Australia, India, New Zealand, Canada, Spain, Japan and Israel.

-- By Nancy Gill McShea

Vitas Gerulaitis

Russ Adams

Italian restaurant of the moment in London in 1977. Vitas Gerulaitis always knew where the hot place was, where to find the people who wanted to laugh the most and stay up the latest. It was a big group, I remember that, because dinner with Vitas in those days was always dinner for just about everyone. He was always the life of the party.

But he could not make himself the life of the party that June night in 1977. He went through the motions, but his heart wasn't in it, because this was the night after the afternoon when he should have beaten Bjorn Borg at Wimbledon. He sat at the head of the table a long time and somehow kept a smile in place, and finally about 11 o'clock he said he was meeting some people at some hot new club.

He was out of Howard Beach, in Queens, which is not supposed to produce the Wimbledon champion. Howard Beach was not even supposed to produce a player who could chase the great Borg around for five thrilling sets that are still discussed in tennis today. But he had done that. Borg was the defending Wimbledon champion. Vitas was 23 years old and a comer, a tennis celebrity already, not just the life of the party but someone who felt like the life of the sport when he was going good, and he was going good at Wimbledon in 1977.

Vitas had stayed with him until 6-all in the final set. He had run and hit all his shots, and Borg, who would turn out to be one of his best friends, had run and hit all his shots. The tennis was something to see. Vitas had his best shot when he was up a service break early in the fifth set. He had a point to go ahead 4-2. The score was 40-30. He had been coming in hard behind his weak second serve all day and getting away with it.

This time he hesitated. Borg took control…won the match (8-6 in the fifth) and two days later he beat Jimmy Connors in the final.

Vitas didn't know anything about that on this night, in the hot Italian restaurant. He just knew he stayed back when he should have come in. He finally stood up and grabbed the check, because he always did that, too.

"That _____ second serve," he said, putting a smile on the obscenity. Then his voice dropped, and he dropped the smile, and Vitas Gerulaitis said, "I could have won Wimbledon…Imagine that, me winning Wimbledon."

He threw some money on the table and walked into the London night, alone all of a sudden.

He was born in Brooklyn, raised in Howard beach, attended Archbishop Molloy High School and even Columbia University for a while. He came from public tennis courts all over the city and Long Island, and the Port Washington Tennis Academy. He owned a mansion in Kings Point once, with all the money you could make from tennis if you could make it to No. 4 in the world, and do it all with style, make the whole thing alive and fun just by showing up. He never won Wimbledon. He won the Australian Open, though. He won the Italian Open. He made it to the finals of the U.S. Open and lost to his pal John McEnroe. He had long blond hair and one of the biggest hearts I have ever known about, and he was my friend.

He is a hundred stories, a thousand stories, from the time he won his first big tournament, the U.S. Pro Indoor. That was in Philadelphia. He came right back to New York and tried to spend all the money on clothes the next afternoon, in about two hours. If you ever knew Vitas Gerulaitis, you understand about the hole cut into tennis…God he was fun.

He beat Borg one time at the Masters tournament when the Masters was still held in New York. I don't recall the exact number, but Borg had beaten him something like 16 times in a row…When he came into the interview area, Vitas looked very grave, very serious. Before a question could be asked, he sat down and pointed a finger at the crowd of reporters and said, "Nobody beats Vitas Gerulaitis 17 times in a row." And brought down the house.

I saw him for the last time during the (1994) U.S. Open final. Now Vitas was a comer in television…So I watched another match with him…And then all these years later, for the first time in a long time, I brought up the Borg match. Vitas smiled.

"I shoulda come in on that second serve," he said.

He should have been 41.

*   *   *   *

John Lloyd stood at the top of the steps outside St. Dominic's Church and watched as the casket slowly came through the double doors. Three of the pallbearers were Bjorn Borg and John McEnroe and Jimmy Connors. There was a time back in 1979 when they were ranked No. 1 and No. 2 and No. 3 in the world. No. 4 was…Vitas Gerulaitis.

"You should have seen Vitas last week in Seattle (at Jimmy Connors' Citibank Champions tour for over-35 world-class players)," John Lloyd said quietly…There was this doubles match, and even with Borg and Connors in it, the show belonged to Gerulaitis.

"After the first set," Lloyd said on the church steps, "I said to Jimmy, The other three of us might as well not be here. This is Vitas' room. And Jimmy said, 'Aren't they all?'"

The last room was a church with a high ceiling at the top of Anstice Street in Oyster Bay. They had come from tennis and television and New York City nights to mourn Gerulaitis. Mary Carillo, remembering the first time she saw Vitas when they were both teenagers at the Port Academy, said, "I remember this big blond streak. He was the most dazzling thing I'd ever seen."

Mary made the church laugh with stories about Vitas, because he was still in the room and that meant you had to laugh. She told of a pajama party Vitas threw in some Pittsburgh hotel on the occasion of his 21st birthday. Then Jimmy Connors was up there, talking about how Vitas still had the magic with people that he took out of New York and all over the tennis map. A fan once mistook Vitas for Borg, even with Borg in the same elevator. Vitas signed Borg's name and when Connors asked him why later, Vitas grinned and said, "Always give them something to make them happy." Connors finished his eulogy and then cried. Because you also had to cry in Vitas' room at St. Dominic's.

After Ruta Gerulaitis had read a simple prayer for her brother, there was this slight pause…Then the three top guys picked up No. 4, and started down the aisle, all laughter gone now from the church, only memories of laughter left behind…

Career Highlights
Highest ATP world singles ranking – No. 3 (June 11, 1979). Ranked No. 4 for the year. Singles winner -- Australian Open, 1977; singles finalist – French Open, 1980; singles finalist -- US Open, 1979; singles winner -- Italian Open, 1977, 1979; singles winner-Canadian Championships, 1982; singles winner -- Tournament of Champions, Forest Hills,1980; singles finalist-The Masters, Madison Square Garden, 1979, 1981; doubles winner -- Wimbledon, 1975. Compiled

11-3 singles record in U.S. Davis Cup competition. One of the most consistent players in U.S. tennis history. Ranked in the 10 ten for six years from 1977-1982 and in the top 20 from 1975-1984. Captured 27 career singles titles (in 55 finals) and nine doubles crowns...Ranked No. 17 in Open Era singles titles...After retiring from the pro tour, moved to the television booth to provide color commentary for CBS, USA Network and ESPN...Ran free tennis clinics for inner-city kids in City Parks Department, 1979-1989...Supported numerous other charities, including cancer and the Special Olympics.

--By Mike Lupica
Excerpted from Newsday September 19 & 23, 1994
Edited by Nancy Gill McShea

Alan King

Alan King at the US Open.

You all know Alan King. He's the famous spectator at the US Open who is decked out in straw hat, chinos and Gucci loafers, the guy you look for in the courtside celebrity box, 52A, every time you walk into the expanse of Louis Armstrong Stadium. You see him at every session and at every match, from Day 1 to Day 14. Just like the blur of colorful uniforms in the ball kids' perch above him, he is part of the ambiance.

"I've been watching the Open for 50 years," said King, 67, who has lived most of his life nearby on Long Island's North Shore. "It's my two-week tennis vacation...About 40 years ago I threw my golf bags into the lake along with the caddy and went out and bought a tennis racquet. I was 27, an old man already in terms of tennis."

King made his name as a standup comic, but he is also a well-known actor -- *Night and the City* and *Bonfire of the Vanities*, and a best-selling author -- *Anyone Who Owns His Own Home Deserves It*, and *Help, I'm a Prisoner in a Chinese Bakery*. He is also a producer of stage and screen -- *Memories of Me* with Billy Crystal -- and a generous philanthropist. But he is being honored by the Eastern Tennis Association for asserting himself as an influential promoter of tennis dating to the early years of the Open era.

"While I was working for Howard Hughes in Las Vegas (in the early 1970s), Dinah Shore and I put on a celebrity tennis tournament as a way of attracting celebs to Vegas," he said. "I saw how the audience reacted, not only to the celebs, but to tennis itself.

"The next year I was negotiating with several hotels for a long-term contract as a comedian and the people at Caesar's Palace came to me and asked, 'What else can we do to sweeten the pot?' I said, 'I want a pro tennis tournament.' They all looked at me like I was crazy, but one boss said, 'Okay, you're faded (covered).'"

King hooked up with oil tycoon Lamar Hunt, one of the first pro tennis promoters in the Open era who founded the World Championship Tennis (WCT) group and the famous Dallas final. Hunt was expanding his tour and agreed to support a $50,000 tournament at Caesar's Palace, which became known as the Alan King Tennis Classic.

"The tournament was so successful that the bosses with their gambling mentality said to me, 'This is too good. Why do we need Hunt as a partner?' The next year they gave me $100,000 for the tournament with all expenses paid for the players." It was the first tournament to boast a $100,000 purse and the first to pick up players' full expenses. American greats such as Arthur Ashe and Jimmy Connors played the Palace, and so did Aussie legends Ken Rosewall and Rod Laver.

"The Australians were the great serve-and-volley players. They don't make them like that anymore," King said in an interview with *The New Yorker*. "They never got better than Rod Laver...ZaSu Pitts could have coached Laver. And they never threw their socks into the stands."

Nine years ago, King and Charlie Pasarell built the Grand Champions Hotel in Indian Wells, California. "We combined his tournament at La Quinta and my tournament in Vegas. It has evolved into the Newsweek Champions Cup with almost $1,800,000 in prize money," said King, who co-chairs the event.

Perhaps because Alan King was exposed to reality early as a high school dropout who grew up in the tough Williamsburg section of Brooklyn and Manhattan's lower East Side, he is heavily involved in humanitarian causes. He founded the Alan King Diagnostic Medical Center in Jerusalem, established a non-sectarian scholarship fund for American students at the Hebrew University as well as an Albert Einstein scholarship fund, and he has led a fund-raising effort for the Nassau Center for Emotionally Disturbed Children, to name a few of his favorite charities.

And for the past three summers, he and Bill Cosby have brightened spirits at the USTA National Tennis Center as emcees of the annual pre-Open Arthur Ashe Aids Tennis Challenge. (The Ashe Foundation has raised over $4 million since the challenge was established in 1992.) King said plans are underway to add the Vitas Gerulaitis Foundation to next year's challenge.

King has received many tributes for his contributions to tennis. Gene Scott points out that "in a game that hasn't always had much humor, Alan King has been a Hall of Famer for contributing this quality to the sport."

King's tennis buddy Dick Savitt, who in 1951 won both Wimbledon and the Australian Open, added, "Alan has done so much for tennis – as a promoter, a fan and as the possessor of a major forehand. And it's ironic that Alan is to be inducted this year along with his friend Vitas. We all had some great times with Vitas at Alan's court…"

MIKE LUPICA INTRODUCES ALAN KING

"…Alan King's court became the oldest established tennis game in New York. Everybody from Hoad and Rosewall and Laver, to McEnroe and Borg and Vitas, you knew you could find them there…during the two weeks of the Open…. tennis wasn't always the laugh riot it later became and Alan brought good humor. But more than that, Alan King didn't show up five minutes ago when tennis became fashionable. He has been going to the nationals and the US Open forever and it began a friendship that became important to all of us…He was there because he loves the game. He put the money down because he thought professional tennis…was a pretty good idea. And the longer you hang around the more important relationships become. I'm happy I get to sit in Box 52A. I'm happy that he's a friend of mine and I'm proud to introduce him tonight…"

ALAN KING ACCEPTS AWARD

"I've been around tennis so long I was too old for Tilden…Helen Moody called me a dirty old man…I have no ability and nothing has given me greater pleasure than to become completely wracked with every bone disease known to man so that I can say honestly that I'm not playing anymore because of arthritis. Had I developed arthritis at age 24 I wouldn't have had all the aggravation and frustration, looking like an imbecile. My coach John Nogrady says "Putz, find another sport." Now I play golf again, a game for drunks and idiots. Am I wearing brown and white shoes today with the pink pants? Tennis is a great leveler, a great lesson in living. Just ask my friend, Dr. Irving Glick, the U.S. Open physician and my sponsor for receiving this noble award. I see Irving more than I choose to. If I don't see him in his office – there are so many cripples there it's like Lourdes -- I call him maybe two, three times a day. I say, "Irving?" He says "What is it Alan?" I say, "I can't get off the toilet." And Irving, with his great medical background, orthopedic giant that he is, says, "I had the same thing yesterday." Whatever ailment I've had in my lifetime he had the day before…My father, an old socialist…used to say to me, "…kid, to be good is an achievement. A genius? Forget about it!" So for me to be around tennis greatness has been so much fun. Before I leave the podium I have to say a final word to Mom (Gerulaitis) and Ruta about our boy Vitas, who lived only 4, 5 blocks from me. I always remember Bjorn Borg and Vitas walking to my court, blond hair down to their shoulders, bandannas around their heads. The bell rang and my wife said, "Two girls are here with tennis racquets." Humility is not one of my attributes, but I appreciate the honor and will accept it with great joy…"

-- By Nancy Gill McShea

King Van Nostrand

King Van Nostrand has been figuring all the angles with his sharp, logical mind and dry sense of humor for half a century now. On tennis courts around the world, in the classrooms of Long Island's Bay Shore school system, where he taught geometry for 31 years until he retired in 1989, and within his own family structure.

When all the math was computed for the 1993 & 1994 tennis seasons, he was ranked first in the world, in the United States and in the East on the men's over-55 and 60 circuits, respectively. "After I won the ('93) world tournament in Barcelona, Ian Hamilton of Nike told me he was extremely proud because I was their only client who was No. 1 in the world," said King, laughing as he recalled beating former top-10 player and Spanish Davis Cupper Juan Couder, 1-6, 6-2, 6-0, in the men's 55 World Senior final. Nike also represents Andre Agassi, Jim Courier and John McEnroe.

King won his second straight world championship last May in Los Gatos, California, routing Florida's Rey Garrido, 6-0, 6-1, in the 60s final. In August, he returned to California and claimed his first of three USTA gold balls in over-60 competition, at the national hard courts in Santa Barbara, where he crushed Buddy Lomax of Texas, 6-0, 6-2, in the title match. One week later, he won the national indoors in Seattle, defeating Russell Seymour of Texas, 6-2, 6-2. In early October, he again beat Seymour, 6-0, 6-1, to win the clay courts in Duluth, Georgia.

Much like the veteran pitcher who finesses the plate with curves and sliders to set up the strikeout, King bisects the angles of the tennis court to set up the appropriate coup de grace. "It starts with court positioning," he said. "I teach the same tactics I use when I play. Depth and consistency, choosing the right shot, and being in the proper position are basic elements of my style. The winner could be a lob or a simple drop volley. It's certainly not going to be a power shot at this stage."

King's court sense, strong conditioning and natural talent help offset the effects of a cumbersome black brace he began wearing two years ago to protect his left knee (on which he had surgery more than 10 years ago). "Last year in Santa Barbara, a spectator at the hard courts asked if he could look at my leg brace to see if I had a motor in it because I ran so fast," he chuckled.

Since winning his first national title in 1971 at the Shelter Rock Tennis Club, King has won 20 USTA gold tennis balls and 10 silver as runner-up, plus more than 17 individual and team trophies in international competition. "The first one is always special," he said. He had lost three USTA finals before beating Lester Sack of Mississippi in the title match at Shelter Rock.

"The USTA gold tennis ball is a cherished thing. I don't believe in just collecting them, so I give them away to special people…family and friends who encourage me."

His family has always been No. 1. Wife Boots, her husband's sweetheart, coach, trainer, scout and nutritionist, first met King in 1953 when they sat next to each other in class while training to become teachers at SUNY-Cortland. They were engaged in 1954, married a year later and then raised a close-knit family that played tennis together for recreation. The couple taught the game to their four children and a group of high school players in a junior program at the Eastern Athletic Club (EAC) in Commack, Long Island, during the late 1970s and early 1980s. (Today, both Van Nostrands teach at the EAC's Half Hollow Racquet Club in Melville.)

"He sacrificed for us. He absolutely loves playing tennis," said King's daughter Molly, who was a singles quarterfinalist at Wimbledon in 1985. King taught his kids math during the school year, but tennis was the focus of the family's summer vacations. He and Boots would pack the kids in the car and, alternately, drive -- south, to North Carolina, Tennessee and Florida; north to Massachusetts; or upstate to Schenectady -- stopping at tournament sites which accommodated multiple age groups. "We took the kids wherever we could afford to go," said Boots. She and King played in the adult events while their children played in four of the five junior divisions.

"We had a little hibachi," she said. "We'd cook out in state parks and stay at Holiday Inns. The kids were free and there was always a pool." Not surprisingly, all four Van Nostrand children received tennis scholarships to college. Jane was recruited by Furman College in South Carolina, finishing up at Simmons in Boston. Young King opted for Pfeiffer College in North Carolina. Molly attended SMU before turning pro. She later earned her degree at North Carolina. And John went to Pepperdine in California before venturing onto the pro circuit.

Tragically, John and New Jersey's Joey Heldman were killed in a 1984 automobile crash while traveling to a satellite tournament in Mexico.

"John is still a very important part of our family," King Van Nostrand said. "He's always with us. It was a very traumatic event, something we'll never get over. But you have to go on."

Molly, currently a graduate student in speech pathology at New York University, believes her parents' relationship and her dad's sense of humor -- "He wore Nike sneakers under his tux at my wedding," she said. -- have kept the Van Nostrand family well grounded. "My parents are best friends and they really respect each other. They taught us not to take life too casually, to remember that love and thoughtfulness are especially important."

King Van Nostrand's angle on competition is less philosophical. "I don't like losing," he said. "I'm a lousy sport. One of my best wins last summer was when I beat Boots at gin rummy out in Seattle three nights in a row."

--By Nancy Gill McShea
Excerpted from Newsday, October 16, 1994

King and Boots Van Nostrand, both nationally top ranked senior players.

Chapter 16

1996: Hartman, Marmion, G. Mayer and Ward

Lewis H. (Skip) Hartman

Skip Hartman congratulates Gina Majmudar at Mayor's Cup tourney.

Until he entered the Peace Corps in 1967, the farthest Skip Hartman had ever been from home was a trip to summer camp in New England.

"When I was young, from when I was born until I finished law school, I spent my entire life in New York City or within 150 miles of it."

After spending time in Mexico and Chile as a Peace Corps volunteer, he felt confident that the place he would be happiest in the world was back in New York. It wasn't the big city that he missed so much as the people who lived there.

"The Peace Corps was a great experience," recalls Hartman. "More than anything it gave me a deeper appreciation of New York.

"I wouldn't have felt comfortable staying in New York if I hadn't explored other places," he admits. "I found that I could be happy pretty much anywhere as long as my friends and family were there, and in my case, that place was New York. It is where my roots are and it made sense to me to stay here."

Tennis in New York City probably would not be where it is today if Skip had decided to move elsewhere.

Three years after his stint in the Peace Corps ended, Skip founded HCK Recreation with partner Bob Kelton. In 1970, they opened Stadium Tennis Center in Mullaly Park, pioneering the use of air structures for indoor tennis on public land.

Hartman's role in the indoor tennis boom in New York City has been a pivotal one, and he is proud of that for a couple of reasons.

"We created jobs through something that wasn't there before and we provided people with a place to play," says Hartman. "That space was unused and then you put a bubble over it, and you can play year round."

The summer after opening Stadium Tennis Center, Skip first became involved with the New York Junior Tennis League when he hired Sydney Llewellyn to run an NYJTL program at Stadium.

In the next few years, as the National Junior Tennis League expanded, with Arthur Ashe and Donald Dell securing national sponsors such as Coca-Cola, the opportunity arose for Skip to become the president of the NYJTL branch. He has been running the NYJTL ever since.

"Because our business (HCK Recreation) was premised on the use of public land, involvement with the NYJTL was certainly a good thing," says Hartman.

Since 1971, the NYJTL has raised nearly $20 million to help provide free tennis programs for New York City youths. Over 170,000 youngsters are involved in the program which is run on converted tennis courts on sites such as school yards and playgrounds throughout New York City.

From 1988-94, Skip served as the Eastern Tennis Association Metro Regional vice president. During this time he worked hard to help make regionalization work in the ETA, finding ways to generate funds so that individual ETA regions could be partially self-sufficient.

"During that time, there was a great group which included Elaine Viebranz, Dan Dwyer and Lou Dimock as presidents," says Hartman. "The leadership was exceptionally good, and we were able to take a fresh look at things and do some effective strategic planning."

Out of the Metro region under Skip's helm grew the innovative program Play Tennis New York, which developed the idea of offering low cost community wide tennis lessons to serve the game and not simply the clubs and court owners. Hartman has also been involved in the implementation and creation of national programs such as the USTA Schools Program and the National Tennis Teachers Conference.

One of the more successful entrepreneurs in New York City, it can be said of Skip that he has given to the game as much as he has gotten back.

"I get a great deal of satisfaction out of the fact that these things that we have been involved with have continued to grow," says Hartman. "I think I have a knack for organizing my ideas and persisting and making it significantly replicable so that others can do it as well. Some of these ideas have been better for me and some have been better for tennis. That's not a lament. It's just how it is."ment Committee as head of junior introductory programs.

--By Cara Griffin

Harry A. Marmion

Harry and Pat Marmion at Hall of Fame.

If you had told Harry Marmion when he was a young man just out of college that his future would hold such tennis accomplishments as being a ranked player in the East, serving as the president of the Eastern Tennis Association, the first vice president of the United States Tennis Association, and ultimately the president of the USTA, he probably would have looked at you a little bit funny.

He was a baseball and basketball player in his youth, and a good enough athlete to play both sports in college. Up until his thirties, Marmion had not even played tennis seriously and in his own words he now admits almost apologetically "I had no real knowledge of or involvement in the game at all."

Once he started playing, it did not take Harry long to get involved in an administrative fashion. He first joined on as an ETA volunteer in 1975 as the Long Island delegate and went on to become the secretary and eventually president of the ETA, from 1980-81. He has been involved in the USTA ever since, with board responsibilities since 1989. A trait that has distinguished Marmion along the way has been his ability to come up with new ideas and follow through with them even when they are perceived as "crazy" at first.

A perfect example is the creation of this very event tonight. After Marmion's presidency ended, he continued on as a member of the ETA board and campaigned for an Eastern Hall of Fame that would be an extravagant event.

"I felt that this had to be big time, with no kidding around," Marmion says. "A lot of people said that it was impossible, that no one would come. People talked like I was crazy."

Harry persisted and even suggested that the ETA commission a sculpture to be received by each recipient. That sculpture, by artist Chuck Clark, is no small part of the event.

"The hall of fame dinner is a major social event in New York," says Marmion. "Don Budge told me that the sculpture is the nicest, most distinctive trophy he has ever received."

Another important suggestion that Marmion followed through on occurred at a national level. After extensive involvement with the US Open, he realized that the average citizen did not connect the event with its governing body and suggested that the USTA change to a more distinctive logo.

Marmion was one of the people who was primarily responsible for sheperding the logo through its formative stages and introducing it at the USTA Annual meeting in 1991. It turned out to be a very important contribution.

"A lot of people had no idea that the USTA ran the US Open," Marmion says. "The logo began to appear at the stadium and people connected the USTA with the US Open."

Marmion's impressive management skills were first honed in 1953, when he served as an infantry officer in Japan at the conclusion of the Korean War. He remained active in the reserves throughout his tenure as the president of two colleges (St. Xavier in Chicago and Southampton College in Long Island) and as a university vice president for academic affairs at Fairleigh Dickinson University. He retired as a colonel in the Marine Corps Reserve.

Harry and his wife Pat have served as the honorary chairmen of the hall of fame dinner in the past and acquaintances point out that Pat is very supportive of Harry's USTA involvement, and no small part of his success. The two have three daughters, Sara, Sheila and Elizabeth, and three grandchildren. Sarah and Sheila are both vice presidents of major public relations firms in New York, while Elizabeth is the president of a health care agency in Westerly, Rhode Island.

Harry has a little tennis administration to take care of at home, and then he has several more ideas for the USTA in the future.

"One of my daughters is married to a professional golfer," says Harry. "They have a son who may need to be swayed. I may need to step in and push the tennis a little."

Marmion feels that issues which need to be addressed in the future at the USTA include bringing the Davis Cup back, winning the Federation Cup and continuing to improve the communications and public relations functions of the USTA so that the public knows exactly what the USTA is all about.

Those who know Harry feel that even with all he has done and continues to do at the national level, his induction tonight is unique because of what he has done for Eastern tennis in particular.

He is someone who has "served above and beyond his duties" according to one colleague, having continued his service to the ETA "even when he had national responsibilities which is a rare thing for someone to do."

"Harry is a true ETA person and that is noteworthy," says former ETA president Dick Scheer. "He has always found the time to contribute to the ETA. He is very dedicated and he is always available."

--By Cara Griffin

Gene Mayer

It doesn't seem quite fair to define Gene Mayer in terms of his family. After all, on his own merit he is one of the top players ever to emerge from the Eastern section. And for that matter, he is one of the top American players of his time. It's hard to escape the facts, though.

Gene's brother Sandy was recently inducted into the Northern California Hall of Fame, which coupled with Gene's induction tonight make it a unique year for the honored brothers. The two were singularly successful throughout their careers, but doubly remarkable when one considers the reality of such athletic success being attained by even one, not to mention two members of a family. Sandy and Gene were the first brothers to win a Grand Slam title together (the 1979 French Open) since the Kinseys in 1929, and the Mayers are the only brothers in the open era to rank in the top ten simultaneously.

Both were coached by their father, Dr. Alex Mayer, a man colleagues held in the highest regard. "He had to be one of the greatest coaches there ever was. He was opinionated and outspoken as most good coaches are, but he was just a great, great coach." This from a man whose program has guided more American champions to maturity (including Sandy and Gene and those other brothers, Patrick and John) than any other, Stanford's Dick Gould.

It was his father who hung tennis balls above Gene's crib as most parents might dangle mobiles of airplanes or teddy bears. And it was Dad who encouraged Gene to spend hours knocking a ping pong ball against the living room wall. This early maturation of his natural ability could account for the quick hands that Gene had on the court, alternately described by spectators as "remarkable," "soft," "creative," "marvelous" and simply "great." Gene developed into a player described by a 1981 journalist as someone who "sparkled in his inimitable way, with his distinctive style of play, featuring two fisted strokes off both sides and marvelous touch on the drop shot, and a game full of rich talent and stroke diversity."

The talent was always there, and the potential first flourished on a grand scale as Gene won the national 12s two years running in 1967 and 1968. He played with a one handed backhand at that time, and with a two handed forehand. Running around that backhand proved successful, until his post Stanford days when the two handed backhand became its own weapon. The forehand was always a weapon.

"Gene had what has to be considered the greatest two handed forehand of all time," Gould offers. "Certainly you would have to consider Pancho Segura who had a good one. Segura is in that league, but Genie's was just incredible."

That wicked forehand certainly made believers out of his competitors as Gene spent the peak of his career as the third rated man in the United States and fourth in the world. It was his bad luck that the men ahead of him happened to be certain Messieurs Connors, McEnroe and Borg. It was in 1978 that he picked up the first of two Grand Slam titles, the doubles with Hank Pfister at the French. The next year he won the doubles at Roland Garros again, this time with Sandy.

He played Davis Cup in 1982 and 1983, winning the Cup in 1982. The 1982 U.S. Davis Cup team featured Gene and John McEnroe at the singles spots. In the finals against France, the U.S. won 4-1, with Gene scoring an important 6-2, 6-2, 7-9, 6-4 victory over Henri Leconte in the second singles match of the opening day.

Beyond tennis, Gene is recognized as a giving individual. He is one of the many distinguished Stanford alums responsible for the state of the art tennis center at the school, and he is a leader among world class players in his devotion to wheelchair tennis.

"He has flown in here a couple of times at his own expense to appear at some fundraising exhibitions," Gould says of Gene's contributions to his alma mater. "That helped us a lot; he was very quick to come back."

Dan Dwyer lauds Gene as being a genuine backer of the disabled, and way ahead of his time in his attention to providing tennis opportunities for all players.

"Gene is the honorary chairman of the National Tennis Association for the Disabled," says Dwyer. "He has always been very involved, from day one, 14 years ago, before anyone else, certainly before any of the top players. Go back about ten years ago, and you can see his sense of humor. There's an incident that I have always wanted to get back at him for. I was playing in a wheelchair exhibition at Madison Square Garden. The match was two able bodied players against two in wheelchairs, and as you can imagine, the noise inside the Garden was just incredible. Genie was the honorary MC. There were shots being hit back and forth, and it was loud, and then suddenly there was this dead silence and a voice over the loudspeaker says: 'People in wheelchairs move faster than Danny.' It was Gene. It was also true."

--By Cara Griffin

Holcombe Ward

The next time you toss the ball up and prepare to strike a serve, remember to thank Holcombe Ward. It was around the turn of the century that Ward, along with some help from Harvard classmate Dwight Davis, developed what is commonly known as the American twist service. It was the first of many contributions that he would make to the game.

Tennis historian Alan Trengove writes, "Ward was so color blind that to him all tennis courts looked brown. He made up for this affliction by continually testing the eyesight of his opponents with sharply twisting services. It was his relatively short stature that prompted him to acquire the twist service as an equalizer. It gave him time to get to the net where he was an adroit volleyer."

At the turn of the century, a time when sports were becoming more and more a part of the American consciousness, Ward joined Davis in "growing the game" both nationally and internationally. It was on a trip to California to promote interest in tennis that Ward and two other Harvard undergraduates were witness to Davis' idea of starting a tennis competition between Britain and the United States. This brainstorm was the origin of Davis Cup matches.

In the first ever Davis Cup tie in 1900, Ward teamed with Davis to clinch the 3-0 victory over the British Isles with a doubles win. Ward even decided the draw when he picked the names out of a straw hat before the matches. The twisting, tricky serve that the duo had been working on is said to have bedeviled the Brits, playing a major role in the United States' capture of the Cup.

The British players, shocked to have been beaten by the Americans, complained that the grass was long, the nets were sagging and the ground was soft at the Longwood Cricket Club in Boston. British player Roper Barrett continued, "As for the balls, I hardly like to mention them. They were awful, soft and mothery-and when served with the American twist came at you like an animated egg-plum. The serve not only swerved in the air, but in hitting the ground, broke surely four to five feet...it quite nonplused us."

Trengove accurately points out that this experience would be the first of many to come where a visiting opponent found that home court advantage, along with local environment and climate, could be all important in a Davis Cup tie.

Ward's individual accomplishments as a player were superior. He was in the United States top ten for seven years, reaching the No. 1 spot in 1904. He garnered seven major U.S. Championships, including six doubles titles and the 1904 singles crown. He was a member of four Davis Cup squads between 1900 and 1906.

After his competitive playing career ended, Ward continued on as a businessman (he was a cotton broker in New York) and as a dedicated volunteer to several tennis associations. Ward was named to the executive committee of the national tennis association by Dr. James Dwight early in the century and went on to become a member of several national tennis committees in the 1920s and 1930s. Appointed to chair the USLTA Amateur Rules Committee in 1924, he resigned from that post in 1931 to chair the Davis Cup and International Play Committees.

Ward's contributions as the Amateur Rules Committee chair were crucial, as he presided at a time when several of the USLTA's finest players were being enticed to the professional ranks. Allison Danzig wrote of Ward's actions during this time span: "Anyone knowing his sensitiveness and extreme antipathy to becoming involved in anything remotely approaching the air of controversy in public can appreciate how strong was the sense of duty that kept him in this work during the years of bitter controversy over the player-writer interpretation of the amateur rules...It was nothing unusual for Ward to stay up all hours of the night, analyzing and sifting evidence against the player and seeking a loophole for him. But once he made up his mind that there had been a violation, he gave no quarter...his work on the committee was unsurpassed in its devotion to the good of the game."

Ward went on to become the Eastern Lawn Tennis Association President from 1932-33 and the United States Lawn Tennis President from 1937-47. He played the game well into his seventies and died at the age of 88 in 1967.

--By Cara Griffin

Chapter 17

1997: Garry, J. McEnroe, McNeill and Myers

Robert J. Garry

When Bob Garry joined the United States Tennis Association as its first controller in 1970, the membership of the organization was 50,000 and the annual operating budget was less than one half million dollars.

Now, 27 years later, a few things have changed. Garry's role within the association has grown, and in turn so has the USTA. Under the recent staff reorganization, Garry is the USTA Director of the Administration Division, and is responsible for the approximately $130 million dollar operating budget which he has aided the USTA in gaining through his expertise over the past 27 years.

And while all of this is impressive, and indicative of the kind of dedication and intelligence which Garry brings to his position, it is his service above and beyond the call of duty that brings him to this induction ceremony here tonight.

"Before I started with the USTA, I was working with Arthur Andersen," Garry said. "My wife was complaining that I worked too much overtime."

When one of Andersen's clients, the U.S. Lawn Tennis Association, was searching for some help, Garry's name popped up and he soon found himself with a new job. Yet, if you are trying to reach Bob Garry early in the morning or in the evening, or even on the weekend, he's probably working. Suffice it to say, his wife Kathy has not solved the overtime problem.

"Right before he took the job at the USTA, I was pregnant," says Kathy. "He was working weekends and nights. Of course, at the USTA he has worked even more, but it has been fun.

"We have been to places we never would have been to and we have really grown up with the USTA."

When Garry first started at the USTA, the association had seven full time employees. That number has now grown to approximately 200, including the sections.

Working with Eastern's Junior Tennis Foundation, Garry has been involved with similar growth. The JTF is the beneficiary of the Hall of Fame, and the success of the event, coupled with Garry's work as treasurer, has enabled the Foundation to donate over $130,000 in grants over the past two years to tennis programs for juniors and for the mentally and physically challenged.

One of his many topics of concern at the USTA lately has been the US Open construction project. The new stadium is sort of a novelty in the building of professional sports stadiums because the USTA is virtually taking the entire cost on itself.

"When he is on his vacation and we are not away, he sneaks into the office at night and checks over all of his mail just to catch up," reveals Kathy. "Otherwise he says it would take him three weeks to catch up."

And when the opening ceremony of the new USTA National Tennis Center and Arthur Ashe Stadium takes place later this year, it will have special significance for Garry. The neighborhood is familiar for him, as he grew up in Woodside, just a miss-hit away from both Forest Hills and the National Tennis Center.

"I went to the same grammar school as (USTA President) Harry Marmion," says Garry. "Of course, 15 years apart. We never played tennis in my neighborhood as kids, that just wasn't a sport that kids played. We were more into baseball and basketball."

This summer when the public facility's new design is unveiled, it will be two boys from Woodside who can stand proudly and say they helped make it happen.

How Garry has found time in addition to his national tennis duties to help out the Junior Tennis Foundation, wheelchair tennis, local little league baseball and various other organizations is a question even Kathy can't answer.

"He is so quiet about it that I don't even know all the things he is doing," says Kathy. "Sometimes I am even surprised. One time we were at an annual meeting and he was being introduced and they were talking about all the things he is involved in and I looked at the person next to me and said, 'Is this the same guy I live with?'"

--By Cara Griffin

John McEnroe

The familiar headbands and youthful mane have disappeared, and the feisty scowl on his face has mellowed a bit since the days when he ruled center court at Wimbledon, the US Open and in Davis Cup play.

John McEnroe is sporting more subdued close cropped locks now, befitting his new image as an authoritative television personality, a connoisseur of art, a philanthropist and chairman of the late Arthur Ashe's Safe Passage Foundation for inner-city children. But the passion McEnroe reserves for the tennis courts he still frequents as a senior player and the memory of his brilliant, often turbulent career remain the essence of his appeal.

McEnroe is one of the greatest tennis players of all time and makes everybody's 20th century list of great New Yorkers and geniuses of sport. For sheer competitive drive, skill and desire, his accomplishments as the world's best player between the late 1970s and mid-1980s defined his sport, while his charisma mirrored the complex intensity of his native city.

John has held the world's No. 1 ranking 14 times during his professional tennis career and has earned the world's No. 1 ranking for the year four times – in 1981, 1982, 1983 and 1984.

He peaked in 1984 and tallied an impressive singles record of 82-3, winning 13 of 15 tournaments while playing his best matches on big occasions. He routed Jimmy Connors, 6-1, 6-2, 6-2, in the Wimbledon singles final and defeated Ivan Lendl, 6-3, 6-4, 6-1, to capture the US Open singles title. He sustained three losses: to Lendl (3-6, 2-6, 6-4, 7-5, 7-5, in the French final), Vijay Amritraj (first round, Cincinnati) and Henrik Sundstrom (13-11, 6-4, 6-3, U.S.-Swedish Davis Cup).

In all, John won 17 Grand Slam event titles – seven in singles: four US Opens and three Wimbledons; and ten in doubles: four US Opens, five Wimbledons and one French Championship.

His 155 combined professional singles and doubles titles – 77 in singles and 78 in doubles – is a record in the Open era. He holds the world record for the longest No. 1 ranking in doubles -- at 270 straight weeks, confirming his longtime partner Peter Fleming's view that "the best doubles team is John McEnroe and anybody else." John is also third on the all-time No. 1 ranking list in singles, having earned the top spot for 170 weeks.

In U.S. Davis Cup competition, John is 41-8 in singles and 18-2 in doubles (14 of them with Fleming) and he holds multiple records: most victories – 59; most matches played – 69; most years played, 12; and most team matches played, 30. He played on five Cup-winning teams – in 1978, '79, '81, '82 and '92.

Hints of his future heroics began in Douglaston, Queens. John's mother, Kay, remembers that at the age of seven-and-a-half, he'd get on his bike at 8 a.m. with a bag of lunch, cross Northern Blvd. and go to the Douglaston Club to hit tennis balls all day. By age nine he was the kid to beat.

The club's head pro George Seewagen was impressed and advised McEnroe's parents to send him to the Port Washington Tennis Academy. "Suddenly here I am with Vitas Gerulaitis, Fleming and all the top Eastern players," John said. "It was like, wow…"

"I first met John when he was 12 and I was 16," Fleming recalls. "I thought he was pretty good, but nothing special…I started bragging that I could beat this kid. I was so sure…I said I would give him a 4-0, 30-0 lead in every set. I lost 5 sets in a row. I realized right then that John doesn't ever give up."

In 1977 John went public. He and his Douglaston friend Mary Carillo won the mixed doubles title at the French Open. Two kids from Queens. The presses started rolling. A few weeks later he qualified for the main draw in Gentlemen's Singles at Wimbledon and went all the way to the semis. At summer's end we rushed to watch him play his first US Open at West Side on an intimate outside court. You could hear people say: "What's all the fuss about? This guy hits all junk." John's reaction to that news brief was succinct: "That was my game plan," he said. "I don't know who accused me of that, but that's why they were sitting watching and I was playing." Only the experts could appreciate the subtle distinction between junk and artistic genius then.

He left for college, won the 1978 NCAA singles championship as a Stanford freshman and turned pro.

In the late summer of 1979, John McEnroe came home to Douglaston and met Vitas Gerulaitis of Howard Beach in the US Open final that crowned a king of Queens. McEnroe emerged with a 7-5, 6-3, 6-3 victory to claim his first Grand Slam singles championship and teamed with Fleming to win the doubles title.

"Vitas was the big shot player in the East who we all looked up to and suddenly I'm 20 and he's 24 and we're playing in the US Open final," John said. "There was an emotional connection there, we were friends, so he was one of the last people I would have wanted to play in that situation. I don't think it will ever happen again – two guys from Queens playing for the US Open title.

"Winning the Open is a combination of everything and every emotion from joy to ecstasy to relief. When you win that final point you feel you can fly for that one second in time."

The neighborhood kids draped his home with toilet paper – usually reserved for celebrating high school sports night victories – and he started to get a little edgy from all the attention.

"It never really hit us, what was going on," recalls his brother Patrick, who was just turning 11 at the time of John's Wimbledon breakthrough. "I remember thinking, 'Wow, he made the semis at Wimbledon.' There were camera crews in our house. It was pretty wild. After that it all seemed pretty normal."

Now thirteen years removed from winning his last major singles title at the 1984 US Open, McEnroe reminisced about his career (although he emphasized that he has still not officially retired). He credits his dad (J.P.) for encouraging him and his brothers. "My father worked hard and took great pride in taking us to Port Washington and to tournaments," John said. "Dad would reassure me: 'You can do it, oh I know you can do it son.' My mom was more like, you get an education. She would only come to matches when she thought I was going to lose. So I knew I was in trouble if she came. But it was good to have mommy and daddy there in case you broke down after a loss. That's when you need them, when you bomb out."

Kay McEnroe said she never liked watching John play because she knew how much it meant to him to win. "John was a very sociable child who early on was competitive and relentless in playing sports," she said. "He was a football quarterback, a baseball pitcher and an All-Ivy soccer player. Once, when he was playing basketball at the Buckley Day School, he was fuming about a team member who didn't try hard enough. The headmaster, Mr. Oviatt, who also coached the basketball team, asked me to come in for a conference and said, 'The problem is, John thinks he's the coach.'"

Kay believes that John preferred tennis because he was in charge, he couldn't blame anyone else. Of course he eventually tried to make officials take responsibility.

Don Budge believes McEnroe was a great inspiration for kids in the modern tennis era. "Kids all over the world imitated him," Budge said. "John was…a genius and could do things with a racquet nobody else could do. And he has character; he always put himself out to play Davis Cup for his country….But out of frustration, John liked every call to be made the way it should be according to John."

Bob Davis, the national director of Ashe's Safe Passage Foundation, believes it was that very quality – McEnroe's reputation for refusing to compromise on the court -- that appeals to the foundation's children. "Kids relate to his passion and honesty…," Davis said. "He expressed the anger they feel in their own lives."

Asked if he has any regrets, John said, "I wouldn't call it regrets. I'm proud of my career. I feel I've represented more positives than negatives. You have to look at the whole package. All people wish they did some things differently, and I know I do a disservice to myself at times, but you can't go back and change anything. It's really up to people to decide what they want to remember. I hope they'll remember the good things I did in the game and not just the times I yelled at an umpire."

And who was his greatest rival? "My matches with [Bjorn] Borg were great because of the quality of the tennis," he said. "My matches with Jimmy [Connors] are memorable from a competitive standpoint. They were packed with intensity."

What was his proudest moment? "It's hard to pin down," he said. "It would have to be my Davis Cup triumphs."

So what is it about your spirit, John? Where did you get the passion and intensity that made you a champion?

"I really don't know; call my parents," John McEnroe said. "I've always been competitive with a will to win. And I believe it came out in a mostly positive way. Most people don't have that chance. I feel lucky."

-- By Nancy Gill McShea

William Donald McNeill

courtesy of International Tennis Hall of Fame

In 1940, Don McNeill had a year that contemporaries such as Jack Kramer, Bobby Riggs and Billy Talbert could only envy. That year he won the U.S. National Championships, the National Collegiate singles title and the U.S. National Clay Courts.

He was only 22, and at the peak of his playing career, but over the next five years McNeill would not be playing much tennis.

World War II called, and McNeill answered, enlisting in the U.S. Navy and spending time as a naval attaché in Buenos Aires before serving as an air commander in the Pacific. So 1940 would stand alone as the best year of McNeill's career, and one might conclude that the years stolen by the war would have been years dominated by Don McNeill.

"I would have to say that Don was the best player in the world in 1940," says Frank Guernsey, a former U.S. Davis Cup player and a doubles partner of McNeill's in the 1940s. "Bobby Riggs had been considered the number one player, but then Don had a great year and he beat Riggs in the U.S. finals. With the war, and Don joining the Navy, he was basically through playing tennis until 1946."

McNeill won his last major championship, the U.S. Indoors, in 1950, but his greatest legacy as a player was his brilliant run in 1939 and 1940.

"The war interrupted many careers back then and unfortunately my father's was one of them," said McNeill's daughter, Margaret McNeill Law. "If not, things would have been much different, to say the least."

And while it is true that McNeill's trophy case would have been a bit fuller had the war not occurred, it is doubtful that you would have heard him complaining.

"By the time we were growing up, he was not playing anymore, at least not seriously," says Margaret of her late father, who passed away in November at the age of 78. "He missed today's game's money, that all came along too late for him. But thanks to tennis he was able to travel the world and really do some amazing things."

McNeill's talents brought him a tennis scholarship to Ohio's Kenyon University in the late 1930s and in 1939 he was one of four American men invited to play an exhibition tennis tour in the Far East. This experience afforded McNeill the opportunity to go tiger hunting in India, to meet the Maharishi and in general, to live the life of royalty.

"I don't think players can do that today because it is such a grind," said Margaret. "But he was very lucky in that way. He led a wonderful life."

In the midst of this traveling exhibition tour in 1939, McNeill was able to fine tune his game against the world's best players. By the time he reached Paris, McNeill was primed and ready to win the French Championships. He did that in fine form, beating nemesis and world No.1 Riggs in the final.

"Don was a baseline player," says Guernsey. "And he just hit the ball so hard. He had a great serve and great ground-strokes. He was not a net-rusher, but he came in when he had the chance."

McNeill grew up in Oklahoma and spent summers traveling throughout the Midwest and Southwest, playing the bigger junior tournaments. He and Riggs had been battling each other since they were boys.

When the two met in the final of the 1940 U.S. Championships at Forest Hills, it was a contrast in personalities. McNeill was known as a gentleman and Riggs was more of a showman. Riggs went up two sets to none, but McNeill won the next two sets to set up an all or nothing fifth set.

After each man took one service break apiece, the score stood at 5-6 in the fifth, with Riggs serving.

McNeill would later recall, "Three things stand out in my memory of the last game with Riggs serving at 5-6. Riggs was unable to persuade the umpire that he had not touched the net and lost a point to make it 0-15. Undecided whether to throw the next point because Riggs swore he hadn't touched the net, I knocked his serve out. Although I had done this unintentionally, the fans cheered wildly, interpreting my bad return as a gesture of good sportsmanship. Score 15-all.

"On my first match point Riggs got to the net and made a fine volley, and I fell flat on my face trying to get a fast start for it. Then he had game advantage, when I hit an impossible forehand cross-court passing shot -- the best I ever hit in my life. It couldn't have come at a better time, as it so unnerved Riggs that he missed two difficult low volleys coming in behind his serve at deuce and match point. I got the feeling he was desperate. Riggs approaching the net after his service was a surprise...several years before his time, and besides, he wasn't that good of a volleyer." McNeill prevailed 4-6, 6-8, 6-3, 6-3, 7-5.

After serving in the war, McNeill settled down into the life of an advertising man on Madison Avenue. He raised his children and continued to play in his spare time. Winning the U.S. National Indoors in 1950 marked one last show of his greatness.

He would work for several advertising firms over the next few decades, playing an integral part in the Sanka "The coffee that lets you sleep" campaign. As his playing career receded further and further into the past, Margaret recalls her dad saying he would be "blown off the court" by the likes of McEnroe, Connors and Sampras.

"He loved to watch," she recalls. "He would watch as much tennis as possible on television. He was an arm chair coach and he would snicker at their antics."

"I asked him once what he was most proud of. And as he thought about it, I was expecting him to say winning the French or the U.S Championships, but he said it was a sportsmanship award. He had won just a little silver plate, but it was what he was most proud of. He was a gentleman."

--By Cara Griffin

Arvelia Myers

Andy Jacobs

Arvelia Myers began her tennis career sitting on a bench as she looked on at her friends playing on the courts. She liked what she saw, got off of the bench and onto the court. She hasn't looked back since.

"I started to play and I just fell in love with the game," recalls Myers. "A friend of mine played and asked me to watch. I started hitting against the wall and I picked it up and then just got a chance to get out on the courts and everything just grew from there."

A shy and humble person, Myers needed a little push from her friends to make her take her game to the next level.

"My friends got me to start playing New York City parks tournaments," recalls Myers. "People were sort of having to push me because I was not very competitive and a bit shy. But I started to do well and I began playing in the American Tennis Association."

Myers went on to become a ranked player in the ATA, at one time achieving a No. 3 national ATA ranking, and winning the ATA women's national doubles in 1973.

"Tennis has been my friend," said Myers. "Just from playing I have met so many people. They see me with a racquet and they say, 'You play?' And they say 'where?' And I tell them."

And what a story it is to tell. In 1973, Myers founded the Pyramid Tennis Association, and in the quarter century since, she has influenced scores of New York City youngsters in a positive way.

"She has this special way about her," says friend and student Sheila Jones. "Because her philosophy is that there is enough seriousness and stress in life. Tennis is just fun."

Making the game fun is important, but Myers will tell you that her main goal is to instill self confidence in her young students, making sure that they believe that they can succeed not only in tennis, but also in life.

"The Pyramid Tennis Association was founded as a program to help young people, particularly African Americans, in building self esteem and a sense of achievement," says Myers. "I am sneaky, because of course the real goal is to be sure they get an education, but I just sneak that in there. Not everyone can be a tennis champion, but youngsters have a lot to gain through sport."

Myers says her idol has always been Arthur Ashe. She met Arthur when he was just a boy and she was playing in adult ATA tournaments.

"He was this little thing, all arms and legs," she recalls. "I remember he was sitting on a bench really quietly watching the adults play. I told people, as they say in the Bible, he was taking names. And he was, because before long he could beat all of the adults.

"I called him my son," she says. "We were really never buddy buddy or anything, but we knew each other. In those days, when our kids played in tournaments, they would stay with people 'in the family' and he sometimes stayed with me n New York. I always knew Arthur would be a champion. I idolized his deportment and felt he was a great example for young people."

The young people in Myers' Pyramid Tennis Association program receive tutoring and are checked up on in school to make sure their grades are satisfactory. This is all part of Myers' aim to be sure each student gives his or her self the chance to get a college education.

"The really skilled players can get tennis scholarships and they may not become pros, says Myers, "but they can certainly get an education and then decide from there where they want to go. It gives them options. If a player is not so skilled, well at least they are building confidence through playing. They must have good grades to stay in the program, so maybe they can get a scholarship that way."

In addition to the Pyramid Tennis Association, Arvelia has worked with countless other programs in the city, serving as a mentor and a role model for literally thousands of youngsters.

Although the programs run year round, Arvelia's favorite time is the summer.

"In the summers we are out in the public parks," says Myers. "It means a lot to me to be out there teaching on the same courts that I learned on."

Even those who might not see her on the public courts may have been touched by her love for the game. Myers is one of the loyal USTA information booth volunteers who helps spread the word to the hundreds of thousands of fans at Flushing Meadows each year.

"Arvelia has always been one of our most loyal volunteers," says long time friend and USTA volunteer booth coordinator Barbara Williams.

"She has been a very important person to children," continues Williams. "In terms of education, she has always been a leader in having people continue on and go to college. Education has always been paramount to her."

What one most gets the sense of from Arvelia Myers is that she has built her life around tennis in order to give back what the game has given to her.

"The most satisfying thing is when they (students) go through college and come back home and call me and let me know how they are doing," she said.

"If a kid does not have a racquet, I try to get one in his hand. I am a shy person and tennis has opened a lot of doors for me. It helps bring people out of their shells. It helped me, and I try to do that for others."

-- By Cara Griffin

Chapter 18

1998: Dwyer, Hammond, Pratt and Reese

Daniel B. Dwyer

H E E E E E E E E R E ' S Danny!

Danny Dwyer is the Johnny Carson of tennis. He disarms audiences with the same sly charm as Carson, the same edgy sense of humor and the tenacity to put himself on the line for decades. Danny doesn't have an Ed McMahon to keep his show rolling, but his staff at the Point Set Indoor Racquet Club helps him tone down the "I want it done now!" mentality he brings to the business of recruiting people to the game.

"When you play Danny, all you have to do is kick your serve to his backhand and you'll win," joked veteran Point Set coach and referee Perry Aitchison. Danny's first retort to that news was unprintable. Then he deadpanned: "Ten years ago I would have run around my backhand; today I'll only play Perry if he's blindfolded."

Danny has the classic Irish temper dipped in honey. He's an optimist his brother, Jim, and sister-in-law, Marty, say. He believes the best is yet to come -- especially to those who are a little less powerful. If he thinks a cause is worth it, he gets involved and never looks back. The Dwyers cited a 1962 national incident Danny became involved in when he was playing tennis on scholarship at St. Edward's University in Austin, Texas. Acting officially in his role as the president of the student government, he sent a congratulatory telegram to James Meredith, the first African-American to be accepted into the University of Mississippi. His gesture showed up in local newspapers, he received death threats from the Ku Klux Klan and 20 classmates stood guard outside his dormitory room.

Brother Raymond Fleck, C.S.C., the university's president, summoned him to his office. Danny said, "You can't tell me that sending the telegram to Meredith was wrong. It's what you taught us." Brother Fleck replied, 'It's not wrong. But maybe you could do it more quietly in the future. We just lost a $10,000 donation.'

"I'm a rebel if there's a cause." Danny said. "I've spent most of my life trying to eliminate prejudice of any kind; it's the biggest waste of human energy."

In the late 1970s, he got a phone call from a wheelchair athlete who wanted to enter a tennis tournament. He quickly made Point Set wheelchair-accessible and began hosting one of the country's first, free wheelchair tennis clinics. By the mid-1980s, he had founded the National Tennis Association for the Disabled and the international Lichtenberg Buick-Mazda wheelchair tournament. He became the USTA's first wheelchair committee chairman, and this past January was one of five people appointed -- and the only American -- to serve on the International Tennis Federation wheelchair committee.

Danny's children, Shawn and Kimberly, grew up feeling comfortable around physically and mentally challenged people. George McFadden once beat Bobby Curran in a wheelchair match, took a shower and walked out of the locker room wearing his prosthesis. Kimberly, then 7, ran to her father in tears: "Daddy, we have to disqualify that man; he beat Bobby, and he can walk."

In Danny's world, tennis-careers-in-the-making seem to depend on who's picking up the tennis balls. In 1952 at age 12, he retrieved balls for Alex Mayer at the Burwood courts in Flushing for 25 cents an hour just to hear what the great coach had to say. Every once in a while, Mayer would give him 20 minutes of his time. "I started as a maintenance person and became a club manager," Danny said. "You never know what's going to happen."

A young Mary Carillo picked up tennis balls for Danny at the Douglaston Club and you know what happened to her: She went on to win a Grand Slam title and become one of the sport's most visible television analysts.

"I would stand outside the fence and listen to him teach," Mary said. "He didn't realize he was teaching two people. We all grew up with Danny. He totally shaped my life. You always wanted to catch his eye. He had such a presence and still does. When I was inducted into Eastern's Hall of Fame (in 1994) my brother Charles said, 'Good God, he looks like a Monsignor now.'

"I asked Danny that night how much he charged back then. He said 8 bucks an hour. I said to him, 'Well, I owe you about $400,000. Will you take a check?'"

Danny tells his junior students that their goal should be No. 1 in the world. When parents tell him their kids just want a respectable ranking for a college scholarship, he says frankly: "You wouldn't complain if I was pushing your child to get into Harvard. Go for the gold even if you only wind up with a bronze. Otherwise, why play tennis?"

He had used that tactic with ten-year-old John McEnroe when McEnroe won a tournament at the Douglaston Club. "You will play at Forest Hills some day," Danny told him, and it worked! He has challenged other famous Eastern juniors he's worked with—among them Sandy and Gene Mayer -- and they took him seriously, too.

"Danny was there at the beginning," John McEnroe said. "He helped me when we first joined the club and started to learn the game. I want to personally thank him tonight on behalf of myself and my family for being there."

Danny has risen through the ranks as a player and coach to become one of the game's most visible national and international administrators. He is the manager and part owner of Point Set in Oceanside, N.Y. He has also been the head pro at the Woodmere Country Club for 40 years. For four years, he was a tournament director at the New York City Mayor's Cup, the world's largest interscholastic event, with over 800 participants. He chaired the Catholic High School

Tennis League when he taught biology and English at his alma mater, Holy Cross, in Flushing. He has served in every volunteer position on the USTA Eastern board -- from Long Island regional vice president to president of the section and the Junior Tennis Foundation. He was among the first sectional leaders to support league and schools programs for recreational players. He has also been inducted into the St. Edward's and Holy Cross Halls of Fame.

"He's compassionate," Danny's brother Jim said. "He could have made more money when he graduated from college, but he went back to teach at Holy Cross to repay them for helping him get a scholarship. He's the champion of those who need a break. He'll push them forward. It doesn't always work but he never gives up. He follows through."

"Danny is a blessing." Marty Dwyer added. "He's Santa Claus."

-- By Nancy Gill McShea

Frank M. Hammond

Chances are you can tap your memory bank and run an instant replay of Frank Hammond's tennis career. Frank was the irrepressible official who was so intensely immersed in his craft, he allowed you to peek into his soul when he was calling a match. His resonant voice still echoes through the corridors of the sport almost three years after his death from Lou Gehrig's disease on November 23, 1995.

"Frank addressed the crowd like a conductor," his friend George Plimpton said at a memorial service for Hammond in his native Manhattan.

"To Frank, being a personality was at least as important as being an official," his friend Gene Scott added recently.

Frank's flair for the dramatic gave him a visibility comparable to the players. When in the chair, he leaned forward with a sense of urgency to get a clearer view, and on the line he virtually grazed the court with his nose and chin. He was so reliable, he was chosen to preside at famous tennis arenas all over the world. He was so recognizable, tennis fans clamored for his autograph.

Known as "Buddy" to his family, Frank was an active junior player in the 1940s who found his niche at age 15 when a dispute was brewing on a California tennis court. "Someone said, 'Get out there Frank and keep score,'" his sister Joan Hammond Brewster remembers. By the 1970s he had become the first full-time professional linesman and umpire. He called lines at the US Open for 34 years and worked the chair for 35 years. He is the only person who has won the Junior and Senior McGovern Awards for umpire service to tennis. He was also a wheelchair tennis board member and worked with underprivileged and handicapped children.

According to Bud Collins' *Modern Encyclopedia of Tennis*, Frank once said he umpired more than 5,000 matches and ran 500 tournaments as a referee without one major incident. But in the blink of an eye during the 1979 US Open at Flushing Meadows, Frank lost control of a second-round match between John McEnroe and Ilie Nastase. The debacle turned into a nightmarish "15 minutes of fame" that would dog the meticulous umpire – yet give him even more celebrity -- for life. Television news broadcasts flashed images of Frank disqualifying Nastase in the fourth set for stalling, and his discourse with the players still reverberates on the air in famous sports clips.

A near-riot had erupted in the crowd. Spectators booed for almost 20 minutes, and some ran onto the court while others began fighting in the audience. The tournament referee, Mike Blanchard, relieved Frank of his chair duties and climbed into the chair himself following a directive from Bill Talbert, the tournament director, who ordered that the match be resumed. McEnroe won and went on to beat his New York friend, Vitas Gerulaitis, for his first US Open singles title.

"That match was one of the few times I behaved," John said, "but Ilie was begging, pleading to be defaulted. Frank was unfairly removed from the chair which basically ruined his career.

"Frank was my favorite umpire. I hope that's a compliment! He always tried to encourage players as opposed to reprimanding them. I wish he had been inducted with me last year (into Eastern's Hall of Fame)."

Frank's rapport with the players seems to be his real legacy. He once told his sister Joan: "Andre Agassi is a very good and thoughtful young man. When he thought I was dying…he came to visit me in the hospital with Brooke Shields and gave me a *Born Again* bible. He wrote inside, 'To the Greatest Umpire That Ever Was. I'm going to miss you. You'll always be in my prayers.'"

Gene Scott can tell you a hundred stories about Frank. "In a world where not everybody is nice -- people can be grumpy -- he was fun to be around. Everywhere we went, he went," said Gene, who enlisted Frank to help him run five professional tournaments (in Westchester; Orange, N.J.; the Bahamas; the Nabisco Masters in New York; and the Kremlin Cup in Russia).

"Frank was a great ally for our tournaments. He was our master of ceremonies, our official on-court announcer, our referee. He was our host."

Gene remembers that Frank also had a very "Frank Mouth." During his illness, Gene kept a constant vigil at his friend's bedside, often accompanied by his daughter, Lucy, and his wife, Polly, who at the time was expecting their second child, Sam. When the disease had sapped Frank of his ability to speak, or even to write, Gene would go alone and devise ways to perk up his friend's spirits. "You can't keep a secret," Gene said to him one day. "No one knows the gender of my unborn child except me. It's a boy, and you can't tell anyone." Frank started crying from laughing so hard. Tears were running down his cheeks. Six days later he died.

Frank once said in assessing his career, "I can honestly say I never showboated in my life. I used my voice to control everyone, tried to thank the crowd in different ways and tried not to use the same phraseology all the time…You don't want everyone imitating Frank Hammond because that would be the worst thing for the game. But what you do want are people in the chair who are going to overrule calls and do the job with consistency."

"Buddy wanted to be a player," his sister Joan said, recalling that her brother worked hard at tennis when he attended Iona Prep in New Rochelle, N.Y., and played first singles for the Blair Academy tennis team in Blairstown, N.J. "He couldn't go too far because he had polycystic kidney disease. Instead, he started calling lines. In tennis, he grew from Buddy into Frank. Tennis gave him his self respect."

-- By Nancy Gill McShea

Betty Rosenquest Pratt

If you're a young girl who takes for granted her right to go the distance in sports along with the boy next door, tip your cap to Betty Rosenquest Pratt, who almost 60 years ago qualified for the second singles spot on her South Orange, N.J., high school boys' tennis team, and didn't give up when she got the boot for winning a match in competition.

Girls' teams didn't exist, Betty said, but the state athletic association decided it would be mentally harmful to young boys if girls beat them at their own game. She practiced instead at the Berkeley Tennis Club with her tennis buddy, Dick Savitt, who went on to win the 1951 Australian and Wimbledon men's singles titles.

Now fast forward about 25 years to 1966, and if you're a woman who plays in a local tennis league to indulge her competitive fantasies, credit Betty for co-founding the National Women's Tennis Association to give you a realistic goal. Until then, women aged 40 to 80 played one of the few nationals available -- the over-40 grass courts at Point Judith, Rhode Island -- and now there are more than 80 national titles up for grabs (in both singles and doubles in multiple age groups).

Betty turned 73 last week and reminisced about her life in tennis with a radiance you would expect from someone who just last month was chauffeured in a bright yellow, 1926 Chevrolet convertible to watch the unveiling of the newly named "Betty Pratt Stadium" at her home courts at the Racquet Club at Heathrow in Florida. She speaks with the certainty of an athlete who was once ranked fifth in the United States, among the world's top ten, and who played on center court at Wimbledon and the U.S. National Championships in the semifinal round of singles.

"I am more competitive than athletic," Betty said, correcting the observation.

The real message in Betty's story, though, is that she has hurdled life's passages with grace, evolving from a four-time *World Tennis* magazine cover girl, who had a youthful fling in Grand Slam events, into a respected senior player. She has managed to juggle career, marriage and family and hang on to her competitive – yet generous – spirit. During the 1950s and early '60s, she helped her husband Carroll Pratt direct the Caribbean tennis circuit and together they raised their three children – John, Anne and Richard. She has taught tennis professionally for over 20 years, won 75 U.S. Tennis Association national senior titles, six ITF world championships and has also captained the U.S. Wightman and Federation Cup teams.

Her trophy shelf is filled with memories of battles won and lost and honors earned for sportsmanship and volunteer service. In 1943 she won the National Junior Tennis Sports Award and was named captain of the first Junior Wightman Cup team. "I made the national junior semis twice," she said. "Unfortunately, Doris Hart was my age, but I once had her match point."

Betty moved on to Rollins College in Florida to study English and psychology, and in her senior year won the Algernon Sidney Sullivan Award for citizenship. "When I was at Rollins we entertained the troops at bases and hospitals by playing tennis against the officers," she said. "The enlisted men loved it when we beat them." In the 1960s the USTA honored her with the Marlboro and Service Bowl Awards for outstanding contributions to the game as a volunteer and player.

"I loved tennis from the start," said Betty, whose family doctor suggested when she was ten that she give up touch football and play golf or tennis to channel her nervous energy. Her dad knew she loved to run so they chose tennis. Her dad also knew she was a tomboy when she came home furious one day because Teddy Palmer had grabbed her books and run. She ran after him, hit him over the head and got the books back. Dad said, "That's a mistake; you're not supposed to catch him."

She first played tennis in Bronxville, N.Y., and Alice Marble was her idol. "I wore shorts and a cap like she did and tried to emulate her aggressive, all-court game," Betty said. She moved to South Orange at age 14 and developed that style practicing with Savitt. "I was two years older than Dick, so I was the aggressor. All he did was run and get the ball back. Then he went away for a year. When he came back he had grown four or five inches and so had his game. He beat me easily."

There were few indoor courts in the East, so Betty's Dad drove her to play at the Harlem Armory in Manhattan every Friday night. She first met Althea Gibson there, who would beat her, 11-9, 6-1, in the semis of the 1956 U.S. National Championships.

Betty made six trips to Wimbledon and considered two of them especially memorable. In 1954 she lost in the semis to Maureen Connolly. "She killed me," Betty said, "but I was thrilled to be there. I won the equivalent of $75 and a bronze medal." In 1957 she played England's new hope, Christine Truman, in the quarterfinals. "When I walked into the stadium I knew I wasn't just playing one person; this was very special. We had wonderful points in a close three setter. There was exhilaration, I was playing at the peak of competition in my mind. I felt in a way I had even won the crowd near the end. When Chris boomed the last forehand away and won, I ran up to the net as though I had won. I was very excited for her because England had waited so long for someone to come through.

"Tennis has been my life," Betty Rosenquest Pratt said. "I've made friends all over the world. When you arrive in a country with a tennis racquet in your hand you get an entirely different greeting. You don't even have to speak the same language. We are welcomed into homes instead of going to museums and looking in from the outside.

"I feel I'll be playing until they pick me up, find another partner for my partner and carry on with the game."

-- By Nancy Gill McShea

John R. Reese

John Reese has attained international stature in tennis circles as the volunteer chairman of the International Tennis Hall of Fame in Newport, Rhode Island. He has taught his daughters, Victoria and Augusta, by example that a regard for humanity and quality volunteer work will determine their legacy more than titles earned in business, or even in tennis -- his lifelong passion.

Arthur Ashe recalled in his memoir, "Days of Grace," that he "felt anxiety rising" as he approached a good friend's black-tie birthday party the day after he told the world he had AIDS. He wondered how the other guests would respond to him. "The first person I saw," Ashe wrote, "was an old friend, John Reese. An investment banker now, in his youth John had been an up-and-coming star with me in junior tennis. He saw me, and hurried over. There was no mistaking the warmth of his greeting, his genuine concern but also his understanding of my predicament. We walked inside together and I had a fine time at the celebration."

Hope Reese, John's wife of 31 years, said, "Embracing a friend who is in trouble is important to John. He knows instinctively that a gesture can have a powerful impact on someone. One of the reasons he has been so successful as a fund-raiser and volunteer is that he finds his own rewards in life. I would use the words integrity and generosity to describe him."

Those character traits can be traced to his origins. John's parents, Frances and the late Willis Reese, brought him up to "participate even if there is no financial reward." Willis was a professor of law at Columbia University and among the first to do volunteer arbitration work in New York for less fortunate community groups. Frances spearheaded the Scenic Hudson Preservation Council, which, together with other groups, won an environmental class action suit against Con Edison to stop polluting the Hudson River.

In 1995, Frances Reese joined co-honorees Leah Rabin and Queen Noor in receiving the Eleanor Roosevelt Award for volunteer efforts.

"The perks of volunteer work are that people appreciate what you're doing and there is a satisfaction in watching an activity flourish that you have a passion for," John Reese said. "It can be exhausting and become politicized but you don't get personal feedback as often in business."

A general partner at Lazard Freres & Company in New York for the past 13 years, John has also served as a board trustee and officer for more than 10 organizations, ranging form the arts, to hospitals, schools and the Cold Spring Harbor Laboratory (a world-renowned genetic research institution headed by James Watson, half of the Crick & Watson team who discovered the code of DNA). The list includes several sports associations, among them the USTA Eastern Section. In the mid-1970s, he was Eastern's vice president and a member or the committee that nominated Barbara Williams to become the first woman president of a USTA section.

Afterward, John took a five-year sabbatical from tennis volunteer work until one day in the early 1980s when he was playing tennis with his friend, Jane Brown. At the time, Jane was the executive director of the International Tennis Hall of Fame. She introduced John to Joe Cullman, the chairman, who invited him to sit on the board. John has since served in every capacity at Newport and was named board chairman in 1995.

A lifelong resident of Long Island, John was ranked first in Eastern tennis boys' 15 and under division, and several times among the section's top-five players, during the 1950s and 1960s. In 1957 he won the sectional junior Chamber of Commerce qualifier and represented New York at the organization's national tournament in Corpus Christi, Texas. "The ETA gave me a special opportunity when I was growing up to have fun," John said.

"We had our heroes. Gene Scott and Herb Fitz Gibbon were a little older, and they were players who really made it. Most of us weren't at that level, but it didn't diminish the joy of dreams and the excitement of legends. The greatest fun was watching Australia play the United States at Forest Hills in the (1956) Davis Cup. Ken Rosewall versus Vic Seixas and Tony Trabert against Lew Hoad. Bill Talbert and Harry Hopman were the captains. They are all hall of famers and reminders of the rich history of our sport."

John took his tennis dreams to the University of Pennsylvania in the early 1960s and captained the tennis and squash teams. He won the Eastern Collegiate singles and doubles tennis championships, and was ranked first in the country in squash in singles and doubles. In 1967 he earned his MBA from Penn and in 1997 was elected to his alma mater's Tennis Hall of Fame.

Victoria and Augusta Reese agree that because sports are so dear to their father's heart, perhaps not so coincidentally, both girls married great athletes. John always offered them advice by using an analogy to sports as the premise. "He'd say, 'See your teacher as your coach and your classmates as teammates. That way you'll get a better focus in learning your subject,'" Augusta recalled. She also said that when she and Victoria were getting married, he was so excited at the idea of having boys in the family; he was out buying Christmas presents at sporting goods stores for his sons-in-law before they walked down the aisle.

Victoria added that her father was always able to beat much younger tennis players, which turned out to be a great screening process for her potential suitors. "Dad would play them, and set me up with blind dates he considered worthy candidates."

Willis Reese would surely give a nod of approval to his son's work at the International Tennis Hall of Fame, especially the museum restoration project and the "City of the Year" outreach program, which provides tennis instruction and competition for inner-city youths. "My father wanted me to be a great tennis player," John said. "And while I wasn't, he would have enjoyed seeing me at Newport sitting between Don Budge and Jack Kramer talking tennis."

-- By Nancy Gill McShea

Chapter 19

1999: Fitz Gibbon II, Savitt, Viebranz and Weir

Herbert S. Fitz Gibbon 11

With a little imagination, you can hear the restless energy of life's rite of passage exploding off young Herb Fitz Gibbon's racquet, as he traversed the world's tennis courts in the 1960s and early '70s and transformed himself from a scholar-athlete into a prominent businessman and philanthropist.

Fitz Gibbon played the U.S. National Championships and the US Open at Forest Hills ten times, from 1961-1973, and was ranked among the world's top 20 during the crossover years between amateur and professional tennis. The U.S. singles draws from that period show that Fitz Gibbon changed his place of residence three times during those transition years in his life.

In the early 1960s, when he captained and played first singles for the Princeton Tennis team, he was listed in the (amateur) U.S. Championships draws as Herbert S. Fitz Gibbon 11 of Garden City, N.Y. (his childhood hometown). He beat Stan Smith in 1964 and was ranked 14th in the country. In 1965 he lost 12-10 (in the fourth set) to semifinalist Rafael Osuna of Mexico. By December of that year, he was a member of the U.S. Davis Cup team and upset Arthur Ashe, 6-2, 14-12, 9-7, at the Victorian Championships in Melbourne, Australia.

While serving in the U.S. Army in 1967, he appeared in the U.S. Championships draw as Pfc. Herbert S. Fitz Gibbon of West Point, N.Y. He beat Erik Van Dillen and lost to his friend Clark Graebner. Earlier in the summer, he had won the silver medal at the Pan-American Games in Canada.

The game turned professional in 1968 and the U.S. Championships was renamed the US Open. Fitz Gibbon became the first amateur to beat a professional at Wimbledon when he upset No. 16 seed Nikki Pilic of Yugoslavia in four sets. But he skipped the Open that summer and played the European clay circuit.

When he returned to the Open in 1969, he had started working as a stockbroker and was listed in the draw as Herbert Fitz Gibbon of New York City. By 1979, six years after he lost to No. 9 seed Jimmy Connors in his final appearance at the Open, he had co-written a book, *The Complete Sports Player* (with Jeff Barstow), and joined Oppenheimer Capital, Inc. Today, he is the managing director.

"Bill Talbert was the model, he did it better than anyone. He went to college and used tennis as an entrée into business, "Fitz Gibbon said. "I wasn't (initially) considered a brilliant analyst but it has been my greatest achievement. I was supposed to do well in sports."

He grew up playing tennis for its own merit and competed at the highest level when there was no financial incentive. The professional game was tempting, but his educational background and the necessity for stability in the real world won out.

"There's something very special about doing one thing very well," Fitz Gibbon says now. "It gives you tremendous satisfaction that you will savor all your life, and it allows you to appreciate the accomplishments of other people."

He started playing tennis at age 7 at the Cherry Valley Country Club in Garden City and went on to win some 50 tournaments, among them four New York State High School singles titles. In his senior year at Princeton, he went undefeated, as his team beat Miami, who had tallied 137 straight victories. He graduated from Princeton in 1964, taught ancient medieval and modern European history for a year at St. Paul's School in his hometown and then headed back to the tennis courts. During his years on the amateur circuit, Fitz Gibbon and his buddies Gene Scott and Graebner sometimes played four or five exhibitions in a week-end -- at the Concord, the Atlantic Beach Club and other Eastern clubs -- to help fund their trips to Australia and Wimbledon.

Fitz Gibbon had met Scott across the net in a member-guest tournament at Cherry Valley. Fitz Gibbon, then 15, and his partner, Harvard captain Dale Junta, beat the Yale teammates, Scott, then 20, and John Clark, in three tough sets. "I was fit to be tied," Scott said. "I had never lost to a 15 year-old in singles, doubles, girls or anything else."

In the summer of 1965 at the US(L)TA National Father-Son Championships at Longwood, Fitz Gibbon and his dad, Les, recorded the most games (76) ever played in that event when they beat Charlie and Manuel Pasarell in the semis, 7-9, 13-11, 19-17. (They lost to the Froehlings in the final but defeated the McNairs for the title in 1967.)

Les Fitz Gibbon remembers the Pasarell match well. "Herb's instructions to me were, 'Just concentrate on return of serve,' he said. "I did that for three sets. But he let me hit one at 15-all in the last game. I knew Charlie would poach when he saw me hit it, so I hit it down the line. He got the ball back, but it flew off his racquet. Herb put it away at ad and then served it out."

After Herb played the Australian circuit in the fall of 1965, he did a tour for the State Department through Southeast Asia in February of 1966 and went to Burma. He was drafted in March, was stationed at West Point and served as coach of the Plebe tennis and squash teams. He finished his stint in the army in February of 1968 and was asked by the State Department to return to Burma to coach their national tennis team in preparation for the Southeast Asia Peninsula Games.

He spent the rest of 1968 touring on the international tennis circuit with Allen Fox and won gold and bronze medals -- in mixed doubles and singles -- at the Olympics in Mexico.

"Herb was the best American on clay that year," said Fox, the former Pepperdine coach and a Ph.D. in psychology. "He beat (Manuel) Santana in his hometown in Spain. Santana was the world's best amateur on clay that year...I never took one set off Herb on clay in 1968, not even in practice...His serve and forehand were enormous weapons on any surface. He was a very good volleyer and cunning on drop shots. On clay especially, he'd work you over with his forehand so you couldn't attack his backhand…

"He is the classiest guy I know," Fox added. "He's honest, thoughtful and understanding. The whole time I traveled with him I never got anything negative. When you live with somebody for a year you know the person very well. You're often driving all night and things come out. Not with Herb."

It's fair to say that Herb Fitz Gibbon's mother Sally knows her son best. He's very caring," she said. "He spent much time in third world countries and became aware of people's problems. So he began raising funds for a charity called Interplast, an organization of plastic surgeons who operate on deformed children. Herb and his friends are sponsoring an Interplast trip to Bolivia this summer, the lives of 100 children will be changed forever."

-- By Nancy Gill McShea

Richard Savitt

Dick and Annelle Savitt.

Dick Savitt is a tennis champion and a modest man who covers up a warm, generous nature with a quick, dry sense of humor, his friends say. If you ask him too many questions about himself or his tennis career, he'll get edgy and deadpan like Jack Webb of the old Dragnet television show: "Just the facts, Ma'am, just stick to the facts."

So we'll stick to the facts here. And the facts are considerable!

In 1951, Savitt was a 24-year-old veteran of the U.S. Navy, a Cornell graduate and a self-taught tennis player from South Orange, N.J., who stunned the tennis world when he swept the Australian and Wimbledon singles titles. By winning two of the sport's four Grand Slam Championships, he established himself as the world's No. 1 amateur tennis player (before the start of the professional Open Era in 1968), and became the first player to win both championships in one season since Don Budge accomplished that feat in 1938.

Budge and Ham Richardson said that their friend Dick Savitt came very close to winning three of the four majors that year when he played "one of the great classic matches" in the semifinals of the French. Savitt lost in five sets to the champion, Jaroslav Drobney, after leading two sets to love with leads in the next three sets.

For the record, Savitt was the first of only two former Eastern juniors who have ever won the Australian singles title (Vitas Gerulaitis won it in 1977), and the second of only four Eastern players who have ever won in singles at Wimbledon (Sidney Wood, 1931; Althea Gibson, 1957 and '58; and John McEnroe, 1981, '83 and '84).

To win the Australian, Savitt dismissed three native Aussie champions, defeating John Bromwich ('39 and '46) in the quarterfinals, Frank Sedgman ('49 and '50) in the semifinals and Ken McGregor ('52) in the finals. "The Australian was a big shock to the tennis world," Savitt said. "It put me on the map." (Incredibly, in December of 1951, he was excluded from the U.S. Davis Cup team that lost 3-2 to Australia in the final Challenge Round in which Sedgman and McGregor combined for Australia's three victories. Earlier that year, Savitt had won three Davis Cup singles matches, against Japan and Canada. When asked for an explanation, he would say only that it's a long story.)

At Wimbledon, Savitt again beat McGregor for the title in one of the shortest finals ever played on Center Court of the

All-England Lawn and Tennis Club. Excerpts from the July 7, 1951 issue of *The New York Times* captured the drama for fans back home: "Savitt beat the Australian Davis Cup player, 6-4, 6-4, 6-4, in 63 minutes before a standing–room crowd of 15,000. The…American culminated his first foreign tour and his initial Wimbledon appearance with the finest array of passing shots seen in this 65th staging of the game's best-known tournament. Savitt showed tension in the first few games, but after that his booming service and forehand and the most devastating backhand he ever has shown proved too much for McGregor…

"The 6-foot-3 Savitt broke McGregor's service -- his best weapon -- five times...He finished with sharp backhand cross-court shots which upset the Australian's net game.

The end came with McGregor lying flat, his drawn face buried in the…grass. He had dived desperately but missed the title-winner, a sizzling forehand drive, by inches. The happy American tossed his racquet high in the air and let go a shout of triumph that echoed above the applause."

Savitt says now that he remembers feeling more relieved than elated when he accepted the Wimbledon trophy from the Duchess of Kent. En route to the final, he had also eliminated Americans Art Larsen and Herb Flam, the singles winner and runner-up at the 1950 U.S. National Championships (now the US Open). Ham Richardson remembers that "Flam had him a set and 5-1 (in the second), but Dick came storming back to win that set 15-13 and won the match in four."

In the late summer of '51, at the U.S. Championships at Forest Hills, Savitt fell in the semis for the second straight year. He had lost to champ Larsen in '50 and in his return to the final four, he lost 6-3 in the fifth to Vic Seixas. "Dick got a boil on the back of his knee which didn't help," Budge recalled.

Savitt played the U.S. Championship 11 times, the first time in 1946 when he lost, 6-2, 6-2, 6-0, to Bill Talbert in the third round. His friend Dan Rivkind reminded him recently, "You know, I remember when you played Talbert at Forest Hills on Center Court," to which Savitt replied, "There aren't too many of you left (who stayed that day). I looked around after the first set and the whole stadium was emptying out. My family and friends left, too."

He quit playing the circuit full-time in the fall of 1952 to work in the oil business in Texas and didn't play at all in '53, '54, and '55. Thereafter, he competed only during summer vacations, and the Australians continued to loom in his draw. When he returned to Forest Hills in 1956, he lost to the champion Ken Rosewall in five sets. In 1958, he beat a young Rod Laver.

Savitt had taught himself to play tennis at age 13 by imitating Eastern's better players (Larry Krieger and Jeff Podesta among them) at the Berkeley Tennis Club in Orange. Russell Kingman was then the president of both the USLTA and Berkeley, and he brought in Jack Kramer, Frank Kovacs, Bobby Riggs and Pancho Segura to play the New Jersey State tournament there. Savitt was a ball boy. "I had never seen tennis like that before," he said. "I immediately got Don Budge's book on tennis to learn how to hit strokes correctly."

Before he made a big splash on the world's famous tennis courts, Savitt had entered Cornell in the fall of 1946 right after he lost to Talbert at Forest Hills. He was a four-year starter at No.1 singles and doubles there, posted a career singles record of 57-2, won the Eastern Intercollegiate singles title in 1949 and '50, and paired with Leonard Steiner to win the doubles title in 1948, '49 and '50. He has combined tennis and business ever since. In 1961, he won the Maccabiah Games in Israel and went into the securities business with Lehman Brothers. In 1973, he got involved with an organization called Israel Tennis Centers, which now has thirteen centers spread all over Israel.

"The concept was to use tennis as a vehicle to improve the quality of life for children," he said. Savitt was interested in the centers as a way to develop world-class players. Ever the businessman, in 1985 Savitt joined Schroder's, a large London and U.S. securities firm.

Savitt won many other elite tournament titles during the years he was ranked among America's top ten, including doubles at the Italian, singles and doubles trophies at the Canadian and three singles crowns at the USLTA National Indoors. Today, he enjoys set weekly games with Bill Colson, editor of *Sports Illustrated;* John Hursh; and his son, Bobby, with whom he won the 1981 USTA Father-Son Doubles Championship at Longwood.

Said Bobby Savitt, once a ranked Eastern junior himself, "He's the greatest father; he taught me everything. He's one of the few guys who played at the highest level, studied the game, adapted to changing techniques and became a great teacher."

Does it take brains to become a tennis champion? "No!" Dick Savitt said. "It takes four things: athletic ability, desire, good technique and experience." Those are the facts; just stick to the facts when you talk to that particular Grand Slam champion.

-- By Nancy Gill McShea

Elaine F. Viebranz

The first thing you notice about Elaine F. Viebranz is that she is an elegant, friendly lady whose gleaming white hair frames a radiant smile. When you get to know her, you realize she is also a very determined, elegant lady with clout.

Elaine has quietly established her legacy in American tennis as a powerful, volunteer executive in the governing body of the game. She has served with distinction as president of the USTA/ Eastern Section and the Junior Tennis Foundation, as a member of the USTA Executive Board, and as a chairman and/or member of 20 USTA and sectional committees. She is also in charge of volunteer operations at the US Open Championships at Flushing Meadows.

She came to Eastern tennis with a strong background in volunteer work, having served as president of the Larchmont Junior League, vice president of the Family Service of Westchester and as a member of the Vestry and Board of Directors of St. John's Episcopal Church in Larchmont.

Elaine joined Eastern's volunteer ranks in 1980, was appointed the first sectional league coordinator of the USTA Adult League Tennis program, when 13,000 players participated nationwide, and she served as the chairman of the league's national committee from 1993 to 1996. Today, Eastern's sectional league coordinator of USTA League Tennis is a full-time paid position and the program fields 340,000 players nationwide.

"It's the best program the USTA has," Elaine said. "That's why I stuck with it as long as I did."

"Elaine has the inclination to promote good causes; she's the ideal volunteer," said her friend Doris Herrick, Eastern's former executive director who has worked closely with Elaine for years. "She has an ability to fit into any group, to draw people out. She is an excellent conversationalist with a genuine interest in others and an uncanny ability to remember details about them."

Elaine also has an uncanny ability to quietly convince you to attend to business her way. For example, if you have occasion to mention her name in print, you know instinctively to refer to her initially as Elaine F. Viebranz -- she's partial to that middle initial -- and thereafter as Elaine rather than Viebranz, or as chairman rather than chairperson. She dismisses rigid journalism rules and trendy terminology as nit-picking nonsense.

On the other hand, Dan Dwyer, who followed Elaine as Eastern's president, will tell you that she can be very proper, specifically when she quietly reminded him about the right dress code for a USTA sectional president. Jacket and tie please!

Elaine feels passionately about tennis and family, say her four children, who have mostly fond memories of playing tennis together at the Orienta Beach Club in Mamaroneck (although Curt admits to boycotting the game for a while). Mom loved to play, they all agreed, but when she made an error she'd look at her racquet, get mad and mutter, "Oh, É-laine!" Her kids actually believed her racquet was named É-laine!

She quit playing when she blew her elbow out (before the medical profession knew how to treat it), but by then she had taken on the role of tennis parent and was running the Metropolitan Inter-Club Tennis League's junior program. "Mom transferred her passion for playing into a passion for supporting the game," said Scott, who did the seeding for his mother's season-ending junior tournament.

Elaine's children added that their mother's accomplishments can be traced to her insistence on consistency, a strong sense of values and a subtle sense of humor, qualities that inspire confidence in others. "Mom creates high expectations for herself and has always expected the same from us. We always knew where we stood whether we liked it or not," said Gayle, once a ranked Eastern junior who earned 11 varsity letters in high school. "She carted me around to all those tournaments, never complained and kept it all in perspective. She allowed me to choose whether or not to play year-round."

"More recently, when I was having my youngest child five weeks early and nothing was ready, she came out (to Colorado) and pulled it all together. I just knew I could count on her. That kind of consistency is reassuring."

Joan and Curt chimed in: "And let's not forget her insistence on good manners!" The Viebranz kids were instructed to greet everybody they knew, even when they spotted acquaintances more than a block away.

Elaine grew up in New York City, worked as an editorial assistant for *Redbook* magazine and then moved on to Sylvania Electric Products (later part of GTE).

The move was a turning point in her life. "I was hired on V-J Day in 1945, met Al (her husband, an electronics engineer), was his executive secretary in 1946 and married him in 1947," she said.

She had instantly become a corporate wife. The Viebranzes settled in Larchmont in 1953, an ideal environment for Elaine to raise her family and start a career as a volunteer.

"Elaine has spent a substantial portion of her life serving other people," Al Viebranz said, adding that his wife of 51 years has always been very pretty, alert and lively with a good sense of humor. "I'm not at all impartial, but I think she's been one of the most effective executives the East or the USTA has ever had.

"Had she stayed in business rather than doing pro bono work, she would have been a top executive. The only person she's never been able to organize is me. That is an impossible task."

During her tenure as Eastern's president, Elaine stamped her signature on many innovative changes. She was involved in the inaugural Hall of Fame dinner in 1988, a major fundraiser for the section's junior programs and special populations. She also worked to strengthen community tennis associations and special programs in the section's five regions, helped consolidate the two umpire groups (the Eastern and New Jersey Tennis Umpire Associations) and organized the first joint annual meeting among the Eastern Section, the USPTA and the PTR. As president of the Junior Tennis Foundation, she awarded the first David N. Dinkins scholarship awards to deserving New York City youngsters.

"Tennis has been a wonderful experience," Elaine F. Viebranz said recently. "I've made great friends. I hope I have contributed to its growth."

-- By Nancy Gill McShea

Dr. Reginald S. Weir

photo courtesy of Carolyn Weir

Within the span of one year during the late 1940s in two of New York City's five boroughs, two very different men forever changed the face of professional sports. In April of 1947, the Brooklyn Dodgers' bold rookie, Jackie Robinson, broke the color barrier in Major League Baseball before a raucous crowd of 26,623 at Ebbets Field, and went 0 for 3 in his first at-bats. In February of 1948, across the Brooklyn Bridge in Manhattan, Dr. Reginald Weir quietly hurdled the same barrier in the U.S. (Lawn) Tennis Association National Men's Indoor Championships before a more polite audience at the Seventh Regiment Armory. And he won his first match.

Weir lost to Bill Talbert in the second round of the 1948 indoors, but after the match, Talbert raved about his ability to Dick Savitt. "What a class act he is; it's too bad he didn't get a chance to play more (national) tournaments in his prime," Talbert said. "He's very quick and a very good volleyer."

Reggie later extended Pancho Gonzalez to three sets in another national tournament and eventually won five USTA national indoor senior titles: three in singles (in 1956, 1957 and 1959) and two in doubles with George Ball (in 1961 and 1962).

Weir was 37 years old and a practicing New York physician and surgeon when he won that historic national match in 1948. He had already played in one Eastern-sanctioned tournament, at the Hamilton Tennis Courts on Dykeman Street (now a New York City housing project). His friend Ernie Kuhn, whose family built and owned Hamilton's 32 red clay courts, ran tournaments there and told Reggie he'd put him in the draw and see what happens.

He had been waiting patiently in the wings for a chance to play the USLTA nationals since 1929, when he was refused entree into the national junior indoors, also held at the Seventh Regiment Armory. Arthur Ashe recalled in his book, *Hard Road to Glory*, that the NAACP had complained about Weir's exclusion at the time, but received the following reply: "...the policy of the USLTA has been to decline the entry of colored players in our championships...In pursuing this policy we make no reflection upon... race but we believe that as a practical matter, the present method of separate associations (USLTA and American Tennis Association)...should be continued."

By 1969, Reggie was widely respected in the tennis community. That year, USLTA President Alastair Martin appointed him to the USLTA Administrative Committee. And in September of 1986, at Weir's 75th birthday reception at the Upper Ridgewood Tennis Club in New Jersey – a little less than a year before he passed away – USTA President J. Randolph Gregson presented him with a plaque which read: "In appreciation to Dr. Reginald S. Weir for outstanding and inspirational contributions to the sport of tennis as a player, sportsman and national champion." Weir was also inducted into the City College Athletic Hall of Fame and a scholarship for youngsters and Eastern's N.J. Men's 35 Sectional Championships were established in his name at the Upper Ridgewood Tennis Club.

"My father was a healer by profession and temperament," said his daughter Carolyn Weir, a graduate of Yale who teaches French Honors and Spanish in New Jersey. "He was a very strong person, fiercely protective of his family, yet gentle withal; an excellent, patient teacher. All his life, he had a Saint Francis-like quality with animals (especially dogs) and children. I once heard him say, at a tennis court, of course, 'I can't imagine not practicing medicine.' But he had to give up both tennis and medicine after a bad heart attack.

"I spent much of my life waiting for daddy at hospitals and tennis courts, especially at Hamilton where all the city high school teams played. Daddy grew up at those courts and formed many lasting friendships there. They were a magical place for me as a little girl...Daddy always played on Court 1 by the clubhouse and so did I when he hit with me."

Although Weir had felt the sting of refusal in 1929 in his first attempt to compete in a USLTA national tournament, he had grown up accustomed to gaining it everywhere else. His father, Felix, the diamond medalist in his violin class at Chicago Musical College, who also attended the Conservatory at Leipzig, Germany, had occasion that same year to work as an orchestra leader at Moulin Rouge in Paris. The elder Weir mentioned to a guest at a private party that his teenage son who played tennis was arriving, and the gentleman said, "Well then, he must become a member of our *Racing Club de France*."

When Reggie traveled to Paris in '29, he had already captained his high school tennis team at De Witt Clinton and was captain of his team at City College. He later won ATA national titles -- in 1931, '32, '33 and '37. After graduating from New York University Medical School in 1935, he married Anna McCampbell, who had just received a master's degree in French from the University of Michigan. They met at an ATA national tournament in Tuskegee, Ala., when Anna's brother, the head ball boy, introduced her to the "fellow from New York (the champion)." By 1939, Weir was an assistant in surgery at N.Y.U. In 1941, he opened his own medical practice and was one of the earliest African Americans to be appointed a New York City surgeon at Gouverneur Hospital on the lower East Side.

"Reggie was very patient, took everything in stride and waited his turn so to speak," said his friend Dan Rivkind, once a ranked Eastern junior/senior player, a dean/teacher in the New York City Public School System and the director of the Columbia University Tennis Center. "I go back 50 years with him; he was like a big brother. It meant a lot to me as a kid who had nothing to be befriended by a guy of his stature. Dick Savitt used to practice with him indoors; that's how good he was.

"He would make home visits to elderly patients and wouldn't refuse a patient who didn't have any money," Rivkind added. "He never feared going into tough neighborhoods to help someone. He was so well known drug addicts considered him a friend and left him alone.

"Reggie Weir exemplified the finest values you would look for in a human being."

-- By Nancy Gill McShea

Chapter 20

2000: Fleming, Herrick, Richards and Tully

Peter Fleming

He is instantly recognizable as the lanky, 6-foot-5 blond who quietly wielded a big forehand as the right half of perhaps the greatest doubles team in tennis history. But anyone who has followed the career of Peter Fleming, who grew up in Chatham, N.J., and holds the Grand Prix record for winning the most doubles titles, 57, with John McEnroe, knows that his low-key court demeanor masks an intense determination.

"I was the stoic one in that partnership," said Fleming, who acknowledged that while he was not quite in McEnroe's league in terms of temperamental court behavior, he was not totally in control all of the time either. "Being cool and collected is not necessarily my personality. I can be pretty intense…but it turned out to be more beneficial to my game. My demons came out in singles."

Individually, Fleming achieved career high professional rankings of No. 8 in singles (1980) and No. 1 in doubles (1984) and won a total of 66 doubles titles while advancing to the finals of 21 other tournaments. He is third in winning percentage in doubles finals, at .759, behind McEnroe and Tom Okker of the Netherlands. He also advanced to the quarters or beyond with partners other than McEnroe, among them Eastern's Fritz Buehning (they won Memphis and Atlanta); Gary Donnelly (Wimbledon finals, French semifinals); Ferdi Taygan (won the NCAA title while at UCLA and Hong Kong); Guy Forget (won LaQuinta); Ray Moore (won Johannesburg); Anders Jarryd (won Toronto); Tomas Smid (won the Italian and Monte Carlo Opens); Brian Teacher (Columbus finals); and Steve Denton (US Open quarters).

Fleming won his first Grand Slam doubles title with McEnroe at Wimbledon in 1979, a 15-minute drive from where he now lives with his wife Jenny and children Joe; 15, Alex, 13; and Holly, 9. "[Winning Wimbledon] was fantastic, really a thrill I had never expected…I felt like I was on top of the world," he said.

These days he works as a consultant/investor of an Internet media company and does television commentary for the BBC and Sky Sports. In addition, he coaches touring pro Laurence Tielman of Italy, who lives in London, as well as three of England's talented 14-year-olds. Fleming gets back to the States six or seven times a year and also plays several events on the ATP Champions Senior Tour, where he catches up with his old tennis buddies.

Fleming and McEnroe won a total of seven Grand Slam doubles titles; three US Opens (1979, '81 and '83) and four Wimbledons (1979, '81, '83 and '84) and were finalists on three other occasions. Fleming ranks seventh in doubles wins among U.S. Davis Cup players, having teamed with McEnroe for a 14-1 record from 1979-1984. The pair also won seven straight Masters titles in Madison Square Garden from 1978-1984.

"To be a good doubles player you need at least two out of three skills: serve, volley and return," Fleming has said in assessing his successful court alliance with McEnroe. "Between us we covered these areas well. Then you need to make sacrifices for the good of your team, which we were prepared to do. Most importantly, there was a great chemistry between us. Mentally we had a great understanding of one another's emotions and our psychological strengths seemed to complement one another."

Of all the titles Fleming and McEnroe won together, Fleming has talked about a 1981 Davis Cup contest versus Argentina in Cincinnati as the most exciting: "Our match against (Guillermo) Vilas and (Jose-Luis) Clerc...had everything you could hope for in a tennis match. The tie was finely balanced and it looked like the winner of the doubles would win the Davis Cup that year. We were heavy favorites, but they played some incredible tennis. Everything happened in that match: players arguing with umpires, players arguing with players, captains arguing with players, and the kinds of momentum shifts that only doubles can provide. It was neck and neck throughout. The game we played when they served for the match at 6-5 in the fifth was probably the highlight of my career. We played four good points to break Vilas at love, and went on to win 11-9 in the fifth. It was a tremendous feeling to play such a dramatic part in a Davis Cup win."

Fleming said his Dad, Alan, played tennis every weekend at the Racquets Club of Short Hills, N.J., and that "his love for the game was so infectious I wanted to have a racquet in my hand hitting the ball from age five." He turned professional in 1976 and influenced the Eastern tennis boom. At the 1979 US Open, McEnroe beat Vitas Gerulaitis for the singles title, and Fleming and McEnroe won the doubles title. All three were friends and had trained together at the Port Washington Tennis Academy. Local kids began signing up for tennis lessons in droves.

"I owed a lot to that whole [Port Washington] program," said Fleming, who traveled by train from New Jersey to Port Washington every weekend and was a guest at the Zausner home. "Mr. [Hy] Zausner put together an environment that bred champions with competitive players and exceptional coaches Harry Hopman and Tony Palafox. When I was 16, Vitas was the top junior in the country and I was like No. 30. Over the next year I improved a lot." Fleming said he developed an attacking serve and volley game and that his greatest strengths were his serve, forehand and return of serve.

He first played doubles on the professional tour with McEnroe in September of 1977 in Los Angeles at the Pacific Southwest tournament. "We both had done quite well and I was one of the few guys he knew," said Fleming, who had transferred from Michigan to UCLA while McEnroe was just entering Stanford. "We figured it would be fun and an ideal situation if we played together and traveled around together."

Said Palafox, who observed the famous partnership from the beginning: "When you think of doubles you immediately think of McEnroe and Fleming. After playing all those tournaments together, they're not enemies, they're very good friends. They practiced together all the time and both of them improved because they had each other. Whether it was Davis Cup or tournaments, they were always in the same place."

Asked for a comment about that partnership several weeks ago, when he was preparing for his second outing as the U.S. Davis Cup captain, John McEnroe resorted to his usual wry humor: "One of us is right handed, the other is left handed. One of us is from New Jersey, the other from New York. One of us went to UCLA, the other to Stanford. One of us is quick tempered…and I'm a team player. But one thing we have in common is the Eastern Tennis Hall of Fame and 7 Grand Slam doubles titles. Congratulations, Peter!"

The famous tennis coach Carlos Goffi, whom Fleming chose to present his award tonight, added, "Honorable comes to mind when I think of Peter. He's a family man and a friend through thick and thin. You can always count on him. He would never look for the limelight…"

"I love tennis," Peter Fleming said. "I couldn't have asked for a better sport to be involved in. I found my niche. I can look back and say I could have done some things differently, but I prefer to be known as a great doubles player than not to be known at all."

-- By Nancy Gill McShea

Doris S. Herrick

If presidential hopefuls Al Gore and George W. Bush are compiling a list of potential cabinet appointees, they shouldn't overlook Doris Herrick. Doris would be the ideal candidate for any post, especially Secretary of State or Ambassador to the United Nations. She is a born leader and a born diplomat.

She is also 5-foot-2 with eyes-of-blue, always cheerful with a quick smile, and everybody's best friend.

Ask all of the people who worked with Doris during the 20 years she presided at the center of Eastern tennis as executive director and they'll tell you she treats everybody like family. They'll say she put on a model clinic of how to succeed as the chief operating officer of a not-for-profit organization, that she was brilliant in the role of liaison to 10 volunteer presidents, the board of directors, the professional staff and the people they serve in the tri-state area. They'll say she was the velvet glove behind the scenes who engineered Eastern's emergence as a national leader in community and recreational tennis development.

"Barbara Williams was president when I began in 1978," Doris said. "We moved from simply doing scheduling and rankings to inventing programming." She explained that together they broadened the scope of Eastern's mission with activities designed to get people playing and keep them playing, such as a traveling caravan to take tennis to the public parks and unranked player tournaments for beginners. The result put Eastern ahead of the national programming boom.

"The key to leadership in my opinion," said Doris, "involves relationships, succeeding at getting people to work well as a team. This job was a challenge in that it involved the dynamics of a small staff and a large corps of volunteers."

"My most important contribution to Eastern tennis was hiring Doris," Williams said. "We got along so well we needed a hot fudge sundae at exactly the same time…Not only did she nurture volunteers, but she also began to hire and train a top-notch staff."

One of those trainees was Laura Canfield, Eastern's first director of the USTA Schools Program and later executive director of USTA/Middle States. "Doris understood that new programs were not going to compete with traditional tournaments," Canfield said. "It was her vision that they would supplement those offerings and reach a broader market. She could see that the schools effort was going to be a big breakthrough, so she made sure she provided the resources for staff, committees and volunteers to make it work...Doris was the boss! She could sell anything to any of us."

Past president Dan Dwyer can vouch for that. "Doris had the unique ability to have an entirely different opinion than mine and in 10 minutes convince me that her original opinion was correct but that it was my idea," he said, still sounding astonished.

"Doris is the ultimate politician because nobody thinks she's a politician," said David Goodman, who headed up Eastern's junior department before he succeeded his boss as executive director in 1997. "Whenever people went over my head because they didn't like the answer I gave them, they'd call Doris yelling and screaming. I could hear their voices through the phone. And the more they yelled the softer the tone of Doris's voice would get. It was only a matter of time before she was in control of the conversation."

When Doris was in her forties she could have been classified as one of the "Great Dames," a tag writer Marie Brenner used in a recent *New York Times* piece to describe a generation of intelligent women with manners and endurance-- Marietta Tree, Clare Boothe Luce and Kitty Carlisle Hart, among them--who came of age before the feminist movement and gained influence as career volunteers in charitable causes, the arts, politics and the diplomatic corps. Doris, too, was the volunteer president and/or board chairman of organizations such as The Woman's Club of White Plains, the First Baptist Church, the PTA and the Jennie Clarkson Auxiliary, a residence for school girls from troubled homes. But she was divorced after 25 years of marriage and had to make the transition to the professional ranks.

"She did what she needed to do when she needed to do it," said Doris's father Jeff Schlesinger, 94, a chemist by trade who added that his only daughter was once the Sweetheart of De Molay in her hometown of Arkansas City, Kansas. He said she was also a cheerleader, editor of the college newspaper at Ottawa University and a member of the drama club, the university honor society, the Pi Kappa Delta national debate society and Who's Who in American Colleges and Universities.

Doris's brother Bill Schlesinger, a Ph.D. from M.I.T. and a professor of theoretical mathematics at Tufts University, said his sister is very genuine and the basis of her leadership is a combination of being sensitive, friendly and responsible. "I think there's always been some ambition there, but it is masked by the responsibility factor which I think is much larger," he said. "She's always had lots of friends and fit in well with all kinds of people. She got that from our mother (Jessie, who passed away last year). Mother helped us with our homework and always gave us a reason for things. I see that aspect of her in Doris."

Friends Kathy and Bob Garry said they are glad Doris traded in her Kansas ruby red slippers for tennis shoes because "as a woman of great faith she became a powerful example for so many people in our sport."

Indeed, people who worked with her responded overwhelmingly with words of love and praise for Doris a few weeks back when I called. The following are excerpts from their thoughts:

USTA Executive Directors:
Peter Herb, Northern California: Working with Doris for 20 years was an honor. Her grasp of...financial matters has been an enormous help to us.
Henry Talbert, Southern California: With her winning personality, she keeps everyone talking so that at the end of a meeting people can part as friends without getting polarized.
Presidents:
Alex Aitchison: For her comfort and smile I would walk a mile.

Louis Dimock: She saw that it's all about the community. I bow to the power of a legend.

Harry Marmion: She is the single most devoted and competent member of any organization I have ever worked with.

Lois Prince: She makes us all look good. It had to be impossible to reestablish good relationships with a new president every two years. She's so clever nobody ever gets angry at her.

Dick Scheer: My favorite person in tennis. I don't know anyone else who is as efficient as she is lovable and warm at the same time.

Bob Schmitz: She filled in the gaps for me; she'll be a friend for life.

Elaine Viebranz: Her ability to work with staff and volunteers and bring out the best in them is the reason the organization is as strong as it is today.

Staff:

Mali Circle: She inspired us; we were indeed a family.

Ann Flint: She's a psychiatrist, diplomat and confidante. I always knew she was on my side.

Denise Jordan: She has a willingness to stretch the human spirit to new heights and a belief that everyone can lead.

Renie Koehnken: She's one of my favorite people to get into trouble with...she knows.

Nancy McShea: She never acts like...ahem...Tiny Alice.

Jenny Schnitzer: She knows how to work the line between boss and friend; that's a gift reserved for a few special people.

Aaron Segal: She gave...our staff tremendous support and guidance...motivated everyone by example.

Herrick Children:

Sue: She's little "Miss Gotta Get to Work."

David: She's a great mother and a real force for good.

Bill: She has a positive attitude all the time, even in grim situations, which gets her through. She can lead the old, the young, liberals and conservatives. She can be all warm and fuzzy with people but at a board meeting she can cut right through trivia and focus. That ability to be honest in both roles is how she pulls people together.

In any given week these days, Doris could be interviewing candidates to head up her church's ministry (in her role as board chairman), serving as vice president of her condo, visiting ill and aging friends or members of her church congregation, or tending to business as executive director of Eastern's Junior Tennis Foundation. You might even catch her slipping out at 6 a.m. in rubber galoshes during a mini-hurricane to collect bittersweet from a friend's garden for luncheon centerpieces at The Woman's Club--because the local florist doesn't have what she wants.

No doubt about it, Doris Herrick is one of the "Great Dames!"

-- By Nancy Gill McShea

Elaine Viebranz worked closely for years with Doris Herrick. They even ordered the same lunch.

Dr. Renee Richards

Renee Richards, the tennis player, needs no introduction. In 1975 Richard Raskind became Renee Richards, and the whole world knows that story. In 1977, Richards, a famous ophthalmologist off the tennis court, began playing on the women's professional tennis circuit and later coached Martina Navratilova to her first victory on red clay at the 1982 French Open Championships and to several other Grand Slam titles.

"New Yorkers have always supported me -- at the Open, everywhere," said Richards, who recalled an incident from 1978 when she was a member of the World TeamTennis New Orleans Nets squad with player/coach Marty Riessen, Bjorn Borg, Wendy Turnbull and her mixed doubles partner, John Lucas, who had played pro basketball for the Milwaukee Bucks. "John and I flew into LaGuardia [Airport]; we were going to Madison Square Garden to play the New York Apples. He was always telling me what a big shot he was everywhere. I said, 'Wait until you get to New York and you'll see what a real big shot is.' When we stopped at the Queens Midtown Tunnel, the guy in the toll booth said, 'Hi, Doc, welcome back.' At the Garden, Apples' captain Billie Jean King implored the crowd, 'Let's hear it for the New York Apples.' Forget it, I told her. Tonight these people are rooting for me because I'm a New Yorker."

Richards comes from a family of medical doctors and would agree that her noteworthy career as a New York ophthalmologist and one of the world's leading surgeons in Strabismus, the correction of eye muscles in cross-eyed children, ranks among her greatest achievements. She would also agree that the joy of hitting a tennis ball ranks among the most constant rhythms in her life.

"That was my thing. I've spent my whole life as an Eastern tennis player," Richards said. "I played the game like a true amateur; I was known for two things: being a deadly competitor and a great sport. I've played in every club and on every court in the metropolitan area."

Born in New York City, Richards moved to Forest Hills at age 6 and was ranked among the top-ten Eastern and national juniors in the late 1940s and early '50s. She was captain of her high school tennis team at the Horace Mann School in New York City, and at 15 she won the Eastern Private Schools Interscholastic singles title. "My first big win," she said. She was later the captain of and played first singles for the Yale Tennis Team in New Haven, Connecticut (1951-1955). When she attended medical school at the University of Rochester (1955-59), she swept snow off the tennis courts through the long winters rather than interrupt the rhythm of hitting the ball.

By the early 1960s, Richards was steeped in the complexities of her internship and residency training at the Lenox Hill and Manhattan Eye, Ear and Throat Hospitals in New York City. But she and Don Rubell, a fellow doctor and Eastern player, found time to escape to the tennis courts during their lunch hour. "I'd pick him up at the Midtown Tunnel and he'd be standing there in his whites," she said. "We'd go to Queens, find a court and then go back to the hospital in the afternoon. Sometimes we'd go up to Baker Field at Columbia and play with Dick Savitt, Ham Richardson and Paul Cranis."

This past January, Richards received the George Seewagen Award at Eastern's Awards Dinner in recognition of her teaching ability, sportsmanship, excellence in competition and love of the game. "I am especially pleased," she said, "because I was taught how to play tennis by George..." She was 12 in 1947 when her father, David Raskind, told her that Seewagen, a top teaching pro in New York, would give her lessons [at the Jackson Heights Tennis Club], and that it was a privilege which would only be continued if she applied herself and worked hard.

Richards said she wouldn't dare address Mr. Seewagen as George until she was 30, that his dignified demeanor and behavior commanded instant respect and became a model for her. "George would rarely verbalize disapproval," she explained. "He would simply shake his head and say, 'I don't know about that.' He taught me tennis but he taught me much more. All of his students were taught how to behave like decent human beings."

Les Pollack, a native of Woodmere, L.I., has known Renee Richards since they played tennis together on the Eastern and national junior circuits, and later on Yale's tennis team. "She was an all-around athlete, a lefty, fastball (pro) pitching prospect who several times in the same day threw complete games for the Horace Mann baseball team, then quickly changed into tennis clothes and won at first singles for the school's tennis team," Pollack said. "When we were freshmen at Yale, she was still eligible to play juniors and was planning on going to the national indoors in St. Louis. She got stomach pains and the doctors thought she had appendicitis, so they put her in the infirmary. She sneaked out, went to the indoors and got to the semis of singles and the finals of doubles."

Pollack believes Richards inherited a great sense of the tennis tradition from Seewagen and her father. "Renee is the fairest player I've ever played against," he said. "Anything close is in. She learned that from Seewagen. And her father, who's 100 now, is a lifelong player. When he earned his first national ranking, No. 18, in the over-85 division, I congratulated him and he said 'It's not so great, we only have 19 players.' He kept at it because he loves the game."

Richards used to bring her dog Rocco, an Airedale, to tournaments. "Everybody knew Rocco," Pollack said. "Whenever Renee started losing, Rocco would start baying at the moon." You might have heard Rocco the day Richards lost to Sidney Schwartz in the finals of the Brooklyn Championships at the Knickerbocker Field Club. "Renee was just 16 and Sid was the king; he was ranked 10th in the country and won the first set easily," Pollack said. "Somehow Renee won the second, and when she started serving to open the third, Sid turned to his claque and said, 'Count the points [in this set].' Renee heard him and hit an ace. Sid said, 'That's one.' Sid won that match, but Renee beat him badly in straight sets next time out at the Eastern Clay Courts."

While competing on the women's circuit, Richards was a 1977 US Open doubles finalist with Betty Ann Stuart--the pair lost a close match to Navratilova and Betty Stove -- and in 1978 she was a mixed doubles semifinalist there with Ilie Nastase. In 1979 she defeated Nancy Richey for the Open's 35s singles title. Richards once extended Chris Evert to three sets in the finals of the Seattle Virginia Slims and posted wins over Hana Mandlikova, Sylvia Hanika, Virginia Ruzici and Pam Shriver. "I think Pam was about 10," she said.

On the Eastern men's circuit, Richards was a New York State champion in singles and doubles, and was ranked among Eastern's top ten for more than five years. In 1964 when she was a U.S. Navy Lieutenant Commander and an eye surgeon stationed at St. Alban's Hospital in Queens, she stood at No. 4 behind Gene Scott, Herb Fitz Gibbon and Rubell. That summer, the Navy provided Richards with daily helicopter flights from Long Island to Newport, Rhode Island, and back again so she could repeat as the All-Navy singles and doubles champ.

In 1973 Richards was ranked No. 6 in the country in men's 35s and had wins over Ray Garrido, Paul Cranis, Tony Palafox and King Van Nostrand. "At the US Open 35s [grass] tournament, I beat Jim Farrin in three sets, a grueling win against a better player," she said. "Then I lost to Gene Scott in a third-set tiebreak after holding double match point. Devastating! Only Gene beat me that summer – twice -- but he's five years younger than I am."

Renee Richards is very comfortable with her life. "It was just the way my life was destined to turn out," she said. "I had little control over it. I'm very fortunate because people with problems not as bad as mine have not been able to end up having such a wonderful life."

-- By Nancy Gill McShea

William J. Tully

Steve Bernian

If you know anything about Bill Tully, you understand that the man is a tennis lifer. So much so that on paper he could be mistaken for a nomadic tennis bum who spends all his time following the path of the sun. Tully plays tennis every day, always looking to improve his serve and volley game. He has already won the five tournaments he entered in his first four months of over-75 competition, beating old Eastern nemesis Tony Vincent in one final at Delray Beach. And he's been playing the sport outdoors year-round since he was a young jet setter commuting between Florida and various residences in Westchester, N.Y.

"My father's business was slow in the winter, so we lived in Florida during those months, and still do," explained Tully, who was captain of both the Iona Prep tennis team up north and the St. Patrick's High School team in Miami Beach.

Tully does have another life, though. He is a veteran officer of the U.S. Navy Air Corps and a 1948 graduate of the University of Notre Dame who has owned a seat on the New York Stock Exchange since 1963. He even once dabbled in the politics of elective office in his native Yonkers until he got so fed up with people calling him at all hours of the night to get their cats out of trees that he fled to Pelham. And he and Kay, his wife of 50 years, are devoted to their nine children and 15 grandchildren.

But if you call him at home, Tully sends a clear message on his answering machine: "Kay and I are out playing a tiebreak." When you reach him, he is quick to point out that all of his children are good club tennis players who have worked as ball kids or in other capacities at the US Open. His father, Leo, was an umpire and linesman at Forest Hills, and three of his grandchildren play Eastern tournaments.

Bill said he was about 12 when he played his first extended set of tennis at the Orienta Beach Club in Mamaroneck before Jimmy Van Alen invented the tiebreak. He wasn't allowed to go swimming for an hour after lunch because his mother, Catherine, believed in the old wives' tale that he might get cramps, so he played tennis to kill some time. "I just liked it, I could beat the kids around my town, it was probably my ego," he said, laughing at his candor. "And my father encouraged me. I was never what you call a champion but always a good Eastern ranked player."

On the contrary, in the 60-something years since Tully hit his first tennis ball, he has won 10 USTA gold tennis balls and hundreds of tournaments, including the men's national Canadian, New York and Florida State Championships. In addition, he has been honored with prestigious tennis awards. In 1985 he was ranked first in the country in men's 60s and *World Tennis* magazine named him the Senior Player of the Year. In 1996 he was the USTA/Florida Player of the Year. And just last month he received the USTA Seniors' Service Award at the organization's annual meeting on Marco Island, Florida.

"Everything revolves around tennis with him," said Tully's daughter Sue Rollins, who played tennis for Fordham and worked the walkie-talkies at the Open. "Every spring [when he returns from Florida] that net goes up in our driveway. He's got to get out there and get those strokes going. He's still a kid who likes to enjoy the moment that's there."

When Tully was 16, he was ranked No. 2 in Eastern junior tennis behind Charlie Oliver and qualified for the 1942 U.S. National Championships at Forest Hills. He lost to Bill Talbert that year but vowed he would return. In 1943 he started playing tennis for Notre Dame where he formed what would become a lifelong friendship with Jimmy Evert (Chris's dad) and his brother Jerry. Bill and Jimmy were ushers at each other's weddings. Jimmy actually met his wife, Colette Thompson, a friend of Kay's, at the Tully's wedding. Jimmy played No. 1 singles for Notre Dame while Bill and Jerry traded places at the second and third positions.

In 1945, Captain Tully's Notre Dame team finished as NCAA co-champions when Pancho Segura of the University of Miami won the singles match to tie them. In the summer of 1947, Tully and the Evert brothers toured the country playing tennis, making stops at the national clay courts in Salt Lake City, Utah; Seattle, Washington; and at Vancouver, where Jimmy won the men's singles title at the Canadian Championships. In 1948 it was Tully's turn to win the Canadian singles title and qualify again for the U.S. Championships.

He would play America's Grand Slam tournament 13 more times over the next 18 years, the last in 1966 at age 40, when he lost to Frank Froehling III. During that same period, in 1965 and 1967, Tully won his first two national titles, in men's 35 doubles. In 1968 he was a member of captain Dick Squires' Olympic Fron-Tennis team in Mexico City, a team doubles exhibition among 16 nations.

Perhaps Tully's most important contribution to Eastern tennis is his consistency as a team player, both off the court as a USTA and Eastern volunteer committeeman and Metro-N.Y. regional vice president, and on the court as a charter member and captain of team events, beginning with the Church Cup. In 30-plus years, he has played on every Eastern team in his age division, most recently at the Atlantic Coast 65 Intersectionals event.

"After many years of competing with Bill in team matches and against him in tournaments, I've concluded that it is better to be on his team than opposing him," said Tully's friend Tony Franco, a popular top-ranked Eastern player.

Tully has been the captain of the USTA Stevens Cup team, a men's 45 Pan American competition; and he twice represented the U.S. on two other international teams, the men's 55 Austria and 70 Crawford Cups. He and his son Chris also played a few Eastern Father-Son events and once faced Peter Fleming and his dad Alan at the Arlington Players' Club in New Jersey.

Last October in Orlando, Florida, Tully added the National Senior Olympics' men's 70 singles trophy to his collection. The 64-player draw included players from every state in the nation. His other USTA national titles include five in doubles on clay -- four in the 55s with Oliver (they once beat Bobby Riggs and Gardnar Mulloy in the final). He has also won three on grass -- one singles and two doubles, the most recent in 1998 with frequent Eastern teammate and national opponent Fred Kovaleski, which earned the pair the No. 1 USTA 70s double ranking.

"Bill and I have known each other since college," Kovaleski said. "He's an excellent sportsman, very fair on the court. If there's a questionable call, I've never seen him take it...He's better on grass than on any other surface, primarily because he's more of a serve and volleyer than any other player in the 70s or 75s. It gets tougher and tougher to play as we get older, but he continues to play every day of the week."

Now, try to imagine a bona fide tennis champion who doesn't curse but prefers to mumble "Jimminy Cricket, darn it anyway" or just plain "phooey" when he misses a shot. No question Bill Tully is a respectable tennis bum!"

-- By Nancy Gill McShea

Chapter 21

2001: Cranis, Jackson, Seewagen and Stockton

Paul Cranis

Ed Goldman

The next time you feel like letting go of a childhood dream and need a jolt of inspiration to keep at it, just call Paul Cranis. He will share anecdotes with you about his storied tennis career that began in 1952, by chance, when he was 17 and pitching for the Tilden High School baseball team in Brooklyn. He is still chasing the dream almost 50 years later in his position as the director of tennis and the head teaching professional at the Norbeck Country Club in Rockville, Md.

"Paul is like a kid, he's still eager to play and improve his ranking; he loves to compete," said his longtime friend Dick Savitt, the 1951 Wimbledon and Australian singles champion. "He teaches all day and at the drop of a hat he'll play. I do not know anyone who likes tennis more than Paul...Not only has he improved as he's gotten older, he's put a lot back into the game. "

His story opens in March of 1952: "...I'm pitching the middle innings for Tilden in a PSAL (Public School Athletic League) game. We win the game and I'm thinking 'Life could not be better. Maybe a career in baseball. Me and Sandy Koufax. [Both southpaws.]' To get to the baseball field I had to cut through the tennis courts at Lincoln Terrace Park. The teaching pro there, Phil Rubell, would bait me and say, 'Come on you sissy, you can't play this game.' One day in May I decided to try but couldn't get the ball over the net. I became obsessed with the game and played my first PSAL tennis tournament in June. By December I won the boys' 18s title at Eastern's junior indoor championships."

Cranis took some lessons that year with Rubell and started playing regularly at the public parks with Rubell's son, Don. In 1965 when *World Tennis* magazine gave Cranis an award for founding the innovative junior training program, Project Upswing, they ran a piece recalling the boys' passion for tennis: "Don was 4-foot-10 and Paul was 6-foot-4.

The two went off to the public courts, looking like Mutt and Jeff...Throughout the winter...they shoveled the snow off the courts and played until there was no more light. They hated to quit and when it got dark they would try to see by the light from a street lamp...Phil Rubell rented an armory on Clinton and Washington Avenue...and put up two courts. There was no baseline because the armory did not have enough room. The highly polished floor was very fast and Paul, from desperation rather than from intuition, learned to hit every ball on the rise."

The following summer Cranis was ranked No. 6 in the East in his only year in the juniors.

"I never saw a baseball again," he said. Except as a spectator, that is. In 1953 he played everyday at the Sterling tennis courts across the street from Ebbets Field, and when he finished at about 4 o'clock he'd go to the side gate of the stadium and sneak in to watch the end of a Dodgers game.

In 1954 Cranis played tennis on scholarship at George Washington University, and after a stint in the U.S. Army, he competed on the amateur international circuit -- at Wimbledon, the French, the U.S. Championships and in tournaments in Europe and the Caribbean. When he returned to New York he completed his education at the Institute of Finance and went to work for the Daniel Construction Company, a business specializing in capital construction of chemical manufacturing and commercial facilities. He also worked as a real estate broker specializing in office leasing, but the game remained a top priority.

Over the years, he has earned 20 top ten national senior rankings and has been ranked first in Eastern men's singles or doubles in every age category. He has won or claimed the runner-up prize in 28 USTA national championships and captured the gold medal in men's 45 singles and doubles at the Maccabiah Games in Israel. A veteran USTA and Eastern volunteer, he has logged 17 years of service at the helm of national and sectional teams, two terms as Eastern's vice president and 15 years as the section's chairman of junior development.

In June of 1970 Cranis played for the first time in the national 35 clay court championships at the Shelter Rock Tennis Club in Manhasset, Long Island, and won his first gold ball by upsetting the top seed and beating King Van Nostrand for the title. "I was obviously sky high," he said. "I'm a power player, a serve-and-volleyer who's constantly at the net. That was my career. To use that strategy on a clay court against King, I had to play really well."

In August of 1970 at the US Open at Forest Hills, he asked tournament director Billy Talbert if they could run a men's 35 event during the Open. Talbert said yes, and you guessed it, in the first year of the tournament Cranis beat both Bill Tully and Bobby Riggs and wound up in the final against Sammy Giammalva.

"That was a good summer, winning my first national tournament on clay and reaching the finals of a national tournament on grass," recalled Cranis, who served for several years as the tournament director of the U.S. Open Men's 35 Championships.

But he had already solidified his legacy in the East in the 1960s by starting Project Upswing, the first group training program for the section's top-ranked juniors. He asked members of the Eastern Tennis Patrons, Alastair Martin and Dan Johnson, to underwrite the program, and they agreed to do it. Luke Sapan, the owner of the Midtown Tennis Club in New York City, donated the courts. George Seewagen was the head coach and Cranis directed the sessions, which ran from 6 to 9 a.m. from October through April.

World Tennis magazine publicized the program: "It is 4:30 a.m. on a Saturday morning and the alarm clock is ringing. Paul Cranis staggers out of bed in his Manhattan apartment because he has to; it was his idea. In 24 other homes around the New York metropolitan area...kids are jumping out of bed...From this group, the official Eastern team will be chosen to play the national junior circuit next summer. Never before has the section sent a full complement of juniors to the nationals. Now everyone capable of getting a national ranking can earn such a trip...Among the stars are Steve Siegel...Dickie Stockton...Jeff Podesta...Mike Fishbach...Eugene Mayer...and Marjorie Gengler."

The New York Times publicized the program, too. In the March 13, 1966 issue, a Charles Friedman piece led with a splashy headline: "Project Upswing: It Leads Tennis Hopefuls to Get Up at 4:30...The group, ranging from 12 to 18 years old, are the top players in their class and have been selected...for Project Upswing, aimed at lifting the section's best juniors to national heights...For years the outstanding juniors in the country generally have come from the South and the West Coast. The present national champion is Bobby Lutz of Los Angeles. His predecessor was Stan Smith of Pasadena...before Smith came Cliff Richey of Dallas."

Cranis was also instrumental in getting Seena Hamilton to found the Easter Bowl in 1968, which is now the largest national junior tournament in the country. "Paul Cranis' Project Upswing was the most progressive program in which a tennis association assumed responsibility for developing its talented children," said Hamilton, the Easter Bowl's tournament director. My son was in the program at Midtown and Paul talked me into running a national tournament there to give Eastern players the opportunity to compete against the best juniors in the country."

It's no wonder that Paul Cranis, who still resembles that enthusiastic 17-year-old from Brooklyn, is linked with a program that helped kids dream.

-- By Nancy Gill McShea

Lee Jackson

Lee Jackson insists she doesn't want to be known as the den mother for the world's best women professional tennis players, but admits that because she's been around so long she's become a constant presence in their lives. Then she says, "They're all my children. I am very blessed."

Indeed, the world's best women professionals literally rolled out the red carpet for Jackson on center court at the 1994 Australian Open. The gesture was part of a luxury trip, a gift given to her by the players, the staff members of the women's tour and the tournament promoters to applaud her professional dedication to the game.

Peachy Kellmeyer, the senior vice president of operations and player relations for the WTA Tour, introduced Jackson on that special occasion and repeated those sentiments last week. "Lee has been the backbone of our tour for the greater part of her life and a second mom to so many of us for the greater part of our lives. No one is more special to women's tennis," she said.

"I've done everything in the game but play pro tennis," said Jackson, 76, a native of Yonkers who called her first junior match more than 50 years ago at the Racquet Club on Park Hill in Westchester. "You name it, I've done it; it's the only thing I've ever done. "I played tennis myself and when my children Whitney and Leslie started, I became heavily involved in the junior game. I joined the Bronxville Field Club and met the umpire Jack Stahr, who became my mentor. I officiated regularly, and before I knew it I was president of the Eastern Umpires Association, vice president of the Eastern Tennis Association and a ranking chair on the Junior Tennis Council...I also wrote a column, "Ask the Umpire," for *World Tennis* magazine, worked for *Tennis Week* and was a member of the USTA Rules Committee when Jimmy Van Alen established the tie-break."

Jackson began officiating at national and collegiate tournaments and then gained clout as a top-notch umpire and referee by working both men's and women's matches at major professional events, including the US Open at Forest Hills. She witnessed great rivalries among the legends Ken Rosewall, Rod Laver, Maria Bueno, Billie Jean King, Evonne Goolagong and Margaret Court. "Everything was very casual then and the camaraderie was incredible," Lee said. "We traveled together, partied together, we spent all of our time together."

Jackson joined the women's professional tour as a full-time traveling referee and umpire in January of 1975. She worked the chair for great women's matches through the 1970s and '80s and developed a strong loyalty to the players.

In the semifinals of her first assignment in San Francisco, she survived a baptism of fire when Virginia Wade disagreed with one of her calls. She knew Wade would come after her as soon as the match was over, she said, "so I got out of that umpire's chair fast, and ran down the corridor...she caught up with me and said, 'You know you just cost me thousands of dollars?' I froze and thought, well, this is all part of the job. But we're good friends now."

Jackson has had to make other tough calls. She remembers overruling a baseline call on a shot hit by Martina Navratilova (from good to out) during a semifinal encounter between Navratilova and Hana Mandlikova. From the look on Mandlikova's face, she thought she might have been wrong. "And I can still see Martina begging me to change my overrule," she said, "but I did not. It cost her the match and also broke her record of most consecutive wins."

Lee has a thousand stories to tell, like the time she trained women umpires in Japan and said "they'd be afraid to call the ball out because they would feel sorry for the player." Or the time a cat gave birth to kittens in a Philadelphia arena during a tournament and Rosie Casals fed them all week. "Every animal Rosie had was a stray," she said. "You can't tell her a sad story about an animal or she'll cry." Lee helped Casals sneak one of the kittens out of the arena by wrapping it in a blanket, stuffing it in her tennis bag and hustling past the guards.

She once endured a humiliating cushion incident in front of several thousand spectators before a featured match in Texas. She walked onto the court and noticed that all the players were milling about. It was unusual, but she figured maybe they just wanted to see the match. "I climbed into the chair and sat down," she said. "...they had put a whoopee cushion on the chair and turned the microphone on. Can you imagine how embarrassing that was? Then they all turned around and left."

The players respect her as much for her sense of humor, intelligence and concern for people as they do for her work in tennis. In fact there's a real mutual admiration, as well as a battle of wits -- and wills -- going on between Jackson and her tennis friends.

Steffi Graf said, "I am so happy to see a special person like Lee get the recognition she deserves. I have known her since I first started playing the Tour and she has...been almost a second mother to me." Yet Graf challenged Jackson in a crossword puzzle duel during both the recent Masters Series tournament at Indian Wells, California, and the Ericsson Open in Key Biscayne, Florida. "Steffi's vocabulary is incredible," Jackson said, adding that the only player ever to win the Golden Slam of tennis (Steffi won all four majors and the Olympic gold medal in 1988) looks adorable and sublimely happy.

Jackson also loves word games, as does Navratilova. They once played scrabble in Tokyo, Japan, she said, "and Martina challenged a word of mine, or I challenged a word of hers...but we refused to give in to one another. She called Dallas, Texas, and had someone look the word up in a dictionary before we continued the game...and she was right..."

She has been so close to Chris Evert she was present at her engagements, her wedding to Andy Mills and the birth of their first child. When Evert said recently that Lee has been a tremendous asset to the game of tennis "and...I love her to death," it brought to mind a piece by Steve Flink that captures the spirit of their friendship. "Lee...and I were sitting on the beach during a tournament at Marco Island," said Evert, "and...this para-sailor came over our heads. I started telling Lee about an experience I had para-sailing once in Australia when I got sick to my stomach...I tried to tell her how wild and dangerous it is...Lee kept saying she could never do it. Then I mentioned that I would give her a hundred dollars if she would go up there and para-sail. I thought she would turn down my offer. But up she went, waving down at me on the beach and smiling. When it was over, she told me she doesn't know how to swim..."

Jackson stepped down from the chair in the pro game in 1990 and assumed her current position as the Tour's Tournament-Player Liaison in charge of operations on the road. She still works the chair at "hit and giggle" pro-celebrity tournaments, like the Chris Evert charity for children, but now she's more involved in the pros' lives off the court. She impresses upon them the importance of education and cultivating good manners.

"I take them to hospitals and when they see less fortunate youngsters, or people at nursing homes, it's a rude awakening," she said. "When they see how thrilled these people are to see them they are glad they went. The same thing happens at sponsor parties. I drag them by the hand and say 'Introduce yourselves...See that gentleman over there? He's writing your check this week. Make sure you go over and thank him. You'll have a fan for the rest of your life.'"

The great tennis champion Billie Jean King deserves the last word here on Lee Jackson: "Mama Lee, the heart and soul of the women's tour." Amen.

-- By Nancy Gill McShea

George Seewagen

An editorial in the sports section of *The New York Herald Tribune* once stated unequivocally: "If George Seewagen...had become interested in tennis when he was roaming the courts and diamonds for Newtown High School [in Queens]...we're certain he would have been the champ of the world."

Seewagen, who passed away in 1990 from the effects of a stroke he had suffered a few years earlier, achieved spectacular success in team sports as a young athlete. But a negative first encounter on a tennis court motivated him to do a complete about-face and become the heroic "Iron Horse" of the individual sport of tennis for more than half a century. By example and dedication, he inspired a passion for the game in others and brought respect and great dignity to the role of professional tennis teacher and coach.

He coached at St. John's University for 49 years and taught all week long at clubs around the Eastern Section in New York, Connecticut and New Jersey. He was Eastern's Junior Davis Cup coach and conducted free clinics sponsored by the Eastern Tennis Patrons, the forerunner to the present Junior Tennis Foundation. His goal was to get tennis into the schools. "If tennis is to thrive...the schools must play a major role," Seewagen said. "Our schools prepare the individual for life...and are remiss...if they fail to teach youngsters...sports which are available to them in their post school years... After graduation...too many boys and girls confine their interest in sports to the role of spectator.

"This is primarily due to the physical education program...sports such as baseball, basketball and football unfortunately have little if any carry over value to post school life."

George's son, Butch Seewagen, said: "My father went seven days a week and seven nights; he was doing clinics all the time. I know, because he would always drag me to them. I'd be eight years old and I'd be demonstrating the forehand. Family time was 4 o'clock Monday afternoons. We'd go to Jones Beach and we'd be shivering."

Added Seewagen's daughter Barbara: "Dad could not say no to tennis. I once said to him, 'you're doing too much, you have to give up something.' He decided to quit coaching at St. John's. His team arrived at the house and gave him a plaque. He looked at me, shrugged and said, 'How can I leave?' and he went back."

George Seewagen always preached the joys of teaching to his students. "Teach tennis, teach tennis," he'd say. He inspired at least 50 members of his St. John's teams to become teachers, even while they pursued other careers. And he inspired his regular students to pitch in, too, like the leading New York ophthalmologist Renee Richards, who coached Martina Navratilova. Richards has said she tried to emulate Seewagen because "his dignity and behavior commanded instant respect and became a model for me." Then there was Ted Zoob, the president of the North Shore Tennis Club and a lawyer who was a teaching pro for years at Alley Pond. Seewagen also taught the public advocate Mark Green, who might be giving a few lessons on the sly. Add to the list the familiar names of Rick Liebman, Don Thompson, Willie Notar, Dick Squires, Eddie Bertram, David Benjamin and Terry McMahon.

"I watched how George acted and thought 'that's how I would like to be.' He was so classy," said McMahon, who has followed the Seewagen method throughout his 40 years as a junior/collegiate coach. "It was the discipline. George would say, 'You're going to wear all white, exercise strenuously, be courteous, be absolutely fair and try your best all the time. Pretend your opponent is your beloved grandmother or grandfather and treat him accordingly, whether you're winning or losing, regardless of how he treats you.'"

Seewagen had been brought up in a team sport environment as a mascot to the Elmhurst Grays, a baseball team managed by his father. So it followed that sports writers would later tout him as a "clouting All-City first baseman on Newtown's PSAL championship team." He also achieved All-City status in basketball and was a member of the winning mile relay team at the Penn track relays. He was offered a contract to play for the New York Yankees farm team out of high school, but turned it down to attend Springfield College in Massachusetts. At Springfield, he lettered in baseball, basketball and tennis and was named All-American soccer goalie for the national intercollegiate championship team.

The folk story about the letter in tennis that unfolds in all the newspaper clippings claims that Seewagen's college roommate challenged him to a game of tennis in his junior year and trounced him. So he took a physical education course in tennis, made the team in his senior year and lost only two matches. From that point on, he was a man on a mission. By the mid-1930s he had started his career as a physical education teacher at his Newtown alma mater and was a top-ten Eastern tennis player in the amateur game for three years before he turned teaching pro.

Seewagen made a couple of appearances at the amateur U.S. National Championships at Forest Hills alongside greats Fred Perry, Bobby Riggs, Frank Shields and Don Budge before they, too, turned pro. When he lost to Budge there in 1936 he wore shorts; it was the only time he ever wore shorts on a tennis court, probably in deference to Budge. (Budge won the Grand Slam in 1938 and turned pro in 1939. He was an early proponent of professional tennis, arguing that with the incentive of financial reward, fewer stars would leave the game before they reached their full potential.)

Teaching pros like Seewagen got to play with former amateur champions--among them Budge, Perry, Bill Tilden, Vinnie Richards, Pancho Segura, Jack Kramer, Lew Hoad and Pancho Gonzalez -- on the pro tour and at pro exhibitions. Seewagen was a leader in the U.S. Professional (Lawn) Tennis Association, serving as the national president from 1948-1953 and again in 1963, and as president of the Eastern division for 12 years. The organization ran the pro game, including the U.S. Pro Championships at Forest Hills, so Seewagen worked them as the tournament director/referee. He bought a tux to referee the pros' matches at Madison Square Garden, and then he'd play exhibitions with the pros at Fordham, at the Notlek Tennis Club (that was owner Frank Kelton's name spelled backward) and at Grossinger's in the Catskills during the second World War to raise money for the troops.

During the war, Seewagen was a member of the National Guard and the tournament referee at the U.S. Pro Indoors at the Park Avenue Seventh Regiment Armory in Manhattan. Butch Seewagen and McMahon were ball boys and saw the world's best players up close, like Tony Trabert, Gardnar Mulloy, Vic Seixas, Bill Talbert and Dick Savitt. Butch got to work Savitt's court the three times he won the indoors. "He liked me because when I was a kid he hit with me at the armory," Butch said. McMahon recalled the time a top player had food poisoning and gave him a hard time during his match: "George followed the player into the locker room and told him, quietly, that he was never to speak to any of his ball boys again in that manner or he'd be banned from the tournament." The player's response? "'Yes, sir!'"

"My sister and I were never allowed to play as kids before our father whitened our shoes the night before a match," said Butch, who along with Barbara was ranked first in the East and among the country's top juniors. "He said you cannot go on the court with dirty shoes. We always felt we couldn't disappoint him with our behavior. And all his students felt the same way." One time when Butch was playing Cliff Richey in the semifinals of the National Boys' 18s at Kalamazoo, he couldn't convert three match points and, in fact, lost by a let cord. He was crushed. But he won the sportsmanship award and his father told him he was more proud of him for that accomplishment than if he had won the tournament.

Perhaps Butch's wife Chris captured George Seewagen's spirit best when she said, "Tennis was the wind beneath his wings that made him soar."

-- By Nancy Gill McShea

Dick Stockton

The men's tennis coach at the University of Virginia could be mistaken for a professor. He is well thought-out, proficient in the language and speaks with authority. He is more interested in recruiting players who look at the school before they hear from him, because that means they're considering UVA for the right reasons. He also likes the depth and diverse lineups in today's collegiate game that can make any match feel like an international Davis Cup challenge.

The coach is Dick Stockton, and he's been winning tennis championships at the highest levels of the national and international game for over 40 years.

He was a junior and collegiate champ; played professionally for 13 years; was ranked No. 8 in the world in 1977 and six times among the U.S. top ten; was a five-year member of the U.S. Davis Cup team; and won his third men's 45 doubles title at the 2000 US Open.

When Stockton turned pro in June of 1972 the game was really taking off in this country, and he and his group of junior tennis buddies -- among them Brian Gottfried, Erik van Dillen, Harold Solomon, Eddie Dibbs, Roscoe Tanner and Jimmy Connors -- were thrust into the limelight of a major tennis boom and unyielding media scrutiny.

Sports Illustrated featured Stockton and Gottfried in a June '72 piece, "Hail the Trinity twosome," to sum up the NCAA Championships: "The bleachers were jammed with spectators and hundreds more watched from the steep hillside when the pair of tanned singles finalists, both as taut as racket gut--and both from Trinity University (in Texas) were introduced...One was four-time All-American Dick Stockton, a native of Garden City, N.Y., the top seed. Across the net: Brian Gottfried, Stockton's roommate...Gottfried won the first set and had Stockton muttering, barking at a ball boy, complaining about the net and throwing his racket down in disgust...When Gottfried lost the seventh game of the second set on a close line call it was his turn to launch into some fine Pancho Gonzalez imitations: a snarl, a grimace, a glare..." Stockton won the title, 4-6, 6-4, 6-3, 6-2.

"I played my last amateur match [at the NCAAs] on Saturday, flew with Brian and another teammate, Paul Gerken, to England on Sunday and we played as pros on Monday," Stockton recalled. "It was kind of a natural progression; we had played a lot of pro tournaments during college. In my second week as a pro I reached the third round of Wimbledon and came away with $300.

"The seventies was the best time to be playing professional tennis, especially in the second half of the decade," he said. There was tremendous interest in the pro game, more and more people were playing, so there were times when the three major networks had tennis on at the same time. PBS had a lot of tennis, too, and this was all before cable.

Stockton points out that Bjorn Borg, Solomon and Dibbs popularized the slower, topspin baseline exchange that became the vogue and influenced a new generation of players. But Tanner's big serve, Connors' attacking baseline style and Stockton's classic backhand, overhead and volley also fared well on the small screen and impressed tennis fans.

Television aired the Stockton-Connors final at the 1977 U.S. Pro Indoors in Philadelphia and Curry Kirkpatrick covered the tournament for *Sports Illustrated*: "Stockton blitzed his way through Gottfried, Ken Rosewall and Jeff Borowiak without the loss of a set...In the final, Connors...after taking a 2-1 lead in sets, fell behind 3-1 in the fourth...he came to 0-40 against Stockton's serve with three chances to break back, tie the match and run it out... Inexplicably, he blew the next three points and lost the game. Stockton resumed serving one-bouncers into the seats, volleying to the corners and dominating the indomitable Connors...In accepting the trophy he said, 'I've never played better for five days in my life.'"

"Dick was playing really well then," agreed Gottfried, recalling that the best thing about the old days was that their group would battle each other on the court and then go to dinner together afterward. "But the thing his friends and I would remember most are the back injuries which cut short his career. He had trouble playing multiple weeks and really struggled with it."

Gottfried said he was 10 and Stockton was 11 when they first played in Chattanooga and "nobody beat Dickie in those days." He was a feared junior champion, winning 20 national titles, the most ever recorded by an Eastern junior (and second only to Scott Davis of the U.S.). He also set a record in doubles with van Dillen by winning the Nationals in each of the four age categories and ranking first in the country for five years. "I was petrified the first time I had to play him, and I was 15 and he was 10," admitted Butch Seewagen, who beat Stockton just that one time.

"There's never been a better junior player than Dickie Stockton," Jimmy Connors said recently. "I loved competing against him. We've played a lot of terrific matches since we were 8 and 9 years old, we've had great times together and still remain the best of friends."

Stockton dismisses his junior titles as "no big deal. You just played and whoever won, won." Yet he admits that you have to be incredibly determined and acknowledges that his mother, Dorothy, once said that his concentration was so good that he could be playing and the clubhouse could be on fire and he wouldn't notice.

He defeated legends such as Arthur Ashe, Ilie Nastase, Rod Laver, Guillermo Vilas, Rosewall, Borg and his junior buddies in notching eight singles and 16 pro doubles titles. He was a singles semifinalist at Wimbledon and the French and was twice a quarterfinalist at the US Open. He won five mixed doubles championships: the US Open, the French and the worlds. He posted a 5-5 record as a playing member of the U.S. Davis Cup team and was a member of the 1979 championship squad. He has also won seven senior titles in the 35s and 45s at the US Open and Wimbledon.

The most exciting match he was ever involved in was in Hartford, Connecticut, at the 1975 Aetna World Cup, an annual competition between the U.S. and Australia. Whoever won four of seven matches was the winner. Stockton, Ashe, Stan

Smith, Marty Riessen and Bob Lutz made up the U.S. roster, while Laver, Rosewall, John Newcombe, John Alexander and Roy Emerson represented Australia.

"It was my first year in the thing and I was shocked when our captain Dennis Ralston said I was going to play No. 1 for the U. S.," he said. "I had to play Laver in the first match. I was terrified. We were the only night match scheduled and there wasn't a seat to be had. I was down 3-0 so fast I was afraid it would be over in 20 minutes. Dennis told me to relax and play one point at a time. I found some air to breathe and then played very well. It was 6-6 in the sudden death tie-break and I had two match points on my serve but couldn't do it. I lost, 5-7, 6-4, 7-6, and we lost the match 4-3.

"I cried when it was over and literally had nightmares about that particular match for eight to 10 years."

Stockton was hitting with Laver this past February at a Washington charity function and said to him, "Hey Rocket, you know one time you hit me with a ball so hard I thought you were going to kill me. Do you remember that? Laver said, 'Yeah, up at the Aetna Cup.' It surprised me that he remembered all these years later."

At the 1983 US Open, Stockton and Gottfried played doubles on the old Court 3, and Stockton's wife Liz, then a Fordham coed and a ball girl, was assigned to work the match. "Everybody wanted Borg's court," Liz said, "but I knew of Dick because he was a New Yorker and my dad (teaching pro Jaime de Carvalho) raved about him. I remember he and Brian were like this cute, tan, All-American team."

In August of 1994 Liz was again assigned to Stockton's court, to work a clinic with him during the Nuveen senior tournament at the Westchester Country Club in Rye. This time Dick noticed her. After the clinic he asked her to grab a racquet and hit with him. Two years later they were married.

-- By Nancy Gill McShea

John Lloyd and Dick Stockton enjoyed their years in the pro ranks.

Chapter 22

2002: Aitchison, Annacone, Horvath and Ryland

Alex. B. Aitchison

Aussie native Alex. Aitchison unleashed a list of humorous asides about tennis in New York.

If you were involved in junior tennis in any capacity during the 1970s and 1980s, and especially if you spent any time at the Port Washington Tennis Academy on Long Island, you remember that everybody was jockeying for position to curry favor with Alex. Aitchison.

During that time frame, which coincided with the tennis boom in New York, Aitchison was one of a handful of the game's administrators who elevated the status of junior tennis in this country and around the world. He was the chairman and chief executive officer of the Port Academy, and in 1977 he founded and directed the famous Rolex International Junior Championships there. At the same time, he was an influential officer of the Eastern Tennis Association, serving as the section's president in 1982 and '83, and before that, as the vice president. He was also the chairman of both the ETA and USTA Junior Tennis Councils and was the first person commissioned to formulate plans for a national junior development program and training center.

Alex. was the right person for the job. Not only did he fit the poster image of a proper tennis official, looking crisp and dignified in his navy blazer while doing Rolex TV commentary alongside John Barrett, the BBC's voice of Wimbledon, but he also had that unhurried manner any executive strives for, particularly one who is directing a frenetic junior tennis tournament.

Aitchison's frame of reference growing up in his native Australia prepared him for the role. He began playing tennis in the early 1940s at age 9 in Essendon, a suburb of Melbourne, where he says "there were public tennis courts on every corner just like there are gas stations here." He gained international experience as an Australian player, yet admits, with a twinkle in his eye, that he moved into sports promotion "when it was decided that I was not going to do anything brilliant [on the court]." In 1971, when he was working as the chief administrator of the Lawn Tennis Association of Victoria which conducted the Australian Open, his friend, the great Australian coach Harry Hopman, called and asked him to join him at the Port Academy as the manager.

Aitchison, then 41, and his wife Marjorie arrived in the United States with their three children -- Perry, Grant and Scott -- and the whole family became involved in tennis. Alex. and the boys were all ranked Eastern players and Marjorie worked side by side with her husband at every tournament he directed. They had such a high profile that in 1987 the Aitchison family was honored as Eastern's "Tennis Family of the Year" and in 1992 Alex. received the "Tennis Man of the Year" award.

"Alex. is handsome, charming, and with his Australian accent, he could have been the pied piper of women's league tennis," says his friend Doris Herrick, who worked closely with Aitchison during her tenure as Eastern's executive director. "Instead, he was the consummate administrator of our junior effort, setting us up to rank as one of the elite junior programs in the country."

He was also a member of more than 13 USTA national committees and the administrator, tournament director and/or chairman of a host of adult and junior competitive events, including several USTA Satellite Circuits: Avon, American Express and Lionel, among them (1972-'78); the 21-and-under World and Amateur Championships; the Girls' 12, 14, 16 National Indoors; the U.S. Olympic National Sports Festival and Olympic Trials; and the US Open qualifying tournament.

"I've worked with juniors all my life, but I've also had some exciting stuff happen with adults," says Aitchison, who today runs adult league programs. He worked with Ivan Lendl on forehand stroke technique and with Martina Navratilova on fitness when he was president of the tennis division of the S.T.A.R.T. program -- an acronym for sports technique and reaction training --when both players were ranked No. 1 in the world.

"I've always appreciated the opportunity to help players, both adults and juniors, to achieve their goals, whatever they may be -- a US Open champ or a happy social player."

But junior tennis has been his legacy. With Aitchison at the helm from 1977 to 1986, the Rolex Championships thrived at Port, becoming the most famous and largest indoor junior tennis tournament in the world. Most Eastern juniors played the Rolex just for the unique experience of competing against someone from a foreign country. At the same time they had the rare opportunity of watching future greats such as Andrea Jaeger, Tracy Austin, Goran Ivanisevic, Stefan Edberg, Mats Wilander, Ivan Lendl and New Yorkers Molly Van Nostrand, Paul Annacone and Kathleen Horvath, among others, play on their home turf.

So it was no surprise when USTA President Randy Gregson appointed Aitchison in May of 1985 as the personal consultant to the president and a special committee to establish a player development program in the United States. He recalls that Gregson asked him if the U.S. needed a player development program and his response was, "Good God, yes, what took you so long...Here we are the greatest tennis country in the world and places like Canada, Sweden and Czechoslovakia have development programs and we don't...I said to Randy, 'I have a job,' and he said, 'Well, leave it.'"

Together, they mapped out a plan, wrote a basic formal program and submitted it to the USTA board, which approved it. The idea was to establish one national facility in a climate where the weather would be conducive to year-round play, and four regional facilities that would feed into it. To expand further, each section would have its own development program so that there would be a real follow through, all the way through from the grass roots to the national level, with the purpose of feeding into the national system.

Aitchison left his job at Port and traveled around the U.S. for a year looking for potential sites. "The system works," he says. "We now have a wonderful facility at Key Biscayne. And I feel very proud of the part I played in getting it off the ground. I knew how to approach it because of my experience in Australia and had every confidence that we could deliver..."

He was also the first general chairman of this Hall of Fame dinner in 1988. "I thought it was a wonderful idea then, and still do, to recognize the people who perform a service to the game in the East," he says. Now it's your year, Alex. Congratulations!

-- By Nancy Gill McShea

Paul Annacone

Russ Adams

Paul Annacone has had more live TV close-ups while coaching Pete Sampras than any celebrity who has ever appeared on CNN's "Larry King Live." He's no publicity hound, though. He has always appeared incognito in the players' box, hiding out behind sunglasses and his trademark navy baseball cap.

It's not that he was trying to elude the paparazzi. He was just trying to soak in the historic atmosphere and urge Sampras on. "It was an amazing seven years. I got to coach and live a close-knit life with the best player of all time and watch him win eight Grand Slam titles," says Annacone, still awed by the fact that when Sampras beat Patrick Rafter in the 2000 Wimbledon final to win his record 13th title, he couldn't walk very well, never warmed up and just went out and played. "That was the most amazing accomplishment...!"

Annacone's childhood friend Jon Grossman explains that while Paul is also very competitive – don't even think about toying with him on the golf course unless you're "athletically challenged like I am," he says, laughing. -- he is really a low-key guy with a self-deprecating sense of humor. What you see is what you get.

The power brokers in the tennis business recognize Annacone's worthy character traits and are equally impressed by his credentials. They point out that because he is still in his late thirties and already accomplished in four high-profile areas of tennis – he was the top-ranked collegiate player in the country, the 12th ranked professional player in the world and a member of the ATP Tour Board and the vice president of the Player Council before he was Sampras's coach -- he is the ideal person to head up the new USA Tennis High Performance program, a support system for America's top prospects.

"Paul is a leader who knows what it takes to succeed at the highest levels of tennis...his experience will be key to programs that support the development of young players into American champions," USTA Executive Director Rick Ferman has said.

Annacone is excited by the challenge. "Here I am, I think of myself as a small town guy and I have the opportunity to have a significant impact on the structure and philosophy of American tennis at the highest level," he says. "It's what I've lived for the last 25 years."

Twenty-five years ago, Annacone was a 14-year-old ranked junior player out of East Hampton, N.Y., who decided to pursue a career in tennis. He moved to Florida to train at Nick Bollettieri's Tennis Academy and then went on to star at the University of Tennessee. He changed his whole game, switching from wood to an oversize racquet, and at the suggestion of his college coach, Mike DePalmer, adopted an unusual chip-and-charge mode on his opponent's second shot, which most players wouldn't even attempt. He was a three-time All-American at Tennessee, in 1982, '83 and in 1984, when he lost just two matches all year and was ranked first in the country. That June at Wimbledon, he came through the men's singles qualifier and went all the way to the quarters before losing to Jimmy Connors.

Between 1984 and 1994, he won 17 professional titles in singles and doubles and was a finalist 22 times, even though he spent some time on the sidelines recuperating from a couple of minor surgeries. He excelled at doubles, winning a Grand Slam title at the 1985 Australian Open and reaching the semis in 1987. He was also a doubles semifinalist at Wimbledon in 1986, a finalist at the 1990 US Open and a semifinalist in 1989.

U.S. Davis Cup Captain Patrick McEnroe recalls that he and Annacone might have won the 1988 US Open doubles title -- they were a game away from defeating the eventual champs, Sergio Casal and Emilio Sanchez -- when McEnroe choked. "I served for the match at 5-4 in the fifth set, choked it away, and we lost like 8-6," he says. "Paul really held me up. He really mentored me. I thought of him almost as a big brother with a slightly different approach [on the court] from my real big brother in tennis. We were both from New York and very few of us made it all the way to the pros."

Paul has a different take on that match. "Patrick didn't choke it away, we were a team," he says.

Annacone is partial to three victories that he's probably already stored among his highlight films. The first was a 1986 Davis Cup match between the U.S. and Australia in Brisbane. Ken Flach and Paul were partners. "We beat John Fitzgerald and Pat Cash, 8-10, 1-6, 7-5, 13-11, 9-7, in a marathon that lasted over two days," he says, recounting the score precisely without skipping a beat.

His second favorite memory took place at the 1985 Los Angeles Open, where he pulled out a 7-6, 6-7, 7-6 barnburner to defeat Stefan Edberg and win the singles title. Paul's father, Dominic, who watched the whole match on a satellite dish, still sounds nervous when discussing it, as though it had occurred last week.

Annacone's third highlight film unfolded at the USTA National Tennis Center on opening day of the 1986 US Open, when he upset John McEnroe in five sets in Louis Armstrong Stadium. Paul was already an accomplished professional at the time, but fans kept milling around the grounds and circling back to check the big scoreboard outside the stadium in astonishment. That match put Paul on the map in Queens and secured his legacy in Eastern's history scrapbook. Whenever he played the Open during the rest of his career, Eastern fans packed the stands to cheer him on.

Yet Annacone's final legacy could well be as a natural teacher, as he goes about the task of grooming future U.S. tennis champions. His friend Grossman says, "I am a mediocre golfer at best, yet Paul continues to encourage me to become better...The last time we played, I beat him by a few strokes for the first time ever (his neck was injured but he stuck it out anyway, making fun of himself over every errant shot). At the end of the round he turned to me and said, 'Ah grasshopper, the student has become the teacher.' That made my year."

Pete Sampras sums it up: "I want to congratulate you, Paul, on an accomplishment you definitely deserve. You are one of the best coaches around our game. I owe you a thank you for all the things you have taught me and wish you the best in your future. You're a great friend and a great teacher. Thanks for all our wonderful years together."

-- By Nancy Gill McShea

Kathleen Horvath

Kathleen Horvath qualifies as the ultimate professional. Within the last two decades, she has been ranked among the world's top ten professional tennis players, graduated magna cum laude with bachelor's and master's degrees from the University of Pennsylvania Wharton School of Business, and is currently a vice president at Goldman, Sachs, specializing in private wealth management.

She values her tennis career as a stepping stone, as a successful experience that gave her confidence. "It's like a do-over," she says. "It's fun when you have wisdom from something that you can apply to something new. You start with the work ethic and discipline and get the analytical tools to back up the tennis."

Horvath began scripting her guide on "how to succeed" in the early summer of 1973 at the tender age of 8 when she lost to the top seed, 6-3, 6-1, in the first round of a girls' 12 tournament at the Poughkeepsie Tennis Club.

"I was devastated. It was my first tournament and I barely knew how to keep score," she recalls, summoning an instant replay of the painful experience. Her father said afterward that if she wanted to win she would have to practice. And practice she did, all day, all summer, often serving 10 buckets of balls at a clip. At summer's end, in a season-ending interclub match, Kathleen defeated the same girl she had lost to earlier in the summer. Not only that, she defeated her in the rubber match to clinch victory for her team.

"I was the hero of the day and I was hooked," she says.

She began to hit regularly with Garry Vander Veer, a philosophy professor at Vassar and a top club player, who encouraged her. She also signed up for lessons with Kit Byron at Rye Racquet in the winter and at the Old Oaks Country Club in the summer. "Kit was my first true coach, he was very selfless and taught me a lot," she says.

"Kathy Horvath was a big-time Eastern player; nobody ever came close to her. She put the Rye Racquet Club on the map in the 1970s as a center for the development of world class juniors, and me along with it as a pro who was capable of training them," says Byron, who at the time was a young teaching pro in his twenties. "Her distinguishing characteristic? When she had you on the ropes, she instinctively came in, cut off the court and volleyed the ball into the open area rather than wait for an error.

"She was so dedicated she would play all day, all summer long," Byron continued. "In the evening, I'd be closing the club pro shop, it would be dark, and I'd hear thump, thump, thump. She'd be out there, so tired, but still pounding balls against the backboard...I'd take the racquet out of her hand and remind her that there's always tomorrow."

Kathleen admits that she worked hard and was really dedicated, explaining that she inherited the strong work ethic and courage from her parents, who emigrated to this country under difficult circumstances. Her mother, Erika, escaped from East Germany and her father, Andrew, fled from Hungary during the 1956 revolution. They shared with her an appreciation of the arts and introduced her to the usual childhood activities of swimming, ballet and tennis, but she gravitated to tennis, she says, because it is "more measurable" than other sports.

She earned her first national 12s ranking by age 10 and zoomed to the No. 4 spot the following year. Andrea Jaeger and Susan Mascarin were her contemporaries, yet Kathleen is the only player who has won all four USTA national junior clay court age group titles in consecutive years. At 13 she was the country's top-ranked singles and doubles player in the USTA Girls' 16s division. That same year, she won the national 21-and-under singles title and a wild card into the US Open qualifier. She became the youngest player to qualify for the Open, a record that still stands.

As a result, she was privileged to play her first pro tournament on her home turf at the 1979 US Open on her 14th birthday, and the next day she and Bjorn Borg were pictured hitting forehands on the front page of *The New York Times*.

She turned pro at 15, played U.S. Fed Cup, was a singles quarterfinalist at the Olympics and in 1984 was ranked No. 10 in the world. She won eight pro titles, including the Ginny Championships Tournament of Champions in Honolulu, defeating Carling Bassett 7-6 in a third-set final. She was also a finalist in six pro events and was twice a singles quarterfinalist at the French Open Championships, the first time in 1983 after she snapped Martina Navratilova's 84-match win streak in the round of 16.

Bud Collins recorded the dramatic encounter in his *Tennis Encyclopedia*: "...Martina Navratilova and Kathy Horvath shared a court in Paris...In retrospect, it may have been the most significant match of the year...it was something special. Navratilova had won her first 36 matches of 1983 before meeting the teenager...a former child prodigy...Horvath had been runner-up to Chris Evert in the German Open the previous week...But nothing prepared her for what happened at Stade Roland Garros...The unseeded American ...posted a stunning 6-4, 0-6, 6-3 victory."

Kathleen became the star of every TV sports highlight film and gained instant celebrity around the world.

By the spring of 1989, she was 23 years old and ready to write the second chapter of her life. After she lost in the first round of the Bausch and Lomb in Amelia Island, Florida, she noticed a few pros doing wind sprints in the darkness and decided right then and there to retire. She called her father and told him she was going back to school. She asked her friend Professor Vander Veer for advice and he encouraged her to look at the Ivy Leagues and play up the tennis experience. Despite interrupting her formal education at 15 and completing high school through correspondence courses, she scored 1300 on the S.A.T.'s and was accepted at Penn.

She returned to New York after graduation and took a job in institutional sales with Merrill-Lynch. She asked people where the best place was to do private banking, and when everybody said Goldman, Sachs, it became her first choice.

"I've been pretty lucky in terms of things I set out to accomplish," she says. "Like having kids, I wanted both boys and girls." Kathleen Horvath and her husband, Phil Fresen, are the proud parents of Erika, 3, and 18-month-old twin boys, Andy and R.J.

-- By Nancy Gill McShea

Robert Ryland

Ed Goldman

Bob Ryland shows only a few signs of slowing down, even though he will turn 82 this June. He is a survivor and an optimist. He still teaches tennis to children a couple of times a week with his friends Arvelia Myers and Leslie Allen, he laughs easily and often, and speaks cheerfully when reminiscing about his unique, 70-year tour of the world's tennis courts.

Ryland was the first African-American to play professional tennis. The promoter Jack March recruited him in the 1950s, when tennis was still an amateur sport, to join the World Pro Tour and compete with Lew Hoad, Pancho Gonzalez and Don Budge. It would be another decade before the onset of the Open era in 1968, with amateurs and pros competing in the same events. Ryland was also the first African-American to compete in the NCAA Championships, the first to lead his team to the small college national championships as a player-coach and the first to play at the prestigious Los Angeles Tennis Club.

Ryland has coached some of the world's top-ranked professionals, among them Harold Solomon, Renee Blount and Leslie Allen. In the early 1960s, he taught tennis to government VIPs Robert MacNamara and members of the Kennedy family in Washington, D.C. Later, he taught celebrities Barbra Streisand, Bill Cosby, Tony Bennett, Mike Wallace and Eartha Kitt at the Midtown Tennis Club in Manhattan, where he worked from 1963 to 1990.

"Bob's name would have been right up there with the great players of his time — Hoad, Gonzalez, Budge, Bobby Riggs and the rest — had he not been born a black man in America," Allen has said. "Still, he endured and succeeded in a sport that was not inviting. We can appreciate his accomplishments and, for generations to come, learn from his experiences."

Born in 1920, the son of an African-American mother and an Irish-Indian father, Ryland learned early to cope silently with restraints imposed on him by racial prejudice. He still vividly recalls the indignities he suffered during his cross-country travels. He was hauled into police stations and ordered to fork over hundreds of dollars — just because he was driving a Cadillac — and forced to sneak in and out of back doors to compete in college tennis matches. He emphasizes, however, that those experiences paled compared to the shock of regularly seeing people of color strung up on trees during his early childhood in Mobile, Alabama. When you witness that kind of horror or feel the jolt of a policeman pulling you into harm's way for no reason, he said, living with fear becomes a way of life. "You're scared to death, but you have no choice, you just go through it."

Ryland long ago adopted a philosophical view of his heritage. "When you're part black and part white you can deal better with prejudice," he says. "You know everybody's the same. But you don't understand that unless you have to deal with the reality of racism."

After his mother, Gussie, and twin brother, Joe, died of pneumonia in 1920 when he was a baby, his father, Robert, sent him from his Chicago home to live with his grandmother in Mobile. While there, he helped pick cotton for the family with his great grandfather, who had been a slave.

He returned to his Chicago roots at age ten and began playing tennis with his father in the public parks. From the early 1930s until the mid-1950s, he was twice the ATA national singles champ and three times the runner-up, during which time he also embarked on a 15-year journey in search of a college degree.

In 1939, he was a student at Tilden Tech High School, won both the Illinois State and junior ATA singles titles and earned a tennis scholarship to Xavier University in New Orleans. "The nuns bought us a station wagon and the five of us [teammates] would travel all over the country playing," he has said.

Ryland left school for a stint in the U.S. Army, from 1941 to 1945, and still managed to play tournaments and exhibitions with players the caliber of Alice Marble, Mary Hardwicke and Dr. Reggie Weir at the Cosmopolitan Club in Harlem. In 1946 he took to the road again, won public parks events in New Jersey and New York and was awarded another tennis scholarship, this time to Wayne University in Detroit. He broke the color barrier that year at the NCAA Championships, advancing to the singles semifinals before losing to USC's Bob Faulkenburg (a future Wimbledon singles champ). Ryland was later inducted into the university's hall of fame.

In 1947, he again abandoned academics and headed for California. He worked nights in the post office and played tennis with Gonzalez during the day. He broke the color barrier at the Los Angeles Tennis Club, losing there in the Pacific Southwest Championships, 6-4, 7-5, to Ham Richardson, the country's No. 1 player at the time. (It would be five years before another black, Arthur Ashe, was permitted to play there.)

In 1954, Tennessee AA&I in Nashville offered Ryland a scholarship to be the player-coach, and he twice led his team to the small college national championships, with help from his New York recruits Vernon Morgan and Billy Davis. (When asked if he could beat Davis, Bob laughed and said: "Billy is a good player but he never beat me. He claims he beat me for ice cream but I don't remember that.") He left Tennessee with his bachelor's degree, came to New York and qualified for the 1955 U.S. Championships at Forest Hills.

Ryland worked as the physical education director of the YMCA in Montclair, N.J., but by 1957 he opted to teach tennis and joined the U.S. Professional (Lawn) Tennis Association. In 1973, the comedian Bill Cosby asked him to accompany him around the world so Cosby could improve his game. A decade later, Allen asked him to tour Europe with her while she was playing the women's pro circuit. "Bob built the foundation for my game, he was always a constant, a guiding force in my life," she has said. "He took me from a teenager dreaming about the pros right to center court at Wimbledon."

-- By Nancy Gill McShea

Chapter 23

2003: Amdur, Casale, S. Mayer and Prince

Neil Amdur

For almost half a century, Neil Amdur has survived the relentless pressure of daily deadlines in his position as one of this country's leading sports writers/reporters, editors and producers -- with a special affection for tennis. He has thrived as the sports editor of *The New York Times* for the past 12 years, from 1990 to early 2003; and before that, as a tennis producer for CBS Sports, between 1975 and 1976; as a daily sports reporter and the tennis specialist at *The Times* over a 15-year period, from 1968-1984; and as the editor-in-chief of *World Tennis* magazine, from 1984-1990. He was also a tennis reporter for the *Miami Herald* in the early 1960s.

Amdur has basically kept tennis in the spotlight throughout the Open era. He has either covered every great player, important match or significant development in the sport's grassroots/business sector himself or assigned reporters to do the job.

How has he coped with the pressure? "I started running 3 to 4 times a week, anywhere from 3 to 6 miles a day, around 1976, and have run everywhere I have gone as a reporter – Moscow, London, Paris," he said. "And I play tennis when I can."

"Neil is a great reporter and writer who became an even greater sports editor," said his friend Tony Kornheiser, a Washington Post columnist and the host of a show on ESPN. "Under Neil's watch, *The Times* set the table for every sports section in the country..."

Ray Corio, a veteran copy editor at *The Times*, concurred: "Like Lincoln, Churchill and Havlicek, Neil has been the right one at the right place and the right time. Black power salutes on the victory stand...Billie Jean crumbling Bobby

Riggs. Rosie Ruiz taking a subway shortcut to Central Park. Renee Richards earning a US Open invitation. Borg outdueling McEnroe in a marathon Wimbledon final."

When the late Howard Cosell reviewed one of Amdur's five published books, he wrote: "Neil Amdur is a writer for his time. He understands the role of sports in contemporary society."

Amdur recently took on a new assignment at *The Times* as the senior editor for staffing/national recruiting. At his farewell party, friends and his staff of reporters, among them Bob Lipsyte, agreed he's a natural for the new job since "he has an almost supernatural gift for picking talent." Bill Pennington called the gift stalking, rather than tracking, talent, and said Neil first called him when he heard "I had shown promise in Sister Grace's second-grade creative writing class." The columnist George Vecsey, a Times colleague since 1968, wrote: "[As] sports editor [Neil] brought… incessant drive and knowledge…It wasn't always pretty…but we produced fast break columns…I can hardly wait to see him in his new calm management recruiter mode…"

Others kidded him for favoring tennis. "Too much tennis, I always told him," Dave Anderson said. "He knows everyone who ever stepped foot on a tennis court to play before a crowd," Kathleen McElroy added. "We gave you tennis shoes with taps on them [when you left the last time]," Fern Turkowitz recalled. "When Neil was with the Miami Herald I was thrilled…a real, honest-to-God legitimate journalist was interested in covering tennis," Billie Jean King said. "…I wish Neil…most improbably: a respectable backhand," Bud Collins wrote.

Hold it Bud, Neil was the president of the U.S. Tennis Writers Association in the 1970s and claimed a Wimbledon doubles title when he and Ubaldo Scamagetta won the press tournament. "I was the beneficiary of a great partner," Amdur said.

Neil first became a member of the media in 1955 at age 15 – and was billed as the youngest sportscaster in the country -- when his radio show "Between the Goalposts" aired weekly on WBAX in Wilkes-Barre, Pa., during the high school football season. "My father bought 30 minutes of airtime and sold it to four sponsors. I wrote the scripts, recorded the show…and sent out predictions to all the high schools," he said. He was also the runner-up among thousands who entered a national junior sports casting contest, sponsored by the New York Yankees. The prize? He taped an inning of a game at Yankee Stadium.

But his voice was more suited for late-night disc jockey work than it was for sports play-by-play, so Neil switched to writing in 1957 during his freshman year at the University of Missouri. He offered his services at the local paper and was assigned to cover the all-black Douglass High School football team. "George Brooks was the coach. I was a kid, 17…I had never had any contact with blacks growing up in northeastern Pennsylvania and I traveled with his team at a time when high schools were still segregated," said Neil, who just last month, 46 years later, talked to Brooks again. "Without doing anything but showing me kindness and a sensitive, caring soul, he showed me how to deal with people from your soul, not just your heart, that what you felt on the inside was more important than what you showed externally…The experience changed my life."

Neil graduated from Missouri's school of journalism in the early 1960s and set out to discover and record the core of the human spirit through the challenge of sport.

Chris Evert believes he succeeded. "Neil was always one of my favorites…fair and human with a great sense of humor," she said. "I felt…when he was interviewing me it wasn't for his own agenda…but rather to ask thoughtful questions… that helped to reveal the real me."

He does that by asking people what kind of fruit they are, and then, to make them feel comfortable, he volunteers that he's an apricot, "a singular fruit, not flashy, but…loyal and consistent. An apricot bruises a little, is a bit sensitive, but it has a tough core and absorbs the blows."

Now famous for his ability to "beam in" on people and hot news items, Neil has been described as a spectacular reporter who would routinely break big stories that had people scurrying for their basements. As an editor, he has been notorious for leaning on reporters every hour of the day or night. Said Joe Lapointe: "My favorite call was on Christmas Eve at 6 p.m. Me: Hello? Neil: 'Uh, Joe, it's Neil. Uh, what are you doing tomorrow?'"

"Life is about timing," Neil said. "I started at *The Times* in 1968 at the beginning of the Open era. The game was opening up, players were being paid, you had to treat it more realistically. Personalities were becoming more public. I tried to look beyond the game for stories that had more than a result. I looked at the people, the issues, whether they're real. "

He was the first to report that Donald Dell would be named U.S. Davis Cup captain in 1968. "I concentrated on the meaning of Davis Cup, a certain level of nationalism." He did the leg work to break a 1970 story on the front page of *The Times* citing rebellion on the pro tour: "Women Tennis Stars Threaten Boycott Over Unequal Purse," and quoted Rosie Casals: "It's discrimination…We play just as hard. We contribute…to the success of the tournament." In the article, Neil's good friend, the late Arthur Ashe, was quoted as saying: "…Men are doing this for a living…They have families, and don't want to give up money just for girls to play."

In 1972, Neil's plane was hijacked to Cuba when he and his wife, Marilyn, were on a flight from Allentown, Pennsylvania, to Washington Dulles. The hijacker released the passengers after 4 hours of captivity and Neil, probably the first reporter to file from a hijacked plane, got a page 1 story in The Times that day.

He scooped the competition with the news that Slew Hester was moving the US Open in 1978 from West Side to a new national tennis center. "The story led the sports section," he said. "There had been no previous thoughts or stories about leaving Forest Hills. This was Slew's mission, and he did not have a lot of popular support, so he searched for confidantes…He was one of the most genuine people I have ever met, true to his convictions…Flushing would have never been built without him."

As early as 1991, after Neil had returned to *The Times* as the sports editor, he sent a reporter to Compton, California, to check out 10-year-old Venus Williams, reported to be a ghetto Cinderella. He has assigned features on many other rising stars and human interest tennis stories as well.

Some of Neil's favorite players: "Arthur Ashe and Chris Evert, because I followed their careers. Billie Jean, because of her determination and spirit. Connors, even with his flaws. Some people I just liked for who they were in the universe…Ion Tiriac because he got so much out of the game and is so intuitively smart…Renee Richards, for her courage in stepping forward…Ellsworth Vines, so smart…George Lott, so thoughtful…Gar Mulloy, ageless and instinctive…Pancho Gonzalez, really true to himself to the end…Bobby Riggs, crazy as a fox but would give his shirt…Agassi, for learning about life and the game…Sampras, who gave the game the best he had and wasn't appreciated for all his natural skills…Virginia Ruzici, a true gypsy…"

Favorite matches: "Borg and Mac at Wimbledon (1980)." Neil reported the match in *The Times*: "…Borg posted a five-set victory over…McEnroe today that gave tennis followers something to cherish long after both players have left the sport…Like well conditioned fighters, they traded shots for 3 hours and 53 minutes…The top-seeded Borg won, 1-6, 7-5, 6-3, 6-7, 8-6, only after the determined McEnroe had saved 7 match points in the fourth set, including 5 in a dramatic 34-point tiebreaker that will stand by itself as a patch of excellence in the game's history…" Neil quoted experts in the story: "'How the guy got up to serve those match points I don't know,' Fred Stolle said in a tribute to McEnroe's courage…"

Other favorites: "Laver-Rosewall in the WCT finals (1971-72, Rosewall won both)…Panatta-Connors at the 1978 US Open (Connors in 5, round of 16)…1984 Super Saturday at Flushing, when every match went the distance (Lendl beat Cash in 5, semifinals; Navratilova beat Evert in 3, final; McEnroe beat Connors in 5, semifinals)…Lots of Martina-Chris showdowns…King-Riggs because it was so socially significant…Laver's Grand Slam in 1969… Virginia Wade winning Wimbledon in '77…Arthur winning Wimbledon in '75…"

Neil Amdur compares life to a five-set match on clay with no tiebreaker: "Clay is the toughest surface to win points. You have to extract every point, think through shots and strategy. That's what life is. It's not about serve and volley, or the true bounce on hard courts, or the insular indoor surface. Clay tests you, as life does. You can think of yourself as down a set and a break, but you have to keep trying. It's survival."

-- By Nancy Gill McShea

Pam Casale Telford

Pam Casale's spirited performances on the world's tennis courts made for the kind of dramatic theatre that could have put her into Oscar contention with the screen divas Sophia Loren and Gina Lollobrigida.

Casale played with such a sense of urgency, in fact, results of a mid-1980s professional-player survey published in a national tennis magazine revealed that Pam and Jimmy Connors were voted "Most Competitive" while Pam and John McEnroe were a lock in the category of "Worst Temperament."

A quick outline of Pam's career stats indicate that she played professional tennis from 1981 to 1989, when a recurring knee injury sidelined her for good. She won her first pro tournament at age 16 in the spring of 1981 and a few weeks later was the runner-up in the Wimbledon Plate (Consolation) Championships. Top schools called with scholarship offers, but she said, "No, no, no…I was on a roll and really wanted to play. It was my time." She turned pro later that year, after zooming in eight months from unranked status to the edge of the world's top 20 and among the U.S. top ten. By 1984 she was ranked No. 15 in the world. She advanced to the quarterfinals or better in some 40 professional tournaments and was the 1986 Domino's Pizza TeamTennis Player of the Year.

The people closest to her say career stats are no substitute for live action, that Pam's performances were compelling because she left her heart and soul on the court. Her mentor and coach, Nick Bollettieri, explained that "she approached a match as if it was a battle, so fiercely fought that the fans felt this same emotion. Her strokes were ugly, especially the backhand which had her elbow out so far in front of her body you thought the elbow would land before the ball… Her success was…directly related to street fighting and competing…giving 110 percent all the time…"

Eastern's tennis diva arrived on the junior scene out of Fairfield, N.J., in the early 1970s after her father suggested that she include tennis in her sports repertoire because she was such an active kid. "It was frustrating at first," she said, "but my father wouldn't let me give up…He said tennis is just like softball. Just keep your eye on the ball and hit it as hard as you can. Then I started hitting the ball over the net."

She left home to train at Bollettieri's tennis academy at 14 after Nick saw her play his protégé Kathleen Horvath at the junior nationals in West Virginia and was impressed by her talent and fight. She lost, 6-4, 7-5, to Horvath that day but won five national junior titles before the age of 15, including the Rolex and Orange Bowl International Championships and the Easter Bowl. Once, after she qualified for a pro tournament in Tampa and was scheduled to play Renee Richards and Andrea Jaeger, Bollettieri sent a busload of kids from camp to cheer her. "It was hilarious," she said, "Every time I won a point they'd scream. We became family. All of us [at Bollettieri's] from the East were good friends -- Kathleen [Horvath], Jimmy [Arias], Tom Fontana and Paul [Annacone]. Paul was really like a brother to me."

"Pam is the epitome of professionalism, integrity and compassion," Annacone said. "We will always have a special bond. She is a true friend...I have vivid memories of watching her 'flawed' backhand zip past her opponents and watching her climb the women's rankings while all the so-called experts said she could not achieve the elite level with a technically flawed game. She has ferocious tenacity on the court, yet can sit down and discuss life's complexities off the court with endless pools of compassion and understanding. She embodied athleticism, heart, desire, focus and knew her game and how best to maximize her strengths while covering her weaknesses. And she did all that with class and humility."

Her flamboyant court presence was on full display at the 1980 professional Volvo Cup tournament at Mahwah, N.J., when she was still an amateur. A fan favorite, Pam came through the qualifier and then beat touring pros Marjorie Blackwood, Wendy Turnbull, Susan Mascarin, Virginia Ruzici and Bettina Bunge before losing to Hana Mandlikova, 6-2, 7-6 (8-6), in the final. Her father underscored the drama by playing the music from "Rocky" to inspire his daughter before each match.

"My father thought I was Rocky," she said. "The year before, I was sitting in the stands and told him 'I want to play this.' He said, 'You will one day.' There I was, a nobody, Bettina misses an overhead on match point under the lights and I get to the finals. It was very special; I was unseeded, it was my home state. Everybody was there -- family, friends, my sister, aunts. It was a real celebration...balloons, music...But I don't get a car, I get a dog! They gave me a Basset hound and I named him Mahwah."

Al Picker, the tennis guru of the *Newark Star-Ledger*, recorded Pam's entire career -- through high school, the juniors and the pros -- and said she was always frank and open in interviews, allowing readers and fans to...gain great insight into...women's tennis. She spoke about the rigors of the worldwide travel, especially for a young player on the women's tour. "A lot of hard work," she would say. "Not as glamorous as one would think...No time for sightseeing...Anxious moments playing against good friends. Always a difficult assignment...Being an athlete, you had to be concerned with results, your ranking. You always made time, though, to try to watch and support your buddies on the tour."

Picker recalled a difficult third-round match Pam played at Wimbledon to describe her character. "She was at the court in time for her scheduled tussle, but her veteran American opponent was very late," he wrote. "Usually, Wimbledon rules would have penalized or defaulted the veteran but leniency was shown and the ...match went on...Not only did the veteran test Pam's resolve, so did the officiating. Numerous balls flew over the baseline and not a single call was made...The famed Casale temper flared several times, and she was positively in the right as I sat behind this veteran official. Close calls I could understand but when they continued to land 10 to 12 inches out, it became a joke. I moved... to get a better look at the linesman and got the shock of my life. He was dozing on and off. Pam received severe warnings from the chair umpire but this was a day that she had every right to complain. Despite her distress, she was the consummate performer and remembered her court etiquette, shaking the hand of her foe and the chair umpire. She is a true sportsman."

Pam Casale feels lucky. "I enjoyed traveling the world playing pro tennis. I loved competing, especially on the slow clay at Paris because I love to run," said Pam, the only player to beat a seed, 6-0, 6-0, at the French when she upset Zina Garrison in the first round. "I was shocked that I did well on grass at Wimbledon. Made it to the quarters of the mixed with [Jaime] Fillol...Also loved the atmosphere at the US Open. I was up 3-1, 40-15 on Tracy Austin the year she beat Martina for the title (1981), and I got so excited I hit an overhead right into the fence.

"Some people are in an office all day, 9 to 5, and hate what they do. How can you be in a lifestyle that you love and not feel lucky!?"

-- By Nancy Gill McShea

Sandy Mayer

If you consider that Sandy Mayer first hit tennis balls over the net at age 2, and that this June, at age 52, he will mark his thirtieth appearance on the grass at Wimbledon, you assume that his life evolved within the confines of the tennis court. But a closer look shows that his affection for the game is a complex tale involving a tug of war over career choices, until he recognized he was born to teach tennis.

Mayer, an independent teaching professional in Portola Valley, California, is proud of his record at Wimbledon. He played at the All-England Club 13 times as a professional and 17 more as a senior. His favorite memory dates to 1973 when he upset top-seeded Ilie Nastase in the round of 16 immediately after winning the NCAA singles and doubles titles as a Stanford undergraduate. He reached the Wimbledon semifinals that year and was twice a quarterfinalist, in 1978 and 1983. In doubles, he and Vitas Gerulaitis became the first American team in 18 years to win the men's title in 1975, and he won the seniors in 2000 with Peter Fleming.

"Beating Nastase was the biggest splash I ever made as a player, it was an out-of-body experience," he said. "I had no clear vision of how good I could be." Yet when he first played Wimbledon [in '72], he lost to Stan Smith 9-8 in the fourth and realized afterward that he could have won the match. He also kept an eye on the rankings, saw that he had beaten the 14th guy on the money list four times and thought, "I can do this." He reasoned that Nastase and Smith were the two best players in the game at that time. He never lost to Nastase and never lost to Smith again.

Yet in early 1974 Sandy was in a quandary. He still had amateur status in tennis and was planning to go to law school, but he was also ranked 15th in the world. "There was pressure to go to law school," he said. "I sort of finessed it and decided to try the pro tour for three years. Right then there was a major uptick in the level of the game, a transition to the big returns of serve and huge ground strokes, no weakness tennis." He was prepared for that transition, having developed an attacking, all court game under the tutelage of his Dad, Alex, a renowned coach who once was a member of the Hungarian Davis Cup team.

The law would have to wait. Sandy turned pro in June of 1974, when he signed with the New York Sets of World TeamTennis, and by December of 1975 his dilemma was the subject of a cover story in Tennis magazine. The writer Barry Tarshis described him as "lean and intense, with dark curly hair, restless brown eyes and the slightly preoccupied manner of a high-strung Shakespearean actor…" Tarshis noted that "…rising young athletes are rarely burdened with the ambivalence that…complicates the lives of people in less goal oriented …work. But Sandy Mayer is an intriguing exception…the more successful he becomes at tennis the more seriously he talks about going to law school.

"As Bill Riordan, an advisor to Mayer, put it: 'Sandy's only problem is trying to decide whether he wants to be the No. 1 player in tennis or a Supreme Court justice. You can't do both."

The three-year trial run turned into an 11-year pro career. He captured 11 singles and 24 doubles titles and was the MVP of the TeamTennis League. He earned career-best world rankings of No. 7 in singles (1982) and No. 3 in doubles (1985). Sandy and his brother, Gene, established pro records as the first brothers to win the French Open doubles title (1979), the only brothers to rank concurrently in the world top ten (1981) and the U.S. top ten (1983).

"Sandy has a very cerebral approach to the game, he is very committed and intense," Gene Mayer said, adding that his brother had numerous injuries but always rebounded and was once named the Comeback Player of the Year. "He had an unrelenting, attacking style and was one of the best returners of serve and volleyers of his time."

The family connection runs deep. Sandy's Dad, Alex, had been a cum laude law student and a successful gentleman farmer in Austria-Hungary before the Second World War. When Hitler took over Hungary, Alex lost everything and eventually moved to Munich, where he met and married Sandy's mother, Ingeborg. They emigrated to the United States in 1951 and Alex took a job as an elevator operator at the YMCA in New York City. The family settled on Long Island and Alex taught tennis all over the Eastern Section, including at the Woodmere Club and at the Martin estate in Westbury. Sandy watched his Dad hit with Don Budge, Bill Talbert and other greats and became firmly entrenched in the game.

"Dad was hands down the best coach that ever was; no chance I'd ever be a decent tennis player without him," Sandy said. "With my brother Gene, Dad had a genius like McEnroe with a feel for the ball. With me, he had to teach me from the ground up how to walk, run and how to chew gum. We discussed every inch of racquet travel, all the nuances of strategy. When I played Kalamazoo at 15 he had me going to the net on all first serves. I didn't stay back for another ten years."

Sandy made it to the finals of the Boys' 16 nationals at Kalamazoo, but he wasn't having fun. "I was heavy growing up, so I decided to quit playing," he said. "I told my Dad I wanted to be the head counselor at his tennis camp. It was just a ploy so I wouldn't have to tell him I was quitting tennis. He said 'Great, we'll talk about salary later.' He didn't even raise an eyebrow.

"Quitting was a good idea. It made me realize I'm a tennis player even though I wasn't sure it was going to be a major league sport."

Sandy refers to "weekend treks" when recounting favorite memories of junior tennis. "We made our own tennis plans," he said. "I would get on the Long Island Railroad, go to Woodside and hit with Bob Kahn and Charlie Masterson on Friday afternoons. They booked a court and let me play. I never paid a dime. I'd go to the city Friday night and at 5:30 Saturday morning I'd play in [Paul] Cranis's Project Upswing at the Midtown Tennis Club. Then I'd go out to Roslyn to Bobby Kaplan's place and hit with Jason Schwartz until the club closed. I also played at Port (Washington Tennis Academy) with King Van Nostrand and Tony Palafox. I had a great time, loved the action."

After Sandy retired from pro tennis in 1985, he became involved in various business ventures, specifically real estate partnerships coupled with personal financial management. But when his Dad died in 1995 he said "what most affected me about the funeral were the number of people who came by and told me, 'Your father taught me how to play and now I'm a doctor or a teacher.' I thought, 'Look at all the lives he affected doing this.'

"My family's goals were education and professionalism. That's why Stanford. Tennis was just a glitch. Becoming a professional athlete was not a sophisticated endeavor. But I started teaching tennis with my Dad at 7 or 8; it was part of the fabric of my life. So I turned to my money management firm and said 'That's it. I'm going to do what I was born to do. Teach tennis!'"

-- By Nancy Gill McShea

Lois Prince

Here in our world of tennis, there exists a true ambassador, a bright, elegant lady who has earned so much respect as a volunteer administrator during her 42-year tenure in the game, insiders simply refer to her as "Lois!" When a local tennis employee once asked Mary Carillo to use her clout to effect an important change in tennis policy, Mary said, "Sure, I'll talk to Lois at the Open."

That would be Lois Prince, who served as the volunteer chairman of the US Open junior tournament from 1992 to 2001.

How cool is it to view your mother as a celebrity? Just ask Wendy Prince, a Manhattan attorney who once won the doubles title at the New York State High School Tennis Championships and also logged time as an Eastern volunteer. "You walk around the U.S. Open with my mother and everybody knows her and stops to talk to her," she said. "All her juniors grow up but they remember her. They know she's rock steady. She cuts through the noise and gets to the heart of the matter."

Wendy recently walked into a roomful of attorneys for a meeting and laughed when one colleague polled the group: "Anyone whose mother appeared in Tennis Week this week raise your hand."

Lois has worked in administrative positions at tennis clubs and within the USTA national and Eastern sectional organizations since the early 1960's. Before being elected Eastern's president in 1994, she was honored as the "Tennis Woman of the Year." She has also served as the section's delegate to the USTA, as vice president, secretary, chairman of the Junior Competition Committee and as ranking chairman of five different boys' age divisions. In addition to chairing the junior open, she has been a member of five other national committees.

And when she was the president of the Junior Tennis Foundation, from 1996 to 2001, she was the epitome of the gracious hostess, welcoming everyone to this Hall of Fame celebration.

"What can I tell you, they kept moving me up," Lois has said. "I could see myself getting in deeper and deeper because I couldn't say no. But I've truly enjoyed it. I love tennis and kids. It's a natural flow…"

Lois is a star because of that willingness to become involved, coupled with her years of experience serving people in the field. Doris Herrick, Eastern's executive director from 1978 to 1998 and now the executive director of the Junior Tennis Foundation, has said, "Lois brought to the office of president a strong history with the organization. She knew the members well – both adults and juniors – and a president who knows the cast has an advantage."

Eastern presidents added similar sentiments:

Louis Dimock: "Lois is among the best of people and has donated thousands of hours. She was great as our president, traveling to all the events waving the Eastern flag and welcoming people into the game."

Alex. Aitchison: "If volunteers were paid for dedication, sincerity and attention to detail, Lois would command a very high salary."

Elaine Viebranz: "Lois has always set an example through a dedication to the section and her loyalty to its people."
A Long Islander to the core, even though she was born in Missouri, Lois strayed briefly to attend the Highland Manor Boarding School in Tarrytown, N.Y., before graduating from Forest Hills High School. She ventured beyond her roots again in the early 1950's and earned a bachelor's degree in early education from the University of Wisconsin but then returned to New York to attend the masters program at Columbia University. She and her husband, Al, settled on Long Island, joined the Renaissance Club in Roslyn and started to play a little club tennis. She also enjoyed a regular game

with friends at Alastair Martin's family estate in Old Westbury. In the early 1960s, she joined the Shelter Rock Tennis Club in Manhasset. She impressed the club's directors by organizing their baby-sitting operation and soon moved into prime time as the tournament director of Shelter Rock's sectional events and the USTA National Men's 35 and Boys' 14 Clay Court Championships.

Lois took a job teaching nursery school in the early 1970s and then survived a Woody-Allen-kind-of-introduction to managing a tennis club when she answered a call to run the Great Neck Tennis Center and their 12-and-under tournaments. "Ron Rebhuhn was the pro," she said. "He'd call me at ten o'clock at night and say 'Lois, the lights are out, the bubble is falling down, the heat is off.' There were leaks in the roof. The boss went out to play in hiking boots. Players complained about water on the court. I'd say 'look, I'll give you two hours of free time.' That only worked for so long. A woman finally said to me before I even opened my mouth, 'And I don't want any more of your free time.' I'd drive down East Shore Road in the morning on the way to work hoping that the bubble had not fallen down. And then I'd think, 'If only I could get a job where they would leave me alone.'"

She admits that in retrospect the Great Neck experience was comical, but she was ready to move on when the club was sold in the early 1980s. The owners of Jericho-Westbury Indoor Tennis came calling and hired her to manage their operation. She tried to take a hiatus after a six-year stint there, but in 1987 Dick Zausner of the Port Washington Tennis Academy called. "He said, 'You've been sitting around doing nothing long enough. Come on over, we can use you over here.' The next thing I know I'm the tournament manager of the International Junior Championships and working with Dick at the USTA Amateur Championships and other tournaments at the Concord Hotel [in the Catskills]. It was almost like going to camp."

You realize Lois has to be on a first-name basis with generations of accomplished Eastern players if you flip through draw sheets dating to the early '60s before the beginning of the Open era. Imagine the stories she could tell about individual personality quirks, stories she will never tell because "I wouldn't want to offend anyone. I just enjoyed the idea of being involved in a tournament, watching the matches and seeing who wins, who loses. Look at all the nice people I met. I bonded with all of them."

The names jump out from the draw sheets and the ranking lists: McEnroe, Carillo, Peter Rennert, Eugene Scott, Renee Richards, Sammy Giammalva, Whitney Reed, Paul Annacone, Kathleen Horvath, Fritz Buehning, Jimmy Arias, Marcel Freeman, Pam Casale, Reggie Weir, Marco Cacopardo, Justin Gimelstob, Melissa Brown and the whole Van Nostrand clan.

"I'm a big fan of Lois Prince," said Kay McEnroe, whose three boys -- John, Mark and Patrick – grew up knowing Lois as their junior ranking chairman and tournament director. "She had to be such a great diplomat to deal with all the personalities of parents, players and fans. You knew when you got to a tournament she would knock herself out to welcome and accommodate the boys. And they knew she would bend over backwards to be fair. Patrick once got so sick to his stomach when it was blistering hot he had to walk off the court. Lois was so gracious she was almost too good to be true."

It is appropriate that the late Barbara Williams have the last word. "Lois Prince has given a lifetime of outstanding volunteer service to tennis. She is eminently qualified and most deserving of being elected to the Eastern Tennis Hall of Fame."

-- By Nancy Gill McShea

Chapter 24

2004: Masterson, P. McEnroe, Russo and Smith

Dr. Charles F. Masterson

Friends say that Charlie Masterson was, by nature, a teacher and a mentor, as much a role model for tennis players who frequented the famous courts of Brooklyn and the West Side Tennis Club -- where he played the game most of his life -- as he was for VIP's in the corridors of higher education, Washington politics and business.

When Masterson died on May 31, 1998 at the age of 80, he was remembered as a scholar-athlete who was admired for his grace, impeccable manners and a classic playing style, on and off the court.

"Charlie was one of my heroes; he practiced with me and encouraged me," said Dan Rivkind, who met Masterson in the late 1940s at Brooklyn's Mammoth Tennis Courts.

"Charlie asked me to play when I was just starting the game and he adopted me," added Dick Scheer, who met Masterson in the mid-1960s at Brooklyn's Highway Tennis Courts. "I was thrilled; he was a legend."

As a player, Charlie was ranked among the U.S. top 20 and often in Eastern's top ten (with highs of No. 4 in singles and 3 in doubles). He collected his share of victories in men's singles at the U.S. National Championships between 1942 and 1959 – once losing to Ham Richardson in the Round of 16 -- and later competed in the men's 35s tournament at the Open. He possessed the talent and tenacity to defeat four Wimbledon champions – Sidney Wood, Vic Seixas, Dick Savitt and Bob Falkenberg – as well as such top-ranked players as Straight Clark, Frank Guernsey, Charlie Oliver, Jack Tuero and the South American champ Enrique Morea, at some point during his outstanding amateur tennis career.

He was a runner up in the national 35 clay courts (doubles) and the national 45 indoors (singles) and once teamed with Eastern's Sid Schwartz to defeat Straight Clark and Hal Burrows in the final of the New Orleans Sugar Bowl tournament. He also participated in Church Cup competition, Gordon Trophy matches and in the Metropolitan Club championships. And he was a member of the International Lawn Tennis Club of the USA.

Off the court, Charlie was a veritable Renaissance Man. It has been noted in the archives of President Eisenhower's Library in Kansas that he was asked to join the White House staff as a special assistant/speech writer in 1953 because "Dr. Masterson…was a man of varied talents…in public relations…as a college professor…an author…and for ten years he was ranked among the top tennis players in the United States."

Before Masterson began his four years of service in Washington, he taught high school English while studying for his Ph.D. at Columbia University (1952) and he was a professor of English, History and Public Speaking at Long Island University and Pace College. In 1954, he became a member of "Who's Who in America." Masterson also authored two textbooks (*World History*, 1949; and *History of Asia*, 1950) and was an elder and delivered sermons at Brooklyn's Union Church in Bay Ridge.

His experience in the business sector included positions as a New York public relations executive with the Rumbough Co., and as the executive director of the Office of Trustees in the N.Y. office of the National Safety Council. In charitable work, he was a director and vice president of the New York City Mission Society, which was established in 1812 to erase poverty through churches and community centers in disadvantaged parts of the city.

One newspaper reporter, who was assigned in 1969 to write a story on Masterson, reasoned correctly that he is "something of a phenomenon on and off the tennis courts…the Charlie Masterson story is too big a thing for a few thousand words to handle."

Yet when Masterson's son Mike was asked recently to try and prioritize his father's major commitments in life, he said, "I would say teaching. He loved to teach. Ethics and beliefs were important to him and the idea that nobody should be left behind. He thought that education gave people the chance to experience a fuller life."

Maybe that's why Charlie chose tennis, because it's an equal opportunity sport. Learning tennis is an education unto itself; anyone can walk onto a local court without previous credentials and there are no age barriers. Scheer had met Charlie exactly that way, by chance, when he was new to the game in the mid1960s. Dick was 34 and an attorney; Charlie was in his fifties and was working for the National Safety Council. A few years later, Kenny Lindner joined them at the Highway courts. "The three of us played together for years and developed quite a bond," Scheer said. "[By then] I was about 40, Charlie was in his late fifties and Kenny [a television broadcasting agent today] was 16."

Rivkind was 17 and Charlie was in his early thirties when those two met. "If you walked past a court and saw Charlie playing, you knew he was a fabulous athlete. He invited me to play tennis in the early winter mornings over a two-year period when he was teaching at Poly Prep, and during that time I was a finalist in two major Eastern indoor tournaments," said Rivkind, the retired director of the Dick Savitt Tennis Center at Columbia University, who also served for 16 years as Columbia's junior varsity tennis coach.

Perhaps the most startling example of Charlie Masterson's commitment to equal opportunity was an incident that occurred in 1961 involving the West Side Tennis Club. Charlie was a member there and had won 16 club titles (eight singles and eight doubles) over a 20-year period, from 1942-1961. That year, Ralph Bunche, the winner of the 1950 Nobel Peace Prize and the Under Secretary General of the United Nations, applied for a West Side membership. He was denied entrée and Masterson resigned his membership, in protest.

In the April 1963 issue of *World Tennis* magazine, Paul Cranis described Charlie, the sportsman, who had triple match point against Gardnar Mulloy: "For five years Gardnar Mulloy had been the best senior in the country. No other player… had even come close to him. Once every two years someone managed to deuce a set. He had been unbeaten on clay, grass and boards. Then he met Charlie Masterson in the second round of the National Senior Indoor Championships.

"Charlie is an extremely hard hitter. He is aggressive as a lion on the tennis court but…he has the disposition of a lamb. He would never take a point from an opponent, and everyone who has known him in competition respects not only his game but his great sportsmanship.

"Masterson played Mulloy at the 7th Regiment…last month…Charlie took the first set 13-11 and led 40-0, triple match point. One linesman and an umpire had been working the match. The balls were not easy to see and the calls had been favoring Gar by about 8 to 2. Mulloy served the first match point against him to Charlie's backhand. Masterson hit a ball that whizzed down the line, past the umpire's chair and by Gardnar. Said the umpire: 'Game, set and match, Mr. Masterson.' Mulloy stood there, hands on hips, and stared at Charlie. 'It was out,' he cried.

"Any other senior would have raced up to Gar, pumped his arm in the traditional after-match handshake, and dashed to the showers…Not Masterson. He walked up to the umpire and told him the ball was out. The umpire thereupon awarded the point to Mulloy and the match was continued. Result: Gardnar won the game, set and match, 11-13, 13-11, 6-2."

Mike Masterson recently said he always felt proud that his father was able to do so many things and do them well. "My father was a giver, not a taker; he was a remarkable, dedicated guy," he said. "And he was my best friend. I miss him."

-- By Nancy Gill McShea

Patrick W. McEnroe

The kid next door has grown up! We watched him play tennis on local courts when he was a child in the 1970's. We watched him work the U.S. Open courts when he was a ball boy and the main heartthrob in the early '80s. And when he turned pro in 1988, we admired the various lengths of his wavy reddish blond hair, along with his lethal backhand. Two weeks ago we watched Patrick McEnroe again -- all grown up now and the captain of the U.S. Davis Cup team -- as he and his young American squad vaulted into the final four of this year's competition, courtesy of a record-breaking serve by Andy Roddick.

The United States defeated Sweden 4-1 in the Davis Cup quarterfinals on April 11 in Delray Beach, Florida, and will play Belarus in the semifinals in September. Roddick announced immediately, "We're halfway to our dream of winning the Davis Cup," while Captain McEnroe high-fived the team for its effort and reiterated his belief that hard work pays off.

Patrick's reaction might sound like a "same old, same old" spin touting the benefits of team tennis, except that in his world, "team effort" and "hard work" are truly operative phrases that can be traced to his family roots in Douglaston, N.Y.

"Patrick was so cute, and shy, always trying to keep up with his brothers," recalled Nancy Lynch Lord, who lived three doors down from the McEnroes when she was growing up. "You'd see the three of them [John, Mark and Patrick] walking back and forth with their racquets to the club across the street. That's what they did. You'd hear the thump of the ball against the backboard, starting first thing in the morning, and there was always a good chance it would be Patrick."

Patrick loves the job of Davis Cup captain because he's a team player, as evidenced by his run as a three-time All American and captain of the tennis team at Stanford University, the NCAA champions in 1986 and 1988. He also understands what it takes to get the most out of players, having worked very hard himself to move forward in the men's professional world singles rankings, from No. 670 in 1989 to a career-high No. 28 in 1995.

That attitude was underscored when Robbie Ginepri was trailing two sets to love against Austria's Jergen Melzer in the first-round Davis Cup encounter this past February in Connecticut. McEnroe asked him if he had ever rallied from two sets down. Ginepri said he hadn't and McEnroe said, "Today's gonna be the day." Ginepri, who according to one writer had "started walking around in concrete soles…staring ahead as if just another male unwilling to ask for directions," perked up and won the match, 6-7, 4-6, 6-4, 6-4, 6-2.

Patrick learned the intricacies of a five-setter -- and probably grew up as a tennis player – in the first round of the 1991 US Open when he was leading Jimmy Connors two sets to love, with Connors serving at 0-3 and 0-40 in the third set. Patrick's mother, Kay McEnroe, had warned Connors jokingly before the match not to be tough on her baby. The battle continued into the wee morning hours and local fans circled the wagons in the courtside boxes to support Patrick. But Connors had it going and prevailed, 4-6, 6-7, 6-4, 6-2, 6-4. "I thought I had it won," Patrick said, "but after experiencing that I came back from two sets down at least six or seven times. That was the positive." His most memorable comeback occurred four years later, in the third round of the 1995 US Open on his favorite Grandstand Court, when he trudged back from a two-set deficit to beat Russia's Alexander Volkov, 4-6, 2-6, 6-1, 7-6(4), 6-2.

"I wasn't the most gifted player," admitted Patrick, the co-author of the 1998 book "Tennis for Dummies" who had doubts about the pro tour and took the law boards when he graduated from Stanford in 1988. "But my mother always called me a plugger and I had been successful in juniors and in college, so I had to give the pros a shot. [I thought] if I'm good enough I'll make it."

He has made it in every phase of a tennis career that went public in 1978 when he was ranked No. 1 in Eastern boys' 12s.

"The first time I met Patrick, he was 10, I was 12 and he was beating us all up at a tournament at C.W. Post College [in Brookville, Long Island]," Allan Van Nostrand said. "He was two years younger than we were…a little boy who had the best backhand of any of us, and he still does."

In the juniors, Patrick won a few major titles – in singles at the USTA boys' 18 grass courts and in doubles at the French Open and the USTA boys' 18 clay courts (both with Luke Jensen) and also earned his share of sportsmanship awards. He turned pro in 1988 and played European Challengers for about a year and a half. "I was doing well in doubles, but I was taking my lumps in singles," he said.

He won a Grand Slam doubles title at the 1989 French Open (with Jim Grabb), and that year broke through in singles, reaching the semifinals of a Challenger in Denmark, which boosted his world singles ranking 314 spots, to 356 by year's end. He returned home and started running twice a day to get into better shape, and in 1990, he had a good run in Asia. He made it to the third round in Tokyo, the quarters in Singapore and Hong Kong and climbed to No. 120 in the world. He played the 1991 Australian Open, advancing to the semifinals of singles, before losing to the eventual champion Boris Becker. He was also a finalist in doubles (with David Wheaton).

Patrick posted a 3-1 record as a member of the U.S. Davis Cup team in 1993, 1994 and 1996. He was a singles quarterfinalist at the 1995 US Open, losing again to Becker, this time in a gripping, four-hour marathon, 6-4, 7-6(2), 6-7(3), 7-6(6). He earned career best rankings of No. 3 in doubles and No. 28 in singles while appearing in 42 ATP Tour singles and doubles finals. Shoulder surgery cut short his on-court career in 1996, but jump-started his new adventure as a tennis analyst for ESPN and CBS Sports. He now does tennis commentary at all four Grand Slam events.

Patrick McEnroe today is a man in transit. He is a co-owner of the Sportime World TeamTennis Team. In the past four months he has shepherded the Davis Cup team to the semifinal round. On February 18, the USTA officially introduced him as the Olympic tennis coach for men, who will compete in Athens, Greece, from August 15 to 22. In between, he returned to his familiar on-camera role with Cliff Drysdale: at the Australian Open, in January; at the Pacific Life Open at Indian Wells, California, in March; and at the Nasdaq-100 Open in Key Biscayne, Florida, in late March.

"I think Patrick's been great for Cliff," ESPN analyst Mary Joe Fernandez has said. "…Patrick keeps him on his toes and hip. That combination has been fabulous. They feed really well off each other. They are not afraid to take punches at each other…that makes for interesting commentary."

Patrick also flew home to New York in late March to see his wife, the actress and singer Melissa Errico, who was appearing at the Oak Room at the Algonquin. Last spring, Melissa received a Tony Award nomination for "Best Leading Actress in a Musical" for her role in Amour. When Melissa's name was announced the night of the awards, the television camera zoomed in on the chivalrous husband, who kissed his wife's hand in appreciation of her inspirational performances.

Maybe because Patrick was a privileged little kid – "He was the baby and we all just loved him to death," Kay McEnroe said. – he finds pleasure in giving back to others, and is an enthusiastic volunteer at Eastern and national junior clinics. "I do it when I'm asked if it fits into my schedule," said Patrick, once a volunteer member of the USTA board of directors. "Kids are what it's about. It's our future. It's pretty simple."

-- By Nancy Gill McShea

Robert P. Russo

Bob Russo, the director of Sport Science Education for ProHEALTH Care Associates in Lake Success, N.Y., and the veteran U.S. Tennis Association athletic trainer for the men's professional circuit, could fill a couple of best-selling books with inside scoops about life on the tour. But he has a reputation for respecting players' privacy, so he talks instead about the great tennis matches he has covered, courtside, in the modern game.

Russo was so impressed when 39-year-old Jimmy Connors rallied from 2-5 down in the fifth set to beat Aaron Krickstein, 3-6, 7-6, 1-6, 6-3, 7-6, during his dream-like run to the semifinals of the 1991 US Open, he told a New York sports writer that Connors "is like a street guy…like somebody the Mets should have…I was electrified…all that stuff about opening night on Broadway and a prize fight at the Garden, he's got it. He's got this New York heart."

It takes one to know one. Bob grew up playing stickball on the streets of Queens across from the West Side Tennis Club in Forest Hills and fantasized about his own dream-like run in tennis. He went to the US Open at West Side every year when he was a kid and worked as a ball boy there. He was such an insider, in fact, one vivid West Side memory dates to the mid-'60s, when he watched from the clubhouse as the Beatles' helicopter landed on the grass and the group scurried out to perform their concert. Nobody could get within three blocks of the place without a ticket. Also special were the hours he spent hitting tennis balls on the club's back courts with his brothers and friends, absorbing tennis history and sometimes pretending that they were part of great matches, like a Davis Cup final between the U.S. and Russia.

Destiny complied some 30 years later, when Bob was part of the action as the U.S. Davis Cup team traveled to Moscow in December of 1995, and Pete Sampras, Jim Courier and Todd Martin defeated Russia, 3-2, in Red Square to win the championship. "It was dramatic, my first visit to Russia," he said. "In my mind I had already played it a million times even though I wasn't playing. Professionally, it was an accomplishment highlight for me."

He had also been the trainer at two earlier U.S. Davis Cup victories -- in 1990, when Andre Agassi, Michael Chang, Rick Leach and Jim Pugh topped Australia, 3-2, in Florida; and again in 1992, when Andre Agassi, Jim Courier, John McEnroe and Pete Sampras beat Switzerland, 3-1, in Fort Worth, Texas. "There were spirited conversations in the locker room," he said. "That had to be the greatest Davis Cup team ever assembled, with four guys who were No. 1 in the world. Who do you sit out?"

It figures that Bob's list of memorable matches would include riveting battles contested in his neighborhood, starring a couple of local heroes:

--1979 US Open Final – John McEnroe defeated his friend, the late Vitas Gerulaitis, in straight sets. "I kept thinking, of all the players in the world, what were the odds that two kids who grew up in Queens would play this final...There were no losers that day."

--1980 US Open final – McEnroe beat Borg in five sets. "You knew history was being made. It was fire and ice and another clean match on the court."

--1984 US Open semifinal – McEnroe outlasted Connors in five, 6-4, 4-6, 7-5, 4-6, 6-3. "[This time] It was fire and fire, Saturday night in New York, a prize fight crowd. After the match we were stretching them both in the trainers' room, John on one table and Jimmy on the table right next to him, for half an hour. There was this long, loud silence....."

Bob earned a master's degree in sports medicine from Long Island University in 1976 and immediately launched his career as an athletic trainer, first for the N.Y. Cosmos soccer team at Giants Stadium in New Jersey (1976-84) -- during which time the Cosmos featured such stars as Pele, Franz Beckenbauer and Giorgion Chinaglia and won four North American Soccer League titles (1977, 1978, 1980 and 1982) -- and then for the US Open (1977-present).

In 1977, the West Side Tennis Club was hosting the Tournament of Champions and needed an athletic trainer familiar with professional sports. Somebody at West Side remembered that Bob was working in that capacity with the Cosmos and asked him to cover the tournament. Later that summer, the USTA asked him to be part of the player medical staff at the US Open. He has since served as the director of trainers for the USTA, establishing a network of certified athletic trainers and assigning them to cover the USTA Men's Professional Circuits. He has also worked for the ATP Tour, World TeamTennis, the John McEnroe Tennis Over America Tour and the AT&T Challenge of Champions, among other pro events.

Off the court, he has authored 14 publications in the area of sports medicine. He is currently the chairman of Eastern's Sport Science Committee, has served as a member of the USTA National Sport Science and Wheelchair Tennis Committees, and has won awards from the Joseph P. Kennedy Foundation and the American Red Cross.

Bob helps tennis players to prolong their amazing careers, or at the very least, helps them to get through a match. He evaluates their physical situations, measures individual capabilities and applies sound scientific sports medicine principles to help them enhance their innate ability. He supervises players' pre-match preparation and post-match recovery, is always available for on-court emergencies and organizes players' rehabilitation schedules at tournaments.

The following testimonials lend insight to Bob's influence in the game:

Peter Fleming – "Trainers…keep players healthy enough to compete day in and day out…Often emotional stress can… undermine an athlete's health as much as physical stress…Bob's peaceful, confident air…is one of his greatest healing tools."

Tim Mayotte – "Trainers are unsung heroes…They make it possible for us to push ourselves…even when our bodies don't…want to cooperate…Bob is one of the best in the business…It was a relief to walk into a tournament locker room at some distant end of the planet or the US Open and see Bob. He did everything from taping my ankles to putting me in touch with the world's best specialists for major injuries."

Paul Annacone – "His knowledge and selfless motivation go beyond words."

Stan Smith – "Bob has done a terrific job working with all the players. He has a helpful attitude and knows his job very well."

Mary Carillo – "This is a very special man…The tennis professionals he's treated, trained and befriended would tell you…this is the…guy you want on your team."

Dr. Irving Glick – "He gives unselfishly of himself. His expertise is a great asset to the game and his profession…Few know of his efforts to help young players, handicapped participants and those less privileged."

Dr. Glick was referring to the ProHEALTH awards, which Bob Russo established in 1997 in memory of his childhood friend, Vitas Gerulaitis. To date, the charity has given more than 100 children an opportunity to play in area tennis programs. Last year, tennis scholarships were awarded to children who had a parent serving in the War in Iraq; and before that, the beneficiaries were families of firemen and policemen who were victims in the September 11th attack on the World Trade Center.

Vitas's sister, Ruta Gerulaitis, has said she is grateful to her old friend for his unselfish dedication, and especially in keeping alive the work her brother did with kids through his youth foundation…Which all goes to prove that while Bob Russo's dream-like run in tennis might not play out with the same dramatic flair that Jimmy Connors created at the 1991 US Open, he's got the same New York heart!

-- By Nancy Gill McShea

Marjory Gengler Smith

When Jeanne Gengler enrolled her nine-year-old daughter Margie in a tennis clinic near the family's home in Locust Valley, Long Island, she couldn't have imagined that the game would become an integral part of her eldest daughter's daily life, or that she had just written the first installment of "A Tennis Legend: The Gengler Sisters."

There have been sisters in tennis before and since – the Everts, the Williamses and the Maleevas, to name a few. But picture five petite blondes marching into an Eastern junior tournament to support one another, or polishing their classic strokes together in a practice session, and they become the stuff of folklore.

"I won my very first trophy in that clinic, at the Piping Rock Club," Margie recalled recently. "There was one other girl in it, and she and I stood at the service line while the pro tossed us the ball from the other side of the net. We were allowed to miss twice. She missed her second shot on the 100th ball and I got 101 and the trophy."

A star was born, and in the early 1960s Jeanne Gengler began waking Margie and her younger sister Louise at 4 a.m. every Saturday to prepare for the drive from Long Island to Manhattan so the girls could train from 6 to 9 a.m. under the watchful eye of the legendary coach George Seewagen. The 7th Regiment Armory was one of the centers for Eastern's top junior development program back then, and Margie said she didn't mind rising at such an uncivilized hour because "I had a huge crush on Butch Seewagen – one of the older guys -- and occasionally he would show up."

When Butch did show up, he noticed that Margie was a very talented player. "She had a textbook classic game, a beautiful game," he said. "Stroke for stroke, she could stay with anybody."

In the mid-1960s, Margie and Louise were asked to be ball kids at the Nassau Bowl Invitational in Glen Cove because they could throw a tennis ball the length of the court as well as the boys could. The Nassau tournament featured many of the world's best players, as it was part of the famous Eastern grass court summer circuit that concluded at the U.S. National Championships at the West Side Tennis Club in Forest Hills. Margie, then 15, was excited when she was assigned to work a match between two 20-year-old college guys, her friend Butch Seewagen and Stan Smith, who had just reached the singles finals at Merion, a leg of the circuit in Philadelphia. "Margie gave me a lucky safety pin before the match," said Seewagen, who beat Smith in three sets. "She was happy for me but then she wound up marrying him."

Not until eight years later, though. After the Nassau match, Margie confided to her mother that Stan was really nice but she was disappointed that he didn't notice her. Her mother advised her to bide her time until she turned 18 and the five-year age difference wouldn't matter anymore. Sure enough, Stan and Margie met again a few years later at a tournament they were both playing in California, and he asked her out on her 18th birthday.

In the 1960s and early '70s, the Gengler girls added dozens of installments to their story. Margie and Louise and their sisters -- Nancy, Jeannie and Marion -- were regulars on the tennis circuit and all five of them earned Eastern's No. 1 junior ranking before starring in college. Margie attracted national attention when she won the Girls' 12s title at the 1963 Orange Bowl and she went on to rank first in the East in every age category and consistently among the U.S. top ten. In 1965, Margie and Alice deRochemont won the USTA girls' 14 national doubles title – "My first and only gold ball," she said – and she was a member of the Junior Wightman Cup team.

Margie later achieved the No. 1 ranking in Eastern women's singles the same year she and Louise finished first in doubles and seventh in the country. She competed in singles at the US Open and played mixed doubles at Wimbledon with Gene Scott, advancing to the third round before losing to Billie Jean King and Clark Graebner.

Margie also set tennis records at Princeton University. Louise did, too, as the captain of Princeton's undefeated tennis team (Louise is retiring this year after coaching the team for 25 years). Nancy also played for Princeton, captained the squash team and was the National Intercollegiate squash champion. Jeannie was the tennis captain and played No. 1

at Colgate University. Marion was the tennis captain and played No. 1 at the College of William and Mary.

But it was Margie who first added clout to the Gengler legend at college. She was thrust into the role of pioneer at Princeton, as Ivy League schools went co-ed and offered athletic programs for women. She was a member of the Class of 1973, the first women's class to graduate from Princeton. She was also undefeated in tennis throughout her collegiate career, and in 1972 was the captain of the undefeated women's team that swept the Eastern and Middle States Intercollegiate Championships. That season, Margie was awarded the white sweater with the orange "P" that had been reserved for men-only captains of Princeton teams that won Ivy League championships, and she was featured as "Princeton's Best Athlete" on the cover of the alumni magazine.

Eve Kraft, her coach at Princeton, said at the time: "…Margie's mastery of the whole court makes her so formidable. She's got all the strokes…she maneuvers her opponent like a puppet on a string from one side to the other and then does a very crisp down-the-line put-a-way…She's disciplined and accurate…and a tremendous ambassador for Princeton."

Margie represented Princeton at conferences such as "Equality and Equity in Women's Athletics" and played in tennis exhibitions with stars Jimmy Connors and Clark and Carole Graebner to benefit charity fundraising efforts. She thought about becoming a stockbroker or working for a tennis promoter and acknowledged that "women at Princeton face a crisis when they graduate. They're not ready to get married and lead a housewife role."

Margie Gengler (r) and her sisters (l-r) Marion, Jeannie, Nancy and Louise won Eastern's Family of the Year. award.

She may have reflected the conflict of her generation, but she had already set her future in motion when she first dated Stan Smith at 18. She played mixed doubles with Stan at the US Open when he was ranked among the world's top ten, in 1973 and in 1974, the year he won the second of his four US Open men's doubles titles. They were married two months later, in November.

Today, Margie and Stan Smith live in Hilton Head, S.C., and are the parents of four children, who all play tennis. Ramsey was born during the 1978 US Open on Labor Day, a few days before his Dad won his third men's doubles trophy there, and the tournament director Billy Talbert announced Ramsey's arrival on center court. Ramsey was a member of Duke's Class of 2001, was the No. 1 player and captain of the tennis team, and later played the pro tour. Trevor, Princeton Class of 2003, was the captain of the tennis team. Logan, UVA Class of 2005, played tennis for one year. Austin, 17, hopes to play at a Division 1 school.

In 1978, the Genglers were honored as Eastern's Family of the Year. Almost 20 years later, in 1995, Margie and Stan Smith accepted the Southern Tennis Association Family of the Year award.

Jeanne Gengler wrote the first installment of the legendary Gengler sisters, and before she passed away, in the year 2000, she added a personal epilogue. At the age of 65, after her husband Herbert died, she began competing in USTA national senior tournaments. Jeanne achieved U.S. top ten rankings in doubles and top 15 in singles. But her biggest thrill came in 1999 when she played an invitational senior match on center court -- right before Jennifer Capriati -- during the women's professional tournament at Mahwah.

One question remains: Who will emerge from the new generation to write the sequel?

-- By Nancy Gill McShea

Chapter 25

2005: Benisch, Kovaleski, Nusbaum and Seewagen

Henry J. Benisch

Read about the late Henry Benisch and you come away with an upbeat script for a sequel to the movie "It's a Wonderful Life." You are inspired by his lifelong concern for people, a character trait he demonstrated through philanthropic commitment to numerous organizations and causes. Benisch was elected the chairman of Big Brothers of New York in 1955, and in a real sense he was a Big Brother to tennis.

Henry was born in Brooklyn and ran a family business there, Benisch Brothers Monuments and Memorials. But he called Forest Hills home for more than 60 years and loved tennis – he won the 1946 Eastern Veteran's singles title, was once ranked fourth among national seniors, and in 1967 won the first Granddad Tennis Tournament – so his membership in the West Side Tennis Club and subsequent volunteer administrative work at the U.S. National Championships were a natural fit. He lived around the corner from West Side, first served as the captain of the grounds and was later appointed the chairman of America's Grand Slam tournament, a position he held from 1963-1965. He served as the president of West Side in 1966-1967, and in 1967-1968 was president of the Eastern Tennis Association.

Benisch was twice honored by the U.S. (Lawn) Tennis Association: in 1960, he received the W. Dickson Cunningham Tennis Trophy for service to senior tennis; and in 1965, he accepted the Marlborough Award for overall service and contributions to the game.

He was also honored at awards dinners held in grand ballrooms such as the Waldorf Astoria – by his alma mater Cornell University, Big Brothers (now Big Brothers and Sisters), the YMCA, the Kiwanis Club, the Industrial Home for the Blind, the Brooklyn Chamber of Commerce, the Henry Street Settlement and the Faith Home for Incurables, among others – in appreciation of his work with those community organizations and charities. Benisch did not limit his support of charities to financial donations, but rather took a hands-on approach and worked personally with the people who benefited from an organization's mission.

"Dad thought people, education, tennis and music were most important," his daughter Peggy Ann Anderson said. "He was sensitive, took things to heart and made time for everyone, no matter how busy he was. He frequently brought guests home for dinner, saying there should always be room for one more."

She added with some amusement that Dad had a good sense of humor, too, and sometimes played his beloved fiddle at tennis dinners. He had grown up playing the violin, and in his youth often used it as a way to earn a little extra money by playing in jazz orchestras at night.

He had been brought up to teach by example and was schooled in the ethic that everybody deserves a chance, so he searched for opportunities to help others. His primary mission involved motivating kids to set goals and pursue their education. His influence on young people was so profound, in fact, that a boy named Robert, whom he had helped in Big Brothers, once made a trip back east from California specifically to paint the family's kitchen ceiling "to thank Mr. Benisch, who has done so much for me."

In that same spirit, Benisch organized the staid, private West Side Tennis Club's first free junior tennis clinic and helped to conduct U.S. Junior Davis Cup tryouts, which were held there. He had a habit of proposing juniors for membership and felt it was important to start tennis when you're young so you would develop sportsmanship at the same time you learned to play the sport for a lifetime.

Henry was involved with the "People to People" sports program, a charity created in the 1950s by tennis fans who, like President Eisenhower, believed that participation in sports was one of the best methods of generating peace among nations. The program's benefactors pooled their resources and invited 80 players from foreign countries to visit the United States. The Benisch family and other members of West Side housed and entertained them. Henry was also the director of the Eastern Patrons program, which sponsored junior tennis activities in parks and schools. After he passed away in 1986, three months after his wife of 61 years, Catharine, had died, the Benisch family honored him in a way they felt he would approve, by establishing an Eastern tennis college scholarship in his name.

The Benisch sisters [Peggy and Barbara] were both junior players. "Not great tournament quality," they said, "we just had a good time." Tennis was obviously a social outlet, too, as Peggy met her future husband Carleton (Carl) Anderson on the West Side courts, when they were both about 16.

Just last month, Carl was awarded a "40-year service medal" for volunteer contributions to the sport, at the USTA Annual Meeting in La Quinta, California. It all started when his father-in-law said he needed some help testing tennis balls. Anderson asked, "How do you do that? And the next day all the equipment was dumped in our front room foyer… then I got the book out." Carl tests the quality of tennis balls year round in the testing lab, at the USTA headquarters in White Plains, checking size, weight, bounce, rebound. "Then we put it in the Steven's machine, compress the ball [18 lbs. of pressure] and release it [after 5 seconds], make sure that when it hits the court or it's hit by the racquet it will reconstitute itself back to round within 5 seconds. After that, we do the forward and return compressions. If it responds it's a real live tennis ball and labeled 'USTA approved.'" Off-the-shelf testing follows, year round, in pro shops, stores, etc. The whole effort is a Benisch-Anderson legacy; the Andersons' son, Carleton J. Anderson III – known as Jay – is the current chairman of the tennis ball testing committee.

Benisch family members say that their Patriarch never lost his enthusiasm for creating ways to help young people and often helped to establish summer camps through organizations like the YMCA, on whose board he served for 30 to 35 years. The Benisch sisters and the neighborhood children staged plays in their basement, charged a fee to get in, and gave the money to the Y camps.

In 1972, the late Phil Dougherty wrote a piece in *The New York Times*, entitled "The Benisch Family: An Institution In Itself." A man had called to ask Dougherty if he knew Henry Benisch, and in response he wrote: "I immediately had visions of this tall, happy grandfatherly type all dressed up in a Santa suit, off to drop in on the local kids on Christmas Eve, or on another occasion playing a sprightly tune on his fiddle at some party…A merry person indeed…a man whose business is closely associated with death, yet he does much more than his share of living for himself and others.…

"He's 72 years old and plays tennis three times a week…His bridge playing borders on a passion; he is an opera buff, frequent traveler, photographer, self-taught handwriting expert…long active as an officer…trustee…president of [many organizations]. Had enough? There's more…

"He graduated from Boys' High School with honors, Class of '16, and from Cornell, Class of '20, as a civil engineer… and before joining the Benisch concern in 1924, worked…in Pittsburgh where he even played his fiddle at the debut party of one of Andrew Mellon's daughters. Who among you can make that statement?"

How did Henry Benisch manage to do it all? Peggy Anderson gives some insight. "Dad had the ability to sleep in 10-minute intervals and wake up refreshed. A typical routine: nap after dinner, then evening activities, then bed-time. Up at 2 a.m., work on a project or business, back in bed by 5 a.m. Up at 7 a.m. to start all over again."

This is either déjà vu or you have just read the latest version of the movie "A Wonderful Life."

-- By Nancy Gill McShea

Fred Kovaleski

Nancy Gill McShea

Whether it's been in the streets of Sudan or behind the shadows of the White House, Fred Kovaleski has spent well over half a century refining his game on the tennis court and in the corridors of the international corporate world.

Kovaleski, who last fall won the men's 80 singles and doubles titles at the International Tennis Federation (ITF) World and USTA Grass and Clay Court Championships, believes tennis is a perfect match for life. A rangy veteran, at 6-foot-3, Fred strolls onto the tennis court with a polite, yet determined demeanor reminiscent of Gary Cooper in "High Noon." He looks calm, with eyes focused, and quickly surveys his surroundings and his opponent in one take. All he needs to complete the picture are a cowboy hat, a holster and two six shooters.

His fascination with the sport defines Kovaleski, who ranked among the world's best players in the early 1950s when he reached the round of 16 at the U.S. National Championships at Forest Hills and at Wimbledon, where he lost to the 1952 champ Frank Sedgman. Tennis gave him entrée to the courts of King Farouk of Egypt, King Paul of Greece and the Maharajah of Coochebehar in India, which helped him put together a VIP career. He worked as a CIA operative with the government in Washington, D.C. – during which time he served in both U.S. and foreign assignments and even enlisted his wife Manya's knowledge of six different languages to translate tapes obtained through taps of the then-soviet embassy -- and also as a high ranking executive of international operations with several blue chip corporations.

Since returning to organized tennis competition on a regular basis in 1990, after retiring in 1989 from his position as a divisional president of Nabisco's international operations, Kovaleski has dominated his senior age groups, winning 59 out of a possible 68 USTA gold tennis balls, and eight individual ITF world singles and doubles titles. On the USTA men's 65 circuit, he was ranked first in the country in singles and doubles four out of five years. In the 70s, he finished first in the U.S. in singles for four years and in doubles for five. In the 75s, he was ranked first in the U.S. five times in both singles and doubles. He has also won a host of European senior titles and has emerged victorious in key matches for winning U.S. International Britannia, Crawford and Bitsy Grant Cup teams.

"Don't let Fred's polite, gentlemanly manner fool you," cautioned Kovaleski's regular tennis partner Ray Benton, the president of KSB Ventures in Washington, D.C., and the former director of the Volvo Masters. "He is as competitive as any player I've ever met. He always hits the right shot and keeps a 'young' guy like me off balance. Sometimes I just want to drop my racquet and watch him because I learn so much."

Fred has enjoyed the whole adventure. He grew up in modest circumstances in Hamtramck, a small Polish enclave in Detroit where his father worked on the production line at the Ford Motor Company. Coach Jean Hoxie, who groomed many of this country's top players -- including Peaches Bartkowicz -- first tutored him at age 11 and was instrumental in securing a scholarship for him to the College of William and Mary in 1942. That same year, he was named to the U.S. Junior Davis Cup team and played in his first of 10 U.S. National Championships.

He detoured briefly, between 1943 and 1946, to serve during World War 11 in the 511th Parachute Regiment of the 11th Airborne Division. "I wanted to be in an elite unit," he said, "and the paratroopers were an all-volunteer group of physically fit, strong spirited men." He returned to William and Mary after the war and was a factor in his tennis team's successful run to the 1947 and 1948 NCAA Team Championships. He and teammate Tut Bartzen also won the 1948 NCAA individual doubles title. After his graduation in 1949, Fred journeyed around the world with the best players of his generation and defeated several of the game's Grand Slam champions.

"In 1950 I played all the major international championships and then decided I better go to work," he said, noting that it would be almost 20 years before the sport would enter the professional era of big prize money and the U.S. National Championships would be renamed the US Open. "I realized I was not going to be in the top five in the world, which back then was the only way you had a chance of joining Jack Kramer's independent professional tour and making any money."

Yet he won tournaments that year in Algeria, Austria, Greece, India (Madras) and Yugoslavia. He was also a finalist in Turkey and again in India, this time in Bombay, beating Jaroslav Drobny (a future French and Wimbledon champ) in the semis before losing to Sven Davidson (the 1957 French champ).

In 1951, he was a runner-up at the Monte Carlo International Championships, defeating Budge Patty (the 1950 French and Wimbledon champ) in the semis before losing to Straight Clark in the finals. Then, during a tour of Egypt, he met Manya, whose family had fled Russia during the Bolshevik Revolution because they were czarsist supporters. He also met the consul of the U.S. Embassy in Cairo, and it was through the consul's introductions that Fred secured his position with the CIA, which, in turn, led to the affiliations with corporations. For the next 38 years, he served alternately as a senior vice president and president of international operations with Pepsi Cola, heading up the Australian division; Revlon, in charge of Europe; Schering-Plough, the international division; and finishing up with Nabisco in 1989.

Fred's career abroad was exciting and sometimes traumatic. While playing the Indian International Championships in Calcutta, the Maharajah invited him to join a tiger shoot. (No, he didn't shoot any tigers!) During the late 1950s, when revolutionaries in Aden were fighting for their independence from the British, his English tennis pal, Arthur Charles, the Speaker of the House in Parliament, was assassinated. When he and Manya were newly married -- 48 years ago this month -- and Fred was working for Pepsi Cola in Khartoum in the Sudan, they were privy to two bloodless coups.

Despite living amidst political upheaval, Manya remembers their time in Sudan as a great adventure. "A young married couple always brings with them a breath of fresh air," she said, "so all the local business and embassy people invited us to parties. It was also a custom for corporations to give employees a month's hardships leave because Sudan was a tough place to live.

"It's not Paris or New York, you know. It's very hot all year long, so we went on leave to Beirut, which was great fun. And once, when Gottfried ("the Baron") von Cramm came to Khartoum on business, he and Fred played tennis exhibitions and everybody came to watch. It was a small place and the people knew who they were because they followed tennis."

"The tennis environment instills a certain degree of self-reliance, confidence and resourcefulness," Fred Kovaleski said. "The game has played an important part in all facets of my life, even in the CIA. It's a perfect match."

-- By Nancy Gill McShea

Jack Nusbaum

Ed Goldman

Jack Nusbaum was once a confirmed Eastern junior tennis parent, an expert in the familiar ritual of pacing and wringing his hands in angst while watching his son Gary compete in tournaments or in team matches for Scarsdale High School. When Gary exited the juniors in 1984 to begin his college career at the University of Pennsylvania, Nusbaum borrowed Marlon Brando's famous "I coulda been a contenda" line from the movie "On the Waterfront" and lamented, "We coulda won Wimbledon!"

Twenty-one years later, Dad is the tennis champion!

Nusbaum, who is a partner and the chairman of the international law firm, Willkie, Farr & Gallagher – which retains over 600 lawyers and 138 partners with offices in Manhattan, Paris, Washington, London, Rome, Milan, Brussels and Germany – recently called his son Gary and announced, "We didn't win Wimbledon but I'm going to be inducted into the tennis hall of fame." He is being honored for his years of volunteer service, dating to the late 1970s when Gary began playing junior tennis. Jack first signed on as Eastern's general counsel during a proxy contest for ETA officers and wound up doing pro bono legal work for the section for 20 years.

"My introduction to ETA affairs was a contested election for control of the organization," said Jack, who heads up Willkie's Corporate and Financial Services Department and specializes in mergers and acquisitions. "I advised the incumbents on how to properly handle soliciting votes, how to use the power of the incumbency to their advantage. We treated it like a proxy fight for corporate control. Happily, we were successful, and in my succeeding years we never had anything quite so exciting."

Other hot items that often required legal attention were complaints about rankings, players' behavior and adult league rating squabbles.

"It's my bet that people don't get involved in the inner workings of a tennis organization like the ETA unless their kids play tournaments," he said, agreeing that the all-encompassing role of tennis parent ropes you in. "It's personal. I still follow some of those kids [from Eastern's junior ranks]. Just being a tennis player or loving the game is not enough to get you into it."

Jack said his own self taught forehand and strong serve were weapons, yet he admits that playing No. 1 singles for the Mamaroneck High School Tennis team and the freshman team at the University of Pennsylvania were the highlights of his tennis career. He became a fan of the game when he was a young kid playing sports in Long Beach, N.Y., and took one lesson from the local pro, Mr. Young. But in the early 1950s, basketball was the "Big" sport when he attended

Camp Arundel in Maine, and Jack and his Long Beach teammate Larry Brown were the starting guards on the camp's basketball team.

Brown and Nusbaum would both become teachers and power players in their chosen careers – one in the NBA (National Basketball Association) and the other in the ABA (American Bar Association). In 2003, Coach Brown led the Detroit Pistons to the NBA Championships; and in 1988, Nusbaum was the lead counsel to the Shearson Lehman group in the high profile deal that was backing management and financing the $27 billion effort to take over RJR Nabisco. It was the biggest leverage buyout in American business history and the subject of the best selling book, *Barbarians at the Gate*, which details Jack's role in the negotiations. He is described variously in the book as a fine attorney, flinty, at one point uncharacteristically tense, cautious and as a common-sensical counsel with an angst-ridden face whose sense of humor permits him to utter a few profanities when called for.

His Shearson group lost out in the deal to Kohlberg Kravis Roberts & Co. (KKR). "It was very deflating, extremely disappointing," Jack said. "It was so close, two groups offering the same money. The issue of who would be chosen was in doubt until the very last second. We were all sitting together at [Nabisco] headquarters waiting for word. A representative of one of the investment banks came into the room looking down at his feet, and we all knew.

"For everybody involved, it was the highlight of their career. $27 billion! That won't ever be replicated."

At the same time Jack was working on the Nabisco deal he was overseeing acquisitions and private restructurings on behalf of Donald Trump, and also working for Ted Turner in his move to take over CBS. He calls it the "go-go" years, a time when he rated TV close-ups and lots of ink in the press for his creativity in putting together tough deals and for his emergence as a leading player in the mergers and acquisitions field. Shearson chairman Peter Cohen once said that Nusbaum is as important an architect of a transaction as the business people. Another client has pointed out that he is terrific on the business aspects and has the ability to bring dozens of warring parties together and arrive at an amicable solution.

Jack graduated in 1962 from Penn's Wharton School and worked part time at Willkie as an accountant while he attended Columbia Law School, from which he graduated in 1965. Asked how he rose from accountant to chairman of the firm, a position he has held for the past 17 years, he mumbled something like "right place, right time, you know, all that stuff." But basically, he said, it's because he switched to mergers and acquisitions. He had started out as a tax attorney but told a senior partner he'd like to do corporate work instead.

His first assignment was to work out the business divorce, the break up of a little firm, Carter, Berlind and Weill. Arthur Carter was leaving and the firm's lawyers stayed with him, so Jack began representing the Sandy Weill, Roger Berlind companies. He handled 27 different acquisitions for them, including Shearson, American Express and Loeb Rhodes, among others. He also became involved in the historic merger of NASDAQ with the American Stock Exchange and the acquisition of McCaw Cellular Communications by AT&T.

He explains that the role of counsel is essentially one of facilitation. He advises clients on how to structure the deal and about barriers such as government regulations. Then he assists in negotiations, including engaging in price negotiations. He also does all the paperwork.

"I take it as it comes," he said. "Being a lawyer is just like anything else. I learned years ago that lawyers sell two things: ability and accessibility. Many, many lawyers have ability and not enough lawyers understand that when the client wants something you have to be accessible. A lawyer takes care of your financial health just as your doctor takes care of your physical health. And when you have a real problem with either you don't want to be told, 'I'll call you back.' It's a lesson I've tried to impart over the years to the lawyers in my firm because it's all that differentiates you; there are lots of smart people out there. It's a fact.

"I have a rule. There are two things in life that get me aggravated in my firm: one is when I get a call from a client saying so and so didn't return my call. And the other is when there are typographical errors in documents that we send out. The former is lack of accessibility and responsiveness and the latter is lack of care. And both of those are easily curable."

Jack is, by nature, calm and well grounded. He is impressed by his clients' accomplishments but not awed by them. He was once having lunch at the Plaza with Donald Trump -- who owned the famous Manhattan landmark -- and Trump said to him, "I'll bet you come from the Bronx and your parents have been married for 50 years. Right?" Jack replied: "On the contrary, I had a very screwed up childhood. I was the only child of my mother and father who lasted together for two years, and then each remarried four more times and I have stepbrothers and sisters around the globe. When you're living under siege with multiple children in the house, one of two things happens: you either go crazy or accept the fact that if that doesn't throw you, nothing will. You learn to roll with the punches. So when you get older life gets pretty simple. I do attribute learning that to my childhood."

Trump still throws up his hands and says, "Can you believe this guy's background? This can't be!"

Doris Herrick, Eastern's longtime executive director who worked with Jack Nusbaum for 20 years, says he is a truly nice man. "I don't believe he treated any of his million dollar clients any better than he did our [tennis] association. He answered every call, solved every problem I ever threw at him and never made me feel insignificant. He really does practice what he teaches...accessibility and accountability...He is both!"

-- By Nancy Gill McShea

Butch Seewagen

Ed Goldman

Walk into the brick building in Rockville Centre, Long Island, with the big CATS sign out front, and you're immediately swept up in a sea of buzzing children. The proprietor, Butch Seewagen, who has agreed to run an inventory of his life, ushers you into a back room far from the madding crowd. You notice that he no longer limps and seems fully recovered from his second hip replacement surgery last November.

Seewagen ranked among the world's top 100 professional tennis players during the 1970s at the same time he coached the men's tennis team at Columbia University and taught physical education there. But in 1975, at the age of 27, he tore a groin muscle while playing the U.S. summer circuit and wasn't able to walk for nine months. The medical consensus was that the injury had inflamed an undiagnosed arthritic condition, and four doctors told him he would never play again. Only Dr. Irving Glick offered hope and said he could resume playing with moderate success.

"I knew I was not going to be what I could be," said Butch, who laughs easily and often, yet admits that he also cried a lot and felt lost when he faced the reality of his life-altering injury. "I was depressed but accepted that I would be a part timer, a recreational tour player. And I loved Columbia, so I made lemonade out of lemons."

He could have settled for the role of celebrity magnet and dashing bachelor-about-town, but instead tried to live down the 'tennis bum' image during the sport's boom years in New York by devising ways to transform himself into a serious entrepreneur.

By 1985, after he had retired from the pro tour and was playing the senior circuit, teaching tennis and also tending to various business interests, Butch and his sister Barbara Steger opened CATS -- the Children's Athletic Training School

– to teach kids basic athletic skills so they would enjoy playing tennis.

"I was teaching one day, daydreaming," he said, explaining that after leaving Columbia in 1979 he was the director of tennis at Manhattan's East River and Murray Hill Racquet Clubs. "If a kid wasn't hitting the ball over the net, he wanted to leave. I wanted to get paid for the lesson and you had to be a clown to keep him there…The kid who can hit over the net loves it and the others go running off. If they could bounce-catch, they could probably bounce-hit. If they could throw a ball, they could learn to serve. If they could catch a ball, they could volley. Kids need skills to have success and I didn't need a court to teach them."

CATS debuted in a Manhattan church gymnasium at 64th Street and Park Avenue and received national recognition for being the first skill-based program in the country.

Duly impressed by those revelations, you ask Butch to continue running an inventory of his life to date:

1949 – His mother, Clella, pitched tennis balls to him at age 3 and drove him to every practice session and tournament between the ages of 8 and 18. "Mom gave up a big chunk of her life for me," he said.

1954 – His father, the legendary coach George Seewagen, began dragging him to clinics at age 8 to demonstrate the forehand. "Tennis gave me everything in my life and dad gave me that gift," he said. "Dad was too nervous to watch me play, thought he'd jinx me, so when he did come he hid out in the woods."

1957-1965 – Butch ranked first in every Eastern junior age division and among the country's top five. He won countless titles – including the Orange Bowl and the Canadian National Championships – and was the runner-up to Cliff Richey while winning the sportsmanship award at the boys' 16 nationals at Kalamazoo. He was named to the U.S. Junior Davis Cup team at 16 with Bob Lutz and Stan Smith and played in the U.S. National Championships at 17.

1966-1968 – Advanced to the mixed doubles semifinals at the U.S. Championships with Kathy Blake (mother of the Bryan twins); member of 'Final 8' Club. Beat future Wimbledon and US Open champ Stan Smith at the Nassau Bowl. He was twice an All-American at Rice, the singles and doubles champion in the Southwest Conference, and was inducted into the university's Hall of Fame.

1969 – Defeated Zan Guerry 6-4 in the fifth to win the U.S. National Amateur singles title. Trailed two sets to one in the televised final (Channel 13) but Dad was there and reminded him at the break that friends back at the Bayside Club – where he had won six New York State Championships -- were watching. "I was ready to lose but Dad motivated me."

1970 – He turned pro and took the Columbia job. At 22, he was the youngest coach at a major university. Opened center court at Wimbledon against defending champ Rod Laver, winner of the 1969 Grand Slam. "Arthur Ashe told me not to look up and not to drink the orange juice or I'd get a bad stomach. After the match I took in the atmosphere and [as a bonus] drank all the juice." Rated a feature in *The Long Island Press* for his induction as a student-athlete into the New York City PSAL Hall of Fame, along with Whitey Ford and Red Auerbach.

1971 – Returned to Wimbledon's Center Court to play mixed doubles with Kristy Pigeon against Evonne Goolagong and Kim Warwick. Butch tripped, curtsied instead of bowing and Kristy smashed him in the head with her big lefty serve. "20,000 people were laughing and she was crying."

1972 – Raised the bar for the Ivy League to match his innovative recruiting tactics. He beat Jimmy Connors, which attracted top-notch players Vitas Gerulaitis, Eric Fromm, Jon Molin, Lloyd Emanuel, Kirk Moritz, Rick Fagel, Henry Bunis, Bob Binns and Larry Parsont. He glamorized New York for recruits, inviting celebrities Arthur and Jeanne Ashe, Dave DeBusschere, Gordon Parks, Phyllis George, Oleg Cassini, George Plimpton and Dustin Hoffman to play tennis with the team. Arranged dates for recruits with top 10 finalists in the Ford Agency's "Model of the Year" contest; squired them to hot spots Maxwell's Plum and Hippopotamus.

1973 – A good year! Notched wins over Wimbledon champ Jan Kodes and Brian Gottfried and founded the Seemar sporting goods company with Columbia professor John Markisz. They had a patent on a new ball hopper, the ball busser, and also represented Australia's titan gut, Kaepa tennis shoes, and they were the exclusive distributor of Yonex racquets in the northeast.

1974 – Detroit drafted him for World TeamTennis. He took a leave from Columbia to play the tour full time. Got right into Wimbledon, "the place to be, the Super Bowl." Dad had never been to Europe and went with him.

1975 – The year of the infamous injury! Players howled: "Osteoarthritis! What's that? Just go play!" During the Open at Forest Hills, he visited a gypsy, who said: "You're a pro athlete; I see you've suffered a severe injury. You'll resume your career in January, and for another $5 I'll put in an extra prayer for you."

1976 – Encouraged, he won 5 Eastern tournaments, the American Express Challenger, and came back from 0 to 200 on the ATP computer. Ranked No. 1 in the East and 37th in the country and returned to Columbia.

1977-1979 – Was proud of his Columbia teams, which won three ECAC and two Ivy League Championships. He's still proud of his Columbia connection, as his son Chad is currently studying in the environmental science masters program there.

The 1980s – Butch opened the Center Court Restaurant opposite Lincoln Center. Attracted celebrities and tennis players from around the world. Gave his Dad a surprise 75th birthday party there; Don Budge and Fred Perry were guests. Enlisted by Neil Amdur, then editor-in-chief of *World Tennis* magazine, to be the equipment advisor and write the "Coaches Corner." Won six USTA national men's 35 doubles titles and was a singles runner-up three times. Won the USTA national 40s and ranked first in the country. Played No. 1 for the 1985 U.S. team that beat Italy for the Italia Cup. Returned to the U.S. and was invited to play a pro-am at the Glen Oaks Country Club. His future wife, Chris, was running the tournament. "She was bossing everyone around, told me I was late getting onto court 3, but we've been together now for 20 years," he said.

After racing through a cliff notes version of some memorable moments in his life, Butch chuckled and said, "I'm resting now, but watch out, I'm gonna come back again when I have the left hip redone." Until then, it's back to the future with CATS and his position as director of tennis at the prestigious Pine Hollow Country Club in East Norwich!

Neil Amdur sums up the inventory: "To know Butch Seewagen is to like him…not just for his skills or his tennis rankings, but for his genuine sense of self."

-- By Nancy Gill McShea

Chapter 26

2006: Gowen, G. Heldman, J. Heldman, Maguire and Vincent

George W. Gowen

George Gowen and his award presenter Henry Talbot.

George Gowen is a senior partner in the Manhattan law firm of Dunnington, Bartholow & Miller and has been affiliated with his firm for almost 50 years. He is also a seasoned tennis veteran, having served 18 USTA presidents – in the roles of advisor, counselor and historian -- and survived countless revolutions within the sport for almost 40 years.

Gowen served as Eastern's vice president in the early 1970s, but he initially established a presence in the game in 1969 when he was appointed general counsel of the USLTA by President Alastair Martin. Martin was working to consolidate tennis's amateur and professional games as the sport moved into the Open Era.

"Bob Kelleher (1967-68) was the first president I worked for but I was officially appointed by Alastair (1969-70), said George, who is known as one of the game's most polished diplomats. "They were both outstanding presidents during a major revolutionary period.

"I was very lucky. It was a position that was 100 percent the president's call…I didn't ever assume that it would continue and I am grateful to those individuals who, for better or worse, selected me."

The late Eugene L. Scott pondered Gowen's role in the Nov. 22, 1975 *Tennis Week* "Vantage Point" column: "[George] has lived and suffered through the gargantuan growth of tennis…He has negotiated license agreements, stadium lease agreements and television contracts. He has been a mediator in player strikes on one hand and player bans on the other. And he has been smack in the middle of thorny anti-trust actions directed against his Association…He has always been cool in crisis, and his integrity is respected everywhere. He also has a nifty sense of humor…rare in administrating or even in playing the game."

Gowen needed a sense of humor and integrity, plus a whole lot of other qualities, along with his instinct for keeping things simple and straight forward.

Open tennis was the first hurdle. The history books report that Open tennis was a done deal in 1968, when in reality the game wasn't completely open. Several groups were vying for power and a classification of registered players existed. "Five of the world's top players boycotted the Open in 1971," George said.

America's Stan Smith won the 1971 Open and the next year George advised USLTA President Robert Colwell in working out an agreement with the players – Gowen-style -- with a minimum of excitement and litigation. The larger issue was to ensure that Open tennis would truly be open. In those days, many tennis organizations felt that the players should do what they were told, which prompted rebellion and a boycott at the 1973 Wimbledon. "The USLTA leadership -- and to the extent that I had influence – believed that the players should be treated as valuable individuals, independent contractors," George said. "It was worked out because we recognized that a new age was coming. It was bound to come with more or less blood shed. And I think it ended up with very little blood shed."

In Gowen's view, many tennis leaders stood up to effect change. The tie breaker, invented by Jimmy Van Alen, was introduced by tournament director Bill Talbert at the 1970 US Open, after Alastair Martin gave the go ahead. It was more than a revolutionary act within the game; it allowed schedule makers and television producers to estimate the timing of a match. "The tie breaker may have been the biggest economic benefit to tennis to date," George said. "The old scoring system…with a match of 22 to 24 games was hardly appealing to television producers."

Litigation defined professional tennis in the 1970s. "It's a pleasant irony that Gladys Heldman is being inducted the same time I am because in 1971 we were on opposite sides of pretty heavy litigation," he said. "They (the "Houston 9") all signed a contract. The good news is that we negotiated a settlement that combined the two women's tours -- the so-called USTA tour and the [Virginia Slims] tour that Gladys put together."

Another revolutionary change occurred in 1975 when Slew Hester, then the USTA's (they dropped the L from USLTA in 1975) first vice president, introduced night tennis under the lights at Forest Hills. George said, "Slew was told he couldn't do it, people would object, but he just went ahead and got the lights. It was revolutionary but he did it rather than endure agonizing studies." Stan Smith was the first leading American tennis player to play under the lights.

The USTA took leadership positions in introducing indoor tennis and in allowing Billie Jean King's World Team Tennis (WTT) players to compete in the Open. "Billie Jean is a historic figure," George said, "not only as a tennis player or as the architect of pro team tennis, but also with respect to women's rights. Tennis in many ways has a broader historical and sociological impact than most sports and Billie Jean is an example of it."

When the Open moved in 1978 from the West Side Tennis Club to the National Tennis Center, the USTA President Slew Hester broke with West Side, which had hosted the tournament since 1914. "West Side got 50 percent of the deal," George said. "Slew said West Side asked for too much. He just walked out and said 'We can do it ourselves.' It was pure guts! The first shovel was stuck in the ground in October of 1977 and 10 months later we were playing the US Open in a stadium of 20,000 and another stadium of 5,000. In retrospect, nobody can believe…that you could start and finish a giant project in that length of time.

"We financed it by getting a loan from Citibank and selling box seats. It was an incredible achievement. I was Slew's counsel and was involved in every aspect of the move. Less people were involved in those days. The USTA didn't have any money so every cent counted. I remember Slew saying, 'We're not going to put in an extra light bulb because we can't afford it.' Now it's matured into this incredible event."

Gowen drafted the contracts for the move to the National Tennis Center. The building was done in less than a year but four park commissioners kept hassling them. "New York was in a decline," George said, "and perhaps that worked in our favor because we were more prone to be creative. I remember getting orders from the park commissioner to shut down construction. I guess I shouldn't say this, but I ignored the order."

When David Markin was president (1989-90), he built the Arthur Ashe stadium, which directly influenced the Open's present success and popularity.

Is there a favorite match, a favorite player? "Any match with Jimmy Connors," George said. "McEnroe had the ultimate touch. Billie Jean transcends tennis. Newcomer Chris Evert made it to the 1971 Open semis…Agassi, in all his phases…And Sampras, sick and reeling on court (in the 1995 Open versus Corretja), put in a second serve ace, won the match and the tournament.

"Every Davis Cup match is memorable, especially…oversees," he continued. "I went to a match in Prague in early 1990 right after the Berlin wall came down (late 1989). It was also historic because the Czech Republic was free again. I went to Zimbabwe in 2000, an unusual place to go. John McEnroe was the Davis Cup captain; Chris Woodruff and Agassi won critical matches and we won."

And how about your tennis, George? "The only strength I had was a good forehand. But at the (1979) USTA Annual Meeting I teamed with Bill Clothier (twice a finalist at the U.S. Championships) and beat Stan Malless (a former USTA president) and Ken Nidrie of Puerto Rico, 6-0, 6-2. That was my greatest moment."

Reminded that he has the most extensive corporate knowledge in the USTA's history and knows all of the inside scoops, he chuckled and said, "Well, some, yeah. That's just because I've been around so long." But you keep your own counsel, right? "Well, it's kind of a lawyer's job to keep quiet.

"If the leadership is open and creative, it's fun. And tennis continues to evolve. We have like 500,000 league players. The emphasis now is in the parks and public playgrounds. That's where it starts. That's a challenge. The US Open continues to get bigger and better. We're on a roll."

-- By Nancy Gill McShea

Gladys M. Heldman

Manhattan-born Gladys Heldman graduated Phi Beta Kappa and first in her class from Stanford University and was the architect of the women's professional tennis circuit. Gladys was described variously as brilliant, indomitable -- and by Bud Collins as "slight and shy, witty and wise, her steel will concealed well." In 1953 she founded and was the publisher, chief editor and writer of World Tennis magazine -- known as the international literary voice of tennis -- and became one of the most influential people in the game. In 1970 she arranged for the Houston Racquet Club to hold a tournament and asked nine of the top women players (the Houston "9") to sign $1.00 contracts with World Tennis to play in the event – among them Billie Jean King and her daughter Julie Heldman -- and enlisted Joe Cullman of Philip Morris to donate prize money and sponsorship, which was the beginning of the women's pro tour. Before she passed away in June 2003, Gladys received many accolades for her dedication to the sport and in 1979 was inducted into the International Tennis Hall of Fame. Nancy Gill McShea.

My mother was an energizer bunny. The words "she started" and "she saved" keep coming up. She started *World Tennis* magazine, she started the women's pro tour, she saved the U.S. Championships at Forest Hills, she helped save the Santa Fe Symphony. There was more. You have no idea how hard she worked.

Her work ethic started when she attended Stanford. My mother always said that she almost flunked out of high school. Well, that's not quite true. Only in her later years did she hint at what a rebel she was. She told me that her teacher once said, "Read Hamlet," and my mother refused, reading Othello instead. My grandfather, a famous New York lawyer, had friends in high places. He got my mother into Stanford on the recommendations of Tom Dewey and Herbert Hoover. At Stanford, she was determined not to let them down, and as she said, "not to flunk out," so she taught herself how to succeed. To be sure, she was smart enough — but to guarantee being a winner she applied her prodigious intelligence to focusing on what her professors wanted, and then spewing it back to them. She taught herself to work harder than everyone else. She ended up with an all "A" average.

From then on, she applied that dynamic focus to each task she undertook. Take her tennis playing. She started the game when she was 23 and I was three months old. She said she did it to see my father [Julius], a tennis champion, on the weekends, which he spent at the Berkeley Tennis Club. She charged hard, practicing hours and hours. She always said she wasn't a natural athlete. So her improvement came out of will and sweat. In just a few years she went from total novice to being ranked number one in Texas and winning tons of trophies.

My sister Trixie and I are her daughters, but you may not be aware that there was another child in our house -- and that child's name was *World Tennis* magazine. From 1953 to 1972 my mother worked like a whirling dervish, performing all the magazine's tasks, from menial ones like managing subscriptions (early on when she got cash, she stored it in her bra), to writing and/or editing all the articles. She was the magazine's graphic designer, but then her tools weren't computers; they were rubber cement and printers' proofs.
She started out with a storefront office near our New York apartment, and when the magazine was going to press, we'd bring her lunch, dinner, breakfast and then lunch again. She'd work 36, sometimes 48, hours in a row. She never let the magazine be printed even one day late.

World Tennis was the most demanding member of the family. All the human members of the family were expected to help take care of the baby. My father, who ostensibly had a day job as a vice president of Shell Oil, did double duty as a tennis analyst and proofreader extraordinaire, while my sister and I stuffed envelopes, filed photos, and manned the magazine's booth at Forest Hills, starting when we were seven and eight years old. We also helped clip tennis results out of the mountains of newspapers from around the world that arrived daily at our home. Those results were printed in six-point type in the back of the magazine. Tennis players around the world turned to *World Tennis* as their bible.

Magazines make money from their ads. My mother sold all the ads in *World Tennis*. She'd invite prospective advertisers to lunch at a fancy French restaurant, and then pitch them her ideas of how to connect the advertiser's name to an event or an award or a column. She was a pioneer of modern sports marketing. If my mother failed to sell the ads she was pitching, she took herself to Tiffany's to buy a consoling treasure. When she died, we discovered her stash of gold pins, gold cigarette cases, and gold necklaces.

My mother didn't sleep much normally, so she had hours to fill with her apparently unbounded energy. During the *World Tennis* years, she wrote several tennis books, did voluminous research in preparation for writing an encyclopedia of Greek Mythology, and became a substantial collector of rare books (another place she would take herself if she failed to sell an ad she was pitching).

Onto this extraordinarily busy schedule she moonlighted several promotions. In 1962 the U.S. Championships at Forest Hills was in dire straits. The best players were skipping the event, instead playing in Europe, where they got lots of under-the-table money. So, my mother turned to her address book, called 9 rich friends, and convinced them to join her in bringing an airplane load of the best international players to Forest Hills. It was a slam-dunk. The airplane came, the top players competed, and Forest Hills was saved.

In 1970, she gave birth to another tennis baby, the Women's pro tour. Without remuneration she began and promoted the tour for its struggling yet exhilarating first three years. *World Tennis* didn't take a back seat, though. To manage both her tennis babies, my mother went on hyper warp speed, even finding the energy to fight the United States Tennis Association, which was constantly battling the women's pro tour. Women's sports can be a hard sell. I was one of the original players on the tour, and I can assure you the media mostly didn't know what to do with us. Often they'd assign the fashion reporter to cover the matches, and we'd have to explain to them what the words "forehand" and "love" meant. Under my mother's passion and skill, women's tennis thrived. No other women's pro sports can boast such fame and fortune. The women's pro tennis tour would not be as successful without my mother's pioneering work.

In 1972, my mother sold World Tennis magazine to CBS publications, although she remained the publisher for two years. She cut back to writing only two articles a month for the magazine. She liked to say that CBS publications hired 7 men to replace her. That's not true. It was 9.

In the mid-1970s, Nana Sato, a highly ranked Japanese tennis player, came to live with my parents for two years. She became their Japanese daughter. My mother loved to speak Japanese with Nana, and in her fifties, in another of her more Herculean efforts, she learned to write in Japanese. She had a wall full of books in Japanese, all of which she read and annotated.

In the late 1970s, she tried to close a trust account at a bank in Houston, and a banker condescendingly went to my father to make her change her mind. He chose the wrong woman. My mother believed that he would have acted differently if there had been women on the bank's board of directors. So she started a service to place women on the boards of Fortune 500 corporations.

Even in retirement, my mother didn't slow down. She wrote a first novel, which was published, no mean feat for someone in her mid-fifties. Once my father retired, they moved to Santa Fe, where my mother worked hard and creatively to help save the Santa Fe Symphony.

My mother was the happiest ever in Santa Fe, maintaining an extremely active social life, learning to have true friendships, and playing tennis six days a week. She continued to hard charge through life, but with more fun. In her eighties, she was still improving her tennis. Earlier in her life she was afraid of going to net, but under the tutelage of Claudia Monteiro, she started serving better and improving her volley. Six days a week she played happily and well. She loved her tennis buddies. The day before she died, she was serving up a storm and attacking the net. Life was good. She went out at the top of her game.

--By Julie Heldman

Julie Heldman

If you recognize that tennis is more than "just a game" and that when it is played at its most challenging level it is a struggle engaging the body, mind and spirit, then you will understand why Julie Heldman's on-court journey reads like a two-act play. The first act was fueled by intensity, the second by joy, and an epiphany in between prepared her for Act III.

"Tennis was my foundation," said Julie, whose collection of tennis memorabilia traces the 15 years between 1963 and 1975 when she ranked as high as No. 5 in the world and No. 2 in the United States. From an early age, her lifestyle was tied to the sport. For years, she and her sister Trixie sold their mother Gladys's *World Tennis* magazines under the stadium at Forest Hills. Julie also wrote articles and captions for the magazine in her teens and cut tennis clippings and scores out of nine papers a day.

"Our family discussed tennis at the dinner table; it became my identity," she said, recalling that she won the Girls' 18 Canadian National Championships when she was just 12.

"I needed it," said Julie, who skipped two grades and felt like an outsider when she attended the Dalton School in Manhattan. "I won the national 15-and-unders one summer and back at school a bunch of us sat around discussing vacations. One went to camp, another had her nose done. I told them I won a tennis tournament." The response? "What's that?"

Julie trained at the Hoxie tennis camp in Michigan at age 8 and also began riding the subway solo to practice at the Heights Casino in Brooklyn. "I was focused from the moment I started playing," she said. "It was all about winning or not losing. My nickname was tiger. My sister saw ferocity across the net. I wasn't aware of it…It was complicated, as most things are."

The obvious clue to Julie's championship tennis game is her intelligence. Not surprising, considering her family background, what she achieved on the court and in her life after tennis.

She entered Stanford University at 16, in 1962, graduated in 1966, and in 1981 was named the UCLA Law School Graduate of the Year. Her father Julius was a national tennis champion, earned a Ph.D. from Stanford and was a vice president of the Shell Oil Company. Her mother graduated Phi Beta Kappa from Stanford, founded *World Tennis* and was the architect of the women's pro tour. Trixie was a national merit scholar finalist, attended Ivy League schools, and played guitar in a rock and roll band she formed in Colorado.

"Our family, fortunately or unfortunately, was distinguished or cursed with being bright," Julius Heldman said recently. "It's difficult, but when all is said and done, I take a great deal of pride in it."

Julie's savvy approach to the game prompted Bud Collins to call her "junk ball Julie." She had good hands, excellent command of the drop shot and hit the ball flat and with topspin. Her on-court image was so mercurial that one writer described her as "both vivacious and pugnacious." She enjoyed entertaining the audience, making fans laugh by way of body language and facial grimaces, but could turn around a minute later and get ticked off.

"I learned from Mr. Hoxie how to outsmart an opponent by using high balls, angles, and using different tactics depending on whom I was playing," she said.

Julie knew that Evonne Goolagong's second serve was weak so she'd run around the backhand and thump a forehand winner down the line. When she beat Billie Jean King in the third round of the 1973 US Open, the temperature was in the 100 degree range and she had already gone through heat prostration. "Billie Jean was suffering from the heat," she said. "I decided to get the ball low over the net so that when she charged it would wear her down." Julie was ahead 4-1 in the third set and Billie Jean retired.

Julie first quit playing tennis in 1966 – "I decided to stop, for good, or so I thought," she said. – when she was not named to play on the Wightman Cup team (she was on the team, but not picked to play) and was also over-reacting to a breakup with a boyfriend. She finished at Stanford, went home to New York and got a job as a secretary at the Wells, Rich, Greene advertising agency.

"I hated being indoors so much that I envied the delivery boys…they could at least be outside," she said. She quit that job, hung out with a hippy group and tagged along when they drove cross-country in a van to California. Once there, she went to live with Dennis and Linda Van der Meer. Dennis was the pro at the Berkeley Tennis Club and ran a summer camp there.

"I was happy to help teach the kids," she said, "but Linda got me out on the court and I felt like playing again. Linda reminded me that I didn't have to push myself; tennis could be just for fun. That was an eye opener for me."

Dennis helped change her backhand and serve and, late that summer she beat Billie Jean in the Pacific Coast tournament at the Berkeley Club. She realized she could still compete at the top level, which ushered in the epiphany and the beginning of Act ll.

"I decided to play again, just for fun, to use my racquet as a passport to see the world," she said. "In 1968 and 1969, I traveled all over, including stops in Europe, Johannesburg, to Mexico for the Olympics, Buenos Aires, Santiago de Chile, Russia and Tel Aviv for the Maccabiah Games."

In 1969, she won the Italian Open, ranked No. 2 in the U.S. and No. 5 in the world (she repeated as the world's No. 5 in 1974). "The travel was exhilarating," she said. "But the women's pro tour started in 1971, so I had diminished opportunities to roam the world. (Julie was one of the "Houston 9" who signed a $1.00 contract with *World Tennis* magazine to help pioneer the [Virginia Slims] tour. She was injured at the time, heard that the players who had entered the tournament would be suspended, so she played one point -- against King – to show her support, and then defaulted.)

"When pro tennis came around it became a job. I gave up my tennis passport …for money and solidarity, losing Naples for Oklahoma City. It was an advantage for so many people, including me, to make my own money. The first thing I did…was…buy a stereo. The next thing I did, when I won a big tournament, was buy a sports car…Plus, I trained very hard, so I saw very little other than the hotel rooms and the tennis courts. There were some successful times, a few more injuries, and I quit the year I turned 30."

Overall, Julie won more than 20 pro titles and played on U.S. championship teams, in Wightman Cup (for which she was twice captain, 1974-75, and the MVP, 1969), Fed Cup (captain, 1975) and Bonne Bell Cup (captain, MVP, 1974). She earned three Olympic medals in Mexico City in 1968 -- gold (in mixed doubles with Herb Fitz Gibbon), silver and bronze -- and three gold medals at the Maccabiah Games. She received the USTA Service Bowl and has been inducted already into several Halls of Fame.

She also enjoyed meeting a wide range of players. She felt honored to play mixed doubles at 14 with the great Gardnar Mulloy, but regrets that she once gave the Wimbledon and Australian champ, Dick Savitt, the chicken pox. "And he got it badly," she said. "When I got the measles a few months later, he refused to have any contact with my mother, even on the phone."

She worked as a tennis journalist and as a television commentator for CBS, NBC and HBO at Wimbledon and at the US Open. "I loved commentating," she said. "I was lively and knew tennis. I had learned a lot from my father and was able to explain what I saw going on on the court."

Thus far, in Act lll, she has practiced law in California, raised her daughter Amy, now 18 and studying film at the California Institute of the Arts in Valencia, California. In 1983, Julie and her husband Bernie started Signature Eyewear and they now have 300 employees.

Julie, by her own admission, is no longer hyper-competitive, but believes her two-act tennis career taught her how to succeed and gave her a sense of accomplishment and confidence to excel in Act lll.

-- By Nancy Gill McShea

Suzanne Maguire

Suzanne Maguire and Pete Sampras at Davis Cup.

Suzanne Maguire may be best known as the US Open marketing director who negotiated the Open's first million-dollar sponsorship, but in truth she has been a tennis insider, in a literal sense, all of her life.

Suzanne grew up in the Westchester Country Club in Rye, N.Y. Actually lived in the building! Her father was an avid golfer there and tried to get her hooked as well. But the club's caddies told her father that golf was not her game, that he should buy her a tennis racquet instead, and a tennis star was born.

She fell in love with the sport and began a lifelong devotion to Davis Cup when she watched Australia defeat Sweden, 3-2, in a 1950 Inter-zonal final on the grass in her front yard at the Westchester Country Club. She was a teenager then, and she and a group of friends wound up going to the movies with the Aussie Davis Cup team.

Suzanne played tennis in the 1950s at the Rosemary Hall prep school in Connecticut under the tutelage of the late Clifford Sutter, once an ETA president and a member of the Eastern Tennis Hall of Fame. After she was married and had children, she returned to the Westchester Country Club to play tennis on the 'B' team in the Metropolitan Inter-Club Tennis League that Barbara Williams created there. She directed the club's women's and children's tennis programs and helped to set up two professional events: the Women's Medi-Quik Open and the Men's Lionel Tournament.

Suzanne worked at those pro events with the tournament director Marilyn Fernberger, the USTA director of women's tennis Edy McGoldrick and the umpire Lee Jackson. "No one could have had better individuals to learn from," she said. Or to be fooled by! Ion Tiriac once asked her at the Lionel event to teach him how to drive a stick shift courtesy car. She struggled, not having a clue about stick shifts. "He was just kidding me," she said. "He raced cars as a hobby."

She returned to the work force full time and represented Avon's interests during the season-ending women's pro championships at Madison Square Garden, working with Ella Musolino. And she also traveled on the Avon Futures Circuit. In January of 1978, Ray Benton of ProServ hired her to work the Colgate Masters at the Garden. "I'm proud to have been Suzie's real starting block in the tennis business," said Benton, now the president of KSB Ventures in Washington, D.C. "She was one of my top administrators at the Masters; she hit the ground running and kept running to bigger and better things to help our sport."

Later in 1978, at the suggestion of Lee Jackson, she applied to the USTA for a job when the US Open was moving from Forest Hills to the National Tennis Center. She was interviewed by Mike Burns, the executive director, and not knowing the politics, expected to hear from him right away. Jackson encouraged her to be patient, advising her that she would have a career-making job if she were to be hired. "I did finally hear from Mike," she said, "and I certainly did have a career-making job."

Working from file cards and a layout of Forest Hills, Suzanne relocated all of the US Open subscribers from the Forest Hills site to Louis Armstrong Stadium at the National Tennis Center. "As I had never been to Forest Hills I did this based on sponsorship, longevity and location," she said. "Mike only changed about four of the subscribers I had placed. Needless to say, I had no idea of the intensity of feelings subscribers have to their seat location. As it turned out it was the safest way to do it. It was done by a fair protocol, all on the up and up, so I survived."

She worked directly for Burns on the US Open for a few years and when the Capital Sports (C.S.) contract was up for renewal, she asked him if they could sell the US Open sponsorships and not renew the C.S. agreement. They met with the USTA president, who agreed to give them a chance. "It went very slowly at first," Suzanne said, "and Mike had to convince the president to give us some more time." It eventually all came together and people started buying what she was selling. Many of the companies that now sponsor the Open came from their early efforts.

She took over marketing of the US Open in the early 1980s. "My best sponsor experiences were landing Coca Cola and Infiniti," she said, explaining that it's very easy to sell something you totally believe in, and she totally believes in the Open. She said that when Infiniti called, they initially asked about renting a hospitality tent. The Open had just lost Avis as the sponsor of the men's singles, so she suggested to Infiniti that they take over that sponsorship.

"Joanne Fairchild and I flew to California," Suzanne said, "and I sold Infiniti the men's singles for a million dollars. It was our first million dollar US Open sponsor…I flew back from California without the plane!"

She also realized a dream to work on Davis Cup when the U.S. defeated Czechoslovakia, 4-1, in 1981 at the National Tennis Center. "I had loved Davis Cup from the beginning and when I was a child that beautiful cup was showcased in the lobby of the Westchester Country Club," she said. "I was fortunate enough to travel with our team for about 11 years -- working with Ed Fabricius, Arthur Ashe and Tom Gorman, and players like Andre (Agassi), Pete (Sampras) and John (McEnroe), Michael Chang, Peter Fleming, Jimmy Connors and Jimmy Arias."

Her friend David Markin remembers a humorous aside involving Suzanne at a Davis Cup match in Paraguay, with U.S. stars Aaron Krickstein and Jimmy Arias. "She broke a front tooth and was moaning and groaning," he said. "I said 'Go to the dentist.' She came to dinner that night with two teeth – one in her mouth and one in her hand. When we asked why two, she said the dentist cautioned 'In case it breaks.' Sure enough, she bit into a roll and it broke."

Suzanne was transferred to the National Tennis Center in 1989 when the Arthur Ashe Stadium was being constructed and she became involved with many aspects of the new stadium – the architectural design, food service and décor. She was responsible for luxury suite sales and, once again, seat relocation.

"Suzanne has very good people skills," said Markin, who supervised the construction of the Ashe Stadium when he was the USTA president. "There were 86 luxury boxes to sell in the new stadium. She was involved in placing and selling boxes. She made sure the appropriate people got the appropriate assignments when she transferred everything from the old Louis Armstrong Stadium to Ashe. Guests were placed in proper seating areas. She instinctively knew who the VIPs were and those who wanted to be. There were no errors in protocol."

In fact, she worked very closely with the USTA presidents and their wives, as she had done throughout her career, in managing day-to-day operations of the president's box, including attending to the décor, menu, linens, flowers, invitations and staffing. At the end of her USTA career, before she retired in 2004, Suzanne worked directly for the USTA President Alan Schwartz.

Andre Agassi and Steffi Graf have sent warm congratulations to Suzanne on the occasion of her induction into the Eastern Tennis Hall of Fame: "Suzanne Maguire has been such a tremendous asset to the game of tennis. She is a talented, dedicated and passionate woman who is very deserving of this honor."

-- By Nancy Gill McShea

Tony Vincent

Bronx native Tony Vincent, a well-known veteran of the world's tennis courts and backgammon tables for most of his 80 years, has a reputation among friends and fellow players for being an enigmatic character who plays his cards close to the vest.

"Tony isn't very forthcoming," said Fred Kovaleski, who, with Vincent as his partner, has won numerous USTA national senior doubles titles. "But everyone who knows him understands his mind-set. He is neat and methodical, loves a challenge and was one of the few young tennis players who maintained a similar level of proficiency as he moved into the senior ranks. Tony is also a great gin rummy player and a master at backgammon. The guy played in the backgammon world championships in Bermuda."

Exactly as billed, Tony was methodical when he recently traced his roots and the chronology of his life in tennis. He may prefer to keep his own counsel, but he laughs easily and often. Chastised for labeling his mother, Mary Campanella, as "just a housewife" who raised Tony and his three younger siblings, he chuckled apologetically and said, "Okay, okay!" He sounded understandably proud, though, when he said that his father, Salvatore De Vincenzo, reputed to be one of the best trombonists in the world, played with the New York Philharmonic under the great conductor Arturo Toscanini at the Metropolitian Opera and other venues.

So where is the tennis connection? When Tony was about 14, after his family moved to Elmhurst, Long Island, he saw kids knocking tennis balls around in the local park, thought the game looked like fun and borrowed a racquet from his Aunt Jenny to teach himself to play. He made it to the finals of a parks tournament there, went on to win the New York City High School Tennis Championships and captained his Newtown High School and University of Miami tennis teams. During the college years, he established a presence in the sport's upper echelon, winning Good Neighbor and other titles with Althea Gibson, Art Larsen and Gardnar Mulloy.

At the height of his 65-year tennis career, he defeated many of the great players of his time and ranked five times among the U.S. Top 20.

In between high school and college, in 1943 at age 18, he took a time out from tennis to aid the World War 11 effort. He joined the Air Force, went to cadet school and became a flight officer, a bombardier. Did he play tennis in the service? "I carried my racquet all over the place!" he said, laughing at the thought, "but I never hit a tennis ball. Not once!" It was your security blanket, right? "Right!"

After the war, from 1946-50, he attended the University of Miami on the G.I. Bill and was a walk-on the tennis team.

Tony had accumulated enough credits to graduate from college in three years, in 1949, but his coach asked him to stick around and play for another year. He said he'd stay if the coach would give his kid brother, Salvatore, a tennis scholarship. "The coach asked me, 'Can he play tennis?' I said no. So I taught him how to play for one year…he went down there and the coach gave him the scholarship."

Tony graduated from Miami in 1950, remained in Florida with his brother until 1954, and worked at the Coral Gables Country Club. He continued to play tennis and during a tournament in Havana, Cuba, he met his wife, Coila, who passed away a few years ago. "We were together for 50 years, we were very close," he said. "She was a model…an actress and was Rita Hayworth's understudy. I was sad when she died, all broken up, but I'm better now."

During his early years on the circuit, Tony won the Men's Open New England championships five times, the Eastern New York States twice, Connecticut four times, Bermuda twice, and captured seven Florida titles. His opponents included Sid Schwartz, Ron Holmberg, Richard Raskind, Gardnar Mulloy, Dick Savitt, Tony Trabert, Chuck McKinley, Billy Talbert and Vic Seixas. "I played everybody," he said.

And what were his weapons? "I had good legs," he said. "I could run. And I had a great backhand. My best shot. No topspin. Flat or spin." And his serve? "The worst!" Did he practice his serve? "I've been practicing my serve for the last 50 years," he said, laughing.

Tony's friend Paul Weinstein, who played tennis with him after the war at Rip Dolman's courts in New York City, agreed with the backhand assessment. Weinstein still remembers the day he was playing at Rip's courts on Sutton Place -- where every ranked amateur and pro in the country played when they were in New York – and suddenly "a great shot maker appeared …Tony Vincent. And then I saw his backhand. I never saw anyone actually follow the ball into the racquet the way Tony did…I could [eventually] gauge how well I was playing by the number of drop shots he hit. If he tried to hit 25 or 30 a set, it meant I must be playing well."

Tony moved to France in the late 1950s and lived in Lyon, Paris and Bordeaux while working as a wine salesman for Chateau La Croix. He played tennis on the European circuit and won 12 international championships – in Canada (1); at Aix-en-Provence (2); in Toulouse (1); LeHavre (1); Biarritz (1); Sagarro, Spain (2); City of Paris (1); Estoril, Portugal (1); Cannes (1); Germany (1, doubles with Budge Patty); and was twice a finalist at Monte Carlo. He was also a singles quarterfinalist at the French and Italian Championships and advanced to the Round of 16 at Wimbledon. During those years, he recorded several wins over French champions Nicola Pietrangeli and Andres Gimeno. He also defeated Wimbledon champ Lew Hoad of Australia, Italy's No. 1 Fausto Gardini and England's Tony Mottram.

Tony returned to Elmhurst in the 1960s and worked in New York for 30 years, 20 of them as a Wall Street investment broker -- 10 with Dreyfus & Co. – and another 10 years as a consultant for RJR Nabisco. During that time, he defeated Tony Trabert at Forest Hills and was the champion at nine national men's 35 clay court events (five singles, four doubles). He also won six senior Grand Slam doubles titles -- one (45s) at Wimbledon with Mulloy; and five at the US Open: one (45s) with Bobby Riggs and four (60s) with Kovaleski.

"Tony was the Beau Brummel of tennis, always well groomed…with creased trousers and a fresh shine on his shoes," Kovaleski said. "And he prided himself on…his 28-inch waist. He would kid around and claim he was the exact height and weight as Martina Navratilova was at the peak of her career.

"He and I used to take on corporate guys who had big egos in the boardroom and on the tennis court and we never lost to any of them."

Weinstein chimed in again with a similar anecdote. "I once walked into the indoor courts on 28th Street and saw Tony playing Jack Dreyfus," he said. "They used the half court to play on, so that Jack only had to hit forehands. Tony would give Jack five games a set, and by the time I finished playing – about an hour later, there must have been three dozen balls at the side of the court, since they used new balls for every set and I was sure Jack hadn't won any of them."

Before Tony retired at age 70, he also played tennis with the Nabisco VIP's, including Ross Johnson and his wife. You socialized with the whole jet set crowd, right? "Right!" And you had fun? "Absolutely!"

"Tony reminded me of Humphrey Bogart," said Lois Prince, once the tournament director of the national men's 35s at the Shelter Rock Tennis Club in Manhasset, N.Y., where Tony often played.

"Not any more, "he said. "I look pretty good, but I don't have any hair."

So what do you think, Tony, you've had a great life, right! "Not too bad," he said. "And I can still play tennis about three or four times a week."

-- By Nancy Gill McShea

*Tony Vincent is a tough competitor on the court
and at the backgammon table.*

Chapter 27

2007: Arias, Cullman, Grimes and Rubell

Jimmy Arias

Two weeks ago when Jimmy Arias was calling the Davis Cup quarterfinal between the United States and Spain for the Versus sports channel, he analyzed the nuances of each point played and told the television audience: "It's tough to break a tennis player's spirit in Davis Cup because you have a captain who won't let you throw in the towel…and a team that's counting on you."

He calls it as he sees it. "If I think you're choking, or tanking…I'm going to say it," said Arias, who does tennis commentary for Versus, the Tennis Channel and ESPN International. "I try to break down the match from a strategy standpoint, explain patterns in the points…and say exactly what I think whether the players like it or not."

He knows what he's talking about. Arias waged legendary five-set battles on the red clay of South America as a member of the U.S. Davis Cup team and in Grand Slam competition. In 1984, at age 19, he was ranked No. 5 in the world on the ATP Tour and was a marquee player during the golden era of tennis that featured Grand Slam event champions John McEnroe, Jimmy Connors, Ivan Lendl, Boris Becker, Bjorn Borg and Mats Wilander. Arias played professionally for 15 years, won five singles titles, reached the finals 11 times and often made it to the semis and quarters of major tournaments. He was a singles semifinalist at the 1984 Olympics and won the 1981 French mixed doubles title with Andrea Jaeger.

He exited the pro tour at the 1994 US Open on Court 18 before 100 fans, a week after he turned 30. *The* New *York Times* reported that Arias, one of the game's original phenoms, who marched out of…Bollettieri's…full of confidence with a howitzer forehand, smacked a forehand wide to lose [to a Swede] and said afterward: "It's tough not to be a tennis player anymore…I've been a tennis player all of my life…"

Now, almost 13 years removed from that match, Arias is still a tennis player and a visible authority in the game. "Jimmy is an expert at evaluating the physical and mental implications of a player's actions on the court," his longtime coach Nick Bollettieri said. "He remembers details of every match he has ever played, which gives him an edge in recalling players' stats when he's analyzing a match…He has a quick mouth and a gift of gab that engages the television audience and allows him to still joke around and talk opponents right out of a match on the senior tour."

Within one week this past March, Arias transmitted match intensity to fans from the television booth -- as Lleyton Hewitt salvaged a tie break to defeat Jurgen Melzer in the final of the Tennis Channel Open in Las Vegas – and then hopped on a red eye to Florida and played McEnroe, Wilander and Aaron Krickstein at Jim Courier's Oliver Group Champions Cup tournament in Naples. He didn't win but said he's having more fun playing now. "It keeps me in shape, forces me to go train and I'm actually playing kind of well." Even fans notice that Jimmy grins a lot, still packs a wallop of a forehand and competes on a high level.

The Arias stats are recorded in the history books, but the stuff that occurs off the court -- the intangible influences of daily life that mold a champion -- is more intriguing.

He began competing in tournaments at age 5 in Buffalo, N.Y. By the time he was 8, people were wowed by his strong forehand and he knew he would someday play pro tennis. His dad, Antonio, a native of Spain and an electrical engineer, taught him the forehand. "My dad didn't know anything about tennis but he was… somewhat visionary because he thought about things mathematically," Jimmy said. "I took a lesson from Ian Fletcher…who made the fourth round of the Australian Open. In those days, players took the racquet straight back, had a Continental or Eastern grip, and stopped the follow through (like McEnroe and Billie Jean King do on the forehand approach). I took the lesson, came off the court and said to my dad, 'What do you think?' He said, 'That's the stupidest thing I ever heard in my life. How can you swing full speed and stop? You have to slow your racquet down to stop. You should let your arm go and finish the stroke.'

"That was one reason I did so well so young. The people I was playing were just guiding the ball and I was hitting as hard as I could (using topspin). That set me apart…My [one-handed] backhand was disparaged a bit when I was coming up but when I was playing well I could hit heavy topspin to my opponent's backhand and hit pretty nice angles…"

Jimmy moved to Florida at age 13 to train with Bollettieri -- he was the first boy to live in Bollettieri's home along with 6-7 girls, including Carling Bassett and Kathleen Horvath -- and he arrived at the academy with his forehand in place.
Said Bollettieri, "After watching him for two minutes, I called my staff together and said that is the way we would now teach the Bollettieri Killer Forehand. Jimmy was very much responsible for changing the whole way of hitting the classic forehand to the new semi-western grip. (Krickstein, Agassi and Courier would all imitate him.)…Jimmy was small in size, but he had that forehand, quick feet…and that quick mouth.

"He had the inner spirit and passion to be a winner and was willing to do whatever had to be done to be a top player," Bollettieri added. "He has a big, big heart…that is why he succeeded.

"He practiced with every level of player with every style of play...to be ready to play against any opponent. He was totally competitive and ready to play satellites at 15."

In 1983, his best year, Arias won in singles at the Italian Open, in Florence, Indianapolis and Palermo and was a finalist at Boston and Washington. He pulled a stomach muscle at the French en route to the round of 16 and pulled out of Wimbledon. He recovered and played his favorite match, against Yannick Noah, in the quarters of the US Open. "Playing the Open at night under the lights is electric," he said. "Noah served at 5-6 and 15-40 in the fifth and I was looking at a second serve. I was so nervous I couldn't swallow. He hit it right down the center and I tried to return it hard down the center but anxiety caused me to hit it so far out in front, it went for an angled winner."

Arias exhaled, relieved, and then fell in the semis to Lendl before a packed house in Louis Armstrong Stadium.

In the fall of 1983 Jimmy was hospitalized with mononucleosis and didn't play again until 1984. He returned to the tour and noticed that some kind of glitch had crept into his forehand swing. At the same time, the game was changing rapidly. Players had switched from wood to composite racquets, creating a plethora of power merchants. As a result, his forehand, once such an explosive weapon, no longer produced winners at will.

But Jimmy still found a way to win matches. He made the semis of WTC/Dallas, Monte Carlo, the Tournament of Champions in New York, Boca West and LaQuinta. He reached the quarterfinals in Philadelphia, Memphis, Richmond, Boston, Barcelona and the French Open, and advanced to the round of 16 at Wimbledon. But he was winning on desire rather than dictating play. "I ran hard and tried hard but I couldn't hit winners anymore," he said. "I basically played on guts alone for the rest of my career!"

In Davis Cup, Arias played for Captain Arthur Ashe on the 1984 U.S. team that lost 4-1 to Sweden. He played in 1986 for Captain Tom Gorman and the U.S. defeated Ecuador, 3-2. Arias lost to Andres Gomez, 7-5, 4-6, 4-6, 9-7, 6-4, in the first match but defeated Raul Viver, 6-3, 6-1, 6-4, to clinch the tie. The tough South American crowd yelled "Aah!!!" every time he missed against Gomez. So Jimmy retaliated. He served an ace at deuce and 4-all in the fifth and said, "I screamed Aah!!! The crowd went bananas. They were screaming, swearing and I just smiled. Then a guy pulled out a flare gun and we didn't play for about 15 minutes…"

In 1987 the U.S. lost 3-2 to Paraguay. Gorman had told Arias to just play and not rile the crowd. "It probably saved my life," he said. "I was down 2 sets to love and match point, came back to 2 sets all and was up 5-1 in the fifth when things spiraled out of control. Lots of bad overrules and line calls. I lost, 6-4, 6-1, 5-7, 3-6, 9-7, and felt so beaten down by the crowd…they were relentless. When the match ended someone threw a brick from the top of the stadium. It glanced my head and I just took off running. After Krickstein lost the fifth match, the linesmen jumped up and raised their hands in the air [in a victory cheer]. It was ridiculous. Paraguay was suspended for 2 years after that."

After Paraguay, he was struggling and felt totally depressed. He went to see Jim Loehr [the psychologist], who suggested that he start joking with the crowd again to have some fun. He posted good results and beat Becker and Wilander along the way.

The Davis Cup debacles in South America did not break the spirit of Jimmy Arias. "That was part of what I was dreaming about when I was growing up," he said. "I was proud that even when I had no confidence or my best stuff, I had the ability to fight to the bitter end [down there]. It makes me sad that I didn't make a late run at some Grand Slam heroics…but as I get older, I appreciate that not many people get to No. 5 in the world…My expectations were higher but I'm proud that I was able to compete with the best players in the world during those last years -- on guts alone."

-- By Nancy Gill McShea

Joseph F. Cullman III

Joe Cullman, the former president and chief executive officer of the Philip Morris Company who passed away in 2004, was, by all accounts, a generous man with a wonderful sense of humor who made significant contributions to many charitable organizations. Cullman has earned legendary status in this venue as the controversial "angel of tennis" who together with Gladys Heldman and Billie Jean King helped underwrite an independent women's professional tour at the beginning of the Open era.

Many people question whether a tobacco company should have been involved with sports. But at a time before Title IX mandated gender equity, few, if any, sponsors were willing to support women's athletics. Without Cullman's commitment to women's tennis, its future could have taken a less predictable path.

"Joe was very knowledgeable and actually wanted to be a history and English teacher," his brother Edgar Cullman said. "But he went with Philip Morris instead and led the company to be very supportive of tennis."

Cullman's influence in the sport dates to 1962, before Open tennis, when he first convinced Philip Morris to support the efforts of Gladys Heldman, who was trying to save the ailing U.S. National Championships at the West Side Tennis Club in Forest Hills. Cullman and Heldman had become friends when they started playing tennis together in the 1950s at the Century Club in Westchester, N.Y. Cullman was the president of Philip Morris at the time and Heldman was the publisher and editor and chief of *World Tennis* magazine. So when Heldman decided to hire a plane to fly 85 European men and women players to New York, who couldn't afford to travel to the U.S. to compete in the tournament, Cullman was the first to write a check.

Cullman then convinced the board of Philip Morris to sponsor the first US Open at West Side in 1968 and he was instrumental in getting that first Open televised. He was chairman of the Open in 1969-70, and served as honorary chairman in 1971. "Joe used to take the same seat near the scoreboard off one of the ground courts so he could watch tennis and hold court," the tennis photographer Russ Adams recalled. "He's say, 'Take a seat, Russ. Let's catch up.' Everybody came up to him. He didn't act like a big deal; he was out there to greet people and see how they were enjoying the show."

In 1970 Cullman etched his name forever in the annals of tennis when he helped Heldman pioneer the women's pro tour by sponsoring what became known as the Virginia Slims Circuit. Every tennis fan knows the story. At the beginning of the Open era, both the men and the women were struggling to establish themselves as professionals. Billie Jean King, one of the top women players, turned to Heldman for help, and together with Cullman they won the battle to set up an independent women's tour. Heldman arranged for the Houston Racquet Club to hold a tournament that would ultimately offer more prize money than a USLTA-sanctioned event that was scheduled to run simultaneously, along with a men's tournament in Los Angeles, California. USLTA authorities would only agree to sanction the Houston tournament as an amateur event. Undeterred, Heldman asked nine of the top women players -- known as the "Houston 9" -- to sign $1 contracts with *World Tennis* magazine so that the tournament would qualify as a legitimate pro contest. King confirmed that fact in the following excerpts from her book *Billie Jean*: "Gladys had…conversations with Joseph Cullman…a tennis nut…[who] said his company would sponsor our tournament…the Virginia Slims Invitational…If we were contract pros the USLTA would have no control over us…Wednesday…eight of us signed…Thursday…We Americans were all suspended by the USLTA."

Richard Evans also documented the historic moment in his book, *Open Tennis*: "…Joe, answering Gladys' call yet again, made his most historic commitment to the game…an immediate agreement to add another $2,500 to the tournament…Gladys and her team…had put themselves out on a limb and even if Cullman had an outstretched hand…the pressure on the women to prove themselves was tremendous…Billie Jean said later, 'If nobody had come to see us play we would have been dead. But they did come. The timing was right.'"

King noted recently, "Without Joe Cullman women's tennis would not have become what it is today. When Gladys Heldman and Joe gave us an opportunity that pushed us into the world's spotlight, he helped a generation of women find our voice. He gave us a reason to face our challenges head on. When we were fearful, he gave us the confidence to push ahead. He taught us about business and whenever we needed him, he was there."

George Gowen, the general counsel of the USLTA at the time, has said, "Gladys Heldman and I were on opposite sides of pretty heavy litigation. The good news is that we negotiated a settlement that combined the two women's tours -- the so-called USLTA tour and the Virginia Slims tour..."

By 1972 Cullman was an influential presence in tennis. He signed on as the co-chair of the first Robert F. Kennedy Pro-Celebrity tennis tournament at West Side, a benefit to help support the activities of the underprivileged youth of the Robert F. Kennedy Memorial. He then served as general chairman of the event for five years.

There's more. Cullman once said that the things he loved most in life were his family, friends, sports and the outdoors. And in his autobiography, appropriately entitled, *I'm a Lucky Guy*, he wrote, "I suppose that when my obituaries are written they will stress my work at Philip Morris...But a person is more than his work. I consider my efforts at conservation through the World Wildlife Fund, the Atlantic Salmon Foundation and the International Tennis Hall of Fame to have been a most important part of my life."

Indeed, Cullman helped rebuild and restore the International Tennis Hall of Fame (ITHF) site in Newport, Rhode Island, and in 1982 he was named the president of the organization. He served as the ITHF chairman from 1985-1989, and in 1990 he was inducted into the International Tennis Hall of Fame.

"Joe Cullman was the primary force in the restoration and resurgence of the International Tennis Hall of Fame," said Mark Stenning, the organization's chief executive officer. "His formidable influence in the corporate community, along with his passion for tennis, made him the perfect individual to spearhead the project, and the Newport Casino was established as a national historic landmark under his guidance."

Accolades for Joe Cullman keep pouring in. Neil Amdur, the veteran tennis writer, sports editor of *The New York Times*, publisher/editor of *World Tennis* magazine and tennis producer for CBS television, echoed the consensus: "Joe Cullman was the chairman of the board, in every sense of the word, from board rooms to salmon fishing to tennis courts to the arts. He loved everything he put his soul into, and tennis became one of those adventures, from women's tennis to the International Tennis Hall of Fame. The notion that a cigarette manufacturer might sponsor a women's tennis tour seemed outrageous in 1970. Before Title IX became a fact of life in American culture, few companies had the faintest notion that women were worth following as athletes, let alone with a sponsorship commitment. Enter Gladys Heldman, a dynamic individualist, publisher and personal friend, who cajoled and convinced Cullman that women's tennis could succeed. Once Chairman Joe made up his mind, the rest is history. Not only did Virginia Slims become synonymous with women's tennis, but 'You've come a long way, baby' soon was replaced by gender equity, a revolution that changed the American sports landscape forever."

Billie Jean King deserves the final word: "Joe Cullman was one of a kind and his induction into the USTA Eastern Section Hall of Fame is a fitting tribute to his wonderful legacy. Joe's generosity, foresight and his commitment to people from all walks of life did not start and stop with the founders of women's professional tennis. All women athletes will forever be indebted to him for breaking the mold. The International Tennis Hall of Fame thrives today because of his dedication. Joe had many, many great achievements -- but his legacy will be that he helped people become leaders -- in business, in sports and in life.

"Joe Cullman was a great sportsman, a great businessman and a true mentor. He loved his family and we all loved that about him. Joe was a great man and one of the best friends any one could have."

-- By Nancy Gill McShea

Jane Brown Grimes

Ed Goldman

Reading the background of Jane Brown Grimes, one has to be impressed by her many years of off court experience in tennis. She comes across as a savvy chief executive officer playing at the top of her game, which is exactly who she is. This past January, Jane began serving a two-year term as the President and Chairman of the Board of the U.S. Tennis Association (USTA). She previously served on the association's board of directors as the first vice president, director at large and as secretary-treasurer.

After an early stint as a reporter and a researcher for *Life* magazine, Jane opted for a career in tennis. She has loved the sport all of her life and has said often that one of her fondest childhood memories was playing tennis all day, all summer long, on local tennis courts near her Long Island home. At summer's end, she and her family would hop into the car to go to the U.S. National Championships at the West Side Tennis Club in Forest Hills. They would spend the entire day there watching greats such as Maureen Connolly, Althea Gibson and the famous Aussies.

One of Jane's 16 first cousins said: "Legend in the family has it that Jane's grandparents used to host Jean Borotra, one of the famous French four Musketeers (Jacques Brugnon, Henri Cochet, Rene LaCoste, being the other three) in their Long Island home when they were here to play in the national championships…A passion for tennis has always been in the genes!"

Jane's brother Sam Gillespie remembers well the trips to Forest Hills. "We would wander the grass courts outside the ivy covered stadium to watch the best amateurs of the day practice and compete," he said. "We would often bring our own racquets (wooden of course) and wear whites on the off-chance that one of the competitors might hit some practice balls with us…During those years Jane competed successfully in [mixed doubles] tournaments, except on those occasions when she was paired with her brother…She has always been devoted to the successful evolution of …tennis."

Only Jane knows exactly what triggered her passion for helping to shape the game, but the record shows that in 1977 she opened the New York office of the International Tennis Hall of Fame (ITHF). By 1981, she was named the executive director of the organization. During her tenure there she functioned as the tournament director for both the ATP and WTA Tour events. From 1986-1991, she served as the managing director of the Women's Tennis Council, after which she returned to the International Tennis Hall of Fame as its president and chief executive officer, from 1991-2000. Today she is President Emeritus of the organization.

John Reese, who has served concurrently with Brown Grimes for over 20 years in lofty positions on the ITHF board -- most notably, as president/chairman and CEO (Reese), and as president and COO/CEO (Brown Grimes) -- described his friend as extraordinary. "The thing about Jane," Reese said, "is that not only has she held prominent positions in tennis for almost 30 years…these are positions that require intelligence and diplomatic skills. Jane understands her audience and can draw them out in a way that no one's feelings are hurt. Besides those attributes, she has the charm and common sense that any chief executive officer has to have. Not an easy combination and she has it.

"Jane's late husband Charlie Grimes was very supportive of her progression -- from the president of the International Tennis Hall of Fame to the president of the USTA. He was a wonderful counsel, a real partner and very proud of Jane. Her success was his success."

Mark Stenning, chairman of the International Tennis Hall of Fame, has watched Jane in action and, like Reese, appreciates the range of her administrative abilities. "Jane's legacy at the hall of fame is unmatched," Stenning said. "She joined the organization at a time when funding was in short supply, the buildings were deteriorating in Newport and there was little public awareness. As president, Jane oversaw the renovation and restoration of the historic Newport

Casino complex, the creation of a world-class Hall of Fame museum and the formation of a strong and supportive board of directors.

"I have had the privilege of working with Jane for over 25 years and have enjoyed her friendship and counsel. And we are fortunate and grateful that Jane is still involved with the hall of fame as our President Emeritus."

Jane will tell anyone who asks that she has always had a racquet in her hand, and still tries to play in two games a week, so it follows that a major priority in her presidency will be to re-energize the schools program. She also plans to create more innovative strategies with the USTA board and committees to increase tennis participation among all ages through local community programs, and to make the sport more inclusive and open to everyone.

To meet this grand challenge, Jane has said that she will continue to campaign to support tennis in the parks, as well as all of the other programs, but that her main focus will definitely be the schools. "My dream would be to have tennis be the sport of choice for kids from seven to 12," she has said. "The way we're trying to do that is [by continuing] to introduce tennis in the physical education classes…By far, the number one thing is the tennis in the schools."

Tennis programs build on each other within the tennis progression. Kids go from the gymnasium to after school programs in the public parks and sign up for Junior TeamTennis. Some players eventually compete on their school teams and in tournaments. To make sure that the tennis progression remains a visible option within communities' sports programs, Jane plans to introduce an advocacy task force so that when funds become available for local recreation centers, tennis advocates will be able to lobby in support of public tennis courts. "The swimmers are there, the soccer moms are there and it's time for the tennis players to be there," she said.

Jane also believes strongly in the power of tennis to change lives. She is a member of the Rodney Street Tennis and Tutoring Association, a community tennis association in Wilmington, Delaware, and she has said that the children affiliated with the program are truly at-risk kids.

"Some of them come to us from the homeless shelter," she said in a recent interview. "And I can tell you we're making a difference in these kids' lives. Long after I have departed the USTA presidency, I know that I will still be a part of this group, because I can honestly see what tennis has brought to these kids in terms of pride and confidence and self respect. It's helped keep them in school and helped us bridge the gap."

Members of Jane's family attest unanimously to her ability to meet challenges -- especially in tennis.

"…When Jane was young she decided she was going to win the…tennis championship [at our local courts]," said her cousin Hester Weeden, who played with her during their childhood. "And, in typical fashion, it was a done deal in a blink of an eye. The rest of the family struggled for years to win it and I for one never did. This only confirms what we all know -- Jane usually achieves what she sets out to do."

Her cousin, Connie Hildesley, added: "It is no surprise to any of us that Jane is focusing her efforts on tennis for children and advocacy. Many of the cousins were able to spend summers together growing up on Long Island. Inspired by a local coach, Fred Eisler, we played tennis from dawn to dusk, until the ball was no longer visible and all you could see were the fireflies. Once, when we were on a spring break in Bermuda, some professional tennis players were there for an exhibition tournament. Jane had the opportunity to talk with…Pancho Gonzalez, Ken Rosewall and others for as long as they would listen."

Jane's brother Sam remembers the trip well. "…The newly-turned pros were staying at the same hotel," he said. "…Barry MacKay…had just moved from being a top amateur to a professional…in those days there was no 'open tennis' and the fledgling pro tour was more like a small, traveling corps of prior top flight amateurs playing exhibition matches against each other…Jane spent time listening to those players talk about their aspirations of what the game could become…

"But there was another strong call for Jane during those teenage years, and that was sailing. While our mother set an example for us as a good competitive…tennis player, our father was a passionate racer of sailboats -- and sails his own boat to this day. He recognized in Jane the ability and dexterity required to do the deck work on his 32-foot Atlantic class sailboat. This required balancing precariously on a wet, slanted deck in high seas, setting a massive spinnaker pole while rounding a mark in close quarters with other racing boats. Our father in almost every circumstance I can recall is the most mild-mannered gentleman I know; however, in the course of these heated races he took on a wholly different personality. I think Jane's ability to withstand the elements, the pressure and the yelling while coolly performing each challenging task on the deck of that ship has stood her well in the tests she has faced in life since then."

-- By Nancy Gill McShea

Donald Rubell

Simon Hare

Trying to keep pace with Don Rubell as he expounds on his changing lifestyle in the diverse roles of amateur tennis champion, mathematician, prominent New York physician, hotel proprietor and world-renowned contemporary art collector – all while he's busy pursuing these passions en route to California from Florida, to New York, Ireland, Berlin, Washington and back again -- makes one's head spin.

Several constants define Rubell. The tone of his quick, dry sense of humor suggests that he's an empathetic guy. His family is all-important, so he and the entire Rubell clan promote the family's ventures together. He credits his wife Mera for "attempting to teach me everything I did not know…but that may be a lost cause." And striving for excellence on the tennis court has been an intricate part of the Rubell family lifestyle for four generations. In addition to Don's credentials, his father Phil was once a runner up in the over-90 world tennis championships; his brother Steve played No. 1 for Syracuse University; his son Jason was an All-American and the ACC singles champ while at Duke; and his four grandchildren are now learning the game.

Phil Rubell taught his son to play tennis at age 6 at Lincoln Terrace Park in Brooklyn. By the mid-1950s, Don was a student at Wingate High School in Brooklyn and led his team to victory at the New York City Tennis Championships. He represented Eastern in the national Tilton Bowl team competition, ranked among the country's top ten juniors and was a repeat winner in Eastern boys' 15 and 18 tournaments. He admits, though, that he lost, 6-0, 6-0, in the first round of the first two events he entered and once choked away a 6-0, 5-0 lead while playing Steve Green at the national junior indoors.

Don attended Cornell University, where he played first singles and was the captain of the tennis team. He was also twice the Eastern Intercollegiate tennis champ, lost only once in a dual match – to Donald Dell of Yale – and was the president of the Cornell Mathematics Society.

"I always liked tennis and mathematics," Rubell said. "Guess I was only half a nerd. "As for my tennis game, I will talk about anything but my forehand. It's still a work in progress."

He graduated from Cornell in 1961, took a job as an actuary with Metropolitan Life and played the Eastern men's open circuit. He later enrolled in medical school at New York University and completed his ObGyn residency there. During those educational years he confined his tennis to the East but competed in the U.S. National Championships at the West Side Tennis Club in Forest Hills and at the Eastern Grass Courts in South Orange, New Jersey. He won singles titles at the New York States, the Eastern Hard Court and Clay Court tournaments and ranked third in the East behind Gene Scott and Herb Fitz Gibbon, followed by Richard Raskind (now Renee Richards) and Bob Barker.

"Those rankings were representative of the era," said Dr. Richards, who recently uncovered tennis records among her late father's papers. "Most of that group was ranked in the top ten for ten years."

From 1973-1975, Rubell was a Lieutenant Colonel in the U.S. Air Force Medical Corps, a member of the Air Force tennis team and he won the U.S. Military Interservice Championships. From 1975-1999, he was a practicing ObGyn in New York City and also chaired the Gynecology Department at the Cabrini Medical Center, lectured at the Beth Israel Medical Center, was an assistant professor at the New York University School of Medicine and was named several times among New York magazine's list of best doctors in New York. During those years he won the USTA and Eastern men's 45 Clay Courts and represented the U.S. in the Dubler Cup and in team competition versus South America.

In Rubell's early N.Y.U. days, Richards was in residency training at the Lenox Hill and Manhattan Eye, Ear and Throat Hospitals and the pair escaped often to the tennis courts during lunch breaks. "I'd pick Don up at the Midtown Tunnel and he'd be standing there in his whites," Richards has said. "We'd go to Queens, find a court and then go back to the hospital...Sometimes we'd go up to Baker field at Columbia and play with Dick Savitt, Ham Richardson and Paul Cranis.

"Don started out as a little guy and learned a retrieving, defensive game, but when he was 21 he grew to 6-foot-3 and developed a big serve and volley. He learned that he could win points quicker that way and his backhand became great. Bobby Riggs once said that Don's backhand was like [Pancho] Gonzalez."

Rubell has described some memorable victories and losses, a few with his amusing slant: Wins -- 1. beat future U.S. Davis Cup player Allen Fox in a 4-hour junior match, 15-13 in the third, after Fox tried to default at 7-all; 2. defeated Vitas Gerulaitis at the 7th Regiment Armory Indoors. Scheduled to play Vitas on lightening fast wood and intimidated by his incredible reflexes and volleys, Don figured "my best chance was to arrange for unlimited tickets the night before at Studio 54. It worked brilliantly. I don't think Vitas woke up before the next to last game of the match;" 3. prevailed over Dick Stockton at the N.Y. State Indoors the first time they played. Next time out, Stockton had switched to the T-2000, Don was barely able to see the ball and never beat him again; 4. routed Tim Coss, reputed to be the world's steadiest player, at the Eastern Clay Courts. Don's father said that if Don could beat Coss at his own game from the get-go it could disconcert him. The first point lasted 174 shots before Coss missed; Don won the match easily.

Every player can relate to No. 5, when Rubell, at 15, upset the veteran Sid Schwartz. "Sid just banged every ball for a winner," he said. "It was not until the middle of the second set that Sid realized most of his shots were missing. I figured if I did not say anything, he might forget he was losing...everybody who was watching also thought Sid was winning. After the match, Sid walked to the net post, systematically broke all of his racquets and threatened to give up tennis forever."

In other wins, Rubell beat both Butch Seewagen and Sandy Mayer at the New York State Championships and once edged Tony Vincent in the finals of the Eastern Men's Clay Courts in Hackensack. Richards was there and recalled the match: "They were both steady baseliners, clay court experts, so it was a grueling contest. After four hours, Tony went up 5-1 in the fifth set. The tournament committee figured the match was over...they brought out a table, put a white cloth and the winner's silver cup on it and placed it next to the umpire's stand. Don, usually a placid man, looked at it and got mad. He suddenly started serving and volleying and won six games in a row to win the match."

Don included three good losses – "It's an oxymoron, I know," he said: 1. lost to Butch Buchholz at Perth Amboy, 9-7 in the third; 2. surrendered to Larry Nagler 3 times in one week, due to rainouts. Don figured it was probably a world record; he had match point in the third match and decided not to ruin the world record; and 3. lost to Wimbledon and Australian singles champ Alex Olmedo at the South Orange Grass Courts. "It was my best tournament," said Rubell, who upset 3 seeded players and played Olmedo in the semis. "It was one of the first televised matches. Somehow, I was up a break and 4-3 in the first set. On the change-over, I tripped on the TV wire, looked up to find myself staring at the TV camera and never won another game."

By the early 1990s, Don and Mera decided to enter the hotel business in partnership with their children, Jason and Jennifer, and to focus on their extensive art collection in Florida. "We wanted to work together as a family, to pool our talents," said Rubell, who for five years endured the New York/Florida weekend commute until he retired in 1999 from his medical practice. "Mera and I have collected art together since we were married 42 years ago and the kids have been involved in the process since they were about 13. Now we collect as a family."

The art collection, open to the public, is housed in the [40,000-foot] Rubell Family Collection Museum in Miami and contains over 5,000 works, which are exhibited on a rotating basis. During the past year, the museum has hosted over 40,000 visitors.

The collection is so well known, in fact, that the *Art Review* has named Rubell 29th on a list of the 100 most important people in the art world and the collection itself as the fifth most important in the world. Don Rubell has been listed among the most influential people in the art world by *Art & Auction* magazine, *Art News*, *Basel Zeitung* and *Frankfurter Allegmaine*, among others.

Not a bad lifestyle and pretty good credentials for a guy who started out liking tennis and mathematics and labeled himself only half a nerd.

-- By Nancy Gill McShea

Chapter 28

2008: K. McEnroe, J. McEnroe, Scheer, Scott and Van Blake

Kay and John P. McEnroe

(L-r) Mark, Patrick, Kay, John and J.P. McEnroe.

A Google search will not reveal the little intangibles that prove why the McEnroes deserve the vote for the "first family of professional tennis." The Williamses qualify as candidates, as do the Everts. Eastern families have also left indelible impressions on the game, among them the Mayers from Woodmere and the Gerulaitises from Howard Beach. But if you look at the whole picture, you would vote for the McEnroes, whose roots are in Douglaston, and whose individual and collective impact on the game spans more than three decades in almost every venue.

Google also will not reveal that the McEnroes have twice been voted Eastern's Family of the Year, or that John P. (call him J.P.) and Kay -- the parents of John, Mark and Patrick -- are being inducted into the Eastern Tennis Hall of Fame to honor their years of volunteer work for the sport. J.P. and Kay are walking endorsements for how best to survive the demanding role of tennis parents. Some of their public stats are included here, but the intangibles, which center on the family dynamic, are mostly private unless you read their son John's memoir, *You Cannot Be Serious*.

John, Mark and Patrick agree that Mom was the glue, the core of the family and that Dad was the cheerleader and the ever present coach.

In private life, J.P., a graduate of the Fordham University School of Law and a retired partner and currently Of Counsel of the international New York-based law firm Paul, Weiss, Rifkind, Wharton & Garrison, is an authority in corporate and sports law. Kay, a surgical nurse who graduated from the Lenox Hill Hospital School of Nursing, includes among her many charitable affiliations outside tennis the role of Trustee on the Lenox Hill board and a board member of the New York chapter of the Alzheimer's Foundation.

Inside tennis, J.P. and Kay were recently the guest speakers at an Eastern junior seminar, which focused on raising a tennis player. They admitted that they were strict with John, the first child, and that by the time Patrick was born they had relaxed and decided he was perfect. In other volunteer efforts, they served together as the honorary co-chairmen of the 1989 Eastern Tennis Hall of Fame. J.P. chaired the 2007 Hall of Fame Selection Committee and was a member of the USTA Davis Cup Committee. Kay is a former vice president and longtime member of Eastern's Junior Tennis Foundation and was a board member of the N.Y. Chapter of Cystic Fibrosis when it was the official charity of the ATP Tour.

John, one of the greatest players of all time, confirmed two family values in his memoir: "Mom and Dad always said, 'Get a college scholarship.' Once they met [the great Australian coach] Harry Hopman, who told them war stories about Davis Cup and playing for your country, it was 'Get a college scholarship and play Davis Cup.'"

J.P. and Kay rallied to the cause themselves and last summer received the 2007 USTA President's Award for giving unusual and extraordinary individual service to Davis Cup tennis. They have supported the U.S. Davis Cup teams, live, for 30 years, since John won his first Davis Cup matches at age 19 (twice in singles during the victorious 1978 final round versus Great Britain and once in doubles versus Chile). Both John and Patrick have competed and served as team captains -- Patrick recorded a 3-1 record as a player in the 1990s and as captain led the 2007 team to victory last December, while John has recorded the most victories, 59, in U.S. Davis Cup history.

The brothers McEnroe respected their parents' emphasis on education and all three attended Stanford University, but John opted for the professional tennis circuit after he won the 1978 NCAA singles title. He ranked No. 1 in the world for the year in 1981, '82, '83 and '84, and held the world's No. 1 spot 14 times during his 15-year pro career. He won 17 Grand slam titles (7 in singles, 10 in doubles) and a combined 154 titles – 77 in singles and 77 in doubles.

Mark followed his father to Fordham Law School, is currently working as a venture capitalist and still plays tennis with his Eastern junior pals. He and Scott Moody were doubles finalists at the 2006 USTA 40 Grass Courts and Mark was ranked a few times among Eastern's top ten in men's 35 doubles.

Patrick took the law boards after graduating from Stanford in 1988 but decided to try the pro tour. He won the men's doubles title at the 1989 French Open, was a singles semifinalist at the 1991 Australian Open and a quarterfinalist at the 1995 US Open. He earned career best rankings of No. 3 in doubles and No. 28 in singles and appeared in 42 ATP Tour singles and doubles finals. Two weeks ago, he was appointed General Manager, USTA Elite Player Development, and will lead a renewed effort to develop future American champions.

But the search to discern motivating factors within the McEnroe family does not show up on Google and would even be an overwhelming challenge for the TV sleuth, Detective Columbo.

You would start with the premise that J.P. and Kay gave their sons every opportunity to succeed while growing up in a typical American household. John confirmed in his memoir that his family was indeed typical: "The McEnroe males were a sports-obsessed group, and we were vocal about it, whether we were rooting or playing...We all loved each other, but we were definitely a family of yellers…blowing off steam or just making friendly noise. We didn't hold back in our household.

"My parents started playing tennis with us when I was about 8," he wrote, "…and took great pride in taking us to Port Washington and to tournaments. Some parents feel they need to do things for themselves. My Dad and Mom were supportive of us…They were encouraging… It was good to have mommy and daddy there if you broke down after a loss. Only problem was, Mom only came to matches when she thought I was going to lose, so I knew there was a potential problem…"

Mom can be forgiven for that. She was the designated driver who ferried her sons to and from daily practice sessions and welcomed a reprieve when they were old enough to drive. Mark said that Mom rarely watched his matches either, but he figured it was a defense mechanism to protect herself from feeling disappointed for her children when they lost. Patrick said that Mom was easier on him and would say: "It's not a bad thing being the best you can be rather than always trying to be the best."

On the surface, the very private McEnroes are a very public family on the move. Kay said that the entire clan spent last Thanksgiving together for the first time in a long time, at Mark's home in Connecticut. She and J.P. then flew to Portland, Oregon, to cheer Patrick as he coached the U.S. Davis Cup team to a 4-1 victory over defending Davis Cup champion Russia, the first victory for the U.S. in 12 years. They returned to New York on Dec. 4 and flew to Paris on Dec. 5 to celebrate their 50th wedding anniversary there on Dec. 7. Last weekend they visited Winston Salem, North Carolina, to cheer again for Patrick and the Davis Cup team. Over the past few months, family members were reportedly vacationing in Puerto Rico, Mexico, or in John's case, competing on the senior tennis tour -- in Naples, Florida; Madrid and Granada in Spain; Manheim in Germany; Belfast in Northern Ireland; Rhode Island; and the Cayman Islands in the Caribbean, where he is tonight.

The telephone is the best way to track down the McEnroes. Reached on his cell phone on his way home from work, Mark pulls over and tells you that his three children play tennis and other sports: Liam, 12 (hockey); Maria, 10 (basketball); and Ciaran, 8 (baseball). Mark also claims that he was the first McEnroe to be defaulted from a match when he attended the Kent School in Connecticut. He was winning but mouthing off at himself and his coach defaulted him. He feels pressure showing up as a McEnroe at senior events because "people who don't know me think I must be pretty good, so when they beat me they think they're pretty good." A trace of childhood sibling rivalry surfaces when Mark mentions jokingly that he used to be the tallest McEnroe, at 6-foot-3, until John's son Kevin surpassed him, at 6-foot-4.

Patrick returned a call a few weeks ago while he was navigating the perils of a busy street in New York City with his two-year-old daughter Victoria in tow, and she was wondering when dinner would be ready. Patrick confessed -- tongue in cheek, as is his wont -- that "Mom was a toughie, but tougher on John. She would say [to him], if you can be No. 1 why would you want to be No. 2? She said the same thing to John when he was second in his class [at the Buckley Country Day School]. The next year he finished first. When Dad was in law school, he worked all day, attended classes at night and then studied…When he finished second in his class Mom said to him, 'If you had tried harder you could have been first.' The next year Dad finished first.

"Parents are allowed to coach [in juniors] when you split sets. My Dad was great; he gave himself credit for coaching me," Patrick continued. "I always did well in three sets and at the split he would say, 'Do whatever you did in that set you won when you hit great angles with the backhand.' I guess that coaching from Dad at an early age made me a successful Davis Cup coach!"

Google will not reveal the intangibles that define the first family of tennis! Neither will most of the McEnroes. And that's as it should be!

-- By Nancy Gill McShea

Richard A. Scheer

The Scheer Family: Killy, Susan and Dick.

Only a gifted athlete would fit the profile of a well known tennis volunteer who for over 40 years has established a reputation as a diehard on the court, and only after he headlined as a major star in both football and baseball in an earlier life.

Dick Scheer certainly fits that profile. He served as Eastern's president in 1984-85 and was honored as the section's Man of the Year in 1993. He started playing tennis at age 33, when his career as a Manhattan attorney took precedence. He has since earned top-ten Eastern rankings in three age divisions and played for several men's teams. In the 1940s, however, Dick was heralded as a running back at Erasmus Hall High School in Brooklyn, and in the early 1950s he was a star center fielder and captain of the baseball team at Harvard University.

"Dick is a great competitor," his friend and long-time doubles partner Harry Keely said recently. "He is a winner. He is what we call a 'tough out.' He will fight to the end."

Accolades for Dick extend beyond the athletic fields. He has been highly regarded as a volunteer administrator during and after the years he was president and was appointed to serve as a member of and/or chair more than ten USTA and Eastern committees and boards. He was also selected to captain two USTA teams that competed on the international ITF circuit – the men's 60 Von Cramm team and the men's 50 Fred Perry Cup team, which won the 2001 world championship in Austria.

He became actively involved in Eastern affairs, he said, "to give back to tennis what the game has given to me…It's been great fun." During his Eastern presidency, he predicted a strong future for key programs and initiatives that were rapidly gaining steam – USTA/Volvo League team tennis for adults, now the highly successful USTA League Tennis program; sectional sponsorship (he was involved in the Head-sponsored Eastern men's grand prix); the early dawn of computer rankings; and the schools program. He believed that promoting tennis in the schools was a natural venue since its pilot program in New York City, under the direction of Skip Hartman, had introduced thousands of children to the game in the East.

Dick still serves on both the Eastern and Junior Tennis Foundation Boards of Directors. He has also chaired the Hall of Fame Selection Committee (1991) and the Charter and By-Laws Committee (1990-2003) and has served on six USTA committees – grievance, chairman (6 years); governance (long-range planning, 6 years), executive, nominating, budget and finance and constitution and rules.

But his athletic life before tennis still looms clearly in his personal history. When he was a star running back at Erasmus Hall, his outstanding play earned him lots of press in Brooklyn newspapers and he was recruited by the University of Tennessee, the country's No. 1 gridiron team in 1949. He also received offers from Cornell, Penn, Lehigh and City College, and then, like magic, transformed himself into the featured center fielder and captain of the baseball team at Harvard University.

Why Harvard? Dick's dad, Max, had said to his son, "Get into Harvard and I'll pay!" And why center field? He grew up in the 1940s and early '50s when the rivalries of the Brooklyn Dodgers, New York Giants and New York Yankees captured the imagination of sports fans. Friends and strangers waged raging debates -- on street corners, in school classrooms, in offices and saloons or at the ball park – to determine which center fielder was the best: Willie Mays, Mickey Mantle or Duke Snider, who was Dick's hero. Not only that, his high school football team won three or four games in Ebbets Field, home of the Dodgers before they fled to Los Angeles. "There would be 15,000 kids cheering in the stands," Dick recalls now. "It was a nice, colorful, screaming event."

After his freshman year at Harvard, the Dodgers and the Brooklyn Eagle newspaper sponsored a team they called "Brooklyn against the world!" Dick said that any kid under 19 who could stand was eligible to try out for a position. Thousands showed up for the audition and he was one of five outfielders who made it.

Then he pulled off a story book ending at Harvard. On the day he graduated in 1954, just a day after he played in the annual commencement Harvard-Yale baseball game, a large photo of his college president appeared on the front page of The Boston Globe with the caption: "Harvard President Nathan Pusey and family watching Harvard captain Dick Scheer running out a triple in the first inning against Yale."

He continued to compete in softball leagues and sandlot football games – and even won a 100-yard dash in a college intramural race -- during and after his days as a University of Michigan law student. He turned to tennis as a logical transition for recreational competition when he went to work as a Manhattan defense negligence attorney of record for an insurance company. (He now represents a few different companies – either by appearing in court to argue a motion, representing them in conference or doing depositions.)

He practiced to improve his game with ranked Eastern players at the Hiway Tennis Courts in Brooklyn and joined a team that featured Steve Ross and Kenny Lindner and they beat the New Rochelle team of Bob Barker and Peter Fischbach in the final of the Metropolitan Club Championships. Finally, in his sixth year of tournament competition, Dick was ranked No. 10 in ETA men's 35 singles. He also earned the No. 5 ranking in the 45s and most recently, right before back surgery, shared the No. 2 ranking in over-70 doubles.

Harry Keely said recently that "we all know about players like Dick. The ball keeps coming back. When will he finally make an error? How many overheads do I have to hit? Why am I working so hard covering cross-courts and shots down-the-line? This was my first contact with Dick Scheer 30 years ago as an opponent in a doubles tournament. We have been friends and doubles partners ever since. It was easier that way.

"Dick has done a lot for us all. He takes his volunteer work seriously and you have all experienced his sense of commitment and his caring for the people who have worked with him.

"Fortunately, though, you have been spared the disdain he reserved for my erratic ground strokes," Keely added. "Picture it: Dick on the baseline as I walked up and back to pick up the tennis balls on my side of the net. I am not complaining. But, for the first half of our weekly hour over the years, he has been running me through the same drill over and over again. It takes 27 minutes, exactly. How much is that over 30 years? And I still do not have his backhand overhead down-the-line. Who can I see for a refund?"

Scheer has also been a member of the Board of Directors of the 1,000-plus member Riverside Clay Tennis Association (RCTA), the 2002 USTA Member Organization of the Year, which was formed to run the 10 public red clay tennis courts in Manhattan's Riverside Park. Dick's wife, Susan Scheer, a physical therapist who treats children with special needs, has for the last several years brought a group of kids to the courts on Friday afternoons. The first year Susan paid for the pro for all of the sessions and then Mark McIntyre, the park's executive director, obtained state/city funding for the program.

Dick's friends and associates talk about his integrity. McIntyre refers to his honesty and gentlemanly demeanor. Another tennis friend, Roger Brach, recalled that when he and Dick were members of the Seventh Regiment Tennis Club, he had a well deserved reputation for never giving a bad line call and always treating his opponent with respect.

Keely, though, offered an aside that indicates even Dick Scheer doesn't win them all. "Dick and I buy lottery tickets together each week," he said. "Now, as everybody knows, Dick is a winner. Every week we each buy a ticket. I give him mine to hold. He will check our numbers. How is it we have never won more than one free game over all of this time? Well, there is always next week."

-- By Nancy Gill McShea

Larry Scott

It's around the world in 80 days for Larry Scott, the traveling salesman of the Women's Tennis Association (WTA), as he scoots around the globe – from Sydney and Melbourne in Australia; to Utah; Miami; New York; abroad again to Doha in Qatar; Dubai in the United Arab Emirates; Bangalore in India; back to the U.S. to California; and on to Miami and New York. No, make that 80 hours. Not an unusual itinerary for charter members of today's speedy tennis caravan.

Scott is the chairman and chief executive officer of the Sony Ericsson WTA Tour and one of the world's most visible authorities in organized tennis. But Eastern veterans remember him as the junior player from Merrick, N.Y., who won the New York State High School singles title and ranked second in the East. Bill Stanley, a longtime friend and rival, said recently, "I have known Larry since we first competed against each other and played doubles together in the 12s. I stole him as a partner from Charles Tebbe so that we could play at the nationals…we lost in the round of 16 to one of the top seeded teams, Matt Frooman and Will Daniels.

"Larry had a two handed backhand, then a one handed backhand and again a two handed backhand. He worked hard on his game…and was a fierce competitor," Stanley confided. "I knew him when he was a baseliner and a serve and volleyer, when he used a wood Bancroft racquet and a Prince Graphite, when he had a big Afro that would have made John McEnroe proud in his heyday. It was the 70's! I am not sure if he had any control of his hairline or if it affected his game… Larry is a people person and always got along with everybody, especially the sponsors. He had a maturity well beyond his years and knew how to get sponsored by the newest and hottest companies of our era, such as Ellesse and Prince, which has served him well…with the ATP and now the WTA."

Bob Binns, Larry's junior coach at the Port Washington Tennis Academy, agrees that his one-time protégé "was always a thinking player looking for an angle to out strategize his opponent. He always found a way to win and that has followed him throughout his life."

Two days ago, on April 16, Larry celebrated his fifth anniversary at the helm of the WTA Tour and acknowledged that his years of experience in the game have helped him deal with the sport's challenging issues. One of his first initiatives was to ink the sponsorship deal with Sony Ericsson. Larry hired the International Management Group (IMG) as the WTA's agent. IMG contacted Sony Ericsson and Larry negotiated the deal personally with the company's worldwide head of marketing.

Tennis Week's news editor Richard Pagliaro, who refers to Scott as a tennis guru, said that "the six-year, $88 million title sponsorship commitment from Sony Ericsson that Larry helped procure dwarfs the Tour's past deals…in its size and scope and remains the largest sponsorship commitment in the history of women's sports…"

Larry also worked the system to get equal prize money for the women at the Grand Slams and received kudos from Billie Jean King, a co-founder of the women's pro tour. "Larry Scott has made a difference in women's tennis – a very big difference," said King, emphasizing that he is making the Tour one of the most viable and successful sports properties in the world today. "Because of his strong marketing skills, he understands the needs of the players, the requirements of the sponsors and the desires of the fans. He worked diligently to help secure equal prize money for women this past year at both Wimbledon and the French Open."

Asked why he felt so strongly about the equality issue, Larry said frankly that "if you're the head of women's tennis it has to be one of your top political priorities. I felt passionate about it and used all the equity in my relationships with the leaders of Wimbledon and Roland Garros. I campaigned very hard for it and made sure to involve our players… particularly Venus Williams…The players were very much front and center on the campaign. I also used a world class public relations firm to help us and we got it done.

"Of all the things I may have accomplished in tennis as an executive," he said, "that will be the most satisfying to me, that I was able to lead the effort to finally get equality for the women at the Grand Slams…It started with Billie Jean King well over 30 years ago. I just happened to be the steward of the organization at a good time where we were able to get it over the line."

Before he arrived at the WTA, Larry spent over a decade as the chief operating officer of the ATP Tour, president of ATP Properties and executive vice president of the International Group. He was also the vice president of the ATP Players' Council and a founding member of the ATP Board of Directors.

His rise in the tennis business is a typical tale of life in transition, or maybe a case of being in the right place at the right time. "I got my start at the US Open," he said. "I was underage, about 15 and playing the junior circuit. Leo Tedesco sneaked me in and got me a job as a runner for Suzanne Maguire (assistant tournament manager) and Mike Byrnes (tournament manager) in the tournament office. They were running the whole show — the Open sponsorship, the box seats, dealing with the players and their agents. For a kid it was kind of like peeking behind the curtain and seeing the Wizard of Oz, to see at a very early age how professional tennis worked at the highest level. I was pretty inspired by that…I loved tennis my whole life and having that experience stayed with me."

He went on to Harvard University, where he earned Tennis All-Ivy and All- America honors, played first singles and doubles and was captain of the tennis team. And his pal Bill Stanley was still with him. "We played against each other and together throughout the juniors and in college," Stanley said. "Besides Harvard, we were teammates on the U.S. Junior Davis Cup team, on the Prentice Cup (a match between a joint Oxford/Cambridge team and a combined Harvard/ Yale team) and the U.S. Maccabiah teams. We were also members of the same finals club at college; he nominated me to join. He was a captain and leader on each team and helped everyone to achieve his best."

Larry graduated from Harvard in 1986 and competed on the pro circuit for three years. He won an ATP event at Newport and defeated NCAA champ Greg Holmes at Wimbledon in 1987. But by 1988 he felt that his game had stalled and he started focusing on some player issues.

"I was in Singapore in April of '88," he said, "and Vijay Amritraj, who was running for president of the ATP Players' Council, asked me to run as his vice president. We were elected and simultaneously elected as founding members of the board. It was a dynamic, interesting time of upset between the ATP and the Men's Tennis Council, which eventually led to the creation of the ATP Tour circuit which was going to start in 1990. I loved the business side and was intrigued at the idea of going from a journeyman player to one of the most powerful positions a player can have."

Larry wrestles with many challenges facing the women's pro circuit, such as a shorter season and more combined men's and women's events in the future. He was an influential leader in the 2007 passage of the Roadmap 2010 initiative, a reform package designed to create a more understandable calendar structure for fans and one that builds stars and rivalries by ensuring that top players remain healthy and consistently play against one another on the sport's biggest stages.

He acknowledges that getting tennis on television is a huge problem, that the sport is being squeezed out and needs a broader distribution…He believes that stars like Maria Sharapova, who were not necessarily born in the U.S. but who do live here, resonate with fans. And that tennis, particularly around the US Open, is not that parochial, that many players from around the globe have star power.

But there is one challenge that Larry Scott refuses to deal with. Asked if he plays tennis with any of the women pros, he laughed and said, "I have resisted the temptation. I figure it wouldn't be a good career move; it's a no win situation. So no, that is not on my agenda."

-- By Nancy Gill McShea

Donald Van Blake

Donald Van Blake, the 86-year-old ambassador of tennis in Plainfield, N.J., is known for the slogan "Tennis, Tennis, Tennis everyone" which is inscribed on the monument in front of the Donald Van Blake Tennis Courts.

Van Blake is one of the most decorated tennis coaches ever, yet he didn't start playing until he was 55. Asked why, he mentioned the expression 'Cherchez la femme' and explained that he was courting a lady who played tennis and wanted to impress her. The relationship faded but he fell in love with the racquet. He has since coached the Plainfield High School Boys' Varsity Tennis team for 30 years (he retired in 2006). In 1983 he helped found the Plainfield Tennis Council and then organized community programs in every nook and cranny available. He has been honored with all sorts of awards in New Jersey — for distinguished service, as sportsman of the year, for his efforts on behalf of grassroots tennis, along with a special commendation as an "Educator, Role Model and Positive Influence to Youth." He was also named the 1991 *Star Ledger* and *Courier News* Coach of the Year and has been honored with Eastern's Southern Volunteer of the Year and Special Services awards. In 2001, the 16 Hub Stine courts in Plainfield were renamed for him.

He likes to say that "you can play tennis with someone for months and not know what their job is. You know their backhand but that's it." In Donald's world, no personal judgment calls exist inside the white lines — no prejudice, no comparisons regarding material possessions or status — only the one-on-one chase to the tennis ball. And his only agenda has been to inspire every kid in the community to share his love of the game and his philosophy of equality. "I was not raised in the kind of community where I could play tennis," said Van Blake, who was born in Plainfield in 1921 and attended de facto segregated public schools there. "One of the challenges of the sport was that it was so closed to blacks. Plainfield did not have a recreational tennis program even into the 1980s. Laura Canfield got me started; she was my guiding light."

When Donald first called Canfield, then the director of Eastern junior programs, he told her he had just retired from teaching metal shop at the Hubbard Middle School in Plainfield and wanted to become a full-time tennis volunteer. "Donald basically retired on a Tuesday, drove to the USTA Princeton office on Wednesday and called me at the Eastern office on Thursday to schedule a meeting," Laura said. She helped him organize a middle school program and develop a schedule of play. She agreed to ship him tennis balls, racquets and anything else he wanted.

"I once met Donald and the pro Willie Washington at about 5 p.m. on a weekday afternoon and they discussed scheduling some future school assemblies," Laura said. "Willie called me at noon the very next day and said the two assemblies he and Donald had done that morning went very well.

"I was dumbfounded and actually asked if he meant to say the two assemblies 'they were planning.' Wrong! Somehow, after I left them, Donald contacted a couple of principals that same night and arranged two assemblies for the very next morning! I envisioned him knocking on the doors of the principals' homes at 10 p.m. and was amazed by his passion and his connections."

Donald said that when Jenny Schnitzer succeeded Laura at Eastern "she was always there for me, too, when I starting getting into the USTA [organization] myself." His big projects have always been in the schools, including gym classes and after school programs, and on playgrounds and in parks.

"Donald's whole focus has been to get kids off the streets and onto the courts and let's see where it goes from there," said his friend of 25 years, Curtiss Young.

"I was not looking for champions," Donald pointed out. "I love it when kids come through the program and make the varsity squad but you never want to lose track of those who don't make the team. I would love every kid to be able to play tennis for recreation now and in later years. So we sponsored Town Tennis summer leagues to keep them playing at every level against teams in surrounding towns and recreational clubs. It's free and parents volunteered to drive them to matches. And the Board of Education got me a bus so I could drive them, too. ..Learning to play tennis is frustrating but that's part of the wonder of it. And you meet all kinds of people…"

In his life before tennis, Van Blake was scarred personally by the reality of segregation. "A whole lot can happen to you in 86 years," he said. He served in the U.S. Army in two segregated outfits – one a harassing mounted artillery unit, and the other, engineering — and saw action at the front during World War ll, in North Africa and Italy. In the early 1950s he earned his degree on the G.I. Bill at Virginia's Hampton Institute (now University), where he trained for a career in painting and decorating. "I wanted to go into my own business to make money," he said. "I had a strong feeling about black men making money…that when you had money you had power.

"I ran the business for 25 years but I never made a million," he admitted with a chuckle.

The civil rights movement exploded in the 1960s and he took on the role of Plainfield's chairman of the NAACP political action committee. "I organized marches for six months," he said. "We marched five days a week. We would have 200 or 300 people carrying signs and singing. It was the time of Martin Luther King's 1963 march on Washington and his 1965 register-to-vote march to the county courthouse in Selma, Alabama, and the sit-ins…There were spontaneous protests in each community. These were the ancestors of black people who over the centuries were trod upon, stepped upon, spit upon. The whole feeling was 'we have had enough!'"

Perhaps inspired by the advancement of civil rights, he tapped into his humanitarian values to focus on helping kids. While teaching metal shop courses in the Hubbard Middle School he also taught his students about black history. "We didn't teach our young people about who they are [like other cultures and religions have done]," he said. "This has been an awful loss to our young people, and to me. Some of my most glorious years were the years I spent in black schools…because they do teach you our history." In Plainfield, he said, black history ran about a page or two in the book and the teachers said Egypt was in Europe. At college he learned that Egypt was in Africa, that the black people had societies on the west coast.

Friends and relatives at Lincoln University in Pennsylvania helped him borrow African American artifacts from the museum there. "We put them on show and related them to the work we were doing in shop class," he said. "The kids loved it. I started an African American history club, told them blacks had contributed to this country, with inventions like stop lights, and with the medical initiatives of people like Dr. Charles Drew, who discovered blood plasma and developed the nation's first blood bank and the storage of blood plasma for transfusions. The kids rushed to join."

In his leisure time, Donald sang second tenor for 13 years in the Ric Charles traveling choral ensemble. Laura Canfield attended one of his concerts and said he was "Awesome!" And about ten years ago, he modeled gentlemen's clothing in newspapers and magazines for a Philadelphia agency. "That's hard work," he said. "You have to go on a lot of 'Go Sees' (auditions) so that potential clients can take a look at you and determine if you're the right type for a job."

Asked if he thinks black people today are as angry as he was, he said "No, especially now since Obama is running. Maybe we will reach some kind of agreement or goal. I'd like my four grandchildren to live in an equal society…"

And how does the sport of tennis rate in the whole scheme of Donald's world? "Everybody has equal footing on the tennis court," he said.

-- By Nancy Gill McShea

Chapter 29

2009: Cash, Schmitz, Schwartz and Snyder

Louise Cash

Louise Cash won the over-45 world singles title.

The tennis reporter Mike Farber wrote in the July 27, 1975 issue of *The Bergen Record*, "Beating Louise Cash in a Bergen County tournament is something like waiting for a bank error in your favor. It could happen but don't hold your breath!"

Louise has rated headlines as a famous New Jersey tennis champion for 50 years, ever since she started playing Eastern junior tournaments at age 11. But she has also won two world tennis championships and is a well traveled athlete whose dazzling 15-foot trophy case spreads across an entire wall. Her road trips around the world and throughout the U.S. are sprinkled with cherished memories and exhilarating highlights, which add up to an inspirational tale of how to succeed in sports.

She has played tennis with and against Grand Slam event champions such as Margaret Court – at the Longwood Cricket Club in Massachusetts; Bobby Riggs – in a mixed doubles exhibition in La Jolla, California; and Virginia Wade – in a national cup team match in France. She upset the No. 4 seed Francoise Durr in the 1982 US Open women's 35 event and then fell in the semis to Billie Jean King.

But it was in the women's 45 field that Louise recorded her most impressive victories. Six weeks after giving birth to her second daughter, Karen, she won the USTA national 45 singles title at Merion in Pennsylvania. In 1990 she and Barbara Mueller shared the top prize in the world doubles event in Yugoslavia. In 1994 she won the world singles title in Buenos Aires, Argentina. To date, she has filled her treasure chest with 29 USTA tennis balls won in senior national events – 11 gold for first place, 17 silver for second, and one bronze for third.

A true Eastern veteran, Louise ranked No. 1 in every Eastern junior age division and this past January she won the Louise Cilla Senior Player of the Year award. She began competing in sectional team play at age 17 and her name has been etched in the lineups of 23 Sears Cup and 15 Addie Cup events. She has also competed for Eastern on every USTA national cup team, from the 35s through the 50s, and still plays on the Addie Cup and the 55 intersectional teams.

With that background, it was no surprise when Louise called from the road in early March with a new tournament update as she headed to Cincinnati, Ohio, to play on the President's Cup team at the National Platform Tennis Championships. Her team finished third and she won 4 of her 5 matches. Tennis is her main sport but she's a 27-year veteran of platform tennis competition and has won national doubles titles in the 40, 50 and 60 age divisions. Reached on her cell in mid-March, she reported that she was on court competing in another platform tennis tournament.

Last fall, she traveled to Tucson, Arizona, to compete in the 4.5 USTA National Senior League Tennis Championships. Her team finished third among 17 entrants.

Louise's husband Paul passed away ten years ago, and she quickly focused on the family's athletic pursuits to help her children Lauren, then 12, and Karen, 9, rebound from their loss. "Life goes on and you do the best you can," she said. "…Being competitive athletes keeps my girls busy and builds their confidence. So you keep moving." When Louise won the national 40 mixed doubles title in California, Lauren was the ball girl for the match. Last spring, Louise accompanied Karen, a high school senior, to Florida to compete in an international junior golf challenge. Karen will play No. 1 on the golf team this coming fall at East Stroudsburg University in Pennsylvania. Louise also accompanied Lauren to national junior tennis tournaments around the country until she started driving north to Massachusetts to watch Lauren, now a senior at Boston College, play varsity tennis.

Beginnings often trigger motivation. When Louise was a kid she had fun playing baseball with the neighborhood boys but switched to tennis at age 9 when her father [Frederick Gonnerman] told her "they'll never let you on the boys' team…Let's start you playing tennis." She took lessons from Frank Brennan at the Oritani Field Club and won her first Eastern junior tournament at the Montclair Golf Club. "I beat Judy Dixon, now the head coach at UMass, to win that tournament," she said.

"Louise has a reputation for being precise," said Nadine Netter Levy, a lifelong friend who first met Louise across the net in an Eastern 13-and-under junior event. "She has great hands and is extremely accurate with her shots. She is agile, light on her feet and a very intense competitor…very tough mentally."

Louise recalls that Nadine beat her soundly back then but Louise, always courageous, pressed onward and decided to try the women's tennis tour straight out of high school in the mid-1960s. "In those days Billie Jean King, Margaret Court, Rosie Casals and Francoise Durr were all playing and I would lose in the first round," she said. After two years she realized nothing was going to happen there, and again, undaunted by defeat, she started teaching tennis all over Bergen County and became a head teaching pro. For her efforts, she was honored with the YMCA Bergen County Woman Athlete of the Year Award, in 1969 and 1972.

Louise's friend Irene Feldsott admires her qualities, including her tenacity. "It is rare and fortunate to meet a person who makes you feel such admiration," Irene said. "My introduction to Louise was at our tennis club in Ridgewood. We developed a bond while watching our daughters play. Louise focused on her family like no other person I know… My daughter Allison and Karen [Cash] played for the Northern Highlands High School Varsity team. Her girls are respectful and considerate and for this I give credit to Louise. When she lost her husband Paul she stepped up, encouraged them to participate in sports and helped them to dig deep to be the best. But what is amazing is that Louise still succeeds in sports herself."

Louise remembers that whenever she lost in the final of a junior tennis tournament her mother Irene would say, "Well Louise, you're a bridesmaid today, not the bride." Louise says now that if her mother is looking down from above tonight she will say, "Well, Mom, this evening I'm a bride wearing a diamond tiara."

-- By Nancy Gill McShea

Robert A. Schmitz

A family friend gave Bob Schmitz a used tennis racket for his tenth birthday, and right then and there he started prepping for a role in every aspect of the organized game. In a tennis career that spans more than 60 years, Bob has thrived on the court as a champion, as the captain of a U.S. team that won a world championship and as a playing member of victorious intersectional team events. Off the court, he has been honored for his work as a high-ranking volunteer and administrator, a community philanthropist and tennis businessman, all while he pursued a successful management career with General Electric and raised a family of tennis players with his wife Barbara.

Success stories can often be traced to a mentor, and Bob said his father Anton hit a few tennis balls with him and got him going. Before long, he and his friends were stringing nets across the wooden floor of the local armory during the rough winters in the Albany area, and he started winning in junior tournaments which in the early 1950s featured a 16-player draw. He moved on to Lafayette College, played No. 1 singles and was captain of the tennis team. In 1958 he earned a bachelor's degree in industrial engineering, joined the U.S. Navy and twice won the All Navy tennis championships.

In 1962 he went to work for General Electric and added a master's degree in industrial administration, which prepared him for a high level management career. After several assignments he achieved the position of Manager, Information Technology and Quality Systems, for G.E.'s Power Generation Division, and he worked in that capacity until he retired in 1996.

Bob says that his business background, which was critical for his G.E. career, also helped him to be an effective leader in tennis. He was the original Information Technology (ITT) Committee chairman for both the USTA and the Eastern section. In the mid-1990s he developed the USTA's first initiative in tennis applications on the computer and then upgraded the Eastern office with broadband servers and internet communication.

He served as Eastern's president in 1986-87, logged three terms as the treasurer of the section, was a longstanding member of the Finance Committee (1984-2005) and is still a member of both the Eastern and Junior Tennis Foundation Boards of Directors. Eastern honored him as the 1996 Man of the Year and presented him with a half dozen other awards -- for management and club service and member organization support – and in 1983, the entire Schmitz clan won the Family of the Year Award.

On the national level, he was the captain of the U.S. men's 45 Dubler Cup team that defeated Germany to win the 2004 world championship, and he was the captain of the USTA Stevens Cup. He chaired or was the vice chairman of the Information Technology, Individual Membership, Olympic and the National Tennis Center Committees, and served on 8 others as well.

His friends say he has juggled the demands of business and tennis well because he is smart, organized, dependable and passionate about his tennis.

"Bob was really my mentor," said Sue Wold, Eastern's Northern Region vice president. "He quietly helped me to understand the big picture in tennis."

"Bob's involvement in our 15-Love program is significant," said Herb Shultz, the president of 15-Love, who pointed out that Bob has served for 20 years as the executive vice president on the board of the inner-city tennis program which has over 3,000 young participants involved annually throughout the Capital Region. "He was instrumental in bringing Eastern into the formation of 15-Love at the outset. He chairs our program committee and makes sure activities are delivered in a consistent and quality manner. Without Bob...our program would not be where we are today.... not even close!"

His friend Nitty Singh explained that her New York Buzz won the 2008 World TeamTennis Championships in Sacramento, California, and that Bob, in his position as the operational owner of the Schenectady Racquet and Fitness Club, had sponsored the team from Day 1. She also confided that when she meets Bob for lunch at Gershon's Deli "he always orders the same sandwich -- with chips. He eats half the sandwich and takes the other half home -- with the chips -- so he'll be in shape to play tennis later that day…

"He even trained before his [double] knee replacement [in March of 2007], rode his bike three miles a day, won a club doubles championship the day before his operation and then checked into rehab right after surgery so he would get back into competition faster."

Five months after surgery, Bob was back on the court playing tournaments, and by year's end he ranked No. 6 in Eastern men's 70s, 52nd nationally and 15th in the USTA Super Senior Father and Son category with his son Tom. That kind of motivation has earned him rankings in 6 USTA age groups and in every Eastern category, from the men's open standings through all the senior divisions. He also played on three 4.5 Northern teams that advanced to the USTA League Tennis National Championships.

"There is no tougher competitor," said his friend Gerry Cuva, who played doubles with Bob in 1985 on the first Northern team that qualified for nationals. "Once he steps over the baseline he's brutal! I remember his epic battle with the marathon runner Don Flynn on a blistering hot July day in (Schenectady's) Central Park. They were both G.E. guys and typically had 3-4 hour matches. Bob, being from the old school, drank very little water, and after he finally won the match the paramedics arrived and carried him off."

"Copy that!" Jack Bauer would say in the TV hit series "24". This reporter recorded a similar Schmitz thriller in a June, 1986 issue of *Tennis Week* magazine: "Eastern defeated New England to win the Atlantic Coast Men's 45 Intersectional Championship, but to reach the finals… Eastern edged Mid-Atlantic 4-3 in a dramatic showdown. With the dual match deadlocked at 3-all, Eastern President Bob Schmitz and Tony Moreno were down one set and 1-4, 15-40 on Schmitz's serve in the second…Schmitz rallied… and with Moreno salvaged the tense three setter, 5-7, 7-6(5), 6-2…That same day, Schmitz's son Tom, a senior and the No. 1 player for SUNY-Albany, was a singles quarterfinalist and won All American honors at the NCAA Division 111 National Championships…

"There was tremendous pressure that day…!" Bob Schmitz said. "Copy that!" Tom Schmitz would say.

-- By Nancy Gill McShea

Bob and Tom Schmitz have been highly ranked in the USTA Super Senior Father-Son category.

Sid Schwartz

Courtesy of The New York Times

Sid Schwartz's daughter Heidi Resnick says there were always people on her family's tennis court when she was a kid. "I came home one day and (the basketball stars) Dr. J. (Julius Erving) and John Havlicek were playing," she said. "My father taught tennis to a bunch of guys who played football for the New York Giants. The Wimbledon champs Chuck McKinley, Arthur Ashe and Dick Savitt came to the court. And we had house guests. Ham Richardson once stayed with us when I was in 2nd grade and he came to my school assembly."

Some of Heidi's neighbors joined her in the celebrity watch on the court that Sid built in 1972 in Kings Point, Long Island. They might have seen Vitas Gerulaitis, Renee Richards, Bill Talbert and John McEnroe all show up in one day to play tennis there.

"He invited all the best players he knew to his court," said Fred Kovaleski, a frequent guest who spent time with Sid on the world tennis circuit in the 1950s. "He was a gracious host and got great pleasure out of entertaining us all."

Sid's peers say he's a charismatic, sociable guy with a great sense of humor. In his day, he was a gifted tennis player and a fierce competitor who was often a featured attraction. In fact, the columnist Stan Isaacs once dubbed him "Fast Sidney" in a piece entitled *The Saga of Lieberman's Leap*, when Sid retrieved an impossible shot on match point at the Eastern Clay Courts.

Isaacs reported: "Sid's opponent Anthony Lieberman said, 'I gave him a twist serve that took him off the court at his backhand. His return was a soft, high bounce left of center. I was coming toward the net...I jumped and hit a high backhand shot that took him off the court at his forehand. I didn't figure he'd be able to go for it, let alone get it.' Lieberman continued running and leaped over the net...ready to shake hands...Sidney...ran furiously...to return the shot. Miraculously, Schwartz got his racket on the ball...it lofted high in the air...over the net and plopped to earth... for a winner." Sid won the match and the tournament.

"We did have a wonderful time," said Sid, who enjoyed entertaining the fans. "There were about 200 people in the stands and I thought they would fall out of the stands. They were doubled up, howling."

Savitt said recently. "Sidney could make a great shot from almost anywhere on the court. One of his best moments was when he won the first set, 12-10, from Lew Hoad at Forest Hills."

Richards concurred: "Here was this charismatic New York kid testing the great Lew Hoad on grass in front of a packed house. It was thrilling."

"Sid had every stroke," added Kovaleski. "He hit the ball very hard and had wonderful touch, a rare combination. He was so talented he frequently risked losing and hit a fancy shot rather than go for a normal winner in critical match situations.

"And we did have a good time. When we were playing the Egyptian International Championships, I was driving Sid to his hotel in downtown Cairo, the traffic slowed and Sid pulled out a water pistol and soaked a traffic cop. I was an undercover CIA agent at the time so I hit the accelerator and took off."

Sid's competitive tennis journey spanned four decades. It began in the early 1940s when his parents Herman and Pauline encouraged him to play, and ended in 1981 after he won his second national senior clay court title with his University of Miami teammate Tony Vincent.

In 1944 he ranked No. 1 in the Eastern boys' division, No. 3 in the U.S., won the New York State Championships at Syracuse and was a singles semifinalist and the doubles champ at the USLTA national boys' tournament in Kalamazoo, Michigan.

He came of age in 1945 at the 7th Regiment Armory in New York, when at age 16 he upset Gardnar Mulloy, then ranked No. 3 in the U.S., and advanced to the quarterfinals of the U.S. men's indoors. He also defeated Savitt that year at the Armory to win the national junior indoor championships and was later a 7-time doubles champ at the memorial tournament there for Fred Scribner, who died in the Korean War.

In 1945, '46 and '47, Sid was a student at Erasmus Hall High School in Brooklyn and won the Eastern Interscholastic singles and doubles titles. In 1947 he was named to the U.S. Junior Davis Cup team and was on his way.

Richards was a ball kid for Sid at the Armory in 1948 when he took Bill Talbert to five sets at the U.S. men's indoors. "He had a big game and great reflexes that were very suitable for the boards," Richards said.

Brooklyn native Jeff Rose watched Sid come to the attention of local tennis fans in the late 1940s at Brooklyn's Mammoth Tennis Courts, a complex of 52 clay courts that was the hub of tennis activity. "Sid would play exhibitions against Charlie Masterson there," said Rose, who played under Coach Masterson at Poly Prep. "Their matches were equal parts ballet and war, not unlike (Jack) Dempsey versus (Gene) Tunney. Sid won most of those battles and even sophisticated tennis folks watched in disbelief as the warriors made one impossible backhand return after another."

A review of Sid's most impressive stats shows that he ranked No. 11 in singles and third in doubles in the United States. He played on scholarship at the University of Miami from 1947-1950 and won the 1953 All Army singles title at West Point. He competed at the French, Italian and Wimbledon Championships in 1955 and '57 and recorded victories over Grand Slam event champs Pancho Gonzalez (1948-49 U.S. Championships) at the Eastern Grass Courts in Orange, N.J.; Vic Seixas (1953 Wimbledon, 1954 U.S. Championships) at a U.S. tournament in Buffalo; Jaroslav Drobny (1951-52 French, 1954 Wimbledon) in Weisbaden, Germany; and Merv Rose (1954 Australian), Budge Patty (1950 Wimbledon), among others. While touring on the Middle Eastern circuit, he was twice a doubles finalist with German great Baron Gottfried von Cramm – in Cairo and Alexandria. Back home, he was a singles quarterfinalist at the 1950 U.S. National Championships at Forest Hills, an accomplishment that netted him elite status as a member of the US Open "Final 8" Club.

What Sid's stats don't show is that he is also a concerned citizen. He lives in Florida now but back in the 1970s he was the president of the Great Neck, N.Y., chapter of the American Cancer Society. His father had been a smoker and died of lung cancer. Sid was also a smoker and after his father passed away he promptly visited a hypnotist to quit the habit, became a big advocate of anti-smoking and hosted tennis exhibitions to benefit the cause.

"I quit smoking on a Monday, August 1, 1970 at 9 a.m.," said Sid Schwartz, a man known for his passion and determination.

-- By Nancy Gill McShea

Sheridan (Sherry) G. Snyder

On his second birthday, Sherry Snyder's mother Edythe wrote a note to her son to save for posterity. "You didn't like your party at all," she wrote, "…As soon as you are old enough you can tell me how you'd like to celebrate it and we'll do it that way…What can you do and what are you like now that you're 2?…You can throw and catch a football very well. You can hit a tennis ball with a racket (sometimes). You don't say much that's distinct enough to be understood."

He certainly speaks distinctly now. Sherry is a world famous entrepreneur in the biotechnology field, and everybody understands exactly how he likes to do things. After graduating from the University of Virginia in 1958 he began a career as a credit analyst for the New York Trust Corporation. But creating new products intrigued him, so in 1962 he founded his first venture, Cambridge Machine Corporation. He has since made a career out of taking new ideas, primarily of a technological and scientific nature, developing them into some 13 major companies and then merging with or selling the businesses to larger companies while retaining partial ownership. In 2002 he was awarded an Honorary Doctor of Law degree from the University of Dundee in Scotland for his contribution to the University's bioscience research center. And in 2004 he received the Officer of the British Empire title from Queen Elizabeth for his contribution to the United Kingdom's science and technology.

But this is a tribute to Sherry's significant contributions to tennis. He revved up his skills at age 4 on his home court in Sea Cliff, Long Island, where his father, George, taught him how to hit a tennis ball more consistently. At UVA, he played No. 1 singles and doubles, was the captain of the tennis team and was named the "Athlete of the Year." Not surprisingly, the game continued to be a passion.

Sherry's longtime tennis friends say that he created a legacy in the sport when he co-founded and supported the National Junior Tennis League (NJTL) in the late 1960s. Sherry got the ball rolling at the Harlem River Playground and today the USTA operates the program in 110 cities and reaches 250,000 inner-city children.

"Arthur (Ashe) and Charlie (Pasarell) challenged me to try to impact grassroots tennis," Sherry said. "They sent me a 14-page memorandum they had written on a yellow pad and helped me raise money to get it started. Les Fitz Gibbon, a president of Eastern, suggested that we create a 'little league' of tennis, with uniforms. I organized the first chapter at the Harlem playground, used it as the beta site while developing the scoring…team orientation, matches without instruction, etc…Skip Hartman offered to help and later ran the New York chapter. He has done a fabulous job."

"Sherry developed ideas into viable businesses and did the same thing for the NJTL," said Skip, who sponsored a site in 1970 and was appointed the president of the NYJTL in 1971. "Sherry initially asked Gene Scott and Stu Ludlum to run the program in New York City and coordinate the expansion of the operation…"

"Sherry's expertise is bringing a product to market," said Ray Benton, who managed the national NJTL program in its early years in Washington, D.C. "Sherry knew how to spot a good idea and made a career out of giving ideas structure, and in the case of the NJTL, setting up local organizations.

"The traditional USTA pathway was that kids needed to learn how to play before they were allowed to play. Our idea was to invite kids to come to the park, put on a team shirt, have fun and then they'll want to play."

"Sherry…is creative, he conceptualizes and then he executes, which is the hard part," said Donald Dell, whose company ProServ enlisted Coca Cola to be the NJTL's first corporate sponsor. "We all had a different role."

Neil Amdur publicized the program in *The New York Times*, including a piece entitled *Disorder on the Court*, in which he chastised the USTA's junior development committee for insisting at its 1970 annual meeting that the NJTL kids wear white uniforms. "With all of the problems of reaching youngsters interested in learning how to play," Amdur wrote, "it took a dynamic…Easterner, Sheridan G. Snyder…to shake the group from its lethargy with a candid explanation of his mass program for reaching youngsters in the inner-city."

Sherry says now: "I explained to the committee that this was a novice program, that the kids would have team names like the Tigers, wear red and blue uniforms and have intra-park competition to get them started…Neil came running out of the meeting and told me not to be discouraged. He stood up for me…

"Neil, Ray, Skip, Donald, Gene, these are my heroes. Solid people! Gene and Donald were natural competitors in tennis (both Yale and UVA law school grads). I was always trying to make peace between them. For my 50th birthday party they walked into my house arm in arm as their gift to me. It brought tears to my eyes."

Sherry chaired Eastern's grass court circuit and promoted other tennis causes in the late 1950s and 1960s and then focused mainly on his business interests. But he resurfaced in tennis to reminisce about his friend Gene Scott who passed away suddenly in March of 2006. Sherry recalled a tennis fundraiser he organized and ran at C.W. Post College on Long Island to energize tennis and benefit the Family Service Association of Nassau County. Billie Jean King and Gene were the marquis players.

"I have known Gene aka "Butch" for 53 years," he wrote. "We started our friendship when he was 16 and challenged me to a match at the Cold Spring Harbor Beach Club and I had to give up my teaching lesson with Jane Fonda. I will always be grateful that I gave up Jane for Gene…Gene was always there willing to help any tennis effort…Gene and Billie Jean King played the first inter gender match at C.W. Post when we needed to create excitement. Gene played Billie Jean a 21 point set, staked Billie 11 points and won 23-21. Billie turned around and donated her appearance money to the charity…I wonder if young ones today will ever understand champions and tennis pioneers like Billie and Gene."

Sherry Snyder (top left) started the National Junior Tennis League on a Harlem playground.

In 1963, *The New York Times* ran a July 11 article that stated: "Sheridan Snyder announced that the Nassau Bowl, one of the oldest and most prized trophies in tennis, is being put back in competition." Sherry revived the grass court invitational with the help of his friend Gene, who recruited many of the world's top players. The U.S. Davis Cup Captain Walter Pate had started the tournament in 1913. In the 55-year history of the event at the Nassau Country Club in Glen Cove, N.Y., players who have collectively won 50 Grand Slam singles titles competed there, including Americans Bill

Tilden, Jack Kramer, Bobby Riggs, Vic Seixas, Stan Smith, Chuck McKinley, Arthur Ashe, Dick Savitt and Australians John Newcombe and Roy Emerson.

But in 1968, the weekend golfers at the Nassau Club balked that the tennis tournament was taking space on the first fairway used for parking. *The New York Times* ran a story, *Nassau Bowl Off; Substitute Event Sought*, and Sherry negotiated with New York City Mayor John Lindsay to run the tournament in the city's public parks. "I rented rooms at the Roosevelt Hotel and gave the players cab fare to get to the sites," Sherry said. "I sent Ray Moore (of South Africa) up to the Harlem River Playground to play his match and kids got a glimpse of the courage needed to play tennis at that level. One kid even yelled, 'Remember the Alamo!'"

Sherry also assisted Joe Cullman, chairman of the US Open in 1968-69, by developing a corporate program along with the US Open Club in the basement of the Forest Hills stadium. Sherry knew it would be smart to create a luxurious environment for executives to entertain their clients, so he hired the set designer from the play "The Fantasticks" who developed a pink and white canvas décor in one day.

At last year's US Open, Sherry accepted the Intercollegiate Tennis Achievement Award, presented annually to past collegiate champions who have achieved excellence in their careers and contributed to society. In 1999, UVA was going to eliminate its major tennis facility and Sherry committed to financially rebuilding a 13 court tennis complex, including an electronic scoreboard, now named the Sheridan G. Snyder Tennis Center. And again, in 2006, he made a large donation to his alma mater to create the Translational Science Research Center, a new UVA Cancer Center and a Children's Hospital. UVA named the structure the Sheridan G. Snyder Building.

What motivated Sherry Snyder to accomplish all of the above? For one thing, his mother suggested a few goals for him at age 2. And you can bet that the thousands of kids who learned to play tennis in the National Junior Tennis League program would say today that he has met those goals.

-- By Nancy Gill McShea

Chapter 30

2010: Buehning, Burling, Flink and Franco

Fritz Buehning

International Tennis Hall of Fame

If you followed tennis during the golden years of the professional game in New York, chances are you remember the 6-foot-5 image of the fiery Fritz Buehning dashing across the court at the US Open. Fritz was out of New Jersey and often met his Eastern junior friends and foes across the net on the storied Stadium Court. In 1982 he defeated Vitas Gerulaitis of Howard Beach in an early round match there. At the 1983 Open, Fritz and his partner Van Winitsky were doubles finalists on Stadium, surrendering to John McEnroe of Douglaston, who once beat Fritz in a boys' 12s match in Bayside, Queens; and Peter Fleming of Chatham, a childhood practice partner at The Racquets Club in Short Hills, N.J.

"Fritz and I go way back, even playing against each other when we were just little kids," McEnroe recalled recently. "Like me, Fritz wore his heart on his sleeve and played the game with a lot of passion. He definitely is one of the most talented players to be inducted into the Eastern Tennis Hall of Fame."

"The game of tennis was made for me," said Fritz, whose goal was to rank among the world's top ten. He fought for every point and admits now that his temper outbursts were basically anger directed at himself. "I was second behind McEnroe in fines at Wimbledon, and if I had made it to the second week I might have passed him. It's ironic because to me Wimbledon is the mecca of tennis."

The record shows that Fritz played the pro circuit full time for five years, from 1979-85, and achieved career high world rankings of No. 21 in singles and No. 4 in doubles. He was poised to break into the world's top ten in singles when a foot injury derailed him and ended his career abruptly at age 25.

Like the fictional Roy Hobbs in the movie *The Natural*, whose goal was to be the best ever before his baseball career was cut short, Fritz suddenly understood all too well the meaning of the movie's famous line – **"We have two lives, the life we learn with and the life we live with after that…"**

…The life we learn with….. Athletic ability was in Fritz's blood. He learned the game at the Racquets Club with his father, Dr. Peter Buehning, West Germany's best gymnast before he moved to the U.S.; and with his mother, Renate, who played on the 1958 U.S. women's national handball team. Fritz's sister Susan was the captain of her high school tennis team and his brothers, Peter Jr. and Jim, both played team handball for the U.S. at the Olympics, but Fritz had the edge in tennis.

He signaled his impending arrival on the world's pro circuit at age 17 when he won the 1977 New Jersey High School State tennis championships as a Millburn junior. The late Gene Scott took notice and gave Fritz his first wildcard into Scott's pro event in South Orange. More wild cards followed and between 1977 and 1979 he vaulted into the tennis spotlight.

"During that two year window I went from being a top junior player to being able to win matches on the pro tour," said Fritz, who told a reporter that he had trained for that opportunity all his life. "I started to play at 7, won my first tournament at 9 and played national tournaments when I was 10."

He skipped his senior year in high school, headed to UCLA on a tennis scholarship and the following spring helped his team reach the 1978 NCAA finals. In the summer of 1978 he was 18 and still eligible for the juniors. He won the USTA national hard court championships and ranked first in the country. He returned to UCLA the next year, won All-American and Pac-10 Player of the Year honors while playing in the first singles and doubles positions, and led UCLA to the 1979 NCAA team championship.

…The pro career… Fritz was 19 and on summer break when he set out to see the world. He traveled to Paris to compete for the U.S. in the International Lawn Tennis Club event and then qualified and won a round in the men's main draw at Wimbledon before moving on to the Pan Am Games in Puerto Rico.

Later that summer, he defeated 1975 US Open champ Manuel Orantes on clay in the first round of the US Open warm-up in Washington, D.C., and then bowed in the quarters to Johann Kriek at the final Open tune up in Stowe, Vermont. Buoyed by his results, Fritz turned pro two weeks before the 1979 Open, and by year's end he ranked among the world's top 100.

In early 1980 he fell prey to the sophomore slump and admitted that a poor work ethic might be the culprit. Luckily, his former coach Harry Hopman asked him to train on the Peugeot-Rossignol team under coach Bob Brett. The team was designed to give structure to young pros, among them Jose Luis Clerc, Andres Gomez and a few other comers. Fritz caught a second wind, inched up the singles rankings to No. 69 and then broke through.

By December of 1980 he had reached his first singles final at the South African Open in Johannesburg, defeating 1977 US Open champ Guillermo Vilas and doubles specialist Bob Lutz before losing to Kim Warwick in the title match. Three weeks later, he won his first Grand Prix singles title at the New South Wales Open in Sydney, Australia. He beat future French Open champ Yannick Noah in the second round and prevailed in the final, 6-4, 6-7, 7-6, over UCLA graduate Brian Teacher.

"Doing well at Johannesburg and Sydney was the springboard," said Fritz, whose singles ranking jumped to No. 21 at the end of 1980. Victories over guys in the top ten kept mounting; he was in the running.

In the summer of 1981 *Tennis* magazine's editorial group singled him out as a player to watch. Another reporter wrote that his blazing serve, savage volleys and explosive temper made him one of the top competitors and one of the leading personalities on the tour.

In 1982 he lost to Clerc in the finals of Richmond but that same year he beat Gene Mayer in Mexico. By 1983 he had posted significant wins over Grand Slam champ Mats Wilander, future Wimbledon champ Pat Cash and top tenners Kevin Curren and Tim Mayotte.

Fritz says that his favorite victories were in singles against the cream of the crop, yet one of his most memorable victories came in doubles at Wimbledon in 1982. He and his partner Ferdie Taygan defeated Heinz Gunthardt and Balazs Taroczy 8-6 in the fifth set to earn a spot in the quarters where they lost in four sets to eventual champs Peter McNamara and Paul McNamee.

Fritz was a well known doubles specialist; he netted 12 titles and reached the finals 15 times. Some were repeats with partners Taygan, a 1981 victory over the Mayer brothers at Rotterdam and a semifinal showing at the US Open; and with Fleming, especially a 6-3, 6-0 route of Tomas Smid and Gundhardt at the 1984 U.S. Indoors in Memphis, and a three setter in 1981 over the Giammalvas at Atlanta.

...The life we live with after that... In 1984 Fritz was 24 and had bone spurs removed from his foot. He returned to the circuit too quickly, developed pain and was diagnosed with a stress fracture. Over a period of two years – from 1985-87 -- he underwent six operations to treat bone spurs in the ankle joint and a stress fracture in the nevicular bone. He walked with a cast and crutches during that time frame.

"If you can't run you can't play tennis," Fritz said, "so that was it!"

He played his last match in March of 1985 and retired officially in 1987.

"I was pretty depressed for a very long time," he said. "I'm [a member of the Open's] "Final 8" Club but I didn't go back to the tournament for 7 years. The guys I came up with were all still out there."

He immersed himself instead in his family's manufacturing business in Hillside, N.J. "My grandfather started the business, we sold plastics machinery," said Fritz, who took on the role of international sales manager. When the business closed, he became involved in selling the company's assets.

Fritz now teaches tennis at Twin Oaks in Morristown, N.J., and works in industrial sales for a Chicago plastics company. He also enjoys the accomplishments of his three children – Gerhard, a senior at Rutgers and the captain of the lacrosse team; Chelsea, who plays soccer on scholarship at USC; and Saxon, a junior tennis player who trains at Saddlebrook in Florida.

Like Hobbs, Fritz has lived the line from *The Natural*. He has closed a few doors and discovered a few new beginnings.

"Tennis was my life," he said, "and it is still my passion. I can play a decent set of singles and a couple of sets of doubles." A good omen, that!

-- By Nancy Gill McShea

Lee Burling

Lee Burling is a celebrated tennis player and a veteran world class athlete in several other sports. Labels don't explain motivation or personality, but a search for clues revealed that Lee, who was born in Manchester, N.H., has mastered a self deprecating New England sense of humor to ease the stress that accompanies her strong personality, competitive drive and strict code of ethics.

When asked on April 6 how she was celebrating her 78th birthday, Lee replied that she had played tennis that morning, was at the moment reading about the survival of wolves in *National Geographic* magazine and was about to walk her dog Gitano. "He's my rescue dog, a gypsy," she said. "His mother was a loose woman and his father was a traveling salesman." She slipped into the conversation the news that her pickup truck was in the shop for an overhaul because chipmunks were living in the air filter so the truck was heating up and smelled like it was about to burst into flames. And oh, by the way, she was a terror in her childhood so her parents steered her toward sports to tire her out.

"I was a trial," she admitted with not a hint of regret. "I was so energetic my mother would tie me to the clothesline. When she came out to check on me the rope would still be there but I would be gone. So when I was 3 she started researching sleep-a-way camps for me."

Some 68 years after Lee first played tennis in a local park with her father, Charles Chadbourne, she is certain that the game has offered her the greatest opportunity to discover who she is, that it has defined her life. "I could be disruptive [acting silly] and I have a short fuse," she said, "but my parents and coaches held me accountable."

And if there is a category in the Guinness Book of World Records that tracks athletes who have won numerous USTA national senior tennis championships and also represented the United States in a variety of other sports, Lee is definitely in the running for a spot in the top 100.

In 2006, Lee was inducted into the Syracuse Hall of Fame to honor her achievements. Years before she earned an international reputation in tennis -- during the pre Title 1X era when she attended Boston University's Sargent College and taught physical education at Smith College in Massachusetts – Lee literally played the field in sports. She was ranked fourth in the U.S. in badminton (1956), toured South Africa and played right wing for the U.S. field hockey team (1958-59), competed in the British Isles and in Ireland while playing center for the U.S. lacrosse team (1954-60) and was a member of the 1960 Massachusetts A.A.U. winning basketball team. She ranked third in the country in squash (1974) and also dabbled in competitive golf for 20 years.

She decided to focus on tennis in the late 1970s after she and her husband Jim, a math professor at SUNY Oswego, had settled in the area. Indoor courts were being built in upstate New York and she could play tennis year round. "That's when I gave up golf," she said. "You can't play a sport six months of the year and really accomplish anything....you can play tennis for the rest of your life."

She won her first USTA national tennis title in 1983 in women's 50 doubles and has since collected an astonishing 46 USTA gold tennis balls and some 31 silver, in singles and doubles. She has represented the U.S. on 10 international tennis teams. In 1987 she competed on the Maria Bueno Cup (50s) squad that defeated Great Britain for the championship in Finland and the next week she was a finalist in the individual world (50s) doubles contest in Germany. She was the 2000 ITF world (65s) singles champion in South Africa and a runner up in doubles. At the 2009 Super-Senior World Championships in Australia, she notched a doubles victory for the U.S. Queens Cup (75s) team. Not only that, hip (1993) and knee (2003) replacement surgeries interrupted her torrid pace.

Lee's friend Brad Mann has played tennis with her almost every week for 20 years. "We missed a couple of weeks after Lee's hip and knee surgeries," Brad said, "although she practiced her tennis swing while recovering in her hospital bed - I caught her in the act…When someone asks, 'Who are you playing tennis with today?' I love to brag and glibly reply, 'Oh, one of the top three players in the world.' If I won that day, I really had bragging rights!"

She played Eastern tournaments before she competed on the national senior circuit. But when she started traveling her family missed her presence and soon began complaining about her absences. So she informed them that she would curtail her athletic jaunts, become the best mother and wife, and would live her life through her husband and two children. For starters, she questioned her daughter Koren's resolve: "You are a runner," she said. "How come you're finishing 10th and not first?" And she challenged her son Temple: "The Burlings say you're very bright but I've seen no indication of this!" Then she posed a rhetorical question to her husband Jim: "You've got a Ph.D. in mathematics. How come you're not publishing?"

A week later, Koren and Temple told their mother they had held a family meeting and decided "we love you best when you leave." There was no problem ever again. "Jim gave me a tremendous amount of space and took care of the kids while I toodled around the country," she said. "I was lucky. When Jim and I were studying for graduate degrees at the University of Colorado, I called my father and said 'I think Jim proposed to me tonight.' Dead silence on his end. I continued and said 'Dad, I'm very nervous about this…It's a real commitment and I don't know if I can hold up my end of the deal.' Without missing a beat Dad said, 'Remember Lee, you haven't had too many offers.' I tell you, you had to have a sense of humor to be part of my family."

When she returned home from her tennis journeys she played and taught tennis at the Eastside Racquet Club in Manlius, N.Y. (formerly known as Limestone). Tennis students and local admirers rallied round her like groupies.

"Lee has been an inspiration for our four sons throughout their childhood," her friends Lisa and Timothy Izant said. "She came into our lives as a tennis coach…and became a part of our family. She teaches tennis as a recreational … competitive…life-long sport and most importantly, as a platform for lessons in life. Tennis is Lee's forum in the education of children for a future to contribute to the tennis community and the community of mankind. She is a role model for the world of tennis, but most importantly she is an example of an exceptional human being. While Lee taught the elements of the game, she incorporated into her tennis lessons the teaching of honesty, kindness, dignity, respect and humility. The gift she has given our children through tennis is the strength and courage to pursue any, and all, of their dreams."

Maureen Anderson, a USPTA pro who coaches tennis at the Manlius Pebble Hill School, said that Lee taught her how to be a better person. "Lee is a caring, yet feisty, opinionated individual," Maureen said. "The first time I had to play a doubles match across the net from her I discovered the true meaning of intensity, focus and match etiquette. I was inexperienced in competing; this was an education for me. There was no chatting, no nice shots, just complete business, quite alarming but a good lesson to learn…Needless to say I did not win!! This taught me to value the mental toughness needed for match play.

"Lee is a very competitive athlete and hates to lose…Her father taught her the importance of sportsmanship so she is always gracious in both victory and defeat and sets the example."

Lee herself offers a reality check on winning and losing in tennis. "Someone told me that 600 million people live in China; 300 million don't even know you played and the other 300 million don't give a damn!" she said. "That's true. I don't think I'm special, but I'm happy. Tennis has been tremendous for my self esteem and gave me the courage to stand up for what I know is right."

-- By Nancy Gill McShea

Steve Flink

Tennis journalists in the media room at the Grand Slams refer to Steve Flink as "Sir Steve." He is a legend in the sport, an encyclopedia of tennis who stores in his mind every box score, court strategy, descriptive adjective and personal history of every world class tennis player. His photographic memory rivals the Dustin Hoffman character in *Rainman* and even Hall of Famers Chris Evert, Pete Sampras and the late Arthur Ashe have deferred to Steve in public interviews to clarify dates, scores and momentum shifts in their matches.

Steve paints graphic pictures to share with fans his unique understanding of the intricacies of every match and to give life to the people he writes about.

No doubt you have read dozens of Steve's 2,000-plus published tennis essays, listened to him on the radio and watched him on television. He currently writes a column for TennisChannel.com. From 1992-2007 he was a senior correspondent for *Tennis Week*. From 1974-91 he was a columnist and an editor for *World Tennis* magazine. Since 1982 he has covered Wimbledon and the French Open for CBS radio. From 1980-96 he was a color commentator for MSG and ESPN. In the 1970s and '80s he worked as a statistician for NBC, CBS and ABC tennis telecasts. He is the author of "The Greatest Tennis Matches of the Twentieth Century."

Steve's career in tennis began as a tale of two cities. His father, Stanley, first took him to Wimbledon at age 12, in 1965. "I was hooked, totally enamored of the environment," he said. At summer's end, he returned to his home base in New York to watch his favorite Americans of that generation – Ashe, Clark Graebner, Dennis Ralston, Nancy and Cliff Richey – at the U.S. National Championships in Forest Hills, thereby setting up a Wimbledon-US Open pattern for the next 45 years.

"I knew by the time I was 15 that I wanted to be a tennis reporter," he said.

Everybody depended on newspapers before the internet surfaced and Steve said that when he was touring Greece at 17 "it was killing me that I couldn't get the tennis results. I hunted down the *Herald Tribune* at Crete, found a place that sold the international issue and got back copies. I had to know every day what was happening.

"Once I saw a score it was locked into my head. I can't explain it; I just had a passion for it." He liked numbers and said that gave him a niche in establishing himself. "Initially, it was the numbers that got me on the board, but I started understanding the game itself much better when I was in my twenties."

In 1970 he moved to England to study at the U.S. International University in Sussex and played college tennis. The word on Flink in team brochures: "He has a well rounded game…excellent student of the sport, practices constantly…main asset is consistency." He jammed his weekly courses into three days and rushed back to his father's abode in London to hang out at the Queen's Club.

"They were important years," said Steve, whose father introduced him to Bud Collins, John Barrett and Graebner. "Queen's was a great education. Everybody floated through -- Ted Tinling, Cliff Richey, Butch Buchholz and Marty Riessen -- and I would have conversations with them. Tinling would hold court in the dining room, regaling me with stories from the latest tournaments…I learned a ton listening to him talk about the game."

He added the French Open to his repertoire in 1971 and in 1973 he walked up to Chris Evert, asked her for an interview and she agreed. He sold the story to *World Tennis*, his first, and a week later received a check from the editor, Gladys Heldman. He wrote another story for *World Tennis* in 1974, and the magazine offered him a job.

"Bud Collins knew I had this memory and hired me in 1972 to help him at Wimbledon and the US Open," he said. "There were no computers, no official head-to-heads put out by the tours so Bud would ask me questions like 'How many times has Ashe beaten Okker?'...I also read *World Tennis* every month and picked up stats from old issues, so it all just got into my system."

At the 1972 Open he met another mentor in Jack Kramer, who was working with Bud on CBS while Steve was doing the stats. "Jack taught me a lot," he said. "We later worked on instruction articles for *World Tennis* and conversations shifted to other relevant topics in the game."

Ashe played Nastase in that 1972 Open final. "Ashe was a hero of mine," Steve said. "I loved it when he won the first Open (in 1968) and this time he was poised to take the title again. He was leading Nastase 2 sets to 1, with a break point for 4-1 in the 4th...which would have put him out of reach. He ended up losing it in 5. He sat down afterward, put his head in his hands and cried. I went off to the clubhouse and cried myself."

Steve's trip to the historic 1972 U.S.-Romania Davis Cup match in Bucharest was a major learning experience. The U.S. team received terrorist threats. Two angry Romanian guards approached Steve, started shouting "American agent, American agent!" and tried to hustle him off the grounds when British writers rescued him.

"It was a great moment in my evolution as a reporter to be there at age 20," he said. "Stan Smith was the hero, beating Nastase in the opening match. Then Gorman was up two sets on Tiriac, who got the crowd chanting to give him extra time between points. Tiriac beat Gorman. It was nerve wracking, but Smith and Erik Van Dillen won the doubles and Stan beat Tiriac 6-0 in the fifth to clinch on the last day, despite a stream of bad calls."

Excerpted thoughts from his media pals -- journalists, editors and television/radio broadcasters – offer an inside view of Sir Steve:

Neil Amdur – "Long before computers spewed endless reams of data, there was always Steve Flink to recall the glorious moments in tennis. And remind us, he could...of a memorable match you barely retained on the fringes of appreciation...There are one-of-a-kind stat freaks in every sport who can recite batting averages, fantasy football numbers and three-point shooting percentages...But Steve's persona is wrapped around more than numbers. He inhabits his own Magic Kingdom filled with the joy and optimism of someone who treasures the true meaning of love, from court to life...he attaches the same meticulous preparation and detail to sartorial coat and tie selections at Wimbledon, Paris or Flushing Meadows, as he does to a thoughtfully researched, well-written original piece of journalism."

Mary Carillo – "Steve can call up matches from decades past and put them in modern day context...Steve can't be spun -- he knows just what he's watched and ably reports what he's seen, every single time..."

Bud Collins – "I've known Steve since he was a kid living in London, a tennis degenerate as we call each other...We covered the uproarious U.S.-Romania Davis Cup final in '72...He, Mary and I formed the TV team for the women's season-ending championships at Madison Square Garden. His facts and figures were as clear on the air as in his writing....Most reporters today resemble ragbags but Steve stands out eloquently in his appearance, much like his mentor, the great *New Yorker* writer Herbert Warren Wind."

Andre Christopher – "I have never known another writer who uses adjectives the way Steve does. If you could get him to describe any activity you were doing, I'm sure it would be like seeing yourself in slow motion. And almost everybody looks cool in slow motion. Not as cool as Steve, mind you, but cool enough...Steve in a press room is like a Rolls Royce in a Walmart parking lot, but he has an Everyman affability that betrays the stuffiness of his wardrobe."

Matt Cronin – "At the Grand Slams, even when Steve is...doing 3 radio reports per hour and trying to fit a column or two into his day, he finds time to check up on his beloved Yankees. He's so obsessed with his boys in pinstripes that I swear, even when his favorite male player, Pete Sampras, was going for his then record 14th Slam, Steve was more concerned about whether Mariano Rivera was losing accuracy off his cutter."

Joel Drucker – "Tennis is lucky to have Steve in its family. As he himself would put it with trademark precision, he has graced our sport with considerable brio and elan. It's an honor to be a colleague of a man so passionate and generous."

Wayne Kalyn – "Other than being the Intel chip of tennis, Steve is an expert on gabardine trousers -- with cuffs, always cuffs -- on the racks of Paul Stuart's, black bean soup, burger and baked potato at Joe Allen's...Perplexed Manhattan doormen are still scratching their heads over Steve's detailed encomium to the Sampras forehand back in the '90s.... the proprietor of China Bowl restaurant—a victim of the wrecking ball—will never forget Steve's weekly panegyric about the lunch specials. The proud proprietor agreed with Steve's assessment and responded, "Thank you, Mr. Frink... The salesman at the shirt department at Brooks Brothers admired Steve's expertise...He imparts his wisdom with the best that Chaucer and Buddy Hackett had to offer --he entertains. ...Passion -- and a laugh -- is always the point..."

Richard Pagliaro – "Steve's writing is to tennis journalism what Rosewall's backhand is to classic strokes...He has unwavering concentration in covering a match, charts every single point with his own distinctive note-taking system yet can simultaneously carry on a running analysis of the match on a point-by-point basis...He is a traditionalist... yet a fiercely independent thinker."

Scott Price – "Steve is always tan; he's our George Hamilton and one of the dearest people I know...We're all professionals, all scrambling around, sort of protecting our turf. Steve isn't built that way. He wants everybody to come in and enjoy tennis. He's as generous with his time and his knowledge as anyone in any sport. I've been covering sports for 25 years and Steve is truly one of a kind, not only as a tennis resource and historian but as a human being...."

-- By Nancy Gill McShea

Tony Franco

Still ruggedly handsome and agile on the eve of his 85th birthday, Philadelphia native Tony Franco, who once had a blind date with Grace Kelly and looks like he could have auditioned for the Cary Grant role in the 1940 movie "The Philadelphia Story," instead left the city in 1938 for more exotic surroundings and landed a role in tennis.

"I was 13 when my Dad was transferred and moved the family to Puerto Rico," Tony said. "And that was the first time I stepped onto a tennis court." He picked up an old, loosely strung racket that looked more like a lacrosse stick and learned the game with local kids at the Condado Beach Hotel and the San Juan Country Club.

In the 71 years since he ventured inside the white lines, Tony has put together a fascinating tennis background at the same time he forged a successful business career with IBM.

A self described late bloomer, he was 80 years old when he earned his first USTA No. 1 singles ranking, in 2005, and the world's No. 1 singles ranking, in 2006. He has won five ITF world championships (1 singles, 4 doubles), 12 USTA national senior titles (4 singles, 8 doubles) and has reached the finals eight times (twice in the 75s and six times in the 80s). In 2009, Captain Franco led the U.S. Gardnar Mulloy Cup (80s) team to the silver medal at the Super-Senior World Championships in Australia.

To get the ball rolling on his long journey, he returned to Philly in 1942 and enrolled at the University of Pennsylvania. He detoured briefly to enlist in the U.S. Navy during World War 11 and served aboard a landing craft tank. "We landed at Normandy in July of 1944, six weeks after the invasion so there were no fireworks," said Tony, who spent time running supplies back and forth from England and up and down the Seine, once that was secure, and was lucky enough to be in Paris on VE Day for one of the bigger parties of all time. He completed his tour of duty and finished up at Penn.

"My Dad is modest and a gentleman who doesn't like to talk about himself so I'll share a story," his daughter Lola said. "When my Dad arrived at Penn he was 5-foot-4 and weighed 90 lbs. The coach of the crew team tried to recruit him and promised a varsity letter as Penn had a tremendous crew team in the 1940s. But my Dad told the coach in his squeaky voice that he was going out for the tennis team because he would rather get a letter for being good, not for being small. He made the varsity tennis team as a freshman."

Tony graduated from Penn in 1949 and has fond memories of playing tennis there. "Fred Kovaleski's William and Mary squad and Dick Savitt's Cornell team clobbered us," he said, "but the last weekend of the season we defeated both Harvard and Dartmouth." He went home to Puerto Rico to work as a trainee with IBM and continued to play tennis regularly with Charlie Pasarell's father – the future pro was 2 at the time – and the pair once split sets in an exhibition at the Caribe Hilton with the famous Fred Perry and Martin Buxby.

In 1951 he was 25, single, and his IBM bosses asked where he'd like to be assigned. "I told them Rio, Havana or Mexico City," said Tony, who understood well that IBM meant 'I'll Be Moving!' IBM passed on exotic locales and sent him to Tegucigalpa, the capital of Honduras, to set up an office and build the business.
Honduras was home for 12 years and at a party he met Edith, the perfect Grace Kelly to his Cary Grant. They were married in 1956 and will celebrate their 54th anniversary this June.

In 1963 Tony and Edith moved on to Mexico City, IBM's Caribbean Central American area headquarters.

Tony continued to play tennis at every destination, of course, and represented Puerto Rico at the Central American and Caribbean Olympics; Honduras at the Central American Championships; and Mexico at the Stevens Cup competition.

In late 1969, Tony and his family returned to the U.S. and settled in Briarcliff, N.Y. He now plays tennis regularly at both Club Fit at Briarcliff and the Saw Mill Club. In 1970, he became eligible to compete in USTA men's 45 senior events. The top four seeds in the first Eastern tournament he played were Bobby Riggs, Ellis Flack, Al Doyle and Tony Vincent, along with national contenders Bill Tully and Alan Fleming. "A pretty tough crowd," he said, yet he managed to rank No. 10 in the East that year. He later ranked first in the East from the men's 50s on up and chaired Eastern's senior ranking committee, a volunteer assignment he handled from 1976 through 1989 when he retired from IBM. He was also the captain of Eastern's Atlantic Coast 45 and 55 Senior Intersectional team matches.

Tony was a national quarterfinalist in the 55s and turned heads in the 60s when, unseeded, he upset Riggs, the top seed and defending champ, 6-3, 6-3, at the 1986 USTA National 60 Clay Courts in Little Rock, Arkansas. Asked if strategy were the key, Tony replied, "I just tried not to miss and I was lucky I was able to move fairly well. It was one of those days when everything seemed to go right, and Riggs was six years older than I was."

Riggs told newspaper reporters that he had run into a buzz saw playing Tony. Curt Beusman, Tony's longtime doubles partner, ordered a batch of T-shirts for their tennis buddies imprinted with "Buzz Saw Franco!"

The good times rolled and longevity ruled. "We've become friends with players and their wives over the years," Tony said. "It's kind of a tight knit fraternity, an interesting group." He played Fred Kovaleski in college and 51 years later lost to him in the final of the 2000 USTA National 75 Grass Courts. The runner-up finish earned Tony a spot on the 2001 U.S. Men's 75 Bitsy Grant Cup team in Australia. Then Tony struck gold in 2004 when he beat his friend Grady Nichols in three sets to win his first national singles title at the USTA Men's 75 Grass Courts at Orange Lawn in New Jersey.

He is now a seasoned veteran on the world stage, having represented the U.S. on five men's 80 world cup teams, most of them played in Antalya, Turkey. Tony won his first world singles title there in 2006, the year

Nichols talked him into playing both singles and doubles in the same event. Together they have captured three world doubles titles: in Turkey and in Australia; and they have won seven USTA national senior titles.

"Tony is a great partner and friend," Nichols said. "He has a joke for every occasion. They just keep flying out of his mouth and he keeps us all loose."

Kovaleski is also a fan. "Tony is a wonderful competitor and a genuine sportsman who always does the right thing," said Fred, who has never lost to his friend. "In the heat of competition senior players will do almost anything to win, but Tony will never give anyone a bad call. Watch out for his forehand, though; it's a weapon."

It's a good thing Tony has a sense of humor because his losses to Kovaleski are a family joke. Lola's oldest son Patrick used to ask his grandfather, "How did you do?" and Tony would say, "Oh, I lost to Mr. Kovaleski." The last time Patrick asked Tony "How did you do?" Tony answered glumly, "Same result," and Patrick said, "Do you think you can beat Mrs. Kovaleski?"

Lola said Patrick's Dad, Kevin Seaman, wasn't laughing the first time he played his future father in law when Tony was 60. "Kevin was 23, in great shape and had played varsity tennis at Hobart," Lola said. "He was certain that he could beat a man 39 years his senior. But Dad is a very smart player. He has a horrible backhand and a lame serve so he covers his weak spots and studies his opponent. Just like in chess, he can see what's going to happen next on the court and it's fascinating to watch him figure it out. Kevin wasn't moving well, Dad saw that right away and whooped him, like 0 and 1. He ran Kevin all over the court, hit all the corners, lobbed him and drop shot him. Kevin thought he was going to have a heart attack."

Tony Jr. says his Dad is a very good parent but he, too, has been stung by that cagey court strategy. "Dad is highly competitive but doesn't mind losing," he said. "He has a heck of a drop shot and he used to take great pleasure in hitting one that I couldn't get to…The first time I couldn't get to his drop shot I was in my late thirties and I could see that he was a little bit sad. I think it showed he felt bad for me that I was getting older…it said something about him, that there's no greater pride than seeing your child do well…"

-- By Nancy Gill McShea

Chapter 31

2011: Brown, Hainline, Litwin and Picker

Melissa Brown

News travels fast in New York tennis circles when a young star emerges from the pack and defeats another young talent soon to be acknowledged as one of the greatest women tennis players of all time. We're talking about Melissa Brown of Scarsdale, who in the early 1980s beat Steffi Graf three times in their early teens.

Melissa was a natural athlete, an honor student who starred on her soccer and basketball teams. But she was surrounded by tennis players -- her dad, Neil, was the captain of his tennis team at New York University; her mom, Nina, was ranked in Eastern Open singles; and her younger brother, Derek, followed suit and ranked first in Eastern juniors and tenth in the country – so tennis ruled in the Brown household.

By 1982 Melissa was ranked No. 1 in the USTA girls' 14 division and newspaper reporters sensed that she was ready for primetime. Charles Friedman reported in The New York Times: "Melissa…tall with long, slender legs was the best junior tennis player in the country in her age group…1982 was a banner year…with a record 90 match victories against 15 losses and a collection of titles ranging from the summer national clay courts to the international Sport Goofy Disney Cup…which she won in Monte Carlo."

Melissa defeated Steffi Graf at the Monte Carlo event, a mini Olympics that showcased eight of the world's best young players from North America, Europe and South America. In that first meeting, Melissa was 14, Steffi was 13.

The most dazzling Brown-Graf encounter was a featured attraction at the 1983 US Open. Local fans lined up 10-deep on the sideline of Court 7 at the USTA National Tennis Center to watch the pair duke it out in the women's qualifier.

This contest would count. They were two teenagers heading toward pro careers. Melissa was 15, Steffi was 14.

Renee Richards coached Melissa that day and gave an account of the match:

"Steffi was seeded second, with entourage of father, mother and assorted other assistants and a reputation already as a top prospect. I went over after practice that day and watched her hitting on a nearby court. Steffi was quick and athletic but…she took her forehand very late, almost off her back foot, and with a big backswing. Melissa had much more classic strokes, was very solid on both sides and more importantly, she hit the ball hard. I told Melissa, 'Listen, you know that Steffi makes big shots with her forehand but it won't stand up to your ground strokes. Play her forehand, she will be late with it.'

"Melissa was smart besides being strong, and she did exactly that, dispatching Steffi, 6-1, 6-2. After Steffi cried courtside in disbelief – to this day that loss is considered one of the worst 10 defeats in Steffi's pro career – she went home to Germany…and came back with the greatest forehand in women's tennis. If Melissa's career had not been interrupted when she went to college, we may have seen more battles between those two young stars."

By the spring of 1984, Melissa was surging and expectations escalated. At the French Open, she had just turned 16 and gained worldwide attention, surprising the No. 6 seed Zina Garrison, 6-3, 3-6, 6-3, to become the youngest singles quarterfinalist in the history of that Grand Slam event.

One month later at Wimbledon, Melissa won the Ladies Plate consolation prize. She outlasted six players who had surrendered in the main draw, including Lea Antonopolis, 6-3, 5-7, 6-2, in the semifinals and Robin White, 6-2, 7-5, in the final. She again gained "a first" distinction, this time as the youngest player ever to prevail in the Ladies Plate event.

"My favorite match was when I beat Zina at the French getting to the quarterfinals," Melissa said recently. "I was just starting out and she was No. 4 in the world…Just the emotion of reaching a goal, trying to do your job…and winning the Wimbledon plate was unbelievable.

"Getting a trophy from Wimbledon; nobody takes that lightly." Her name is engraved on the trophy in the Wimbledon museum.

Later that summer, Melissa prevailed over Steffi Graf again in an exhibition at the Rye Town Hilton. They had become friendly and Melissa invited Steffi to her home for lunch. They prepared for the match by practicing together on the courts of the Scarsdale Junior High School.

Melissa's first coach, Kit Byron, said she outslugged Steffi in that match, basically hit her off the court. "Melissa was a very strong girl," Kit said. "She hit through the ball, very flat, and could drive the ball off both sides. And she was a quick learner, one of the most coachable pupils I've worked with. She dominated everyone in her age group. She was also one of the loveliest young women I have ever met in my life and one of the hardest workers I ever had on the court."

Yet on August 16, 1984, Jane Gross commented in The New York Times that hazards awaited young kids who played pro tennis: "Miss Brown, currently ranked No. 43 in the world and a quarterfinalist at the French Open, is neither the first nor the youngest tennis prodigy to switch from amateur to professional play at a time when most of her friends are worried about junior proms, learner's permits or the availability of Michael Jackson tickets. In recent years -- outgrowing the age-group competition, uninspired by the prospect of collegiate play -- a parade of teen-agers has joined the women's circuit, among them Tracy Austin, Andrea Jaeger, Kathleen Horvath and Carling Bassett. The phenomenon has had mixed results and has stirred debate about whether teenagers are particularly susceptible to disabling injuries, like Miss Austin's, and to symptoms of emotional burnout, like Miss Jaeger's."

Melissa said she was aware of the hazards of being one of those young pros in the early 1980s. She said it was like a free-for-all before the WTA adopted an age rule (January 1, 1995) which helped longevity.

She trained at Nick Bollettieri's tennis camp while she toured on the pro circuit. Nick was impressed with her upbeat personality and her ability. "Melissa was a real fighter, she would do anything to win," he said. "She was part of a talented group -- Arias and Andre (Agassi). They all worked hard."

"I'm dedicated when I do something," Melissa said, "but I wanted some balance, to be well rounded. Tennis becomes like a business, it requires a lot of preparation. I started to think about life after tennis so I went to college, which kept me grounded. It held me back with the tennis but I thought it was better for the long run."

She enrolled at USC and then transferred to Trinity in Texas, from which she graduated in 1991. She continued to compete on the pro tour part time and won the USTA Circuit in San Antonio in 1987 without losing a set. In 1988 she defeated Pam Casale and Michelle Jaggard in advancing to the third round of the Australian Open before losing to Claudia Kohde-Kilsch.

Kathleen Horvath, who also turned pro at 15 and quit the tour to attend college and graduate school, said she thinks of Melissa "as friendly, smiling, bubbly. Melissa and I…sometimes trained together…Unlike most pro tennis player peers, Melissa was open, honest and sharing. She would happily divulge everything she did without me even soliciting information…I knew exactly what fitness drills, exercises she did…and how her practice match went…She would honestly ask for feedback without hesitation or concern that she was giving away anything. It was…endearing and I was touched that she trusted me and valued my opinion. I think this was a testament to her drive and desire to be able to put ego aside…to become a great player."

Butch Seewagen played mixed doubles with Melissa at a tournament in San Diego and said, "I was already in my thirties and Melissa was just a kid; she was a great player and we had fun."

Nicole Arendt remembers playing the same tournaments as Melissa and said, "Wow, what a talent!!!"

Another contemporary, Patti O'Reilly, said that Melissa was a "beautiful competitor on and off the court."

Melissa's friend Nick Greenfield called her a role model. "She was a tall, lean, quick and graceful player…an Amazon beauty…who punished the ball," he said. "She hit clean winners from anywhere on the court and achieved tremendous success and fame facing older, top ranked players who were ruthless competitors. Had she not been so nice, there's no doubt she would have been a top-10 player…but then she wouldn't have been Melissa."

Melissa finished college and retired from the tour in the early 1990s. "It was a difficult transition to focus on getting a normal job," she admitted. "Nothing can be as rewarding as playing professionally where you grew up or getting to the quarters of a Grand Slam tournament. You think about the millions who are playing tennis and trying to strive...I cherish the past a lot more now than I did during the moment itself. I'm like wow, that's not so easy to do. When you're in the thick of things you're just trying to reach the top and don't realize the accomplishment until you're older."

But it was time for a change. Over the next ten years she first worked at Tennis Week with Gene Scott – "He helped me get started," she said – and she ran successful pro-am charity fundraisers at Tennisport for Skip Hartman's New York Junior Tennis League. She worked at Planet Hollywood in their event department and enjoyed a successful advertising career with Conde Nast's Self magazine and Hearst's House Beautiful.

Melissa and her husband Herb Subin are now busy raising two children: Brianna, 7, and Benjamin, 4. What's next? "I'm going to use tennis to do something big again -- a charity fundraiser For Juvenile Diabetes," Melissa Brown said. "I'm going to really start focusing on that now!"

-- By Nancy Gill McShea

Brian Hainline, M.D.

Brian Hainline counseled Pete Sampras when injury forced him to pull out of the 1999 US Open.

"Brian Hainline has literally saved the US Open tennis tournament at times by making sure a player was prepared to go on court for the final," confided David Brewer, USTA managing director, professional operations. "Brian was also central to the initial effort to establish the tennis anti-doping code. He did the heavy lifting – research and writing -- that put tennis ahead of the curve in establishing a systematic approach to the issue."

Not surprising. Dr. Brian Hainline is on a mission to make certain that the game of tennis is the model sport for protecting players' health and safety. He has the credentials to get it done.

Brian is the chief medical officer for the United States Tennis Association (USTA), which oversees the US Open and all of American tennis. He is also the chief of the division of neurology and integrative pain medicine at Pro Health Care Associates in Lake Success, N.Y., and a clinical associate professor of neurology at the New York University School of Medicine.

"I have always been interested in the study of the mind and I've been playing tennis as long as I remember walking – since about the age of 2," said Brian, who earned Phi Beta Kappa status at the University of Notre Dame in South Bend, Indiana, and played first singles and doubles for the tennis team there.

He brought his tennis game and fascination with the mind to New York in 1983 to begin his neurology residency at N.Y. Hospital, Cornell Medical Center after completing studies at the University of Chicago. On the court, he has engaged in knock-down-drag-out battles for 25 years with his tennis buddy Jim Malhame.

"Brian is a fierce competitor and he kicks my butt most of the time, but the guy's got character, he has never given me a bad line call," said Jim, who's equally impressed that his friend has logged 20 years teaching religious instructions to pre-teens and 25 years volunteering in tennis. "He's an inspiration, a physically fit doctor who practices what he preaches. To win in tennis, the nerves and body have to hold up and technique has to be solid so a player won't fold under pressure. Brian attends to all three components to prepare himself and tournament players for the contest."

"I have observed the 'extraordinary' in motion working with and observing Brian in his gentle but confident care of an athlete in the most important match of her career…," said Kathleen Stroia, WTA (Women's Tennis Association) vice president, sport science/medicine & player development.

Brian's interaction with players is confidential, of course, and he admits "it's a lonely place to be. It's a challenging balancing act between helping a player prepare to go on court or helping a player make a decision to retire.

"Everybody is always searching for answers," he continued. "Whether I'm practicing neuroscience, teaching religion or developing policies and procedures for the USTA, a unifying theme is to help people become aware of how they can take steps to improve their level of self care, sense of awareness and well being, to develop that and give it back to life."

He met the ideal adviser in that effort in the late Dr. Irving Glick, the US Open tournament physician for over 25 years who established a medical department that became the model of medical care at tournaments throughout the world. "Dr. Glick was my mentor in medicine and in life," Brian said. "He taught me the essence of what it's like to be a compassionate and knowledgeable physician."

In 1986 Dr. Glick invited Brian to follow him as a consultant at the Open. In 1992 Brian became the Open's chief medical officer and started working closely with the WTA, the ATP (Association of Tennis Professionals) and the ITF (International Tennis Federation).

Brian, a prior USTA board member, remains a committed volunteer beyond his professional responsibilities. Back in 1989 USTA President David Markin was expanding a sports medicine advisory committee. Brian wrote to Markin, said he would be honored to serve and became a founding member of the USTA Sport Science Committee. Since 1993 he has served on and now chairs the ITF Sport Science and Medicine Commission, which oversees 202 Olympic countries. Since 1999 he has been a member of the ITF Wheelchair Tennis Medical Commission and has written the rules of eligibility for international wheelchair competition. In 2005 he chaired the USTA Professional Council, which oversaw five interrelated committees.

"Everyone has an agenda, but when it comes to medicine and safety there is no other agenda," said Brian, who gathers expertise from all the constituents in tennis to help create an environment in which players can thrive. "We're all about building bridges…We sit down together and…realize we have the same mission."

A few colleagues indicate the reach of the mission.

Kathleen Stroia – "Leadership has many definitions, but the one closest to articulating Brian's style is how he creates a way for people to contribute to making something extraordinary happen, as when he guides a committee to come to consensus and action on a critical health care initiative."

Patrick McEnroe, head of USTA Player Development -- "Dr. Brian is a very thoughtful and measured individual. You sense immediately that he wants to do what is best for our kids…"

Brian Earley, director, USTA Pro Circuit – "Brian has re-written the medical timeout rule used at every level of professional tennis, including the WTA, ATP and Grand Slam rule books. If I can find any fault whatsoever, it's that the rule uses terms like 'musculoskeletal', 'subcutaneous' and 'kinetic chain.' Maybe…he wants us referees…to travel with a copy of Gray's Anatomy along with our rulebooks!"

Dr. David Cooper, CEO of Pro Health Care Corp. – "Brian is a complete physician…Whether it be an elite athlete or a weekend warrior in need of care, he goes one step beyond applying his knowledge…to heal and rehabilitate his patients. He is a humble, honest man, yet when I asked if he could help my game, he replied, 'I am just a physician, not a miracle worker!'…."

Brian's origins trace the history of his destiny. He and his six brothers and sisters grew up in Detroit. "My mother, Nora, was the glue and the faith of our family," he said. "We'd wake up, see seven lunches already prepared and a huge breakfast on the table, Midwestern style."

Brian's late father Forrest, also a tennis lifer who chaired the USTA Grievance Committee, was the family's first coach. Brian later trained at the Hoxie Tennis Camp in Hamtramck, Michigan. "I had a love-hate relationship with the walls there," he said. "You had to qualify to get on the courts. There were two huge cement slabs and you'd have to hit ten forehands in a row between the two lines, then backhands and volleys and serves. Sometimes you'd be at the wall all morning and finally they'd feel sorry for you and let you go on the court. They had a boxful of steel racquets and steel strings so when it was raining we'd hit against the wall with all steel."

At Notre Dame, he majored in philosophy within a pre-professional program which allowed him to concentrate on liberal arts and take subjects in other areas. He loved science but wasn't yet certain he wanted to be a doctor. He took all the pre-med courses in pre-pro and in his junior year did a year of independent study on Carl Jung.

"My main interest was the study of the mind," he said, "so after studying Jung, who interwove psychiatry with the human condition – not the individual neuroses but the sense of the human connection -- I decided to go to medical school and be a psychiatrist…as it is the human connection and lack thereof that is responsible for shaping our genetic predispositions, insofar as that is possible.

"But when I attended medical school, psychiatry was taking a turn into the pharmacologic revolution, branching into neuroscience – the discovery of peptides and neurotransmitters that had an immunologic, physiologic and behavioral counterpart, the discovery of opioid (pain relievers) and serotonin (helps feelings of well being) receptors…Clinical psychiatry and pharmaceutical companies took these receptors and their neurochemical counterparts and made them one-dimensional. Serotonin the happy neurochemical?…

"Before my eyes I saw psychiatry turning to clinical diagnoses…I had this uneasy sense that they were treating the brain like it was a mixing bowl. And neurology was just coming out of a black box. For the first time we had cat scans and neuroscience was on the verge of a major breakthrough into thought, emotion and disease. So I concentrated on that discipline."

Neurology gave Brian the opportunity to delve into the humanity of thought and emotion…expressed in the mundane of daily life. He reasoned that the physician has the unique opportunity to listen to a patient who has had part of his or her humanity taken away. It is the physician who tries to help restore that sense of lost humanity to the patient. And the nervous system is the essence of how that humanity is expressed. All sensation, all motor activity, all thought is communicated through the nervous system.

"That reality, and the excitement of understanding brain function better, convinced me to explore neurology," he said. "But to this day my favorite thing to read is philosophy. Maybe there will be a way of fully returning to Carl Jung…"

Brian is devoted to his family – his wife of 31 years, Pascale, who works in private wealth management; his daughter Clotilde, who is completing medical school and will go into neurology; Arthur, a college physics major; and Juliette, a high school freshman.

Asked where he finds time to spread himself so thin, he said, "I tell my children that a disciplined life with a purpose gives us the most freedom."

But seriously, who is the real Brian Hainline? Dr. Cooper has the answer -- "My fondest images are of seeing this brilliant, articulate man transform into a mush when he holds his 3-year-old granddaughter Sophie in his arms. Extraordinary…!"

-- By Nancy Gill McShea

Robert L. Litwin

Sports icons Phil Jackson and Andre Agassi have been defined as evolving Zen Masters. Add to the list the name of Bob Litwin, the world and national senior tennis champion who has been ranked first in the world. Bob confided that he started to evolve personally and win major senior titles after he created "The Focused Game" concept, a series of Zen-like self-affirmation techniques he began teaching in 1978 at mental training seminars.

Today, 35 years after he began writing about his focus philosophy, interviewing coaches, national champs and training others in the discipline, Bob works full time as a mental training performance coach with Wall Street hedge funds, traders and athletes. He uses the athlete as a model for high performance to help people get into the ideal space to bring their best to their jobs.

Brian Cheney, ranked No. 1 last year in USTA men's 60 singles/doubles and the son of the legendary Dodo Cheney, believes that Bob's gift is his ability to convey his thinking in his writing. "When I read his writing, I relate to what he's saying about his own experience and that helps me grow in my own life," he said. "That's why he's a successful life coach."

To get to this point in his personal history, Bob has experienced and come to terms with a full range of life's highs and lows. In the process he has learned that "we are not our roles; all roles are transient. We evolve as we get older and what's left is who we really are. Many know the journey but few actually take it."

The tennis angle is obviously a huge part of the story. Bob played the game casually when he attended Great Neck South High School but didn't compete in national tournaments until he was 35. "I was awed by tennis's elite," he admitted some years ago. I kept thinking you can't start at 35 and be a great national player."

He changed that story when he won his first national title at the 1990 USTA Men's 35 Grass Court Championships in Southampton, N.Y. He was 43. Less than a year later, he silenced skeptics when he beat California's Dave Bohannon 6-2, 6-4 in the final to win the USTA Men's 40 Grass Court singles title at Santa Barbara, proving to himself that his victory in the 35s had not been a fluke. He capitalized on his strengths – mental toughness, great foot-speed and what many consider his wicked southpaw serve – and committed just two unforced errors. He called on his focus techniques to concentrate on the short term task at hand and keep his attention in the present to banish anxiety.

He forged ahead and claimed victory in 14 USTA national championships, ranked 21 times in the U.S. top ten and played on and/or served as captain of countless USTA-sponsored national and international team events. He's a legend in the East – undefeated for 11 years while ranking first in his age group 18 times and 29 times among the top three. *(Bob's national and international tennis achievements in singles, doubles and team play fill 5 pages. E-mail requests will be honored.)

In 2002 he was honored as the USPTA National Senior Player of the Year and on 16 occasions he took home Eastern's USPTA Player of the Year Award.
In 2005 Bob stood on the mountaintop when he won the ITF (International Tennis Federation) Men's 55 World Championships in Perth, Australia, and achieved the world's No. 1 ranking for the year. He has twice been a world finalist (he defaulted once on Yom Kippur) and has notched a trio of top three world rankings.

His peers say he is the classic good guy. Mike Silverman, director of Sports, City Parks Foundation, targeted Bob to receive the 2008 Vitas Gerulaitis community service award for his support of the foundation's junior programs. "However big a heart Bob has as a tennis champion, he has an even bigger heart as a person. He's been an inspiration to many, including me," Mike said.

When Bob hosted "Tennis Talk" -- a live audio stream, call-in talk show – which aired on the USA Network during the 2000 French and US Open Championships, he invited his doubles partner Kirk Moritz to work as co-host. "Bob is like a brother to me. Asking me to join him was a nice gesture and very good for my spirit," said Kirk, who had endured open heart surgery shortly before the show.

Kirk let it slip that Bob is not completely perfect, however, that he used to engage in a bit of hostility on the court. "He had a feisty basketball attitude like the other left handed Aquarian [John McEnroe], but he's more relaxed now. His writing helps his play, it helps him to visualize."

Visualizing not only helps his play, it also refreshes his memory. Bob was a basketball player in high school and said "tennis was a fill sport." He went to college at Michigan, tried out for the freshman tennis team and, coincidentally, met

Dr. Brian Hainline's brother, John, across the net. John was heavily recruited and trounced him 6-0, 6-0. Bob put his racket back in the closet and didn't hit another tennis ball for five years.

In the early 1970s he taught history at the Franklin School in Manhattan and the members of the school administration decided to start a tennis team. They checked resumes to find a coach, saw that Bob had played tennis in high school and told him "You're it!" Kids at liberal private schools in those days were politically sophisticated and more interested in debating the Vietnam War than learning a new sport. Only two students showed up for the team. No problem; Bob had instant practice partners!

He got a summer job stringing rackets at a club in Great Neck. The head pro, Joe Fischbach, was passionate about golf and often AWOL when people showed up for tennis lessons so Bob started teaching.

You know the rest. He left the classroom to teach tennis full time, and during that period he welcomed into his life his two daughters, Jody and Amy. He played a few tournaments and thought his game was looking good as he moved toward his thirties. At 33 he tried out for the Maccabi Games and qualified for the nationals. A young kid from Harvard beat him but a spectator told Bob he was close.

"That triggered a positive reaction," Bob said. "It was a double elimination. I won the next two matches and lost the fourth but decided I would try again in four years to make the 35s team. I played some before the next tryouts – met all the great Eastern players -- the Steve Siegels, the Doug Barrows – but I got the experience and made the team. I went to Israel, won a bronze in singles and a gold medal in doubles with Steve Gottlieb."

In 1983 he won all his matches in the East but didn't meet the top two players and ranked third. His goal was to be ranked at the top of his age group so he kept going.

"I was always evolving as a player," he said. "Even back then I had a sense that I could be better. I wasn't stuck on a point in time. Every year was a mountain and I thought that was cool. I once told Brian Cheney I thought it was amazing that I was up there with the best players – with him, the Larry Turvilles, the Armstead Neelys, the Charlie Hoevelers. Brian said, 'Bob, you've beaten the top players; guys are looking up the hill at you.' Yet after I achieved the No. 1 world ranking in 2005 I still wanted to play a perfect match."

But in the fall of 2007, Carol, Bob's devoted wife of 26 years, was diagnosed with cancer while he was playing the grasscourts at the Rockaway Hunt Club. Dealing with Carol's illness from 2007 to the summer of 2010, when she passed away, was the toughest battle of his life.

To complicate matters, in early 2008 during a national event in St. Petersburg, Bob flipped over a cement wall. "I was lying there for about five minutes waiting to see if I was paralyzed," he said. "I got up, attempted to finish the match but had to stop."

He was in pain for a year, thought it was a muscle problem and eventually went to see Dr. Hainline to help eliminate the pain. The X-ray showed that he needed a new hip. Bob was shocked, said he went into instant denial but had surgery in July of 2009 and then a total revision of the surgery in November of 2010.

He is now on the comeback trail, getting ready for a tournament in May and writing a new chapter in his story after two years away.

"If I'm ready to play I'm not going to lose," Bob said. "The more complete I am as a human being the better tennis player I am. When you gain perspective about what's really important and then think about the importance of winning a match, the pressure disappears. I feel like the work I've done over the last several years – the spirit work of accepting and non judgment and being more forgiving of myself – these are the things that free you up as a player. So I didn't hit my backhand today. Big deal. All the things I needed to get through the last four years I bring to the court. I'm going to look like I don't even care.

"That is the new story I'm writing for myself right now."

-- By Nancy Gill McShea

Al Picker

Imagine getting arrested while running through a tunnel and suddenly Superman swoops in to save you. That would be Al Picker, alias The Newark Star-Ledger columnist Clark Kent -- sans cape but with famous glasses intact -- who took on his Superman persona to rescue his friend John Korff.

"I ran through the Lincoln Tunnel…while training for a 100 mile race," said Korff, a USTA board member and Mahwah pro tournament organizer. "I got arrested in the middle of the tunnel. The only way I stayed out of jail was by showing the police a story Al wrote about me in that day's paper…I got Al on the phone to say I was a real person. He wrote about the incident in the next day's paper. It's good to have a pal like Al."

Al was everybody's pal during his amazing 60-year run (1946-2005) as a columnist and reporter for The Star-Ledger. Tennis players respected him because he showed up at tournaments in every nook and cranny and was fair, positive and accurate in his reporting. He understood the sport, was passionate about it and always had a smile on his face. Add that all up – it's Superman!

John McEnroe will vouch for that. "Al has covered tennis and has written about me for a very long time," John said. "I appreciated Al's sense of humor and his interest in the game...he is one of a very few tennis writers who actually knew me, understood me, and even recognized that I also had a sense of humor."

Justin Gimelstob, the journalist/broadcaster who ranked 65th in the world, cast his vote, too. "Al taught me from a very early age to respect the quality of a person's work and helped my entrée into this field," he said. "He came to watch me play for 25 years; he didn't sit behind a computer and file a story. In our interviews I learned about loyalty, that the relationship between an athlete and a writer is a partnership of trust invested in together."

Dick Savitt, the 1951 Australian and Wimbledon champ who never misses a tennis news tidbit, was impressed that "Al was thorough, his articles always accurate and he never wrote anything negative about anyone."

Nicole Arendt, ranked 49th in the word in 1997, still has articles Al wrote about her. "I looked forward to our little interviews [juniors to the pros]...lots of them...all over the world," she said.

Neil Amdur, The New York Times sports editor/beat tennis writer, echoed the consensus: "Al was a hard-working journalist who loved tennis and covered it well."

The tennis writer Steve Flink said that watching Al work for the first time was an eye opener. "I was 19, a reporter in training and I went to South Orange (N.J.) with Clark Graebner to watch him play a final," Steve said. "Clark won the tournament and Al kept asking him questions in his straightforward way...Al was polite yet persistent, low key yet forceful, smart yet unassuming. Clark rolled his eyes...but he respected Al, knew that he was a professional doing his job...That left an indelible impression; I wanted to be like Al, to gain the respect of the players yet not make a nuisance of myself."

Bud Collins said "tennis fans in New Jersey were lucky that Al was their man about tennis...His reportage and columns...kept his readers well informed. He knew the game, the players, the coaches...and came up with many a scoop. This went on for years, then decades as he made his name as the dean of American tennis writers. He covered other sports, too, but his heart was in tennis. I have fond memories of sharing press boxes with Al at Mahwah, Forest Hills, Flushing Meadows, Madison Square Garden, Orange and too many date-lines to recount."

Al's career goes so far back he actually filed his stories in the mid-'50s with Western Union, which would send them to the paper in Morse code. In those days the Associated Press (AP), UPI and Reuters did not have reporters on the spot, so Al sent stories to all three wire services in addition to handling his own assignments.

The Superman image gained momentum in 1945 while Al was a student at Newark's Weequahic High School. At 14 he took on two jobs. He worked as a copy boy at The Star-Ledger and then began writing about high school sports. He played piano in a combo and during summers performed for shows at hotels in the Catskill Mountains. In 1949 he won the Scholastic Magazine prize for Best Short Story.

Next stop was Montclair State. He earned bachelor and master's degrees in secondary business education and was the sports information director there before continuing studies in the doctoral program at New York University. "I refined my typing skills at N.Y.U. and hit 126 words per minute," Al noted. "That speed proved invaluable in making deadlines."

When Al retired from The Ledger in 2005, he had spent 99 years combined in two jobs. He devoted 39 years to education, first as a school teacher (24 years) before taking on a supervisory role (15 years) at his Weequahic alma mater.

He simultaneously covered sports and tennis (60 years) for the state's largest paper.

"A most rewarding and satisfying period," said Al, who also provided radio coverage in the '50s and '60s for CBS Sports and ABC WorldWide Sports. An advanced intermediate tennis player with a couple of jobs, a marriage and family – wife Anita, daughter Susan and son Michael; that's more complicated than it sounds.

As tennis grew in prominence, The Ledger elevated it to a featured sport. In 1954 Al expanded news of the game with "On Tennis" columns and on-site coverage of Wimbledon, French Open, the US Open and Davis Cup matches plus important junior events.

He also covered the New Jersey State and Gene Scott's Eastern Grass Court Championships in South Orange, Anne Cummings (18s), senior grass courts, the Hamlet Cup, the Mahwah event, the Concord Hotel juniors (1973-91, the Easter Bowl, the Port Washington Junior Championships and numerous ETA events.

Al's informal style captured the excitement and ambience surrounding big-time tennis so fans could experience the passion and heat of action on courts thousands of miles away. Readers began to understand the emotional day-to-day life of athletes involved in a world-wide sport played on a year-long basis. In a sport known to keep writers at bay, his easy personality helped him form relationships with players on the way up, like Pam Casale, and with established stars like Arthur Ashe.

He followed Pam through high school, the juniors and the pros, said she was frank in interviews, allowing readers and fans to…gain insight into…women's tennis. She spoke about the rigors of worldwide travel. "A lot of hard work," she would say. "Not as glamorous as one would think…No time for sightseeing. Anxious moments playing against good friends…

"Al became part of my family," said Pam, who in 1984 ranked No. 15 in the world. "I once played Chris Evert on Wimbledon's Center Court and asked my mother to find Al and invite him to sit in the Friends' Box. I was getting killed, 6-0, 4-0, came back to win the second 7-5 but lost the third. Al was there cheering. When I beat Bettina Bunge to get to the Mahwah finals, my father couldn't wait to open the paper and read what Al wrote. Al rooted for us all. We were the boxers and he was the trainer sitting in our corner supporting us."

Patti O'Reilly, one of the famous O'Reilly triplets of Ridgewood, N.J., another Mahwah veteran, said she would turn around at almost every ETA tournament she played and "Al would be sitting in the front row, smiling. He had a warm and welcoming manner and you knew that tennis was his passion."

Al saw Arthur Ashe play when he was 15. "I followed him and after he retired we spent hours viewing US Open matches in the press box," Al said. "In 1989, after I had heart bypass surgery and returned to work…at the Forest Hills Invitational, I received a surprise call from Arthur. He wanted to know how I was feeling, advised me not to overdo it, to make sure I covered myself from excessive sunlight. A warm and thoughtful expression that made you realize how special he was.

"The following year, Kean University…needed a replacement commencement speaker. My wife, Anita, an assistant registrar, asked if I could get Arthur…He graciously accepted and came through with one of the most memorable and stirring addresses in the school's history."

Tennis beat writers shared some memories. "Al became a trusted friend," said Doug Smith, a tennis correspondent/reporter with USA Today and other papers. "In the mid-90s we helped our newspapers save expense-money by sharing a house when we covered Wimbledon…Most tennis journalists covering Grand Slam events…for major newspapers wrote one story (800-1000 words) per day. I felt overworked …my daily workload included a major story, two side bars (300-400 words) and a package of notes (700 words). I complained until I watched Al punch out a major story, side bar, package of notes and a 1,000-word column/commentary daily while covering Wimbledon and the US Open. He never complained."

Steve Flink mentioned that he, too, shared a room with Al at Wimbledon in 1982 to save on expenses…"…the pre-computer days when writers still worked on typewriters," Steve said. "Al would work on his daily piece in the press room but finish the writing back in our room. That meant that sleep was simply out of the question. Al would be up as late as possible and would dictate his stories over the phone. He…taught me that there is no substitute for persistence."

Sid Dorfman, 91, a columnist for The Ledger, said it may be a cliche, but "Al Picker became Mr. Tennis, as well known in England and France as he was in the U.S. He covered the sport as one of the most important tennis writers in the country."

Al has been honored with multiple awards --Tennis Week Magazine, Tennis Writer of the Year, 1977 and 1983; the U.S. Tennis Writers Association, Lifetime Achievement Award, 1994 (he was vice president of the association); and the New Jersey Sportswriters Association, Journalistic Achievement Award, 1997, along with the Key to Newark City Hall, for outstanding coverage of tennis events. Al has also been a voting member of the media for over 20 years in selecting the annual recipients to the International Tennis Hall of Fame in Newport, R.I.

Does Al Picker miss his tennis beat? "Sure I miss it," he said. "I loved covering the tournaments, writing profiles and meeting the people but I certainly don't miss the deadlines!"

-- By Nancy Gill McShea

And Finally......

U.S. OPEN Special '98

BY RICHARD PAGLIARO AND NANCY GILL McSHEA

You can watch the world stand still outside the National Tennis Center. For the next two weeks, the tennis world will be watching the action inside the National Tennis Center.

Standing on the steps of Arthur Ashe Tennis Stadium at the USTA National Tennis Center in Flushing Meadows provides a scenic view of the tree-lined lane that starts at the south gate entrance of the grounds, moves past the outer courts and stretches to the Unisphere that remains a global reminder of the World's Fair that was held in the park decades ago.

The link between the site's past and present status as a world center is as visible as the view from the stadium to the giant globe. Twenty years ago, the U.S. Open moved from Forest Hills to Flushing Meadows. A year later, several players who grew up in Queens attending the Open as spectators -- John McEnroe, Vitas and Ruta Gerulaitis and Mary Carillo -- played the Open as pros and the tennis world watched. "Some of us did better than others," Carillo said. It was a unique moment in New York.

In 1979, McEnroe met Vitas Gerulaitis in the U.S. Open final that crowned a king of Queens. McEnroe emerged with a 7-5, 6-3, 6-3 victory to claim his first Grand Slam singles championship and first of eight U.S. Open titles (four in singles and four in doubles) before a strangely subdued crowd.

"The good news was winning my first Grand Slam singles title and the bad news was that no one wanted Vitas or me to be there because most people wanted to see a Borg-Connors final," said McEnroe, who teamed with fellow New Yorker Peter Fleming to win the doubles title that year. "It became an awkward situation because we played in the same places growing up. Vitas was the big shot player in the East who we all looked up to and suddenly I'm 20 and he's 24 and we're playing in the U.S.

Open final. There was an emotional connection there so it was almost like he was one of the last people I would have wanted to play in that situation because we were friends. I don't think it will ever happen again - two guys from Queens playing for the U.S. Open title."

McEnroe, Carillo and Vitas Gerulaitis grew up training at the Port Washington Tennis Academy, all three were inducted into the USTA/Eastern Tennis Hall of Fame, and when their careers on the pro tour came to a close they returned to the Open reunited as prominent television analysts.

"A couple of years back, I was up in the booth with John and Vitas," said Carillo, who teamed with McEnroe to win the 1977 French Open mixed doubles title. "And I was thinking: 'Here we are, three kids from Queens. This is a pretty big deal.'"

Carillo and McEnroe continue to cover the Open as broadcasters. Gerulaitis died suddenly on Sept. 18, 1994 at the age of 40 of carbon monoxide poisoning in Southampton, N.Y.

"Vitas was a very special person," McEnroe said. "He was like Broadway Vitas - he was like our Joe Namath. He was very charismatic, he had a style all his own and he influenced a lot of us. For his life to end so abruptly is numbing. Even now I feel sick to my stomach just thinking about it. Quite honestly, I still can't believe he's gone."

In this special U.S. Open issue we profile Gerulaitis, McEnroe and Carillo and explore their impact on the U.S. Open. In addition, we feature a group of New Yorkers -- men's locker room supervisor Carl Munnerlyn and husband and wife hosts Larry and Donna Lopater -- who play significant roles behind the scenes during the tournament.

Nineteen years ago, two local players from Queens stepped onto the court to compete for the U.S. Open championship. The moment lasted for a match. The memory lasts a lifetime.

"Winning the U.S. Open is a combination of everything and every emotion from joy to ecstasy to relief," McEnroe said. "When you win that final point you feel you can fly for that one second in time." •